How We
Became
Hedonists

MORAL DARWINISM

BENJAMIN WIKER

IVP Academic

An imprint of InterVarsity Press
Downers Grove, Illinois

InterVarsity Press
P.O. Box 1400, Downers Grove, IL 60515-1426
World Wide Web: www.ivpress.com
E-mail: email@ivpress.com

InterVarsity Press® is the book-publishing division of InterVarsity Christian Fellowship/USA®, a student movement
active on campus at hundreds of universities, colleges and schools of nursing in the United States of America, and a
member movement of the International Fellowship of Evangelical Students. For information about local and regional
activities, write Public Relations Dept., InterVarsity Christian Fellowship/USA, 6400 Schroeder Rd., P.O. Box 7895,
Madison, WI 53707-7895, or visit the IVCF website at <www.intervarsity.org>.

Scripture quotations, unless otherwise noted, are from the Revised Standard Version of the Bible, copyright 1946,
1952, 1971 by the Division of Christian Education of the National Council of the Churches of Christ in the U.S.A., and
are used by permission.

Cover illustration: Roberta Polfus

ISBN-10: 0-8308-2666-1
ISBN-13: 978-0-8308-2666-7

Printed in the United States of America ∞

Library of Congress Cataloging-in-Publication Data

Wiker, Benjamin, 1960-
   Moral Darwinism: how we became hedonists/Benjamin Wiker.
      p. cm.
   Includes bibliographical references.
   ISBN 0-8308-2666-1 (pbk.: alk. paper)
   1. Hedonism—Religious aspects—Christianity. 2. Epicureans (Greek
philosophy) 3. Ethics, Evolutionary. 4. Christian ethics. I. Title.
   BR115.H43.W55 2002
   261.5'1—dc21

                                                                              2002004052

P   21   20   19   18   17   16   15   14   13   12   11   10   9   8   7   6
Y   22   21   20   19   18   17   16   15   14   13

Contents

Acknowledgments *7*

Foreword *9*

Introduction *15*

1 / It All Started with Epicurus *31*

2 / Lucretius, the First Darwinian *59*

3 / Christianity Versus Epicureanism *75*

4 / The Fall and Rise of Epicureanism *95*

5 / Newtonianism: *The New Face of Epicurean Materialism* *111*

6 / The Moral Revolution of Materialism *143*

7 / The Taming of Christianity, or Scripture Declawed *178*

8 / Epicureanism Becomes Darwinism *215*

9 / How We Became Hedonists *255*

Conclusion *289*

Subject Index *323*

Scripture Index *329*

Acknowledgments

I would like to thank the following for kind permission to quote at length from the listed works.

Epicurus excerpts from Brad Inwood and L. P. Gerson, *The Epicurus Reader*, reprinted by permission from Hackett Publishing Company, Inc. (copyright © 1994 by Hacket Publishing Company, Inc.).

Lucretius excerpts from *De Rerum Natura* reprinted by permission of the publishers and the Trustees of the Loeb Classical Library from *Lucretius*, Loeb Classical Library Vol. L 181, translated by W. H. D. Rouse, rev. by Martin F. Smith, Cambridge, Mass.: Harvard University Press, 1924, 1975. The Loeb Classical Library® is a registered trademark of the President and Fellows of Harvard College.

Excerpts from *Leviathan* by Thomas Hobbes reprinted with the permission of Simon & Schuster, Inc., from *Leviathan* by Thomas Hobbes, edited by Michael Oakeshott. Copyright ©1962 by Macmillan Publishing Company.

Excerpts from D. F. Strauss reprinted from *Life of Jesus Critically Examined* by David Fredrich Strauss, copyright ©1972 by Fortress Press. Used by permission of Augsburg Fortress.

Excerpts from Charles Darwin's *Descent* from Darwin, Charles, *Descent of Man*. Copyright ©1981 by Princeton University Press. Reprinted by permission of Princeton University Press.

Excerpts from Spinoza reprinted from Benedict de Spinoza, *A Theologico-Political Treatise and A Political Treatise*, translated by R. H. M. Elwes, copyright © by Dover Publications, Inc., 1951.

Excerpts from Margaret Sanger reprinted from Margaret Sanger, *The Pivot of Civilization*, copyright © by the heirs of Margaret Sanger (represented by Alexander Sanger).

I have made multiple requests for permission to quote excerpts from James H. Jones, *Alfred C. Kinsey: A Public/Private Life*, W. W. Norton & Company, copyright ©1997. The publisher has not responded to my requests.

Of course, I take full responsibility for all that appears in this book, but I would also like to thank the following persons and institutions, all of whom contributed to making this book not only possible but actual. To begin with, Jay Richards and William Dembski, without whom my manuscript proposal would still be gathering dust in a large stack of unopened manila envelopes, and for the encouragement of other friends at Discovery Institute. Thanks also go out to all the many informed members of Phylogeny who kindly answered research questions almost immediately after my asking them, and to the ever cheerful and always helpful Gary Deddo at IVP. I also would like to express my appreciation to the *New Oxford Review*, which first published "The Christian and the Epicurean," the article which, in seed form, gave rise to this book, and to Frank Clark, whose appreciation for the article gave me the courage early on to make it into a book. Special thanks also go out to Jonathan Wells and Richard Weikart, who saved me from my own typographical errors. Finally, I must thank my best friend, editor-in-chief, spirit-lifter and wife, Teresa, without whom I never could have finished such a task, and my children (Jacob, Anna, Faith, Clare, Nathaniel and Beatrice), who mourned my absence during so many long days and late nights.

This book is dedicated to the memory of my greatest teacher, Ernest Jay Walters.

Foreword

William A. Dembski

According to John Maynard Keynes, great intellectual and cultural movements frequently trace back to thinkers who worked in obscurity and are now long forgotten. Of course, the converse also holds. Great intellectual and cultural movements are often also associated with thinkers who worked in the public eye and remain wildly popular. Some thinkers are both famous and influential. Others are only influential.

This book focuses on two such thinkers, one largely forgotten, the other a household name. The largely forgotten thinker is the ancient Greek philosopher Epicurus. The household name is Charles Darwin. The two are related: Epicurus set in motion an intellectual movement that Charles Darwin brought to completion.

Understanding this movement is absolutely key to understanding the current culture war. Believers in God often scratch their heads about Western culture's continual moral decline. What was unacceptable just a few years ago is today's alternative lifestyle and tomorrow's preferred lifestyle. Abortion, euthanasia, divorce, sexual preference and drug abuse are just a few of the moral issues that have undergone massive changes in public perception.

Too often believers in God take a reactive approach to the culture war and throw their energy into combating what they perceive as the most compelling evil of the moment. In the back of their minds, however, is an awareness that something deeper and more fundamental is amiss and that the evils they are combating are but symptoms of a more underlying and pervasive evil.

Several authors have attempted to get at the roots of the current culture war. James Davison Hunter has traced its sociological roots. Robert Bork has traced its political roots. Phillip Johnson has traced its Darwinian roots. But none of them has traced the historical roots of the culture war back to its metaphysical foundation. Ben Wiker does that brilliantly in the present book.

Insofar as traditional theists sense an underlying cause for the moral decline of Western culture, all roads lead to Epicurus and the train of thought he set in motion. Though hardly a household name, Epicurus is best remembered for making pleasure humanity's chief good. What is largely neglected these days is how he conceived of pleasure and why he gave pleasure such a high status.

For Epicurus pleasure consisted in freedom from disturbance. Two forms of disturbance stood out for Epicurus: the disturbance of God intervening in nature and the disturbance of an afterlife. For Epicurus, to allow that God might intervene in the natural world and to take seriously the possibility of an afterlife (with the moral accountability and judgment it implies) were incompatible with the good life.

Although religious believers tend to think of belief in God and the promise of an afterlife as a comfort, Epicurus and his disciples (ancient and contemporary) held precisely the opposite. A God who intervenes in the natural world and thus in human affairs is a God who can derail our plans and mess up our day. Moreover, an afterlife in which accounts from the present life get settled places undue restrictions on how we live this present life. Thus, for Epicurus belief in a God who is actively involved in the affairs of this world and who judges us in the next is a surefire way to destroy one's personal peace and happiness.

To short-circuit belief in such a God, Epicurus proposed a mechanistic understanding of nature. Accordingly, Epicurus conceived of nature as an aggregate of material entities operating by blind, unbroken natural laws. God or the gods might exist, but they took no interest in the world, played no role in human affairs and indeed could play no role in human affairs, since a material world operating according to mechanistic principles leaves no place for meaningful divine interaction. Moreover, since humans belonged to nature and consisted entirely of material entities, death amounted to a dissolution of a material state and thus precluded any sort of ongoing conscious existence.

All of this has, of course, a very modern ring to it. Typically we identify it with the "modern scientific worldview." What Ben Wiker is at pains to help us realize, however, is that the materialism or naturalism of Epicurus is nothing other than an ideologically driven metaphysics that masquerades as science but in fact serves as a stick with which to beat religious believers and disenfranchise them in the square of public discourse. Phillip Johnson (see his *Wedge of Truth*) has argued this point in the context of Darwinism. Wiker traces it to its fountainhead and then draws out its moral implications for the present.

Epicurus's most prominent disciple is without question Charles Darwin. Darwinism is not only the most recent incarnation of Epicurean philosophy but also the most potent formulation of that philosophy to date. Darwinism's significance consists in the purported scientific justification it brings to the Epicurean philosophy. But the science itself is weak and ad hoc. As Wiker shows, Darwinism is essentially a moral and metaphysical crusade that fuels our contemporary moral debates. Furthermore, Wiker argues that the motivation behind Darwinism today is its alternative moral and metaphysical vision rather than the promotion of science.

Wiker's project has nothing to do with scapegoating Epicurus, Darwin or anyone else for that matter. To be sure, it is a temptation to find a target and blame all evils on it. There's even an old joke about Satan standing outside a congregation Sunday morning weeping. Asked why he is weeping, Satan responds, "They blame me for everything." Ultimately the problem is not Epicurus, Darwin or their contemporary disciples. Ultimately the problem is whether reality at its base is purposive and intelligent or mindless and material.

This is the great divide. All the ancient creation stories come down on one or the other side of this question, making either blind natural forces or a transcendent purposive intelligence the fundamental reality. Wiker brilliantly traces this divide to its metaphysical foundations. In so doing, he shows how the challenge of intelligent design to the evolutionary naturalism of Darwin is not the latest flash in the pan of the culture war but in fact constitutes ground zero of the culture war.

Intelligent design is a moral and metaphysical threat to Darwinism. That is why Darwinian critics of intelligent design are so quick to conflate it with theology. But intelligent design is a legitimate form of scientific inquiry that already subsumes many special sciences (like archaeology, forensic science, cryptography and the Search for Extraterrestrial Intelligence [SETI]). Still, Darwinists like Kenneth Miller and Robert Pennock, who write full-length books against intelligent design, lament that it is theology masquerading as science. To this, theologians like John Haught and Ian Barbour add that intelligent design doesn't even succeed as theology.

Why is that? The problem is not that intelligent design fails to raise legitimate topics for scientific research. The key questions that intelligent design raises for science are these: Are there natural systems that are inherently incapable of being explained in terms of blind natural causes, and do such systems exhibit features that in any other circumstance we would attribute to intelligence? These are legitimate scientific questions. Moreover, the answers cannot be decided on philosophical or ideological grounds, but must be decided through careful scientific investigation. Nonetheless, Darwinian critics of intelligent design remain adamant that it is a misbegotten form of theology.

A little reflection shows why Darwinists take this stance. Indeed, why does Kenneth Miller write a book titled *Finding Darwin's God,* and why does John Haught write a book titled *God After Darwin*? The juxtaposition of God and Darwin here is not coincidental. As Wiker shows, this preoccupation with theology results from critics of intelligent design having built their own theology (or antitheology as the case may be) on a foundation of Darwinism. Moreover, because intelligent design challenges that foundation, critics reflexively assume that intelligent design must be inherently theological and have a theological agenda.

Freud, if it were not for his own virulent Darwinism, would have instantly seen this move by critics as a projection. Critics of intelligent design resort to a classic defense mechanism in which they project onto intelligent design the very thing that it is unmasking in their own views, namely, the extent to which Darwinism, especially as it has been taken up by today's intellectual elite, has itself become a project in theology, metaphysics and moral philosophy.

Consequently, the fundamental divide between intelligent design and Darwinism is this: Is reality fundamentally mindful and purposive or mindless and material? Wiker shows that how we answer this question undergirds all our moral decisions. Moreover, insofar as the moral decline around us is systemic, it is because we have answered this question incorrectly. "Thou shalt have no other gods before me," reads the first commandment. Naturalism substitutes Nature (writ large) for the true God and in so doing distorts all our moral judgments.

This book is above all a call to clarity, clarifying the moral structure that God has placed in the world as well as the distorting power of naturalism to undermine that moral structure. If you really want to understand why our culture is in its current state, you must read this book.

Introduction

The last decade of the twentieth century witnessed the revival of a very ancient argument, the argument for design in the universe from the evidence provided by nature. The new proponents of this argument consider it to be the most ancient possible insofar as the evidence was written into nature itself from the very beginning. The scientists, philosophers and mathematicians who are now busily reading evidence of design from nature have dubbed this intellectual renaissance the "intelligent design movement."

The intelligent design movement differs from older approaches that sought to demonstrate God's existence from nature. There is now far *more* evidence than ever dreamed of by any ancient apologists for design.[1] Ancient apologists had only their naked eyes and their reason, and argued for design on the basis of the obvious indications of intricate complexity and amazing order visible before them, from the regular motions of the heavenly bodies to

---

[1] A complete listing of sources is beyond the scope of this work, but a good beginning can be had from the following sources: Michael Behe, *Darwin's Black Box* (New York: Free Press, 1996); William Dembski, ed., *Mere Creation* (Downers Grove, Ill.: InterVarsity Press, 1998) and *Intelligent Design* (Downers Grove, Ill.: InterVarsity Press, 1999); Michael Behe, William Dembski and Stephen Meyer, *Science and Evidence for Design in the Universe* (San Francisco: Ignatius Press, 2000); William Dembski, *No Free Lunch* (Lanham, Md.: Rowman & Littlefield, 2001); J. P. Moreland, ed., *The Creation Hypothesis: Scientific Evidence for an Intelligent Designer* (Downers Grove, Ill.: InterVarsity Press, 1994); and Michael Denton, *Evolution: A Theory in Crisis* (Bethesda, Md.: Adler & Adler, 1986).

the integral beauty and purposeful organization of living things. But the contemporary intelligent design movement in science is gathering evidence from sources far below and beyond the reach of the naked eye. The advances of modern technology have enabled us to discover ever more layers of won-der-full intricate order. From the astounding complexity of DNA and the amazing, beautifully orchestrated inner workings of cells to the discovery of the anthropic nature of the universe created in harmonious concordance of its finest details for human life, the deeper science digs, the more the evi-dence points to an intelligent cause.

But there has nearly always existed a rival to the argument that nature must have an intelligent cause—the materialist argument.[2] Materialists, both ancient and modern, assert the contrary position, that ultimately *chance* is the cause of what appears to be completely and beautifully designed. Unlike the ancient argument for design, the strength of this appeal lies beyond the senses, both physically and temporally.

On a physical plane, materialists argue that what we see is deceiving, for if we could look below the surface, below the level of appearances, we would discover the ultimate, completely material source of the visible world. On the visible level, it appears that we have a well-ordered world, one of such stun-ning complexity that it would require a divine intelligence as its cause. On the invisible level, however, the random motions of brute matter jostling without purpose, but acting according to physical laws, are the real cause of the order on the visible level. As for the heavens, their seemingly perfect and eternal motion is not the result of a designing intelligence, but is likewise reducible to the purposeless dance of chance and material necessity on the microscopic level.

On a temporal plane, materialists argue that while it may seem that such beautifully contrived things as we see every day in nature could not have been brought about by unintelligent matter shuffling through random possi-

---

[2]I prefer the term *materialism* as opposed to *naturalism*. Many prefer *naturalism* because they believe that with the modern discovery of the convertibility of matter and energy, *materialism* is too narrow a descriptive term. I prefer *materialism* because (1) condemning naturalism sounds as if one is condemning nature, thereby tainting the whole natural order by association, (2) it sounds as if the opposite position would be "supernaturalism," the denial of the importance of nature, and (3) I believe the introduction of energy destroyed materialism, rather than extending it, by eliminating the eternal nature of matter, and the materialist habit of mind simply does not understand the ram-ifications.

bilities, that is because we cannot see the infinite stretches of time which brought it all about. Chance cannot do what intelligence can in a short amount of time, but given an infinite length of time, anything is possible. If we realize the infinite stretches of time available, we would have no trouble grasping that not just one world as complex as ours could be produced by almighty chance, but an infinite number of worlds.

From ancient times up until the Renaissance, there was no satisfactory way to settle this greatest of debates, for the one side, that of intelligent design, appealed to the visible complexity, and the other side, materialism, appealed to the invisible world (both physically beneath our vision and temporally beyond our vision). Modernity, for the first time in human history, has sought to settle the argument by uncovering the invisible world. In great part, at least in regard to science, modernity may be defined as the attempt to increase our vision, to augment our natural abilities with nearly supernatural strength, so that we can *see* who is right. The great debate has been fought largely, for these last four hundred years, by telescope and microscope. The light from distant galaxies has taken millions of years to reach us; therefore, when we peer into our telescopes, we are looking back into time. Microscopes, especially those made within the last fifty years, allow us to see things that are as small as the galaxies are far away.

As the reader shall see in the later chapters of this book, by the nineteenth century the materialists had declared victory in the great debate, and indeed today *science* often seems synonymous with *materialism*. The standard reigning argument is that chance and material necessity have been shown scientifically to be sufficient causes of visible reality, even and especially of the most complex things.

Thus, to use the now famous words of Richard Dawkins, one of the chief spokespersons for the materialist view, "Biology is the study of complicated things that give the *appearance* of having been designed for a purpose."[3] Complex natural objects may give the *appearance* of having been designed, but that was merely the result of our primitive understanding. Upon closer inspection, we find that chance and material necessity were and are sufficient to explain the existence of the most astounding complexity. Appearances are indeed deceiving.

---

[3]Richard Dawkins, *The Blind Watchmaker* (New York: Norton, 1986), p. 1, emphasis added.

The contemporary intelligent design movement arose in the midst of this seeming victory of the materialist side precisely because the evidence uncovered by science as defined by materialism is (ironically) proving the exact opposite. When we look through our telescopes, we do not find that there is an infinite time available for the blind actions of chance to work, but (in accordance with Big Bang cosmology) a finite amount of time. We also find that conditions necessary for complex life are so peculiar, so unlikely, that there is almost no chance that there exists the kind of rich intricate biological diversity and complexity we find on earth anywhere else in the universe. Nor on the microscopic level do we find what materialists promised. Instead we find even *more* complexity, not brute simplicity; this complexity is so intricately woven that it could only have come about through the agency of a designer. The intelligent design movement declares, contrary to the reigning materialist view of science, that science wherever it turns finds more and more evidence of design, and that the realm which can reasonably be assigned to almighty chance is shrinking with every advance of science. And as it shrinks, the only alternative grows proportionately: the universe has an intelligent cause.

The obvious question, then, is why, if what I say is true, is science generally considered to prove the exact *opposite* of the intelligent design conclusion? That is, why is science taken to be (at best) indifferent to the existence of a designer, or (at worst) methodologically hostile to the existence of design? If there is significant evidence for the existence of a designing intelligence, why does contemporary science, as an intellectual and cultural institution, choose to ignore or dismiss it? Why has it sided with the materialist?

Much of this book is undertaken to answer that very question. Why *has* much of modern science set itself against a designing intelligence? As I shall argue in the following chapters, modern science itself was *designed* to exclude a designer. Even more surprising, modern science was designed by an ancient Greek, Epicurus, "born . . . in the third year of the 109th Olympiad, in the archonship of Sosigenes on the seventh day of the month of Gamelion, seven years after Plato's death," that is, in 341 B.C.[4]

This would seem to be an absurd claim. How could *our* science—our sophisticated and intricate science, which has gained us more extensive and

---

[4]Diogenes Laertius, "Epicurus," 10.1, 14 (hereafter DL). *The Epicurus Reader,* trans. Brad Inwood and L. P. Gerson (Indianapolis: Hackett, 1994), pp. 3-4. Since Epicurus is so important for the argument of this book, I have used this inexpensive, readily available version for referencing.

intimate knowledge of nature than ever dreamed possible by any premodern—have been designed over two millennia ago when knowledge of nature was primitive by comparison?

Before answering the question, I'll pose another. If my central claim is that modern materialism, to be properly understood, must be traced back to Epicurus, why is the book titled *Moral Darwinism: How We Became Hedonists* and not, say, *It All Started with Epicurus* or *How We Became Epicureans*?

I'll answer the question about the title first, for this will allow me to answer the prior question more clearly. A thing may be named according to its origin (where it came from) or its end (where it is going to, or what it has resulted in). An ironing board is named after its origin. Ironing was originally done by a heated piece of flat metal with a handle, the whole thing made of iron. A dishwasher is named after its goal, or end, to wash dishes. This book is named after the historical result of the modern acceptance of Epicurean materialism, and that is moral Darwinism.

There are at least two good reasons for this. First, the end result, Darwinism, is far more familiar to us than the origin, Epicurean materialism. A title that depends on something unfamiliar to entice readers will end up largely unsold, entombed in boxes in a warehouse because it was, on the surface, encrypted in obscurity. Darwinism is more familiar to us because our current intellectual and moral situation is directly formed by Darwinism. Epicureanism is the root of Darwinism, but Darwinism is the flower, or better the vine which, growing from the root, entangles nearly every aspect of our contemporary culture. Second, Darwinism is a well-developed scientific argument which, as part of the entire project of modern scientific materialism, developed far beyond what Epicurus could ever have imagined his thought could be (but not beyond what he had hoped for). That means, interestingly enough, that there is more evidence for the truth of Epicurus's assertions in Darwin than in Epicurus's own arguments.

That allows us to return to the first question, How could our sophisticated science possibly have been designed by a comparatively unsophisticated Greek? I hope that this claim, that Epicurus is our intellectual forebear, will seem less and less absurd as the lines of his argument are traced from his philosophical school in third-century B.C. Athens to the present day. The point of tracing this lineage is not primarily historical. The reason for returning to the beginning point is that our understanding of the end point, the world we live in now insofar as it is defined by Darwinism, will become much more clear if we do so.

Readers need not fear, however, that they will be subjected to a tedious, seemingly endless historical analysis. I will only give an overview of the strictly historical connections, enough so the readers may follow the trail to see that it does indeed lead where I point. The focus of each chapter will always be the arguments themselves, and I will take care to show, all along the way, how they bear on our understanding of contemporary secularized culture and the view of science which secularized it, for it is the materialist view of science which permeates our culture, and this view is a modern form of ancient Epicurean materialism.

The argument of this book, then, is that the ancient materialist Epicurus provided an *approach* to the study of nature—a paradigm, as the historian of science Thomas Kuhn called it[5]—which purposely and systematically *excluded* the divine from nature, not only in regard to the creation and design of nature, but also in regard to divine control of, and intervention in, nature. This approach was not discovered *in* nature; it was not read *from* nature. It was, instead, purposely imposed *on* nature as a filter to screen out the divine.

How did the views of an ancient Greek form the materialist paradigm of modern science? To be brief, Epicurus's approach to nature was revived in the Renaissance, and became the foundation of modern materialist science. The Western view of science was secularized, not (I shall argue) out of some inner historical necessity, but because it accepted the view of nature designed by Epicurus to exclude the divine.

This secularization culminated in Darwinism because it was with Darwin that materialism, which had been slowly but surely permeating and re-forming the predecessor Christian culture, finally reached and devoured God the creator and the immortal human soul, leaving behind a completely Godless, soulless universe.

But if the victory was this complete, and modern science was defined by materialism, then how can I then claim that the advances of modern science

---

[5]Thomas Kuhn, *The Structure of Scientific Revolutions*, 2nd ed. (Chicago: University of Chicago Press, 1970).

have actually resulted in undermining materialism and in supporting intelligent design? Precisely because nature is independent of human opinion (and hence independent of any scientific hypothesis defining scientific inquiry), nature always has the last say. Thus, the very attempt to uncover the subvisible and supravisible realms must eventually reveal whether materialism can reduce these realms to a few simple material principles.

Intelligent design theorists argue that the materialist attempt at such reductionism has backfired, and wonderfully so, for the dream of reducing apparent complexity to brute material simplicity has fallen victim to the discovery of actual microcosmic and macrocosmic complexity of geometrically greater magnitude than either side, using only the naked eye, could have suspected. In this respect, there is nothing more likely to lead to the ultimate collapse of Darwinism than the advance of science. That is why the intelligent design movement itself arose from *within* science, rather than as an external critic of science.

Sadly, Darwinists all too often hold to materialist principles even when their own science turns up startling evidence questioning those very materialist principles. This refusal to see what is before them, the evidence of their own making, is what makes intelligent design theorists question whether there is something else motivating the materialist scientists with whom they debate, something that makes them resist the mounting scientific evidence for a designer.

Precisely here, the present study of the origins of such motivations in Epicurus will prove most illuminating. In regard to Epicurus's motivations for clinging to materialism, we need not make an abstruse and tenuous argument to prove that his goal was the exclusion of the divine from the universe. As we shall see, he himself confessed it boldly. The entire aim of the study of nature, asserted Epicurus, should be to liberate us from the belief in gods, in the immortal soul, and in the afterlife, and so make it easier for us to live in *this* life.

The Epicurean assertion that a godless, soulless universe makes for a more comfortable world in which to live runs counter to the opinion of many modern materialists. To cite an important example, in the first quarter of the twentieth century Sigmund Freud, one of the great modern priests of the godless, argued that religious belief was an irrational and cowardly escape from the hard realities of a godless universe. In his words, "We shall tell ourselves that it would be very nice if there were a God who created the world and was a benevolent Providence [sic], and if there were a moral order in the universe and an after-life; but it is a very striking fact that all this is exactly as we are bound to wish it to be." And so, asserted Freud, we must recognize that all these "religious doctrines" are "in their psychological nature, illusions."[6]

But Epicurus would surely have realized that the opposite is true. A universe without gods (or at least, without gods who interfere in human affairs) and without immortal souls (which can suffer in the afterlife) is a universe with much *less* anxiety. A godless, soulless universe is one without judgment, one without peril, one in which, rather than our every thought and movement being watched by an omniscient deity whose claims for absolute justice are unremitting (although Christians believe his mercy is unfathomable), we are instead free of any such brooding, unblinking divine eye. Epicurus's goal was to close that divine eye, so that we could make the most of this world without the anxiety brought on by its imperious stare.

To put it in its most concise form, Epicurus was seeking a view of science and nature to fit the way of life he was advocating; that is, he needed a cosmology to support his morality. He very astutely realized that every way of life, every view of morality, is groundless unless it is grounded in the way things actually are, in nature. This is one half of a most fundamental law, which we might call the great law of uniformity. Every distinct view of the universe, every theory about nature, necessarily entails a view of morality; every distinct view of morality, every theory about human nature, necessarily entails a cosmology to support it.

Thus, all scientists making scientific arguments are—at the same time and whether they know it or not—making moral claims, for statements or presuppositions about nature necessarily include human nature. In the same way, all moralists making moral arguments are—at the same time and whether they know it or not—making scientific claims, for statements or presuppositions about human nature necessarily rest on nature itself. Because nature and human nature are necessarily connected, there is no way to escape the interrelationship of science and ethics, and no one should

---

[6]Sigmund Freud, *The Future of an Illusion*, trans. James Strachey (New York: W. W. Norton, 1961), 6:42.

be relieved of the responsibility that this interrelationship entails.

Epicurus did understand this necessary connection completely, and therefore, when he put forth his materialist view of human nature and morality, he knew that it had to rest on a universe that supported it. He therefore created a complete materialist universe, designed so that it would be entirely devoid of anything but material atoms and the void, completely exorcised of all immaterial entities, and absolutely free of all divine intervention.

That means, of course, that if modernity did follow Epicurus's lead, then it would inherit his entire uniform cosmology. Thus, it would inherit the moral universe that was necessarily part of his materialist universe, even if it originally accepted only the materialist premises of that universe. To be blunt, materialist-defined science must necessarily lead to materialist-defined morality. And that is exactly what happened historically. As I shall demonstrate, materialism was fully enshrined as the scientific paradigm by the eighteenth century. Once enshrined, it worked (if I may borrow a famous phrase from Daniel Dennett's *Darwin's Dangerous Idea*) as a "universal acid," dissolving all that did not fit the materialist universe.[7] Epicurus designed a view of nature to fit his desired way of life, a cosmology to support his morality. Modernity began by embracing his cosmology and ends by embracing his morality.

Why, then, do Darwinists all too often hold to materialist principles even when their own science turns up startling evidence questioning those very materialist principles, very often dismissing the intelligent design movement without a fair hearing? This tendency, I shall argue, is ultimately rooted in the desire to retain the secularized world of Epicureanism intact. That, of course, is a *very* serious charge—but, it is no more serious than materialists' charge that the arguments of intelligent design theorists are not ultimately scientific, but based on their desire to reinstate a theistic cosmology, so that intelligent design theory is mere faith in the disguise of science. I am only returning the charge. Since materialism has a necessary moral component (that is, a materialist account of human action and the human good), the debate between scientific materialists and intelligent design theorists is only part of a larger cultural conflict between those who believe that human

---

[7]Daniel Dennett, *Darwin's Dangerous Idea* (New York: Touchstone, 1995), p. 63.

nature has no intrinsic moral design (and therefore, human beings must construct their own "value systems") and those who believe that human nature has an intelligent designer who created a moral order intrinsic to human nature (and therefore, human beings must act in accordance to the designer's natural moral order). And that is why this book is entitled *Moral Darwinism* rather than merely *Darwinism*.

The so-called culture wars are the result of this great conflict. Our analysis will make clear why contemporary moral debates, which are the front lines of battle in the culture wars, are both so strident and so hopelessly irreconcilable. The complete moral gridlock over moral issues such as abortion, euthanasia, and homosexuality, a gridlock that seems to make peaceful coexistence impossible in our culture, is ultimately caused by two rival moral universes colliding.

If Darwinism historically defines one of these moral universes, what about the other? The other is that of the Christian, because it was Christianity that historically was both the most important bearer of intelligent design arguments in the West, and also the most influential antithesis of Epicurean materialism. As our analysis shall make evident, Epicurean materialism and Christianity have been implacable foes since the very origin of Christianity. Indeed, as we shall find out, central to the aim of the *modern* recovery of ancient Epicureanism was the destruction of Christianity, root and branch.

Theoretically, Epicurean materialism was defined against every account of nature leading to an intelligent designer, and so it also always set itself against any religion which asserted that the universe was created and controlled by divine power. Epicurus himself, living three hundred years before the birth of Christ, forged his materialism for the particular task of eliminating the pernicious influence of Greek religion. But when Epicurean materialism was revived in the Renaissance and Enlightenment, fifteen hundred years after the birth of Christ, its modern adherents reforged ancient Epicureanism for the task of destroying Christianity. Not only was Christianity the particular bearer of intelligent design at that point in history, but modern followers of Epicurus considered Christianity to be even more pernicious and anxiety-producing than Greek religion ever could be. The hostility of contemporary science to intelligent design arguments is just the tip of an iceberg, then, an iceberg designed to sink the titanic influence of Christianity in the West, thereby removing it once and for all from the horizon of this world. All sincere protestations to the contrary by advocates of Darwinism, *that* is precisely why the historical effect of Darwinism has been the destruction of Christianity.

In order to make this more clear, I shall spend a significant part of the analysis outlining the rival moral arguments of Epicureanism and Christianity, and tracing their historical paths down to the present conflicts in our society over moral issues such as sexuality, abortion, infanticide, euthanasia, eugenics and cloning. In doing so, I shall take care to demonstrate how their rival moral conclusions are necessarily rooted in their rival cosmological accounts. Our analysis will make quite evident why our culture, informed by these two rival and irreconcilable accounts of nature and human nature, must of necessity be plagued by irreconcilable moral positions. To be blunt, because these fundamental disagreements between the Epicurean and the Christian historically define the rival sides in our moral debates, our society can only become more and more deeply divided. And as a house divided against itself cannot stand, so also our society, defined by two ancient and antagonistic accounts of nature and human nature, cannot withstand this fundamental disagreement for long.

With great seriousness, then, I present the arguments in these pages. For those within the intelligent design movement, I hope that it makes even clearer the nature and magnitude of the antagonism they face. Further, by examining the historical roots of Darwinism, I hope my analysis allows them to see its presuppositions far more clearly (for these presuppositions, as we shall see, are also the weak points in the materialist argument). Although the present book is not a direct contribution to the ongoing work in contemporary science by the intelligent design movement itself, I do hope that it proves quite useful for putting the debate between materialism and intelligent design in the proper historical context. To cite an important example, Darwin's evolutionary arguments are often taken to be quite novel. But as will become clear, nothing could be further from the truth. Darwinism should really be regarded as in no way novel, but rather as a necessary and ancient part of the entire materialist creed. Modern evolutionary theory is not modern—we find it full-blown in the first century B.C. in the Roman Epicurean poet-philosopher Lucretius—and its rise was assured with the victory of materialism in the seventeenth century. Rather than looking at

Darwin as *starting* a revolution, as some are inclined to do, we ought to look at him as *ending* it, as the last piece of the materialist worldview snapping into place. That means, of course, that there is more to Darwinism than Darwin. There is an entire cosmological framework that Darwinism presupposed, and it can be traced all the way back to Epicurus.

However, this book is written not only for those in the intelligent design movement but for Christians as well. While intelligent design arguments are not essentially Christian, they are compatible with and supportive of Christianity. Intelligent design seeks to show, through science, that natural things have been designed, but unlike theology it goes no further. It does not investigate or speculate on *who* the designer is or *what* he is like, but focuses on the *effects* as signs of an intelligent cause. Natural and revealed theology begin where intelligent design theory ends, making reasoned arguments about the person and nature of the designer (natural theology) or elucidating what the designer has made known about himself and his relationship to humanity (revealed theology). Thus, even though the proper goal of intelligent design is to identify the marks of intelligence in natural things, it also removes the obstacles to natural and revealed theology that the reigning materialist account of nature has put in their path.

For those on the Christian side of the culture wars, I hope that this book makes clearer not only the importance of intelligent design arguments for the support of Christian faith, but also defines more exactly the ultimate presuppositions behind the moral conflicts in which Christians in our society are increasingly engaged. In regard to Christian theology, intelligent design arguments help to clear up obstacles to faith by removing a cosmology directly opposed to the Christian belief in a creator God who is able to act in history as well. In regard to morality, Christians must understand that the moral revolutions of the twentieth century mark the end of the materialist revolution in morality, not the beginning. The real origin of those moral revolutions was the cosmological revolution in ancient Greece begun by Epicurus. The cosmological and moral revolutions are essentially one revolution. This book traces this revolution from its source to the present day.

Two aspects of the argument of this book should be clear. First, while Daniel Dennett may have been engaging in playful hyperbole in describing Darwin's idea as a "universal acid" that "eats through just about every tra-

ditional concept, and leaves in its wake a revolutionized world-view,"[8] I will
argue that Dennett's description is entirely accurate, except that its acidic
quality is the result of Darwinism being merely a modern form of Epicureanism. Epicureanism, as we shall soon see, was designed as a universal acid to
dissolve everything opposing the materialist universe.

Second, because Epicurus's acid was designed to eliminate (or make
utterly impotent) every form of religion, and Darwinism accepted the acidic
formula, there can be no reconciliation between Darwinism and Christianity.
Any attempt to reconcile the two—either from the side of theology, as for
example Kenneth Miller's *Finding Darwin's God* or John Haught's *God
After Darwin*, or from the side of Darwinism, as for example Michael Ruse's
Can a Darwinian Be a Christian? or Stephen Jay Gould's *Rocks of Ages*[9]—
can only end in conjuring up a superfluous deity or cobbling together an
incoherent and unstable "two spheres" approach (where the universe is tidily
divided between science and religion). The problem with a superfluous deity
should be obvious. What will be quite clear by the end of the book, however,
is that Epicurus designed his materialist system to make any deity superfluous, and that evolutionary theism (or any of its variants), rather than providing anything new, is merely following in the ruts of Epicurus's wagon. As
for the two-spheres doctrine, it will be equally clear that the great law of uniformity abhors it. Darwinism could not and cannot remain merely a scientific theory. A materialist cosmos must necessarily yield a materialist
morality, and therefore Darwinism must yield moral Darwinism.

To give readers an overview, the first chapter of this book examines Epicurus's arguments themselves, but (as I mentioned above) I will take the liberty during this analysis to draw connections between Epicurus's arguments
and contemporary scientific and moral debates. Doing so will reassure the
reader that the historical analysis is not a meandering goose chase. (For the
same reason, all other chapters will likewise draw connections between the
arguments of the historical figures under analysis, and contemporary scientific and moral issues and debates.)

---

[8]Dennett, *Darwin's Dangerous Idea*, p. 63.
[9]Kenneth Miller, *Finding Darwin's God* (New York: Cliff Street Books, 1999); John Haught, *God
After Darwin* (Boulder, Colo.: Westview, 2000); Michael Ruse, *Can a Darwinian Be a Christian?*
(New York: Cambridge University Press, 2001); Stephen Jay Gould, *Rocks of Ages* (New York: Ballantine, 1999).

The second chapter focuses on the Roman poet Lucretius, Epicurus's adoring spokesperson to the Roman world. Even more important, when his Epicurean apology was rediscovered in the Renaissance, Lucretius became a most effective advocate of Epicureanism (maybe *the* most effective advocate) to the modern world, and his influence can be seen everywhere throughout modern scientific and moral thought.

The third chapter analyzes Christianity, which arose less than a century after Lucretius. Christianity was the main historical rival of Epicurean materialism after the first century A.D., and it was largely responsible for driving it underground by the time of the fall of the Roman Empire. When Epicureanism was revived in the Renaissance, the two immediately resumed their battle. Even more important, since Christianity was historically the most influential bearer of intelligent design arguments in the West, we cannot understand how modern materialism gained ascendancy without understanding its necessary and fundamental antagonism to Christianity. Furthermore, Christianity was also the main historical bearer of the moral arguments of natural law, and such moral arguments, being based on the assumption that God designed the natural order and the natural order was the source of the moral order, were and still are directly antagonistic to Epicurean moral arguments. So, whether we are Christians or not, it is simply a historical fact that the shape of our scientific and moral debates over the last half millennium can only be understood as the result of the two principal antagonists, Christianity and Epicureanism.

The fourth chapter follows the historical fate of Epicurus's and Lucretius's writings, for if they had been lost (or more properly, if Christianity had successfully destroyed all remnants of Epicurean theory), it is quite unlikely that modern secularized culture would even exist. That, of course, is speculation impossible to prove, but when readers see how influential these writings were in starting the materialist revolution of modernity, they will at least understand that such speculation is not implausible.

The fifth chapter looks at the theoretical victory of scientific materialism that occurred between the sixteenth and seventeenth century. This victory assured that materialism would strongly influence much of science, down to the present day.

The sixth chapter focuses on the moral revolution that occurred during the same period as the scientific revolution. As with the scientific revolution, it was fundamentally Epicurean, and defined very clearly what *moral* would come to mean for the modern world. In this chapter the reader will begin to understand why this book is subtitled *How We Became Hedonists*.

The seventh chapter examines the modern battle between Christianity and Epicureanism that took place in regard to understanding and interpreting Scripture. Modern Epicureanism, I argue, realized that Christianity was the greatest obstacle to its successful bid to transform Western culture. Rather than simply rejecting Christianity, the early modern Epicureans realized that they had to remove it by subterfuge. Instead of rejecting biblical authority outright, they redefined the "science" of scriptural analysis according to the tenets of Epicureanism. This method of scriptural interpretation, which formed the modern approach to scriptural analysis (insofar as it is modern), worked as an acid poured onto the text, destroying the authority of Christianity from within. It is only with the resultant weakening of Christianity, which began in the seventeenth century, that Christianity became too enfeebled to resist the spread of Epicurean materialism in the nineteenth and twentieth centuries.

In the eighth chapter we at last come to Darwin. Here I show that Darwin's arguments were not revolutionary but, as I have said, a necessary part of the whole materialist cosmos, already well defined long before the nineteenth century. I also focus on Darwin's moral arguments, arguments that are often "overlooked" (even and especially by materialists themselves) because they are so startling. Startling they may be, but, following the great law of uniformity, we find that they are fully consistent with his evolutionary arguments, rather than aberrations from them.

The ninth chapter examines several influential arguments by representative moral Darwinists. We do this first of all to show that contemporary moral debates, especially the "hot" issues of eugenics, embryonic stem cell research, cloning, abortion, infanticide, homosexuality, and so on, are simply the result of the clash of the Christian moral universe with the Epicurean moral universe. But second, it becomes clear that a great deal of the cultural weight thrown behind scientific materialism (and hence against intelligent design) is moral in origin. There is more at stake than first appears in the sometimes rather abstruse scientific debates between materialists and intelligent design theorists—far more.

I conclude by showing that there is no possibility for compromise in the current moral debates between the rival sides in the so-called culture wars. The fight over abortion, for example, will not go away until either the Christian worldview or the Epicurean worldview goes away; the Christian universe forbids it, while for the Epicurean moral universe it is not even a moral problem. The same is true in regard to other conflictual moral issues.

I hope the reader will understand the true seriousness of the current debates between scientific materialism and intelligent design. These are not side issues related to arcane academic disciplines. No more serious debates could occur, for we are faced with two rival and irreconcilable views of the universe and human nature; we must find answers to the two most important of all questions: What is truth? and How shall we then live?

A final warning: The order of these two most important questions is itself most important and must not be reversed. We cannot begin with the way we believe we should live and fashion the universe accordingly. That, as we shall see, was Epicurus's error. The truth about nature and human nature must precede moral questions concerning how we ought to live, for the moral answers depend on what we are. If we, as a part of nature, are ultimately derived from purposeless material forces, morality should be defined as moral Darwinism has defined it. If, on the other hand, we are ultimately the result of an intelligent designer, morality must follow that design. Since this book is largely focused on the moral implications of these rival views, it cannot settle the moral debate itself. The fundamental debate is about the nature of science and the nature of reality, the debate between materialism and intelligent design. With that warning firmly in mind, let us now turn to an analysis of Epicurus.

It All Started
with Epicurus

One definition of *Epicurean* is "a person fond of luxury and sensuous pleasure." Since most of us have not read Epicurus's writings, we are thereby led to believe that Epicurus himself must have been an unreserved sensualist, immersed in every form of sexual and culinary excess, resting only long enough to gain strength for the invention of further debauchery.

If we turn to Epicurus's surviving works, however, we find him to be a complete ascetic, a man who counsels us to *avoid* every kind of sensual excess, and to be content with living on "barley cakes and water."[1] Thus, Epicurus, the very founder of Epicureanism, turns out to be quite different from what we might have expected; that shows us the importance of going back to the original sources.

Although the point of our analysis is not the study of Epicurus and his writings as such, but instead the connection of Epicurus's arguments to contemporary scientific and moral debates, it is essential for us to grasp what he

---

[1]Diogenes Laertius (hereafter DL), "Epicurus," 10.131, in Brad Inwood and L. P. Gerson, *The Epicurus Reader* (Indianapolis Hackett, 1994). Almost all of the material in this chapter—except for Aquinas and Plato—is found in Inwood and Gerson. Since Inwood and Gerson use the standard notation for citing Epicurus's writings as contained in Diogenes Laertius, I shall simply use the standard notation. Inwood and Gerson also use standard citation for all other ancient authors, such as Cicero, who report the sayings of Epicurus, and I follow them in that as well.

actually said, rather than merely relying on second-hand knowledge. However, since our goal is to show the relevance of Epicurus as the great-great-great-grandfather of modern materialism, I will draw connections throughout this chapter to contemporary materialists' arguments. Such a procedure will help the reader to see where our analysis of Epicurus is headed.

The first thing we must investigate is why Epicurus put forth the kinds of arguments that he did. This may seem an odd approach, for we are used to thinking that we ought to study what someone said first, not why he or she said it. But for Epicurus, the what was determined by the why.

Epicurus counseled his followers to study nature. The reason is rather strange. The goal of the study of nature was not, as one might think, the discovery of the truth. The goal, oddly enough, was to produce and maintain a certain condition of mind, a state of being undisturbed or untroubled. As he cheerfully told his followers, "Do not believe that there is any other goal to be achieved by the knowledge of meteorological phenomena [i.e., knowledge of the sun, moon, stars, planets, etc.] . . . than freedom from disturbance and a secure conviction, just as with the rest [of physics]."[2]

This dual goal, creating "freedom from disturbance" and "secure conviction," is worth dwelling on because it defines the why of his whole system. The Greek words *ataraxia* (freedom from disturbance) and *pistis bebaios* (secure conviction) mean, literally, "not stirred up" (hence, "undisturbed") and "firm faith."

Freedom from disturbance as the goal of science? A secure conviction about what? What did Epicurus have in mind here? Let's begin with his desire that the goal of science be defined in term of science (somehow) freeing us from disturbance. Naturally we ask, disturbance from what? Or from whom?

According to Epicurus, there are actually two related causes of disturbance, the second following upon the first.[3] The first is the belief that things in the sky—whether lightning, thunder, sun, moon, stars, comets or eclipses—

_____

[2] Ibid., 10.85. The Greek *kai epi tōn loipōn* translated by Inwood and Gerson as "just as with the rest [of physics]" may mean simply "as with the remainder of all studies," and not just physics.

[3] In Epicurus's words, the "worst disturbance occurs in human souls because of the opinion that these things [the heavenly phenomena] are blessed and indestructible and that they have wishes and undertake actions and exert causality in a manner inconsistent with those attributes, and because of the eternal expectation and suspicion that something dreadful [might happen] such as the myths tell about" (Ibid., 10.81).

are themselves either gods or the effects of the gods' trying to communicate their pleasure or displeasure to human beings. Such suspicion that things in the heavens are divine (or are the media of divine communication) is, for Epicurus, the cause of all the anxiety and dread associated with religion. The belief that there are gods who not only continually watch over us but are trying to make their wills known to us through astronomical phenomena keeps us in a continual state of disturbance, worried at every clap of thunder or searing drought that we have crossed the will of the gods and are therefore ripe for even worse punishment.

The second cause of disturbance is the belief in an afterlife. Even if we think we can escape the wrath of the gods in this life, we still dread their hold on us in the next. Rather than spend our lives in a state of contentment, we fritter them away, scurrying about trying to placate the gods with sacrifices and prayers, cowering at each bolt of lightening or eclipse, and being eaten away by fear of the horrible impending punishments recounted in the myths about Hades. If only we could rid ourselves of this dark cloud, Epicurus argued, then we would be free from the "worst disturbance [that] occurs in human souls," the fear of hell.

But science, understood in a particular way, can cure us of such dread, and can thereby bring us this-worldly contentment. Such, for Epicurus, was the *whole point* of natural science, for "if our suspicions about heavenly phenomena and about death did not trouble us at all and were never anything to us . . . then we would have no need of natural science."[4]

Clearly, then, science for Epicurus was not primarily truth-seeking, but therapeutic. For this reason, not just any view of natural science would do. The cure for our anxieties resides in a view of nature and natural science that (ironically) *by design* would completely eliminate any possible divine influence and, beyond that, eliminate the immaterial soul; for those who believe that they are completely extinguished at death certainly have no fear of punishments in the afterlife.

As a consequence, Epicurus defined science with this therapeutic goal in mind, the establishment of a kind of tranquillity. This goal of tranquillity, or freedom from disturbance, was moral in the broadest sense: it directed all

---

[4]Epicurus, *Maxim* xi, in Brad Inwood and L. P. Gerson, *The Epicurus Reader* (Indianapolis: Hackett, 1994).

one's thoughts and actions to achieve a particular goal, establishing *habits* of thinking and acting—the Latin root of "morality" is *mos*, which means "habit"—that determined one's entire way of life.

To establish this freedom from disturbance in the minds of the adherents requires "a continuous recollection of the general and most important points" of a particular view of natural science, one which rests in turn on a particular view of nature. We must meditate continually on nature constructed as a closed system, closed to any influence by the gods, and closed to any possibility of the existence of an immortal soul that could live after death. This continued reflection makes materialism a habit of mind, that is, a firm faith, or "secure conviction," as he called it, that nature really is that way.[5]

What view of nature (and hence science) could advance Epicurus's moral goal? He found such a view of nature ready at hand, the materialist atomism of the philosopher Democritus.[6] If we are to understand the hold which materialism has on contemporary minds, we must very carefully examine the reasons Epicurus offered for why and how the materialist account of nature was so useful for his moral goal, and that will mean we must carefully investigate the way he supported this materialist atomism by argument.

We must first make an obvious point, since it is the obvious we are most inclined to overlook. Microscopes were invented near the close of the sixteenth century, and were only powerful enough to peer into the subatomic world by the twentieth. *None* of Epicurus's arguments in favor of materialism was based on direct evidence. That means, of course, that other, nonmaterialist arguments were viable alternatives as long as they explained the visible phenomena equally well or better.

Since Epicurus could not rely on direct evidence, he had to rely on argument alone. I beg readers to sharpen their wits and pay close attention to these arguments, for in their truth or falsity, the fate of religion and the soul hang in the balance. Epicurus began his argument with a principle that

---

[5]DL "Epicurus" 10.82.

[6]Much of Democritus's moral argument finds its way into Epicurus; however, Democritus's ethical reasoning is far less coherent than Epicurus's and is not clearly connected to his account of nature. Epicurus himself, if we are to believe his ancient biographer Diogenes Laertius, claimed that his thought was original, but it is difficult to take this assertion very seriously, and the first-century B.C. philosopher Cicero was right to ridicule it. See DL "Epicurus" 10.13 and Cicero *De Finibus Bonorum et Malorum* 1.17-21.

every sane person should accept, "that nothing comes into being from what is not."[7] "Nothing" cannot be a cause. There cannot be creation *nihilo ex nihilo*, creation "by means of nothing, out of nothing." That is impossible.

But the next intellectual move is questionable, and we need to be wide awake to see what Epicurus was really up to. We see all around us, Epicurus rightly argued, that things in nature grow and decay, come into being and pass out of existence. But if nature itself were not, at bottom, eternal, then soon enough everything would have been reduced to nothing. However, we see that such is not the case, for the universe is full of things. Since nothing itself can give birth to nothing, Epicurus reasoned, there must be something which never comes into being and never passes away. Therefore, the universe itself must be eternal.[8]

But the eternality of the universe does not follow from the truth that "nothing" cannot be a cause or source. An alternative to his view is that nature is not itself eternal, but contingent (that is, *not eternal*, mortal, subject to decay, etc.). This alternative argument would run as follows. Nothing in nature comes to be from nothing. But we see around us that things in nature really do exist. These things are *not*, however, eternal; we see that they come into being and pass away, grow and die, form and disintegrate. Therefore, there must be some source outside nature that is eternal. That source is called God. This argument, in sum, is that of Thomas Aquinas.[9]

But even though the eternality of the universe did not necessarily follow, treating it as if it did allowed Epicurus to remove the possibility of divine influence in nature. Why? If the universe is eternal, it obviously has no need of another, higher, eternal being to create it. Nature stands in no need of an intelligent, eternal cause; it always has been, it is, and always will be.[10] It is self-existent.

This shift of eternality from the divine to nature was essential to Epicurus's therapeutic goal. The universe itself, in being eternal, takes on immor-

---

[7]DL "Epicurus" 10.38.

[8]In his words, "If that which disappears were destroyed into what is not, all things would have been destroyed, since that into which they were dissolved does not exist. Further, the totality [of things] has always been just like it is now and always will be" (ibid., 10.39).

[9]Thomas Aquinas *Summa Theologiae* 1.2.3. See also his *Summa Contra Gentiles* 1.13.

[10]One cannot help but think of the opening lines of Carl Sagan's television series *Cosmos*: "The Cosmos is all that is or ever was or ever will be."

tality, and hence one of the essential characteristics of divinity.[11] The universe does not inherit, however, the other characteristics of divinity, intelligence and will, which are the chief causes of human anxiety according to Epicurus. In one very short argument, Epicurus rid nature of the need for a divine creator, and by implication, any possibility of divine intervention in human affairs.

We should note two things about the rival arguments of Epicurus and Aquinas. First, everything depends upon whether the things of nature are or are not eternal. If they are, Epicurus is right, and nature is self-contained, having no need of a divine source; if they are not, Aquinas is right, and nature is contingent, existing in a state of dependence on the source of its existence, a source outside of nature.

Second, Aquinas's argument is not based on revelation. It is not a scriptural argument. The Bible is never mentioned. It does not count on accepting the dictates of supernatural revelation. It depends entirely on natural reason. The importance of this point for contemporary debates about the status of intelligent design arguments cannot be overemphasized. The intelligent design movement is heir to Aquinas in that it also distinguishes arguments based on nature and natural reasoning from arguments based on revelation, and focuses *only* on the former.[12]

We will have more to say about this later, but for now the essential point is that the great divide between a view of nature closed to the divine and a view open to the divine begins with the question of whether or not nature itself is eternal, and therefore self-contained. Epicurus's assertion that nature is eternal, is (at this point in his argument) only a bare assertion. Epicurus had no microscope, nor telescope; he had no way to peer into the smallest elements of the universe to test whether they were everlasting, nor any way to stretch his vision to see the universe as a whole, in either the present or

---

[11]Epicurus does allow that gods exist—although his sincerity might be questioned—but they are eternal because they partake of the eternality of nature. This point shall be taken up below.

[12]This is in no way to deprecate the latter. Aquinas distinguishes between what is understood by reason and revelation for two reasons. First, you cannot argue with someone unless there are shared principles, and if the opponent does not understand the Bible to be revealed truth, then using the Bible as a beginning point not only is pointless but will lead almost invariably to scorn of the Holy Scriptures. Second, revelation has as its source and goal the things that are *above* reason, so that it cannot serve as a strictly rational foundation, but only a suprarational foundation received by faith. See *Summa Theologiae* 1.1.1-8.

the past, to see if it was eternal. Furthermore, because nature itself does appear to be contingent, the Aquinas-like argument was (at least) equally viable.

Since Epicurus's reasoning was not based on evidence, it must have had another source. The acceptance of the great leap from (A) nothing comes to be from nothing, to (B) the universe is eternal, is supported only by Epicurus's desire to rid nature of divine influence. Moreover, that same desire is today the only bridge from (A) to (B), for there remains absolutely no hard evidence that the universe is eternal; indeed, since the advent of Big-Bang cosmology in mid-twentieth century, it certainly seems that the great weight of evidence points to the contingency of the universe.

Returning to Epicurus, the next step in his argument is a mixture of truth and questionable assertion. Since the universe is only the sum of its parts, the elements which make up the universe are the real source of eternality. The entire universe, Epicurus claimed, is made up of bodies and the void (that is, space between the bodies), and the bodies themselves are either "compounds" or "those things from which compounds have been made." The fundamental bodies "are atomic and unchangeable, . . . not being subject to dissolution in any way or fashion . . . [so that] the atoms and the void are eternal."[13] (A-tomos in Greek means "not able to be cut.") The immortal atom and the void take the place of the immortal gods.

Again, we must pause to consider his argument. It is certainly true that bodies exist, and that such material wholes have material parts, as the periodic table of elements attests. But that there exists an eternal, smallest point, out of which everything is made, is questionable; that is, there are other, equally viable alternatives that explain the material parts without ascribing to them the eternality of the gods. Material parts do not have to be eternal to function as parts; but they do have to be eternal if the goal of physics is to replace the eternality of God with the eternality of the fundamental constituents of nature.

We are forced to conclude that the foundation of Epicurus's materialism was not empirical evidence, but the desire to shift the locus of immortality from the gods to nature. This led him to posit, without evidence, the existence of eternal atoms (and hence the eternality of the universe). The eternality of

---

[13]DL "Epicurus" 10.40-41, 44.

the atoms themselves gave the faith of materialism an object to which it could cling with all the tenacious zeal one normally associates with religious faith.

This charge is not calumny on my part. Epicurus spoke in just such terms. The modern reader of Epicurus is often confused by Epicurus's repetition that one must "become accustomed to" this or that aspect of his theory, and "not become accustomed to" some other rival, nonmaterialist approach. We, who are generally quite accustomed to materialism, think that he should simply have said that *this* is true and *that* is false. But Epicurus himself nearly always speaks of training the mind to a kind of belief, and the word he uses most frequently is *nomisdein*, the etymology of which is quite illuminating.[14] As a verb, it means to hold or own as a custom or usage, or to recognize by custom. Ironically, its extended meaning includes recognition of the religious beliefs acknowledged by the customs of one's city, or more generally, the recognition of the existence of the gods as such. The root of the verb is *nomos*, custom or convention, or the laws based on custom. Epicurus was self-consciously creating a new habit, a new custom to replace the old. Meditation on his eternal principles, the immortal atoms, was meant to displace the habits of mind brought about by belief in the eternal gods. His use of *nomisdein* reflects the gap between his invisible fundamental principles, and the visible universe they purport to explain.

To go a step further, the *faith* in the existence of atoms defines beforehand what can and cannot be found in nature, and hence defines what science should and should not look for. To put it another way, the faith in the existence of eternal atoms defines both nature and science as essentially materialist. Ironically, the evidence which would actually support the claims of materialism is *not* available at the beginning—Epicurus could not, we recall, have seen an atom—so his materialist science could not be built upon the atom as a certain, demonstrated foundation. On the contrary, the evidence that would support it defines the goal which it is seeking. The goal—to find the eternal atom (or today, to unify the laws of physics by a single, simple equation)—defines what the materialist believes is real. And so when Epicu-

---

[14]The frequency of *nomisdein*, or some compatible word, where we would expect an assertion of fact is too great to ignore. See the following (I have noted where he used a word other than *nomisdein*): DL "Epicurus" 10.49, 52 ("it is necessary to hold the opinion," *dei tēn doxan katechein*); 10.53-56, 58-59, 60 ("it is necessary not to proclaim," *ou dei katagorein*); 10.63 ("it is necessary to view," *dei sunoran*); 10.73-74, 7-77, 78 ("it is necessary to opine," *dei doxasdein*); 10.80.

rus commanded his students to accustom their minds to the belief that eternal atoms exist, the existence of eternal atoms was not an established fact, but a questionable assumption that acted as a filter to screen out the serious consideration of other, nonmaterialist possibilities.

In much the same way, when a contemporary materialist physicist such as Stephen Hawking asserts that the "eventual goal of science is to provide a single theory that describes the whole universe," a grand unification of the general theory of relativity and quantum mechanics, "a quantum theory of gravity," that predefined goal, which is as yet unachieved, defines the habit of mind of the scientists searching for the grand unification. The grand unification theory functions, for Hawking and others, just as the eternal atom did for Epicurus: a hypothetical entity that becomes the object of materialist faith that the universe is indeed as the materialist believes it to be.

That is why Hawking, in his bestselling *A Brief History of Time*, speaks about God continually, but does so in the context of continually phasing him out of a job, a point that the late Carl Sagan, who wrote the introduction, makes with evident Epicurean relish: "This is a book about God . . . or perhaps the absence of God," intones Sagan in the introduction, for Hawking's conclusion is that the universe has "no beginning or end in time, and nothing for a Creator to do."[15] The eternal physical laws (just like Epicurus's eternal atoms) make a creator God unnecessary.[16]

So while it may seem that the materialist mind (ancient or modern) is open, it is really a habit closed to evidence contrary to its assumptions, assumptions derived from a predetermined goal. While Epicurus encouraged his students to consider alternative theories in an effort to explain natural phenomena, he added that "we must not accustom ourselves to hold that our study of these matters has failed to achieve a degree of accuracy which contributes to our undisturbed and blessed state."[17] And so Epicurus admon-

---

[15]Stephen W. Hawking, *A Brief History of Time* (Toronto: Bantam, 1988), pp. x, 10-12.

[16]In his conclusion Hawking seems, at least briefly, to allow that God could have created the universe with another set of laws than those which his grand unified theory seeks to discover, but the overall thrust of the work bends almost exclusively to the conclusion that God (if indeed he exists) "had no freedom at all to choose initial conditions" in creating the universe. That makes the laws completely binding, even on a divine source, which is to say, the laws are then coeval with God, or eternal, and God is as helpless to break them as we are (ibid., p. 174).

[17]I have substituted "accustom ourselves to hold" for Inwood and Gerson's "believe" as a more accurate translation of *nomisdein*.

ished his students, "Thunderbolts can be produced in several different ways—just be sure the myths are kept out of it! And they will be kept out of it if one follows rightly the appearances and takes them as signs of what is unobservable."[18] That is, to "keep the myths out of it," one must always habituate one's mind to hold that the unobservable but ultimate cause of such disturbing phenomena is the eternal atom. The only *real* choice, according to Epicurus, must be between materialism and mythology, so any explanation which is not naturalist must be mere groundless theologizing.

This point is important today because one of the chief difficulties in advancing intelligent design arguments in the public square is that this square is guarded by those who are trained to believe that there are only the two stark alternatives: materialist science (which defines the very meaning of rationality) or immaterialist irrationalism. That there are rational arguments for the existence of an intelligent cause is simply ruled out by declaring that if the argument is not materialist, then it must be irrational (or, more kindly, "theological").

At this point we must examine another way Epicurus designed his view of nature to exclude the divine. There is something else about the Epicurean atom, other than its eternality, that should not escape our notice: its utter simplicity. Atoms, according to Epicurus, differ only in shape, size and weight.[19] Beyond this, they are blandly homogeneous. All complexity in the universe is merely *apparent*, for at bottom everything can be reduced to something utterly lacking in complexity.

How does the assertion of the atom's utter simplicity help to advance Epicurus's materialism? The assertion of atomic simplicity was actually a purposeful destruction of the "lure" of believing that "apparent" complexity has a divine source. As Epicurus realized, wonder (the kind of wonder that borders on religious awe) springs naturally from the realization that the thing before us is so complex and well ordered that it must be part of a divine conspiracy of order. To counter this natural awe—indeed, to redefine it as *un*natural—Epicurus posited the eternal, simple atom to numb such wonder at its very root. Things may *seem* to be so complex as to need a deity for their explanation, but at bottom we know the cause of such apparent complexity is

---

[18]DL "Epicurus" 10.104.
[19]Ibid., 10.54.

the utterly simple, wonderless atom. Instead of being infected by wonder, we might then give an Epicurean sigh of relief, "Oh, is *that* all? It all comes to that." Whatever we can grasp completely, we do not hold in awe; what we do not hold in awe does not disturb us.

To achieve this reductionism even more completely, Epicurus found another ingenious way to help eliminate our natural awe. It may sound, at first, a strange way to do it, but he reduced the universe by expanding it. The universe, according to Epicurus, is unlimited, both in respect to size and in respect to the "number of bodies and the magnitude of the void."[20] That means that, given an infinitude of time with an unlimited number of atoms in an infinite expanse of the void, there will be "an unlimited number of cosmoi [the plural of "cosmos"], and some are similar to this one and some are dissimilar . . . [for] there is no obstacle to the unlimitedness of worlds."[21]

Whether the universe is infinite or limited has been a continual subject of debate among philosophers and physicists of all kinds for over two thousand years, for the merely human mind cannot seem to understand how either is possible. How could the universe be limited? If we traveled to the "edge" of it, what is on the other side? But how could it be unlimited, for it cannot go on forever. That also seems impossible. Consequently, one does not have to be a materialist to believe that the universe is infinite.

But given the next step in Epicurus's argument, the hypothetical infinity is useful for asserting that, since there is an unlimited number of atoms and they move eternally and combine easily, then there must be an unlimited number of worlds. This "plurality of worlds" argument is essential to Epicurean materialism, and is used again in the Enlightenment as a weapon to undermine Christianity (and continues to be used to the present day for the same purpose).

Why, then, would a plurality of worlds be so useful to Epicureanism? The assertion of a plurality of worlds both rests on, and reinforces, the assumption that creation of complexity is easy, so easy that the combining and recombining of atoms creates not just one world, but many. So easy, indeed, that invoking a divine cause is completely superfluous. There must be a plurality of worlds, the materialist reasons, because an infinite universe during

---

[20]Ibid., 10.41-42.
[21]Ibid., 10.45.

an infinite time using an unlimited number of atoms in perpetual motion, simply must produce a multitude of complexity out of simplicity. This belief is the origin of the "monkey-at-the-typewriter" argument, where even a monkey, randomly pecking away, can produce Shakespearean sonnets, if only it has an infinite amount of time to do it. The goal of this belief is to allow enough time and material so that chance can replace intelligence: if the monkey can replace Shakespeare, then almighty chance can replace almighty God.

And so, even though there was no empirical evidence of eternal atoms, no empirical evidence that such atoms combine easily to form complex structures, no empirical evidence that the universe was infinite or the number of atoms unlimited, and no empirical evidence that there actually was a plurality of worlds, the *belief* in a plurality of worlds actually functioned, for Epicurus, to sustain the undemonstrated arguments on which his system itself rested. That is, the belief in a plurality of worlds reinforced the belief in the simplicity of the atom and the ease with which it could combine to create complexity. Whether for Epicurus or the modern materialist, the circular reinforcement ultimately serves to release adherents of materialism from the disturbing thought that a divine Intelligence is behind it all. Are we surprised to find that the late Carl Sagan, the chief spokesperson for materialism in the last quarter of the twentieth century, calculated that in the Milky Way galaxy alone, there would have to be one million civilizations capable of interstellar communication?[22]

Yet as I have pointed out above, the potential infinity of the universe or unlimited number of galaxies is not the central issue in the debate. Such things are being used as a kind of backdrop for the assertion of the ease with which complex life must be created given an unlimited amount of time. Interestingly enough, the assertion of the ultimate ease of the production of complex life has recently fallen on hard times. Peter Ward and Donald Brownlee, scientists who are not trying to support intelligent design, argue in their *Rare Earth: Why Complex Life Is Uncommon in the Universe* that the conditions of complex life are so improbable—approaching zero, in fact—that complex life would be extremely rare in the universe

---

[22]See the discussion of Sagan in Peter D. Ward and Donald Brownlee, *Rare Earth: Why Complex Life Is Uncommon in the Universe* (New York: Copernicus, 2000), p. 271.

no matter how many galaxies there are, so that the earth may be the *only* locus of complex life.[23]

To turn again to the arguments of Epicurus, it might seem, from what has been said so far, that he would have been an atheist. There was some debate about this in antiquity,[24] but if we take Epicurus at his word, then he was very pious—after his own fashion. His new form of piety is worth noting because it became all the fashion in the Enlightenment 2,100 years later. Even more important for the present purposes, his account of the gods provided a bridge to his account of morality.

For Epicurus, the gods were rendered harmless because they were a part of nature, made of atoms just like everything else in the universe. The point of having them as corporeal was not to uphold the anthropomorphism of Greek and Roman religion but to undermine it and replace it with his new and innocuous form of piety.

> First, be accustomed to hold[25] that god is an indestructible and blessed animal, in accordance with the general conception of god commonly held, and do not ascribe to god anything foreign to his indestructibility or repugnant to his blessedness. Become accustomed to hold of him everything which is able to preserve his blessedness and indestructibility. For gods do exist, since we have clear knowledge of them. But they are not such as the many believe them to be. . . . The man who denies the gods of the many is not impious, but rather he who ascribes to the gods the opinions of the many.[26]

There are several interesting assertions here. To begin with, it should seem very odd to us that Epicurus would call a god an indestructible and blessed animal *(zōon aphtharton kai makarion)*, and translators often ignore it.[27] But the assertion was essential to his argument. He classified the gods as animals because their indestructibility was the result of their being a part of nature, not above nature. If it were otherwise, the totality of the universe would not be reducible to atoms and the void. Somehow—and Epicurus was not at all clear how—the quasi-bodily form of the gods is immortal as the

---

[23]Ibid., esp. pp. 243-75.

[24]See Cicero *De Natura Deorum* 1.1-3.

[25]*Nomisdein.* I have substituted "accustomed to hold" for Inwood and Gerson's "believe."

[26]DL "Epicurus" 10.123.

[27]See, for example, Hicks's translation in the Loeb edition of Diogenes Laertius, and Bailey's translation in his *Epicurus: The Extant Remains*. Other ancients classed the gods as animals, but for different reasons. See Porphyry, *Isagoge*, "On Difference."

result of the eternality of atoms of which they are constituted.

Epicurus's proof that the gods exist is both strange and incoherent, and so weak as to crumble and disappear under the least criticism. Following is a general summary.[28] The first argument was based on his peculiar epistemology wherein, because the senses do not err, and there is universal belief that the gods exist, it must be that material images of the gods, cast off by their "quasi-bodies," have reached us and given us a kind of innate knowledge of them. A second argument as odd as the first was that the universe must be balanced by an equal distribution of mortal and immortal beings, a principle he called "isonomia"; therefore, because there are mortals, there must be a counterbalancing number of gods.[29] Suffice it to say that the very weakness of these arguments caused them either to be discarded by Epicurus's heirs, or simply let pass into desuetude. That is one reason why Epicureanism, which was originally an attempt to redefine piety, almost invariably became atheistic.

An additional but complementary reason why Epicureanism became atheistic, however, was that, since nature itself was defined as eternal and self-contained (i.e., completely independent from the gods in its source and workings), Epicurus's divinities were idle concepts. They could safely be jettisoned without the least damage to his account of nature. And so they were in antiquity, and so again they would be in modernity. For when Epicurean materialism was revived in modernity while Christianity was the reigning religion, various well-intentioned attempts were made to reinsert God back into Epicurean cosmology. However, it was soon enough realized that, since nature was defined as self-contained, God had nothing to do. As a result, by the nineteenth century he was forced into retirement like an old train conductor who had been kept too long on payroll in an age of jet planes.

But even if we cannot make sense out of the jumble of Epicurus's reasoning concerning the existence of the gods, we will be rewarded by seeing how the gods function as part of his overall cosmological and moral project.

We have seen that Epicurus described the gods as indestructible and blessed, and charged his disciples not to ascribe to them anything foreign to their indestructibility or repugnant to their blessedness. What is more

---

[28]Cicero gives an account of Epicurus's reason in his dialogue *De Natura Deorum*, as well as a harsh critique. See especially 1.43-56, 69, 71-76, 103-10 and Epicurus *Maxims* xxiii-xxiv.

[29]Cicero *De Natura Deorum* 1.50.

repugnant to their blessedness, Epicurus argued, than if the gods were the caretakers of the universe, or if they were in control of nature and human affairs? These would indeed be "burdensome services," completely at odds with their detached blessedness. Yet in so magnanimously releasing the gods from toil, Epicurus was really releasing nature, and hence human nature, from any divine interference. His "piety" ran directly against the belief (found not only in Greek and Roman religion, but also in Judaism, Islam and Christianity) in God understood as a creator, who is provident over human affairs. His piety had the effect, not of raising the gods to blessedness, but of raising indifference to a virtue, both on the part of the gods and on the part of humankind.[30] By making the gods sublimely indifferent, he was only liberating humanity from disturbance by the divine. The essence of his account of the gods, then, was the same as the goal of his cosmology: *our* freedom from disturbance. The essence of Epicurean theology was the subordination of the gods to nature so that they could not interfere with human affairs.

Furthermore, Epicurus was not only eliminating the most primitive notions of animism, such as believing that the sun is a god and the moon a goddess. He was also eliminating the most sophisticated accounts of natural theology and intelligent design, placing the most primitive and most sophisticated on equal footing, then washing away the ground on which they both supposedly rest. Because nature is self-contained, "when it comes to meteorological phenomena, one must believe that movements, turnings, eclipses, risings, settings, and related phenomena occur without any [god] helping out and ordaining or being about to ordain [such things]."[31]

We recall Epicurus's original admonition: "Do not believe that there is any other goal to be achieved by the knowledge of meteorological phenomena . . . than freedom from disturbance." We also recall that the "worst disturbance," according to Epicurus, came from the belief that the gods have power over nature through which they express their "wishes and undertake actions and exert causality" in relation to human affairs. By subordinating

---

[30]Thus, while Epicurus praises friendship, which is of immediate benefit to us (*Maxim* xxvii; Epicurus *Vatican Sayings* 23, 39, in Brad Inwood and L. P. Gerson, *The Epicurus Reader* [Indianapolis: Hackett, 1994]), he admonishes his followers to remove themselves from political life, which would smack of the same burdensome toil on behalf of others as, on a larger scale, governing the universe would for the gods (Plutarch *Against Colotes* 1127d-e).

[31]DL "Epicurus" 10.76.

the gods to nature, Epicurus made them impotent to interfere. Ostensibly, Epicurus dressed this impotence in a kind of piety, "for troubles and concerns and anger and gratitude are not consistent with blessedness." But it is this "piety" which allowed him to insert a completely material account of the origin of nature, and to keep the gods from interfering in it. Thus, in regard to the "movements, turnings, eclipses, risings, settings, and related phenomena" Epicurus insisted that "one must hold the opinion that it is owing to the original inclusion of these [material] compounds in the generation of the cosmos that this regularly recurring cycle too is produced."[32] We have no need of invoking a god as the designer of the complex dance of the stars and planets; a purely material account will be sufficient.

This materialist cosmology led directly to a materialist account of morality. By painting the gods as sublimely indifferent (and also powerless to direct nature), nature would be completely self-contained. Of course, since human nature is a part of nature, and human actions are a part of human nature, Epicurean materialist cosmology yielded materialist morality—morality not just in the broadest sense, as a habit of thinking and acting, but in the more strict but common sense of having to do with actions concerning justice, honor, and prudence (prudence being the ability to judge which actions are moral, and the best means to produce them). This meant an account of human action that was purely materialistic, and which (as we shall soon see) had as its goal the maximization of physical pleasure and the minimization of physical pain. The materialism also set a limit for all human endeavor, hope, and worry: the soul itself, made up of finer atoms than the body, dissipates at death along with the body. Since the soul is the source of our personal awareness, personal awareness is likewise extinguished at death.[33] As a consequence, Epicurus was able to eliminate the second aspect of the "worst disturbance" for human beings, "the eternal expectation and suspicion that something dreadful [might happen to us after death] such as the myths tell about." Epicurus therefore admonished his disciples:

> Get used to accustoming oneself to hold[34] that death is nothing to us. For all good and bad consists in sense-experience, and death is the privation of sense-

---

[32]Ibid., 10.77.

[33]Ibid., 10.63-67.

[34]Again, deviating from Inwood and Gerson.

experience. Hence, a correct knowledge of the fact that death is nothing to us
makes the mortality of life a matter for contentment, not by adding a limitless
time [to life] but by removing the longing for immortality. For there is nothing
fearful in life for one who has grasped that there is nothing fearful in the
absence of life. . . . So death, the most frightening of bad things, is nothing to
us; since when we exist, death is not present, and when death is present, then
we do not exist.[35]

The longing for immortality, which is so omnipresent that other philosophers took it to be natural, was declared by Epicurus to be unnatural, a kind
of pervasive mental illness which he intended his materialism to cure. The
"mortality of life" could be transformed into a "matter of contentment" if we
would only realize that death is natural, and there is no reason to fear such
extinction because, once our atoms have dissipated, *we* are no longer around
to experience the lack of life. The fear of nonbeing was thereby made
groundless: "We are born only once, and we cannot be born twice; and [after
death] one must for all eternity exist no more."[36]

Obviously, if at death we are no more, then we have no hell to fear, nor
heaven to long for. Consequently, we are released not only from all fears and
groundless desires in regard to life after death, but also from all religious
"toil" in this life undertaken to avoid such eternal punishment or purchase
such eternal bliss. The gods in their blessedness are indifferent to us, and we
are now completely free to be indifferent to them.

It is equally obvious that recasting human beings as purely material necessarily entails a purely materialist ethics where good and evil are identical
to physical pleasure and physical pain. Here we should not be confused or
misled by Epicurus speaking of pleasure and pain in the soul as distinct
from pleasure and pain in the body. The soul and body, we must recall, are
both material for Epicurus. Thus, disturbance in the soul is just as much a
physical pain as a splinter in the foot.

Epicurus therefore argued that we must "refer every choice and disturbance to the health of the body and the freedom of the soul from disturbance, since this is the goal of a blessed life. For we do everything for the
sake of being neither in pain nor in terror."[37] Pleasure is the "starting-point

---

[35]DL "Epicurus" 10.124-25.
[36]Epicurus *Vatican Sayings* 14.
[37]DL "Epicurus" 10.128.

and goal of living blessedly," so that "every pleasure is a good thing, . . . but not every one is to be chosen. Just as every pain too is a bad thing, but not every one is such as to be always avoided."[38]

We have reached the core of Epicurean asceticism, and it is absolutely necessary that we truly grasp what is being asserted here, because it is precisely from this point that nearly every modern account of ethics springs, either directly or indirectly.

We are surprised to find that Epicurus was an ascetic. When we hear that he identified pleasure with the good and pain with evil, we immediately infer that he must have been a shameless hedonist. But Epicurus, anticipating just such an inference, stated that

> when we say that pleasure is the goal we do not mean the pleasures of the profligate or the pleasures of consumption, as some believe, either from ignorance and disagreement or from deliberate misinterpretation, but rather the lack of pain in the body and disturbance in the soul. For it is not drinking bouts and continuous partying and enjoying boys and women, or consuming fish and the other dainties of an extravagant table, which produce the pleasant life, but sober calculation which searches out the reasons for every choice and avoidance and drives out the opinions which are the source of the greatest turmoil for men's souls.[39]

Two reasons emerge for his asceticism. The first is that nature itself often punishes us with severe pain when we indulge in sensual excess. We must obey nature, then, for it will have the last word. Epicurus therefore argued, "One must not force nature but persuade her. And we will persuade her by fulfilling the necessary desires, and the natural ones too if they do not harm [us], but sharply rejecting the harmful ones."[40]

This is common sense, indeed so common that it is found in ethical systems radically opposed to Epicurean materialism, such as Aquinas's. Although it is beyond the scope of the present work to give an adequate account of the ethical arguments of Aquinas, we should at least note the following. Epicurus took the limits of nature to be imposed by the restrictions of unintelligent matter, matter which by chance *happens* to make up our bod-

---

[38]Ibid., 10.128-29.
[39]Ibid., 10.131-32.
[40]Epicurus *Vatican Sayings* 21.

ies and souls in a particular way. Aquinas, on the other hand, took the limits
of nature to be imposed by a designing intelligence; the limitations are indications of the natural law, written into our very nature by God. In Epicurus's account we must avoid indulgence because the blind laws of nature
have so formed us, albeit unintentionally, so that sensual indulgence causes
pain; in Aquinas's account, the natural law, which is the direct result of a
provident, creating intelligence, warns us by pain that we are transgressing
an intended moral boundary. In Epicurus's account moral boundaries are
the result of physical boundaries, and physical boundaries are the result of
the chance concatenations of atoms that happen to make up our material
bodies and material souls. In Aquinas's account, physical boundaries are the
result of moral boundaries designed by God to limit and direct human action
to the good of the material body and, above all, to the good of the immaterial, immortal soul.

What was Epicurus's second reason for advocating asceticism? A rather
peculiar one. The greatest pleasure, he claimed, is the *absence* of pain.[41] No
other pleasure is greater because after all pain is removed, all pleasures are
equal.[42] Therefore no other pleasure is more worth seeking than mere
absence of pain. This assertion was so peculiar, so contrary to common
sense, that it was soon ridiculed out of existence.

Why put forth such a peculiar argument? By it Epicurus hoped to undermine the longing for immortality, for "unlimited time and limited time contain equal [amounts of] pleasure, if one measures its limits by reasoning."[43]
We would get no more pleasure than the absence of pain even if we lived for
an unlimited time, so there is no reason to long for immortality.

Why do so many people of so many different cultures seem to share a
longing for immortality? According to Epicurus, it is the result of the unnatural desire of the body for unlimited physical pleasure. "The flesh took the
limits of pleasure to be unlimited, and [only] an unlimited time would have
provided it." But we can use reason to dispel such silly desires, as long as we
reason according to the materialist presupposition that our souls are not
immortal, for "the intellect, reasoning out the goal and limit of the flesh and
dissolving the fears of eternity, provided us with the perfect way of life" so

---

[41]DL "Epicurus" 10.128, 131; Epicurus *Maxim* iii Cicero *De Finibus* 1.37-38, 55-57.
[42]Epicurus *Maxim* ix.
[43]Ibid., xix.

that we have "no further need of unlimited time."[44]

To take a moment and compare Epicurus to Christ—a comparison that will help illuminate both—perhaps the best example of the profound difference between Epicurean asceticism and Christian asceticism is this: whereas Epicurus would have us turn all wine into water, the first miracle of Christ was the turning of water into wine. Epicurean saints, then, will eat barley cakes and water to purge themselves of the desire for a heavenly banquet; Christian saints will fast on bread and water to get a better seat at the heavenly banquet.[45] Epicureans are ascetics in regard to bodily things for fear that sensual indulgence will lead to a desire for spiritual things; Christians are ascetics in regard to bodily things so that they may indulge in spiritual things.

Many of Epicurus's moral arguments seem insightful and salutary. For example, "It is impossible to live pleasantly without living prudently, honorably, and justly and impossible to live prudently, honourably, and justly without living pleasantly."[46] Who could have a problem with this? It sounds as if it could have been said by Socrates.

But if we look beyond the surface, we find that for Epicurus there were no intrinsically evil moral actions. "No pleasure is a bad thing in itself. But the things which produce certain pleasures bring troubles many times greater than the pleasures."[47] Consequently:

> If the things which produce the pleasures of profligate men dissolved the intellect's fears about phenomena of the heavens and about death and pains,[48] and moreover, if they taught us the limit of our desires, then we would not have reason to criticize them, since they [the profligate men] would be filled with pleasures from every source and would contain no feeling of pain or distress from any source—and that is what is bad.[49]

---

[44]Ibid., xx.

[45]One might also add that the bread and wine of the Eucharist understood as the body and blood of Christ would be the most profound rejection of Epicureanism possible, for it links eternity with the ordinary sustenance of bread and the joyful and festive nature of wine. It is no accident that the first miracle of Christ was to turn water into wine at a wedding feast.

[46]Epicurus *Maxim* v.

[47]Ibid., viii.

[48]As we shall see in later chapters, modernity asserted that such pleasures were the very things we needed to dissolve the lure of eternity.

[49]Epicurus *Maxim* x.

Cicero reported the following as a direct, famous and blunt summary by Epicurus of the goodness of all pleasure:

> Nor do I know what I could understand that good to be, if I set aside the plea-
> sures we get from sex, from listening to songs, from looking at [beautiful]
> shapes, from smooth motions, or any other pleasures which affect any of
> man's senses. Nor, indeed, can it be said that only mental rejoicing is [to be
> counted] among the goods; for this is my understanding of mental rejoicing: it
> lies in the expectation that our nature will avoid pain while acquiring all those
> things I just mentioned.[50]

Readers of Epicurus often have trouble reconciling such bald assertions of seemingly unbridled hedonism, with other equally famous remarks of high moral tone such as the one quoted above. What could he mean by asserting that "it is impossible to live pleasantly without living prudently, honorably, and justly and impossible to live prudently, honorably, and justly without living pleasantly"? Let us look at each of the virtues he lists, and see how his account can be reconciled with the identity of the good with pleasure.

According to Epicurus, no pleasure is bad in itself. But since nature imposes limits to our desires, then if we are to avoid pain and disturbance we must *prudently* calculate whether any pleasure will outweigh the difficulty in acquiring it and the pain that might follow upon it. We must emphasize *any* pleasure, however, because there were no intrinsically evil pleasures for Epicurus. Nature does not intend to set any limits, moral or otherwise. Atoms, by their random configuration, did not intend to impose limits on our actions and desires; such limits and the pain that reinforces them were ultimately the result of chance.

It is not as easy to see what Epicurus meant by living *honorably*.[51] What he seems to have meant is this: one lives honorably by doing those actions that are publicly held to be good because they are also those actions which have proved to be useful, either immediately (by limiting our desires) or mediately (by keeping friction to a minimum between ourselves and others who live in common life). For example, to be a public drunkard is dishonorable, while being sober is honorable. But being sober is useful because it

---

[50]Cicero *Tusculan Disputations* 3.41. See also DL "Epicurus" 10.6.

[51]The primary meaning of the root word in Greek, *kalos*, is "beautiful," and by extension, "good," as in serving a good purpose. Thus, by extension, it comes to mean a morally good action.

keeps us from both the pain of excess and the pain of public humiliation. The ultimate root, then, of what is honorable is what is useful for avoiding pain. I infer this from Epicurus's account of justice.

Justice for Epicurus was not some independent standard to which we must conform our actions. Justice was merely "reciprocal usefulness" arising from a kind of negative agreement "neither to harm another nor be harmed." However, there is no natural justice independent of such agreements. Justice was purely conventional, and therefore relative to each society. Epicurus stated quite bluntly, "There is no justice or injustice with respect to all those animals which were unable to make pacts about neither harming one another nor being harmed." For "justice was not a thing in its own right, but [exists] in mutual dealings in whatever places there [is] a pact about neither harming one another nor being harmed." Consequently, "Injustice is not a bad thing in its own right, but [only] because of the fear produced by the suspicion that one will not escape the notice of those assigned to punish such actions."[52]

There are two important ramifications of Epicurus's assertions that return full-blown in modern political theory, and hence in contemporary political and moral debate. First, justice itself is relative to time and place. When new practical circumstances arise, new things become useful, and previously useful things become harmful; therefore justice changes with circumstances.[53] Second, the only reason Epicurus gave for not doing an unjust act was this:

> It is impossible for someone who secretly does something which men agreed [not to do] in order to avoid harming one another or being harmed to be confident that he will escape detection, even if in current circumstances he escapes detection a thousand times. For until his death it will be uncertain whether he will continue to escape detection.[54]

Thus Epicurus warned his disciples, "Let nothing be done in your life which will cause you to fear if it is discovered by your neighbor."[55]

But what about those who do manage to escape detection and in fact live

---

[52]Epicurus *Maxims* xxxi-xxiv.
[53]Ibid., xxxviii.
[54]Ibid., xxxv.
[55]Epicurus *Vatican Sayings* 70.

quite happily in the pleasures they have gained at other's expense without the least gnawing of fear that they will be caught? For those devoid of such timidity, Epicurus had no cure.

We have focused primarily on pleasure in Epicurus's account of morality. How does pain enter into Epicurus's moral system? For anyone, pain is a disturbing element in human life, and the more severe it is, the more disturbing. As we have already seen, Epicurus quite reasonably noted that much of our pain is self-inflicted, caused by our own foolish indulgence. But what about the pain that besets us through no fault of our own? Epicurus, wishing to preserve tranquillity, assured his disciples that such pain, if it was severe, was "short in duration" because the severity was a sign of impending death, and death "is nothing to us," for the soul dies with the body. Those pains that do "last a long time in the flesh cause only mild distress," Epicurus assured his disciples, so we can bear them cheerfully.[56]

Of course, the problem with this reasoning is that one would have to be a blind devotee of Epicurus to believe it. Many diseases are both very painful and long-lasting. As with the assertion that the greatest pleasure is the absence of pain, so also here we sense that Epicurus was putting forth a strained argument. But we can see why he would have to strain at this point. Unendurable, long-lasting pain often turns people to the divine in search of relief, seeking either a miracle in this world or a pain-free paradise in the next. Of course, that would undermine the whole materialist project. Therefore, Epicurus was forced to maintain an absurd position, that there are no long-lasting, severe pains.

We have one final aspect of Epicurus's moral account to cover, one even stranger than his treatment of pleasure and pain. It might seem that Epicurus, being a strict materialist, would also have been a strict determinist, and if he were a strict determinist, then offering any moral account at all would be pointless. If our very actions are completely determined, then we cannot choose between alternatives, and all moral direction and exhortation would be vain.

To avoid such determinism, Epicurus introduced an element of arbitrariness into nature: he claimed that atoms, while moving through space, suddenly and without cause, swerve. This swerve allowed for contingency in an

---

[56]Ibid., 4.

otherwise fully determined material universe; this contingency, in turn, allowed for free will, and hence moral action. [57]

There was an obvious problem with the swerve, as Cicero and other ancient critics pointed out. It was a theoretically arbitrary and utterly groundless addition. A fiction that serves a good function is still a fiction. It should not surprise us that, when Epicurean materialism was revived in modernity, the swerve was left quietly aside, but with the following predictable result: modern Epicureanism, both cosmological and moral, became utterly determinist.

Enough has been said to grasp Epicurus's overall cosmological and moral arguments. Let us end with a summary that highlights the aspects and assumptions of his arguments that have had the most effect in defining contemporary scientific and moral debates.

First of all, it is incontestable that Epicurus's primary goal in regard to physics was therapeutic. As we have shown, he was not primarily a truth seeker, but a philosopher in search of a cosmological theory to support his moral project. He himself said so. That is not to say that he did not really believe that the universe was made up solely of atoms and the void. He really did *believe* it. In other words, he wanted it to be true and used his materialism as an explanatory filter that eliminated *a priori* the possibility that the universe could be intelligently designed. But he did not and could not have proved in the third century B.C. that the universe consisted only of eternal atoms and the void. At best, his materialist account would be a promising hypothesis to be tested.

We have seen the essential assumptions that characterize the Epicurean materialist hypothesis, that there are invisible things called atoms that are indestructible, and that these atoms are simple. These immortal, simple atoms, along with the equally immortal void, make up the entirety of the universe, and therefore make the universe itself eternal. The materialist hypothesis is promising because it takes the form of a promise: if we follow the materialist paradigm, then we shall find that there really are indestructible atoms, and we shall demonstrate that the apparent complexity of nature is ultimately reducible to easily comprehended atomic simplicity. These are

---

[57]In the extant remains of Epicurus we do not have an account of the "swerve," but must rely completely on others. See, for example, Cicero *De Finibus* 1.18-20; and Lucretius *De Rerum Natura* 2.218-20.

promises, however, not established facts; they guide research, determining what is worth looking for. These promises are at the heart of Epicurus's materialist faith.

As we shall see, these very assumptions were taken over by Epicurean materialism when it was revived in modernity—again, as working hypotheses, not as established facts—and became the foundation of modern materialist faith. In saying this, I am not accusing modern materialists of *bad* faith at this point, that is, of purposely misrepresenting the status of their arguments. It is enough to accuse them of faith. That is, it is of the utmost importance to see that both in Epicurus and in the founders of modernity, the very evidence needed to prove the materialist hypotheses was not there at the beginning.

We hasten to add, however, that using hypotheses to guide scientific research is not peculiar to the materialist view of science. The use of such hypotheses is both common and necessary in any view of science, materialist or nonmaterialist. All scientists work according to promising hypotheses because all human knowing on the universal scale that science attempts to reach, begins not by knowing but by guessing. Thus, far from faith being bad in science, we must realize that, without faith, there would not be any significant advance in science.

However, there are better and worse guesses, and the true test of the merit of any hypothesis is that it passes the test of nature. Is nature really this way, or are we trying to shoe-horn it into conformity by ignoring substantial counter-evidence to our theory? Such faith can become bad faith, if the working hypotheses cease to work, that is, when a theory that has worked for some time begins to work increasingly against nature. Contradicting nature around the fringes of one's theory is not fatal; a good working hypothesis can undergo minor readjustments. But if after probing ever more deeply into nature, we find that nature continually and directly contradicts the fundamental assumptions of our view of science, then good scientists question these very assumptions.

If instead the scientist is merely a bad patriot of human theory, declaring "My theory, right or wrong!" then we may accuse him or her of bad faith. The hypothesis has then become not something to be tested, but an intransigent habit of mind. It has become bad faith because it has become blind faith.

There are (at least) two reasons for leveling the charge of bad faith against contemporary scientific materialists, reasons that I hope are clearer from our examination of Epicurus (and will be clearer still after we analyze modern materialism directly). First, if modern scientific materialism, after practicing science according to its theoretical commitments for hundreds of years, discovers not only that atoms are not indestructible but that the universe is not eternal, and nevertheless remains entrenched in the materialist faith which depends on the eternality of atoms and the universe, then we may accuse such materialism of bad faith. But at the end of the nineteenth century and beginning of the twentieth, atoms were found to be quite destructible, and near the middle of the twentieth the universe was found, via the discovery of the Big Bang, not to be eternal. What, then, is the foundation of that faith?

And again, if after practicing science as defined by materialism for hundreds of years, what is continually discovered is not some fundamental, easily understood simplicity, but ever-increasing, irreducible, fundamental complexity, and in the face of this undreamed-of complexity, materialists still hold tenaciously to the belief that the reduction of complexity to simplicity is just around the corner, then again they are open to the charge of bad faith.

Further, the materialist habit of mind shows itself as bad faith when it suppresses, distorts, or ignores compelling counter-evidence that undermines or severely questions it. One mode of suppression we have already seen in Epicurus is the characterization of all nonmaterialist accounts of nature—no matter how sophisticated, intricate and powerful their explanations—as mythical. Contemporary materialists tend to reject intelligent design arguments, even prior to consideration, as irrational, classifying them as warmed-over versions of creationism (which in turn they suppose to have the intellectual character and caliber of ancient Greek myths). That is bad faith.

Could it be that much of the impetus keeping materialism as the reigning view of science today is, as it was with Epicurus, moral in origin, both in the broader and in the more confined sense? I believe, in many cases, that it is. To be blunt, materialists often suppress (or simply dismiss) evidence of intelligent design because, consciously or unconsciously, they realize that the Epicurean moral world they comfortably inhabit (for it was Epicurus's goal to make the world comfortable) would be completely undermined if materialist cosmology were overthrown by intelligent design.

In this, materialists rightly embrace that most fundamental law mentioned in the introduction, that every distinct view of the universe entails a view of morality, and every distinct view of morality needs a cosmology to support it. Many materialists therefore rightly fear the intelligent design revolution because they realize that a moral revolution necessarily follows upon it. If an intelligent designer exists, then a divinely mandated moral code for which we are accountable might exist. If an intelligent designer is not part of nature, and hence is not material, then he could have created other immaterial entities such as the immortal and immaterial soul. If the immortal soul exists and God exists, and he mandates a moral code, then heaven and hell might exist. If heaven and hell exist and God exists, then we might be held accountable for actions that are mandated or prohibited. All of this is quite disturbing, and materialists rightly fear it. Those who wish to be freed from it realize that materialism remains the therapeutic cure.

Before too many hackles get raised, I must make clear that this is not a charge leveled only or even primarily at practicing scientists. Most scientists practice their craft according to the materialist creed only because they were trained to do so, not because they are materialists themselves. Either they do not see the implications at all or they are nine-to-five materialists who commute between two universes. Twenty-four-hour-a-day, seven-day-a-week scientific materialists, such as Stephen Jay Gould, Richard Dawkins and the late Carl Sagan, are more rare; however, they generally make up in volume for what they lack in mass.

The greater charge of intellectual suppression I level at the moral Epicureans who are not scientists, but the keepers of the culture, those who have gained cultural power through a variety of institutions from funding agencies and the various media, to academia. They are protectors and promoters of materialism in science. Their desire to suppress or ridicule intelligent design arguments is purely moral in origin. Their support for materialist science is in no small part fueled by the realization that if the materialist cosmology were to crumble, the Epicurean moral world would crumble with it.

Later chapters examine this Epicurean moral world more thoroughly; its principles and implications become more clear when compared with its historical antithesis, Christianity. If the Epicurean moral world is the real source of the cultural support for materialism, and Christianity is the historical antithesis of Epicureanism, then our cultural wars are really cosmological wars between the rival and irreconcilable cosmological and moral worlds of the Epicurean and the Christian. To substantiate this, we must first illuminate the path connecting ancient Epicurean materialism to modern scientific materialism, for it is by establishing this connection that we establish that modern scientific materialism is truly the heir of Epicurean materialism and that we are not connecting the two by mere surface similarities. Along this path we shall see the Epicurean moral arguments first in direct conflict with Christian moral arguments, then seemingly vanquished by Christianity for a thousand years, but finally being taken up and transformed in modernity, where they eventually gain the upper hand again. The next stop on this complex journey is Rome, where we find the great Latin expositor of Epicureanism, the poet-philosopher Lucretius, whose poem *De Rerum Natura* was largely responsible for transmitting the spirit of Epicureanism to modernity. Here in Lucretius we shall find the first well-formed evolutionary argument, the seed of Darwinism, as it were.

T W O

Lucretius,
the First Darwinian

W hy worry about Lucretius? One reason, the one mentioned at the close of the last chapter, is that Lucretius's great Epicurean poem *De Rerum Natura (On the Nature of Things)* was even more influential than Epicurus's own writings in reintroducing Epicurus's thought to the West. Written near the middle of the first century B.C., Lucretius's poem was rediscovered in the fifteenth century, and both the thoroughness of its presentation in Latin and the sweetness of its poetry helped Epicurean materialism to charm its way back into the West after a hiatus of a millennium. We are materialists in modernity, in no small part, because we were lovers of Lucretius at the dawn of modernity, and that means the culmination of Epicurean thought in moral Darwinism was made possible by Lucretius.

We shall examine the historical path by which this occurred in later chapters. Here we must concentrate on Lucretius's poem itself. While seeing the roots of moral Darwinism in Epicureanism takes a good bit of digging and explaining (as the last chapter should make evident), seeing moral Darwinism in Lucretius's *On the Nature of Things* is almost effortless. Not only is the Darwinism quite clear—Lucretius gives the West the first clear evolutionary argument[1]—but the moral Darwinism is especially clear. The entire materialist account of human nature, society, morality and religion, which forms the stream of modernity flowing toward its culmination in Darwin, is found clearly and succinctly stated in Lucretius. Lucretius seems so modern because we are so Lucretian.

So as not to keep the reader in suspense, we may go right to those parts of Lucretius that are such obvious precursors of Darwinism. In the following analysis, there is no need to rehearse all the points wherein Lucretius faithfully followed his master Epicurus. The basic arguments are nearly identical. But as will become evident, Lucretius was not just a copyist-versifier. He added many insights and arguments to the main body of Epicurean materialism, thereby making the Epicurean approach much stronger. We will focus on his contributions, and take the elements of agreement as given.[2]

First of all, Lucretius made it very clear—even more clear than his intellectual mentor, Epicurus—that the universe is the result of chance, not intelligent design. The very birth of the universe—which assuredly neither Epicurus nor Lucretius could have witnessed—was devoid of guidance or

---

[1]Empedocles (c. 490-430) is usually given the honor of stating the first evolutionary argument. There are two good related reasons for this. First, Empedocles, as reported in an important passage in Aristotle's *Physics* (198b17-33), argued that animals come into being by the chance coming together of limbs and parts (which were themselves "wandering about") and that monstrosities that were unable to survive, perished (such as the famous ox-faced men and man-faced oxen). See G. S. Kirk and J. E. Raven, *The PreSocratic Philosophers* (Cambridge: Cambridge University Press, 1960), Empedocles fragments 442-451. Kirk and Raven even title this section of fragments the "Four Stages of Evolution." Second, and related, Darwin himself draws attention to this passage of Aristotle in the "Historical Sketch" which begins the later editions of the *Origin* (of course, his point is that Empedocles was on the mark, and Aristotle was hopelessly confused.) There are, however, several difficulties with attributing to Empedocles this honor. He was most likely a Pythagorean (or a slightly fallen away devotee), and was essentially religious, believing not only in the gods, but that we human beings had fallen away from our divine state, and into the cycle of birth and death ruled over by the twin powers, Love and Strife. Love and Strife, which put together and tear apart, are the quasi-evolutionary forces that allow parts of animals (limbs, heads, etc.) that are wandering alone to be put together randomly. Lucretius, on the other hand, believes that human beings are completely mortal, for there is no such thing as the immortal soul, and while he has a vague Epicurean account of the gods, he is purely secular in outlook and aim. Even more important, however, is that Lucretius grounds his account of evolution in materialist atomism (as does Darwin) and gives a very clear description of the purely natural forces of the development of species and the effects of natural selection.

[2]We do note, however, that part of Lucretius's power for future generations came from the paucity of Epicurus's writings that survived. Epicurus wrote a tremendous amount. Diogenes Laertius reports that Epicurus eclipsed all others before him in regard to the number of works written, "about three hundred rolls." See DL "Epicurus" 10.27-28 for a partial list. All that has been left to us are three short letters, some aphorisms and scattered fragments. Lucretius must have had a

purpose. The mindless jostling of Epicurean atoms, not the gods, brought order out of chaos.

> For certainly it was no design of the first-beginnings that led them to place themselves each in its own order with keen intelligence, nor assuredly did they make any bargain what motions each [atom] should produce; but . . . struck with blows and carried along by their own weight from infinite time until the present, [atoms] have been accustomed to move and meet in all manner of ways, and to try all combinations, whatsoever they could produce by coming together, for this reason it comes to pass that being spread abroad through a vast time, by attempting every sort of combination and motion, at length those come together which . . . become the beginnings of great things, of earth and sea and sky and the generation of living creatures.[3]

Lucretius's materialist account of the genesis of our world is repeated throughout the poem,[4] and it supplied for later generations a ready-made cosmology where chance, not design, became the cause of the natural order.

But Lucretius added an important element to the argument. Even if on theoretical grounds he had not already come to the conclusion that chance concatenations of atoms were the causes of the orderly world we now experience, Lucretius assured the reader that he would have rejected the notion that the world was made by divine power because the orderliness is shot through with "faults."[5] The world is not only full of diseases and wild animals, both of which prey on humanity, but a majority of it is a worthless wasteland which, without human labor, would produce little or nothing.[6] In fact, Lucretius ended his great poem with an account of the horrors of a plague, not only to argue that diseases have a purely natural origin (rather

---

far greater number of Epicurus's writings available than we do today, so for us he fills in quite a few gaps.

[3]Lucretius, *De Rerum Natura,* Loeb Classical Library vol. L 181, trans. W. H. D. Rouse, rev. Martin F. Smith (Cambridge, Mass.: Harvard University Press, 1924, 1975), 5:419-31. I use the Rouse translation because it is readily available, and does not try to versify in imitation of Lucretius, an attempt which nearly always ends in distorting the original to make it poetic. In addition, Rouse is generally very literal.

[4]Ibid., 1.1021-51; 2.167-81; 2.1058-1104; 4.823-57; 5.76-90; 5.198-234; 5.417-31.

[5]Ibid., 5.195-234. Lucretius used the Latin word *culpa,* which has moral overtones, as if assigning the design of the universe to a divine source would impugn that divine source on moral grounds for having done such shoddy work.

[6]These assertions will later be picked up and transformed in modernity by Francis Bacon and John Locke. I elaborate how below.

than being a judgment by the gods), but also to reinforce belief in the very imperfection of nature. The presence of imperfection, so the argument goes, proves that the universe has no designer, for a divine designer surely would not commit such engineering blunders.

Let us now see how the earth itself, imperfections and all, came into being. Again, we shall find that many modern theories of the origin of the earth are actually ancient in origin.

> In the beginning *[principio]* the earth gave forth the different kinds of herbage and bright verdure about the hills and over the plains, and the flowering meadows shone with the colour of green; then to the various kinds of trees came a mighty struggle, as they raced at full speed to grow up into the air. . . . So then the new-born earth put forth herbage and saplings first, and in the next place created the generations of mortal creatures, arising in many kinds and in many ways by different processes. For animals cannot have fallen from the sky, nor can creatures of the land have come out of the salt pools.
>
> It remains, therefore, that the earth deserves the name of mother which she possesses, since from the earth all things have been produced. . . . [And so] the earth, you see, first gave forth the generations of mortal creatures at that time, for there was great abundance of heat and moisture in the fields. Therefore, wherever a suitable place was found, wombs would grow.[7]

Thus, reasoning purely from the supposition that eternal atoms do exist, Lucretius concluded that in their continual jostling they eventually form the earth and everything on it. We even have a sort of prototype of the contemporary chemical origin of life theory, where a "great abundance of heat and moisture" gives rise to complex, organic life. No intelligence. No design. Chance (the randomness of atomic movement) and necessity (resulting from necessary interactions of weight, shape, and size of the eternal atoms themselves) are sufficient to cause all that we see.

But what exactly was the mechanism by which such jostlings were translated into the variety of living organisms? A very familiar one: natural selection (entailing survival of the fittest) and the successful passing on of beneficial characteristics by procreation. The whole surprising passage must be quoted in full—it is almost pure Darwin, two millennia before the appearance of *The Origin of Species*.

---

[7]Lucretius 5.783-808. Rouse overplays the similarities to the Bible's Genesis account.

Many were the portents also that the earth then tried to make. springing up with wondrous appearance and frame: the hermaphrodite, between man and woman yet neither, different from both; some without feet, others again bereft of hands; some found dumb also without a mouth, some blind without eyes, some bound fast with all their limbs adhering to their bodies, so that they could do nothing and go nowhere, could neither avoid mischief nor take what they might need. So with the rest of like monsters and portents that she made, it was all in vain; since nature banned their growth, and they could not attain the desired flower of age nor find food nor join by the ways of Venus. For we see that living beings need many things in conjunction, so that they may be able by procreation to forge out the chain of the generations. . . .

And many species of animals must have perished at that time, unable by procreation to forge out the chain of posterity: for whatever you see feeding on the breath of life, either cunning or courage or at least quickness must have guarded and kept that kind from its earliest existence; many again still exist, entrusted to our protection, which remain, commended to us because of their usefulness. . . .

But those to which nature gives no such qualities, so that they could neither live by themselves at their own will, nor give us some usefulness for which we might suffer them to feed under our protection and be safe, these certainly lay at the mercy of others for prey and profit, being all hampered by their own fateful chains, until nature brought that race to destruction.[8]

For anyone even mildly familiar with modern evolutionary theory this is a remarkable passage. We suppose that Darwin discovered evolution in the early nineteenth century, but in reality he was mainly repeating an ancient argument, and adding to it what he took to be a body of supporting evidence. In this passage, we find nearly all the essential ingredients of Darwin's argument (lacking only a direct statement about the transition of one species of animal into another):

(1) Random variation at the atomic level brings about a diversity of creatures at the level of species.[9]

(2) Monsters (later called monstrosities by Darwin) do not survive because

---

[8]Ibid., 5.837-77.

[9]One might argue that since Darwin himself said fairly little about the physical foundations of his theory, it would be better to say that Lucretius was providing the foundations of neo-Darwinism. While Darwin was largely silent in this regard, I will show in later chapters that such atomism was presupposed by Darwin.

they cannot defend themselves, nor provide sustenance, nor procreate by "the ways of Venus."

(3) Whatever animals have survived must have been the most fit, having greater cunning, courage or quickness (or greater utility to human beings), and so are "able by procreation to forge out the chain of the generations."

(4) Like the monsters, those species that are less fit do not survive, for they "lay at the mercy of others for prey and profit . . . until nature brought that kind to destruction," that is, extinction.

Again, we need to remind ourselves that Lucretius had no more evidence of the mechanism of evolution at work through the ages than he did of the existence of the eternal atom. The basis of his confidence in these things was (following Epicurus) the desire to rid the universe of divine influence, as is clear from his extended attack on religion at the beginning of Book Five, where his evolutionary account occurs.[10]

We may now turn to Lucretius's account of the evolution of human society and morality.

As with the above evolutionary account, we are surprised that many modern political and moral theorists (as well as later social scientists and anthropologists), whom we took to be progressive, were merely repeating arguments made by Lucretius in his account of the evolution of human society and morality. But we should not be surprised. For history repeats itself (in this instance, at least) because of the first part of that great law of uniformity: "Every distinct view of the universe, every theory about nature, necessarily entails a view of morality." To put it in terms of its historical culmination, Darwinism and moral Darwinism necessarily go hand in hand, because a materialist account of the universe can only yield a materialist account of morality.

And so, if human beings (along with all other creatures) are an accident of blind physical forces, then human society and morality must likewise be explained in terms of their accidental rise and development. Just as in evolutionary accounts (both ancient and modern), the nonliving gives rise to the living, so also in Lucretius's narrative of the evolution of society and morality, the nonsocial (or better, *a*social) gives rise to the social, and the nonmoral (or *a*moral) gives rise to the moral. Our social and moral natures

---

[10]Lucretius 5.1-180.

cannot have been designed or intended. *Nothing* is designed or intended.

At the same time, however, Lucretius (just as Epicurus) designed his account with a definite goal in mind: to convince readers that they should follow the Epicurean way of life, and thereby rid their lives of disturbance. For this reason, we must recall Epicurus's moral goal when we read Lucretius's narrative conjectures about primitive man. Not only is his primitive man asocial and amoral, but he is an Epicurean ascetic precisely because his assertions about primitive man were designed to show that only Epicurus's view of human nature was really natural. The Epicurean "saint" will be the one who most closely matches the carefree existence of the Epicurean "Adam" precisely *because* the Epicurean saint was the model for the Epicurean Adam.

The Epicurean Adam is indistinguishable from an animal, stripped by Lucretius of anything that would make him distinctly human. He has no speech, no tools, no thought about the past or future, no arts, no music, no fear of death and no religion. These primitive men roamed the fields like wild beasts because they were wild beasts, "tougher than the men of today," utterly unaccustomed to consuming or using anything beyond what the earth spontaneously produced.[11] Existing in a blissful asocial, amoral condition, the first human beings "could not look to the common good; they didn't know how to govern their intercourse by custom or law. Whatever prize fortune gave to each, that he carried off, every man taught to live and be strong for himself at his own will." This animal-like existence pertained in sexual matters as well: "Venus joined the bodies of lovers in the woods; for either the woman was attracted by some mutual desire, or caught by the man's violent force and vehement lust, or by a bribe—acorns and arbute-berries or choice pears."[12] In sum, primitive human beings were completely tranquil, undisturbed by any desires or fears beyond their immediate self-preservation and self-gratification, living a blessed, "barely cakes and water" existence.

If we take a closer look at Lucretius's rather startling account of sexuality, we will see most clearly the alleged asocial and amoral nature of human beings. The only natural goal in the above-described act of "Venus" is the immediate satisfaction of sexual desire. This desire is essentially and com-

---

[11]Ibid., 5.925-57, 1029-54. My translation.
[12]Ibid., 5.958-65.

pletely defined by sensual pleasure, which is, we remind ourselves, the Epicurean good. That sexual intercourse results in procreation is an accident unforeseen and unintended by Epicurean Adams and Eves. They have no natural desire for children, but desire only the release of sexual passion, a simultaneous experience of pleasure and removal of the pain of unfulfilled desire. The original sexual act, therefore, is both asocial (for children are the very beginning of society) and amoral (for the focus is solely on the satisfaction of desire).

This historical account of our natural, original sexuality accords with Lucretius's later explanation of sexuality in terms of his cosmology. Before tackling the subject of the nature of sexuality, he reminded the reader that in *no* case are any of our bodily organs created for a purpose—that would mean that we were intelligently designed. "That is a vice in such things that you should vehemently desire to escape and [you ought] to avoid [such] an error with dreadful apprehension."[13]

Since our bodily organs are not designed, we cannot read any moral purpose from our physical sexual constitution. Given that we human beings (and everything else, for that matter) are an accidental result of the random motions of atoms over time, it is only accidental as well that sexual passion happens to be linked to procreation (and hence to marriage). The gods certainly do not link the two, since they are not creators. It follows that there is no necessity that *we* link the two. We are not surprised, then, that Lucretius gave some very modern advice to men: "Ejaculate the liquid collected in the body and do not retain it."[14] In imitation of primitive human beings, we should keep the cure for sexual pain, as well as the experience of sexual pleasure itself, as close as possible to ourselves, thus allowing us to imitate, as best as possible, the original asocial state of the Epicurean Adam.

We must emphasize that it was not because Lucretius was a shameless sexual hedonist that he gave such an account of primitive man or offered such frank advice about how to deal with the turgid nature of sexual passion. These things emanated from his Epicurean asceticism, both in regard to the material body and the material soul.

We recall that Epicurus argued that the desire for immortality is a kind

---

[13]Ibid., 4.823-24. My translation. From a historical perspective, it is very interesting that he uses the example of the eye in this passage, which Darwin focuses on as well.
[14]Ibid., 4.1065-66, my translation.

of echo effect of the desire for indulgence on the part of the body. In regard to sexuality, easily the most vivid and powerful source of bodily indulgence, Lucretius was counseling independence from the entanglements that produce the pain and anxiety of the lovelorn. Such suffering of the pangs of unrequited love has always been the stock and trade of the love poet. But the normal goal of love poetry is singing the praises of the beloved to the heavens, and that is precisely what both Epicurus and Lucretius wanted us to avoid. In doing so, Epicurean asceticism set itself dead against the greatest love poems of all times—among them, Plato's *Phaedrus*, *The Song of Songs*, and Dante's *Divine Comedy*—which all happily link earthly sexual desire and love to the desire for immortality and the divine. For Lucretius, the advice to masturbate was part of the general ascetic admonition that "it is fitting to flee images [of the beloved] and drive away fearfully from oneself the foods of love, and turn the mind elsewhere and ejaculate the liquid collected in the body and do not retain it." The "foods of love" might drive us heavenward. Masturbation was the local cure for this pesky cosmic perturbation.

And so, strange as it may sound, Lucretius was preaching an interesting form of abstinence: sex leads to love, and love disturbs our tranquillity (not only in regard to the normal turmoil of human relations, but in the possibility of sliding from human to divine love); avoid sex if possible; if impossible, then be quick about it, and return to tranquillity. The amoral account of sex, both in regard to his narrative of primitive sexuality and in regard to his frank advice for his disciples, is determined by his larger moral goal: the release from disturbance for the sake of this-worldly tranquillity on every level.

But even that does not exhaust the depths of his peculiar account of sexuality. We may ferret out more by reading a contrary account of sexuality from Aristotle.

> The most natural of the works of living things . . . [is] the making of another like itself—an animal, an animal; a plant, a plant—in order that they may share, insofar as they have the power, in the eternal and in the divine. For all desire this, and for the sake of this do what they do according to nature.[15]

---

[15]Aristotle *On the Soul* 415a23-415b2, my translation.

The desires for immortality and to be as divine-like as possible are for Aristotle the actual desires behind all procreation, even on the level of a plant, let alone the level of the rational animal, human being. The parents receive a kind of natural immortality through the lives of their children who continue after the natural death of the parents. But this desire for natural immortality would, for Lucretius, be a danger, because it would not only disturb one's tranquillity by entanglement in the family (and thereby in the larger affairs of the greater political whole), but kindle the unnatural desire for one's own immortality after death.[16]

Yet regardless of Lucretius's philosophic goal, and despite the Epicurean Adam and Eve's desire to remain asocial and amoral, children are the natural result of sexual intercourse, intended or not. Society happens. But Lucretius put a materialist spin on it. It is important to note that the description of the coming into being of society (and hence morality) closely parallels the materialist account of creation out of the random jostling of atoms. In the same way that atoms, moving through the void in their primitive state happened to bang into each other and accidentally create larger wholes that *appear* to be designed, so also atomic individuals, moving through forests, happen upon each other in a primitive state devoid of all natural connections and moral restrictions, and quite by accident create complex societies with complex moral codes, all of which may *appear* to be natural but are actually deviations from our proper, original condition. The reason for this parallelism should be clear: the theoretical foundation for atomic individualism *is* materialist atomism—or to put it the right way around in regard to Lucretius, atomic individualism is merely an expression of the larger moral goal of Epicureanism, and (in accordance with the great law of uniformity) the moral goal must be supported by a materialist cosmology.

And so it is by accident (both locally and cosmically) that a male and female happen to meet in the forest, and since sexual desire and procreation are likewise linked only by accident and not divine intention, there is no

---

[16]Epicurus (or perhaps the early Epicureans) seems a bit less harsh in regard to childbearing. In regard to sexual intercourse, there is the simple admonition not to have it "with a woman in a manner forbidden by the laws," which accords with Epicurus's utilitarian-conventional view of justice. And he does say that "a wise man will marry and father children." However, such advice is not that of someone impassioned about love and the family, for "sexual intercourse never helped anyone and one must be satisfied if it has not harmed." DL "Epicurus" 10.118-19.

unnatural sexual desire; therefore, it could just as well be a male and male, or female and female, or other combinations too sickening to suggest (although, as we shall see in a later chapter, even these will be affirmed with gusto by the unabashed modern Epicurean Alfred Kinsey). But somehow, males and females do unite and, after intercourse, stay together long enough to make the first society.

Why don't they just happily go their separate ways after intercourse, as apparently they had so many times before? Lucretius suggested the following, which provided the blueprint for Rousseau and others eighteen centuries later. Men built huts to stay out of the rain, and to guard against the heat and chill (i.e., to avoid pain). A male and female both happen to inhabit the same hut, and they use each other for sexual satisfaction (and hence procure pleasure). Rather than disappearing back into the forest never to see each other again, they remain in the hut long enough for a child to appear, a child who is an unintended effect of the natural desire for sexual pleasure and the release of sexual pain. For some reason (not all that clear in Lucretius) the parents desire to watch over and protect their offspring. Soon enough, "Venus has weakened manly strength," and the original Epicurean freedom of primitive man has been traded for the softer common life of the family. With this common life comes the origin of all law, for the separate families make a compact *(foedus)* among themselves not to harm one another.[17] From this social compact, all morality evolves.

In Lucretius's account, then, society was purely artificial, cemented by a merely negative agreement, and all later laws, rather than being reflections of some natural or eternal law, are rooted in what each particular society has found to be useful. Not only is society unnatural—that is, purely conventional—but it represents a kind of falling away from an original blissful state, an Epicurean Eden, where human beings were utterly untroubled by unnecessary desires, and able to express what desires they had without the fetters of morality or society. As we shall see when we get to the chapters on modernity, such arguments were the source and framework of all modern social contract theories from Hobbes, Locke and Rousseau on. These, in turn, formed part of the great stream of materialist arguments about the nature and origin of human society and morality that rushed to culmination in Darwin, and the

---

[17]Lucretius 5.1011-27.

Darwinist accounts of human nature, society and morality that have flooded Western culture ever since.

We may now turn to Lucretius's account of religion. Although last in our presentation, it is at the very heart of Lucretius's entire poetic argument. Of course, as we would suspect, primitive human beings were not only asocial and amoral, but areligious, completely oblivious to the gods and utterly devoid of any gnawing fear of death or the afterlife. They do not yearn for anything beyond the simplest existence, and death is nothing to them. Before going to Lucretius's narrative of the rise of religion, we should recall its ultimate source—not direct, empirical evidence, but the larger moral goal and the materialist cosmology that supports it.

One of the "benefits" of Epicurean materialism is that it allows its adherents to claim omniscience. Lucretius's *On the Nature of Things* claims to tell the truth about everything because (as with Epicurus) Lucretius maintained that he had "seen" the very fundamental constituents of all that there was, is, or could be: atoms and the void. And as with Epicurus, these constituents are utterly without complexity; that is, completely intelligible to the human mind. Once we know what an atom is—and who could fail to grasp it, it is so simple—and we know how atoms move through the void, we know everything.

On the basis of this omniscience, Lucretius was able to eliminate the gods, not by denying their existence, but (following Epicurus) by declaring them to be utterly innocuous. Epicurean materialism allows the gods to exist, as long as they are unable to interfere in human affairs. Thus, Lucretius asserts that the gods exist, but in a state of blissful, indifferent tranquillity, unable to control nature even if they desired to do so.[18]

As for those who believed that the gods do care for and intervene in human affairs, Lucretius was a much greater and more direct rhetorical critic than Epicurus. His barbs appealed particularly to those at the dawn of modernity who had a secret discontent with Christianity and a barely hidden streak of worldliness. Lucretius's attacks against religion provided the critics of Christianity, as they became more and more public in the seventeenth and eighteenth centuries, with a string of high-minded Latin slogans, the most famous being *tantum religio potuit suadere malorum*, "only religion

---

[18]Lucretius 2.1090-93, 5.147-80.

was able to persuade men of [such] evil things."[19] What things? Almost every evil imaginable, from child sacrifice to war.[20] Even though Lucretius's criticisms were directed at Greek and Roman religion, the Renaissance and especially the Enlightenment took him to be a prophet speaking the truth about all religion, including Christianity.

Furthermore, Lucretius's theoretical omniscience enabled him not only to render the gods impotent, but to eliminate hell, for after scanning the entire universe he declared, "Nowhere appear the regions of Acheron" (the river in Hades made famous by the Greek poet Homer, where Odysseus consulted the spirits of the underworld). Thanks to Epicurus, Lucretius declared, "The fear of Acheron may be hastily sent away, the fear which disturbs the life of humanity at its foundations, and suffuses all things with the blackness of death, leaving no pleasure clean and pure."[21] And so, corresponding to the more dedicated attack on the evils of religion, we find in Lucretius a more sustained jeremiad against the evils caused by the belief in Hades. As we shall see, the early moderns made this attack on the Christian doctrine of hell (a doctrine, by the way, that Darwin himself considered "damnable").[22]

This fear of Hades which "suffuses all with the blackness of death" is part of a larger fear, the fear of death itself, which is for human beings "the very fountainhead of their troubles." [23] Religion and the fear of death are thereby linked together in Lucretius right from the beginning of the poem as twin evils that Epicurean materialism can cure, "for, if men saw that a definite end was set to their hardships, they would find strength, in some way *[ratione]*, to stand against religion and the threats of the prophets. As it is, there is no way *[ratio]* of resisting, because everlasting punishment is to be feared after death."[24] But an antidote is available in the Epicurean account of the soul.

---

[19]Lucretius 1.101, my translation.

[20]The passage where the phrase first occurs refers to Agamemnon's sacrifice of his own daughter, Iphigeneia, to placate Artemis and bring a wind allowing the Greeks to cast off to fight the Trojans.

[21]Lucretius 3.24-40, my translation.

[22]See Gertrude Himmelfarb, *Darwin and the Darwinian Revolution* (Chicago: Ivan R. Dee, 1996), p. 12.

[23]Lucretius 3.82, my translation.

[24]Ibid., 1.102-12, my translation. I provide the Latin *ratio,* which means (primarily) "reason," for what we need, according to Lucretius, is a way, a reason, or a reasoned account that will dispel these fears.

In regard to the soul, Lucretius chanted the Epicurean dictum *Nil igitur mors est ad nos*, "death is nothing to us."[25] The soul is purely material, and therefore its accidental unity is subject to dissolution at death—or more accurately, death *is* that dissolution. "For which reason, it seems, the soul is neither deprived of a birthday or a funeral."[26] As with the other points above, the denial of the immateriality and immortality of the soul, which seems so characteristic of modernity, is really quite ancient.

Now that we have spelled out Lucretius's larger cosmological and moral goal, we may (as he himself did) simply transport it all into the original condition of primitive humanity so that we will see that religion, the belief in hell and the belief in the immortality of the soul are all unnatural. Natural men, according to Lucretius, knew neither fear nor wonder. Night provided no terrors of the unknown, nor did the stars call forth any wonder in their unperturbed breasts. They had no more desire for immortality nor fear of death or hell than any other brute animal of the forest.[27] How did all these unnatural evils, beginning with religion, arise then? What "implanted in mortal men the awe [Latin: horror] that raises new shrines to the gods all over the world, and drives them to throng together on festal days"?[28]

Lucretius's answer was a bit strange. It relied on the peculiar epistemology of Epicurus that bodies continually cast off thin films of atoms that fly through the air and hit our eyes. (That is why we see things at a distance.) The air is full of these films, including the films cast off by the immortal gods (for remember, Lucretius was not an atheist). In dreams we manipulate these images of the gods, and attribute to them actions they themselves would not undertake, such as actions of vengeance or interference in nature. We therefore come to believe that the gods do these things in real life. Religion, therefore, was born from bad dreams.[29]

But religion also receives additional force because of the ignorance of the

---

[25]Lucretius 3.830, my translation. This *Nil* is ultimately the source of modern nihilism.

[26]Ibid., 3.711-12, my translation. It is important, however, that Lucretius added to the basic Epicurean assertion of the mortality of the soul many compelling arguments that the soul could not possibly be immaterial and immortal. Why, he asked, does bodily sickness affect the mind? Why does the mind seem to age with the body? We see, then, that Lucretius was not simply repeating the master in poesy, but adding to the substance of the Epicurean position by adding to its strength. See the entire section of Lucretius 3.417-829.

[27]Ibid., 5.970-80.

[28]Ibid., 5.1165-67.

[29]Ibid., 5.1160-83.

real—that is material—causes of the regularity of the heavens.[30] Such wonder is unwarranted, however, and can be dispelled easily by recalling that the regularity and splendor of the heavens is purely random in origin, and at bottom made of the same material as we are. This intellectual exercise is absolutely essential for our tranquillity, for from our ignorance of the heavens, we likewise ascribe awe-full phenomena to the gods, such as earthquakes, lightning, thunder and tornadoes, and fall to propitiating the gods, who are actually utterly indifferent to our fate and utterly impotent to control any aspect of nature whatsoever. In the grips of wonder and fear, we are well on the way to being ensnared by the evils of religion.[31] Our salvation from such evils lies in embracing materialism.

Now that we have gone through Lucretius, I hope one thing is clear. Epicurean presuppositions determined every detail of his entire evolutionary account—and I use evolution here in the very broadest sense to include not only the generation by chance of animal species, but the generation by chance of everything, from the universe itself to human society, morality and religion. But if Lucretius seems so very modern, we ought to wonder whether we too haven't deduced our narratives of the origin of the universe, of species, of human society, morality and religion, from the same materialist presuppositions. Perhaps we are merely following the ruts of Lucretius.

If this is so, how is it that this Roman poet came to exercise so much influence? As brilliant as his great Epicurean poem was, a new religion was about to arise which would oppose Epicurean philosophy (and hence Epicurean poetry) so vehemently that Epicureanism would be driven underground for nearly a millennium and a half. That new religion was Christianity. But fifteen hundred years after the birth of Christianity, the West was suddenly ignited by the love of all things ancient, especially of ancient Rome. The rebirth (for that is the meaning of the word *Renaissance*) of classical learning was part of a general shift of temperament, which often included a brooding discontent with Christianity and the Christian culture of the Middle Ages (now considered to be "dark" as compared with the blazing light of pagan antiquity). The Renaissance intellectuals loved Latin, the more elaborate and pure the better. Elaborate Latin, however, was the Latin labored

---

[30]Ibid., 5.1184-94.
[31]Ibid., 5.1161ff.

over by the great pre-Christian and early A.D. non-Christian Romans, not the seemingly more dry and theologically constrained Latin of the medievals. Pure Latin was the Latin of the original Roman civilization, directed to life in that civilization, to life in the world; the Latin borrowed by monks to dwell upon life in the next was impure. So it seemed to the Renaissance.

In that regard, aside from the content, Lucretius's *De Rerum Natura* was inviting, even enticing to the Renaissance because of the artisanship of its Latin alone, for Lucretius was an excellent poet. In fact, he told his readers that, like the physician who tricks children into taking bitter medicine by smearing the rim of the cup with honey, so he would set forth Epicurean philosophic doctrine with the honey of poetry in order better "to unloose the soul from the tight knots of religion."[32] Lucretius's trick worked far better than he could have imagined, for when his poem was rediscovered in the Renaissance, it seemed to be a great treasure buried for centuries by ignorant monks, a treasure which nearly blinded its new patrons by its poetic brilliance. The convincing power of its content, in no small part, followed upon its form. Yet the content had its allure as well, and it was the content that, even after the honey of the poetry was long forgotten, eventually helped to reverse the Christianization of Western culture and initiate the march of secularization that is now all but complete. Before we see how the West was secularized, however, we had better investigate first how it was Christianized, and especially in what ways Christianity and Epicureanism were so diametrically opposed cosmologically, morally and hence historically.

---

[32]Ibid., 1.931-50, my translation.

THREE

Christianity
Versus Epicureanism

The reason we need to examine Christianity in the present work is not confessional or dogmatic, but historical. Whether we are Christian or not, it is simply true from the very beginning Christianity set itself completely against Epicureanism at all points. The victory of Christianity in the first five hundred years A.D. necessitated the defeat of Epicurean materialism. The two could not coexist.

Nor could they coexist when Epicureanism was revived in the Renaissance. As Epicurean materialism took greater and greater hold of Western culture, the grip of Christianity was correspondingly weakened. By the time of Epicurean materialism's culmination in moral Darwinism, cultural secularization was all but complete. Thus, the antagonism between moral Darwinism and Christianity in the nineteenth century and beyond was and is simply a continuation of a very ancient animosity. As a consequence, even detached observers would have to understand why these two rival and irreconcilable cosmological and moral views must inevitably collide. That means that we must have at least a general grasp of the essentials of Christianity.

In focusing on Christianity for historical reasons, we should not forget the fundamental cosmological and moral agreement between Christianity, Judaism and Islam. Since all three share a common foundation in the Old Testament, all three will be in basic opposition to Epicurean materialism (and hence, moral Darwinism). Consequently, much of what is said about Christianity in its opposition to Epicureanism could be said of Judaism and Islam as well. However, mentioning all three throughout this chapter, or throughout the whole book, would not only be tiresome but would remove the essential focus on Christianity as the dominant historical rival.

Before beginning our analysis of Christianity, we must make a very important distinction. There are two central doctrines of Christianity that, depending on which is emphasized, result in two distinct approaches to our natural knowledge of the created order: the doctrine of the goodness of creation and the doctrine of sin. Both approaches agree that God is the creator of the natural order; the difference arises in consideration of the effects of sin.

If, on the one hand, the effects of sin are so great that the goodness of the human intellect has been destroyed, then nothing can be read from the natural order by human intelligence. Therefore, apart from revelation, true knowledge is impossible. Since the moral order is part of the natural order, sin makes it impossible for the human intellect to grasp the moral order as well, so that apart from the revealed divine commands included in the Bible, there is no moral knowledge. This view of Christianity is obviously incompatible not only with intelligent design theory, but with natural law accounts of morality.

If, on the other hand, the goodness of creation is not entirely destroyed but only wounded by sin, then enough of the goodness of the human intellect remains for it to engage in fruitful scientific inquiry, and to draw moral conclusions from nature via the natural law. This view of Christianity is compatible with intelligent design theory, and with natural law accounts of morality as well.

In this chapter, and indeed in the rest of the book, I am only concerned with the latter view of Christianity. In order to avoid the tiresome repetition of this distinction, from here on (unless otherwise noted) when I say "Christian" or "Christianity" I will simply mean the kind of Christianity compatible with intelligent design.

This leads to another important distinction. While Christianity (in the sense just mentioned) is compatible with intelligent design theory, not all intelligent design theorists have to be Christians. While grace builds on a particular view of nature, having the particular view of nature does not inevitably lead to grace.

According to Christian doctrine, grace is a gift from God, therefore belief in the strictly supernatural aspects of Christian revelation is likewise a gift. For this reason, intelligent design theorists who are Christians not only keep intelligent design arguments distinct from natural theology, but keep both distinct from revealed theology. This is done not out of a lukewarm attitude toward revelation, but out of deference to faith. Only God can empower us to believe the supernatural mysteries of faith.

To give an example, according to the intelligent design movement, from scientific evidence open to all, we can infer that nature has an intelligent designer. Further, we can extend these arguments philosophically, demonstrating that the intelligent designer is God, and thereby have *knowledge* that God exists through his effects, that is, through a study of the natural order. Knowledge that God exists, then, belongs to natural theology, as supported by contemporary intelligent design arguments. But we can only have belief or faith that God is triune—Father, Son and Holy Spirit—through supernatural revelation, and the power to believe in the Trinity is itself a gift. Belief in the Trinity, then, belongs, to *super*natural, or revealed, theology, *super* in Latin meaning "above," for the content of revealed theology, strictly speaking, is truth above our natural capacities.[1]

Futhermore, intelligent design theorists who are Christians are very careful to distinguish themselves from creationists. The problem with creationists for the intelligent design movement is not their belief that nature was created by God in an orderly way, but that they often confuse, by not clearly distinguishing, what can be known by natural reason, and what can be known only by supernatural revelation. Creationists have given many sound insights and arguments against materialism, and indeed, prior to the emergence of the intelligent design movement in the 1990s, they were the torchbearers of intelligent design arguments, if only by providing cogent criticisms of Darwinism. But the tendency of strict creationists was and is to use Genesis to defeat materialism, thereby giving the impression that one had to believe in the Bible to reject materialism. But belief in the Bible *as revealed*,

---

[1]We should note that it is possible to *believe* what can actually be *known* by natural reason, because the two domains overlap; that is, it is possible to believe that God exists based only on supernatural revelation, in the same way that it is possible to believe that King Cyrus was a Persian based only on the information given in the Bible. But just as the knowledge that there was indeed a King Cyrus can be had independently from his appearance in the books of Esther, Isaiah and Daniel, so also can the knowledge that God exists be gotten independently from his appearance in the Bible.

is itself a gift of grace, and a sign that purely natural arguments could be used against materialism was that creationists themselves often pointed out the defects of Darwinist materialism on purely natural grounds. The intelligent design movement is only saying, "Stick to the natural grounds."

It is true, however, that precisely because Christian supernatural revelation builds on nature itself, Epicurean materialism contradicts Christianity on both levels. For example, since Epicureanism insists that God can interfere with nature, then it will deny that Jesus Christ could turn water into wine or raise Lazarus from the dead. Both levels are important, then, for our historical analysis of the way that Epicurean materialism and Christianity have done battle with each other, especially (as we shall see) in regard to modern Epicureanism. However, in referring to the Bible as the source of authority for all Christians, most of the time I focus on the general parameters of the Christian approach to nature, the parameters shared with a non-Christian intelligent design approach, and particular examples from the Bible are used to help make those parameters clear. Further, as with the previous chapter, I draw immediate connections to contemporary debates, so that the reader will be clear that the historical analysis actually leads to a clarification of our present situation.

To begin at the beginning, even a completely disinterested reader of the first chapter of Genesis can see that the Christian God is a creator God. He is not, like the god of Epicurus, a part of nature, nor is nature coeternal with him. He exists as an independent immaterial being. Furthermore, the Christian doctrine of creation *ex nihilo* (creation out of nothing) strikes directly against Epicurus's contrary doctrine that the universe, atoms and the void are all eternal. At one time, or rather before time, there was only God. For Christians, God preexists nature, and calls it effortlessly into being out of nothing.

This effortlessness on the part of God means that nature, being his creation, does not and cannot oppose his will. His omnipotence extends from before time to all of time. Therefore, unlike the Epicurean gods, the Christian God is not only a creator but a miracle worker, and examples of miracles abound throughout the Old and New Testament, from the parting of the Red Sea by Moses to the miracle of the resurrection of Jesus Christ.

There is another important aspect of the Genesis account. Creation is from the top down, so to speak, whereas in Epicurus, it was from the bottom up. That is, God is portrayed in Genesis as an intelligent designer, creating according to the plan of his intellect and will; therefore, the material follows the design—or to put it another way, the form (or design) is prior to and superior to the matter. For Epicurus and Lucretius, by contrast, the visible form a thing takes is caused by the accidental relations of matter. It is obvious from Genesis, however, that creation occurs according to intention and not accident. No Christian can hold that it came about by chance, just as no Epicurean can hold that it came about by design.[2]

Furthermore, the Genesis account is not an exhaustive scientific account. That is, the general parameters of an intelligent design approach to nature are present, but there is no attempt to fill in the details about the inner workings of nature. There is no account, for example, of what the elements are, or what (if any) are the smallest constituents of nature, or how large the universe is. The closest Genesis comes to offering a scientific particular is the presentation of the heavens as a firmament, literally a dome over the earth (1:6-8). There is also a general order of creation, divided into "days," but the order seems, for the most part, to stick to the obvious: dry land has to appear before plants and trees, and so forth. There is ample room for scientific discovery as long as one avoids a completely literal reading.

By contrast, Epicurean materialism, as we have seen, is exhaustive; that is, it designates beforehand the fundamental constituents of the universe—atoms and the void—and their sole qualities of shape, size and weight. All else that is discoverable must be rendered according to these material confines. The job of science, in the most fundamental respect, is finished. That is why Lucretius could claim scientific omniscience on behalf of Epicurus and himself.

_____

[2]However, Christians are free to admit that chance enters in as a subordinate cause—in fact, they are commanded to, since they are not allowed to be determinists. Materialists, however, are not free to admit that there is design anywhere in nature, and, unless they, like Epicurus, introduce a fiction like the "swerve," they are commanded to be determinists. As Aristotle noted long ago, the irony of such strict materialism, is that it posits chance as a first cause, and denies it everywhere else, when every sane person sees that it is the other way around: intelligence is the cause of the heavens, and a certain amount of chance exists in the natural order (Aristotle *Physics* 196a31-196b9). Or as G. K. Chesterton remarked on the "madness" of materialism, "The Christian is quite free to believe that there is a considerable amount of settled order and inevitable development in the universe. But the materialist is not allowed to admit into his spotless machine the slightest speck of spiritualism or miracle. . . . The Christian admits that the universe is manifold and even miscellaneous, just as a sane man knows that his is complex. . . . But the materialist's world is quite simple and solid, just as the madman is quite sure he is sane" (*Orthodoxy* [New York: Doubleday, 1959], p. 24).

However, there is an important area of agreement between these rival views. Both Epicurus and the Bible agree that the sun, moon, stars and planets are not divine (Gen 1:14-19). Both, then, can say with equal fervor, when discussing heavenly phenomena, "Just keep the myths out of it!" for mythology is the attribution of divinity to something which is purely natural. Mythology confuses the creature and the creator. The difference between Epicurean materialism and Christianity, as we have seen, is that Epicureanism classes the notion that there *is* a creator as mythology.

In regard to humanity, according to Genesis 1-2 human beings are distinct from other animals. They are the pinnacle of earthly creation, somehow made in God's image, not, as with Lucretius, a happy accident of chance, ultimately no different from other animals. Following upon this, it is clear from reading the entire Bible that human beings have an immortal, immaterial soul; that death, rather than being the natural dissipation of atoms, is an unnatural punishment; and finally, that the immaterial soul lives on after the death of the body. We see the opposition of Christianity to materialism on this point throughout the Old and New Testaments, and there is no need to belabor the point here.[3] But we ought to be clear about the kind of opposition that the two really have, otherwise we shall end up distorting Christianity.

The Christian doctrine of the relationship of the soul to the body is the contrary of two extremes, not just one. One extreme is, of course, materialism, which denies the immateriality or existence of the soul. The other extreme, to which Christianity is equally opposed, we might call "immaterialism," that is, the belief either that material bodily reality is actually an illusion or a mere projection of an immaterial mind or minds, or that our bodily nature is not natural but a kind of punishment or trap that the immaterial soul naturally desires to escape.[4] Christianity proclaims to both extremes that both are half right, but in taking themselves to be completely right, they are both all wrong.

In regard to the relationship of the body and soul, this puts Christianity

---

[3]The entries in a standard concordance under "spirit" and "soul" go on for pages. As we shall see, modern Epicureans, who were either trying to combine Epicureanism with Christianity, or subordinate Christianity to Epicureanism, championed a scriptural exegesis that "discovered" that, all along, the Jews and early Christians had never believed in an immaterial and immortal soul, but such was an alien import from Greek philosophy.

[4]So it was that Christianity was historically opposed to Manichaeanism and Gnosticism, and was always on guard in relation to the excesses of Platonism.

in a peculiar position. To the materialist, Christianity looks like airy immaterialism; to the immaterialist, Christianity looks like crass materialism. Christian apologists often get into difficulty by overplaying their opposition to one extreme, and thereby becoming not the mean between two extremes, but the other extreme.

To dwell on an important instance in regard to Epicurean materialism, because Christianity claims that a human being is defined by the intimate and essential union of the body and immaterial soul, the material aspects of our nature—including our intellectual nature—are not a source of embarrassment, but a matter of doctrine. No more radical affirmation of the essential unity of body and soul could be imagined than the Christian doctrine of the resurrection, which asserts that the immaterial soul *does* exist after death, but exists in a state of incompleteness until it is reunited with a resurrected body. In regard to materialism, then, Christians need not fear evidence offered by materialists—if it is really true evidence, and not a distortion or half the story—that our intellect is intimately related to our bodily nature; a Christian need only be on guard against the materialist attempt to reduce the soul to the body completely.[5]

To return to our comparison, in regard to the original condition of humanity, once again the Bible and Lucretius are completely at odds. Lucretius asserted that we are asocial by nature, but according to Genesis 2, man and woman were made for each other, and exist in a natural state of interdependence, not Epicurean independence. Adam and Eve do not happen upon each other in a jungle, but are made for each other in a garden. Human beings are, therefore, social by nature, not by accident. Furthermore, they are commanded to be fruitful and multiply. The goal of our sexual nature is our social nature; sexuality is an intrinsic good that naturally unites male and female in the first social nexus, the family. The goal of sexuality is not pleasure or the release from sexual pain, but the intimate union of male and female for the sake of the family.

As opposed to Lucretius's belief that we are amoral by nature, the biblical

---

[5]In regard to the purely natural level, it was Aristotle who fit best with this position, for he argued that human beings are constituted by an immaterial soul (form) united essentially to a body (matter). See *On the Soul*, esp. 412a3-413a11. Therefore, Aquinas relied upon Aristotle's account. See his *Summa Theologiae* 1.75-90. For a recent appreciation of this synthesis, see J. P. Moreland and Scott B. Rae, *Body & Soul: Human Nature & the Crisis in Ethics* (Downers Grove, Ill.: InterVarsity Press, 2000), esp. pp. 199-228.

account clearly presents human beings as moral by nature. This is seen not only in regard to the example of sexuality just given, but also in the command of God not to eat of the tree of the knowledge of good and evil (2:16-17), God's anger when he is disobeyed (3:11), and the moral blame assigned to Cain for killing his brother (4:11-13). This sets the pattern for the whole Bible: from the ten commandments (Ex 20:1-17; Deut 5:6-21) all the way to the last judgment depicted in Revelation (20:1-15), there is no doubt that some acts are intrinsically evil whether or not they might happen to give us pleasure and pain, and the moral commandments are explicitly tied to God's will, both in regard to creation and redemption.

That the moral code is natural—that is, written into our very nature as human beings—is clear from Paul's letter to the Romans.

> For the wrath of God is revealed from heaven against all ungodliness and wickedness of men who by their wickedness suppress the truth. For what can be known about God is plain to them, because God has shown it to them. Ever since the creation of the world his invisible nature, namely, his eternal power and deity, has been clearly perceived in the things that have been made. So they are without excuse; for although they knew God they did not honor him as God or give thanks to him, but they became futile in their thinking and their senseless minds were darkened. (Rom 1:18-21)

A passage more opposed to Epicurean materialism would be hard to imagine. Not only does Paul insist that God is immaterial, but that his creative causality is evident in nature. According to Paul, the rejection of this natural knowledge leads through idolatry directly to all manner of wickedness, and he lists quite a few manifestations, ranging from every kind of sexual sin to murder (Rom 1:24-32).

It also takes no more than a casual reading of the Bible to make manifest that the God of the Old and New Testaments is anything but aloof from human affairs. He is, as we have seen, not only the source of the moral commands imposed upon human beings, but he also commands human beings to worship him. The covenant God makes with Abraham (Gen 12:1-9; 17:1-14), and hence with all of his descendants, is as personal a relationship of a deity to human beings as one can imagine. But the incarnation goes beyond what can be imagined, and is therefore an even more personal and intimate connection between the divine and the human. As Paul made clear, the incarnation changes everything, shifting our focus from this world to the God-man who shall take us to the next.

> For the grace of God has appeared for the salvation of all men, training us to renounce irreligion and worldly passions, and to live sober, upright, and godly lives in this world, awaiting our blessed hope, the appearing of the glory of our great God and Savior Jesus Christ, who gave himself for us to redeem us from all iniquity and to purify for himself a people of his own who are zealous for good deeds. (Tit 2:11-14)

Since this intimate relationship of God with humanity extends into the next life as well, it is especially clear in the New Testament that death is *everything* to the Christian, for death seals the relationship, for better or worse, of each individual human being to God. Rejection of God and his moral order mean eternal damnation—and the pain involved is neither small nor of short duration, as Epicurus promised all pain would be.[6] Belief in God and conformity to his moral order bring eternal happiness, and the New Testament gives every indication that paradise is not the absence of pain, but the presence of unimaginable bliss.[7]

Death, therefore, does not bring extinction, but judgment, the very thing Epicurus and Lucretius both thought to be the worst of disturbances. To return to the same passage of Romans, the Christian God, unlike the Epicurean gods, will both punish and reward.

> For he will render to every man according to his works: to those who by patience in well-doing seek for glory and honor and immortality, he will give eternal life; but for those who are factious and do not obey the truth, but obey wickedness, there will be wrath and fury (2:6-8).

There is also included in Christianity a far different understanding of pain and death, especially insofar as both bear on life after death. In the Old Testament, pain, toil and death are ultimately tied to moral disobedience, and become an inescapable punishment that all human beings must bear (Gen 3:16-19). In the New Testament, where everything is turned on its head, or perhaps better, things are turned right side up again, pain, toil and death become the windows to eternity—and worse yet, in regard to Epicure-

---

[6]For example, Mt 5:22-30; 10:28; 18:9; Mk 9:42-46; Lk 10:15; 12:5.
[7]For example, Jn 3:15; 6:27-55; Mt 25:46; Mk 10:17-30; Lk 18:18-30.

anism, the very window opened by God himself in his passion, death and resurrection.[8] In regard to Epicureanism, the cross is not just a folly or a
stumbling block; it is Epicurus's and Lucretius's worst nightmare. That a
God-man's pain, suffering and death should lead to the end of our troubles,
not by annihilating us, but by ushering us into eternal life, contradicts Epicurean materialism at every point.

Furthermore, the "imperfections" in the universe, imperfections that
were for Lucretius a certain sign that the universe was made by chance and
not divine design, were linked by Christianity to the violation of the moral
order of the universe. With Epicureanism, Christianity likewise denied that
we should attribute these imperfections to God as a creator. But against
Epicureanism, Christianity argued that the original creation was good, and
the imperfections come about, directly or indirectly, as a result of moral disobedience. Again, toil and pain are a punishment for the disobedience of the
first human beings (Gen 3:14-24), and plagues, diseases, droughts and the
like were, as clearly seen in the account of Moses and Pharaoh (Ex 3:1—
14:31), directly brought on by God as well. Even more opposed to Epicurus,
the entire New Testament, from the Gospels to Revelation, is quite adamant
in the assertion that demons—immaterial fallen angels—also use various
sicknesses to afflict humanity.[9] Finally, and most peculiarly Christian,
nature *itself* somehow participates in the fallenness of humanity, so that the
imperfections of nature are in part a kind of echo effect of human sin which
only the return of Christ and the resurrection will cure (Rom 8:18-23).

Since there is such deep, irreconcilable disagreement between Christianity and Epicureanism on the cosmological and larger moral level—both in
regard to their respective natural foundations and in regard to Christianity's supernatural elements and goal—there will also be radical disagreement between the two on the particularities of morality, even when there
appears to be agreement on the surface.

In the following analysis of the particularities, we must recall the goal of
the present study: to make clear the presuppositions of the two rival intellectual and moral views that historically came to define our contemporary intel-

---

[8]In addition to the obvious Gospel passages about Christ's intention to suffer and die (Mt 16:21; Mk
   8:31; 9:11; Lk 9:2; 17:25), see especially Col 1:24; 2 Cor 1:3-7; and Rom 8:18-25.
[9]One need only consult a concordance under "Satan" and "unclean spirits" to see how essential this
   belief is to Christianity.

lectual and moral debates. It is not a study of every ancient view, or even every ancient view with which Christianity had to contend. Thus, for example, while abortion existed in many different ancient societies completely untouched by either Epicureanism or Christianity, the cosmological views of these societies and the moral conclusions drawn from them did not historically define our contemporary debates. The reasons given in favor of abortion today do not come directly from ancient Roman culture, but from Epicureanism which flourished within it (as carried forth by moral Darwinism). The reasons against abortion today do not come directly from the ancient Assyrians (even though the Jews, who likewise prohibited abortion, would have been in contact with the Assyrians, and the prohibition of abortion in Christianity was taken over from Judaism). We also note that other historical studies could be done that follow the debates Christianity had with other cosmological views, such as for example, Christianity's struggle with radical Platonism,[10] but radical Platonism does not inform the current moral debates.

We must also realize that Christians were not the only ones arguing from an intelligent design position. Much of what is said in this chapter of Christianity, insofar as it is based on the natural law, could be said of Stoicism and Aristotelianism as well, but historically, Stoicism and Aristotelianism were influential in the long run because they supported the approach of Christianity, and therefore, Christianity took up their arguments and carried them forward. I hope, then, that the reader will excuse me from offering a pan-historical analysis of every cosmological and moral view, and allow me to focus on the historical interactions of the two main rival views which directly affect us, Epicureanism and Christianity.

In regard to sexuality, there may seem to be agreement on the surface between the two because of Epicurus's asceticism, but since the reasons for his asceticism are in direct contradiction to the fundamental principles of Christianity, such surface agreement only hides the deep and abiding opposition. For example, as we have seen, Epicurus admonished his disciples to avoid the "pleasures of the profligate" such as the "enjoying [of] boys and women," but that was not because such actions were intrinsically or naturally evil. For Epicurus, there were no intrinsically evil actions because

---

[10]Such as documented in Denis de Rougemont's famous *Love in the Western World,* trans. Montgomery Belgion (New York: Harcourt Brace, 1940).

nature itself is amoral.[11] Since human beings are ultimately a random con-glomeration of atoms, there is no intrinsic unity causing or defining "human being" to which we can refer moral judgments. The locus of moral judg-ments therefore must be the pleasure or pain any particular accidental unity, which we call a "human being," might feel. As a consequence, no sexual act is intrinsically evil, for as Epicurus himself said, "every pleasure is a good thing." Since only the individual can affirm or deny whether something gives him a pleasing sensation, then no other individual can deny the "goodness" of what someone else finds pleasant. No one can be wrong about what hap-pens to *feel* good.

As we have seen, moral restrictions arise in Epicureanism from two sources, our bodily constitution and the peculiar moral boundaries of the society in which we happen to find ourselves. As to the first, since sexual indulgence, like any other indulgence, often happens to cause bodily pain, then on Epicurean grounds we ought to avoid such indulgence. But again, we must remind ourselves that, since the natural constitution of our bodies is ultimately the result of chance and not the intention of some agent higher than nature, these limitations, however real, have no cosmic sanction. Had the atoms turned out some other way, we might well have felt little or no pain at such actions.

According to Epicureanism, the peculiar moral boundaries of the society in which we happen to live are founded upon what that society deems useful. If it is polygamy, then we may be polygamous; if monogamy, then we may be monogamous; if we are allowed concubines, then having them is moral; if homosexuality is permitted or promoted, then we may follow suit. But there is no one moral code that is naturally superior, for nature itself is amoral, and since, even in a single society, utility changes when conditions change, then moral codes even within one society are malleable over time.

As a consequence, for Epicureanism a particular relationship of sexuality to marriage can only be considered a social convention which may be useful but is not essentially good. The only judgment of such customs will be in terms of how useful the practices actually were or are for a particular society (for example, does the society continue to practice monogamy, which was

---

[11]Or to be more exact, atoms themselves are amoral: they are indestructible (hence nothing is either good or bad for them) and they have no goal, moral or otherwise, in their random motions and associations with other atoms.

originally useful given a shortage of females, when the supply of females becomes abundant?), or in terms of how much a particular society restricts the original, amoral sexual desire (for since pleasure is the only good, then customs that restrict pleasure must ultimately be bad).

With Christianity it is precisely the opposite. Human beings were made in a particular way by God, so that morality is written into their very nature and precedes and overrides any particular person's desires or what any particular society finds useful or pleasant. Thus, when Jesus was asked about divorce, he did not question whether divorce might be useful, or allow for greater pleasure, or reduce the amount of pain; rather, he rejected divorce as contrary to the natural, created order.

> And Pharisees came up and in order to test him asked, "Is it lawful for a man to divorce his wife?" He answered them, "What did Moses command you?" They said, "Moses allowed a man to write a certificate of divorce, and to put her away." But Jesus said to them, "For your hardness of heart he wrote you this commandment. But from the beginning of creation, 'God made them male and female.' 'For this reason a man shall leave his father and mother and be joined to his wife, and the two shall become one flesh.' So they are no longer two but one flesh. What therefore God has joined together, let not man put asunder." (Mk 10:2-9)

This was taken not only to be a corrective of Judaism, but also a blanket statement concerning the proper relationship of male and female. The exception was made for adultery, but this exception was rooted in the nature of the sexual act: sexual intercourse is a union of male and female; marriage is the only place where this union may take place, for however pleasurable it may be, the pleasure is secondary to the natural goal; the sexual union, where two become one flesh, is a making of one flesh out of two; therefore the child, as one, stands for the permanence of the marriage union. In direct contrast to the Epicurean account of sexuality, the child is not an accidental effect of sexual pleasure; the child defines the proper goal of sexual pleasure.

Contrary to Epicureanism, then, the goal of marriage, for Christianity, is written into the very nature of male and female. Since Christianity[12] rooted its moral teachings in natural law, rather than taking moral commands to be simply the direct commands of a deity, then the way human beings were

---

[12]The kind of Christianity compatible with an intelligent design approach.

made is a moral sign of a moral goal. Male and female are essentially sexual distinctions, and, as any biological textbook attests, the distinction between male and female exists throughout the animal kingdom. Human beings do not differ from other animals in being divided into male and female; nor do they differ insofar as the anatomical parts that distinguish male and female are all for the sake of procreation. Human males and females differ only in that human procreation results in the creation of another being made in the image of God, with an immortal soul and an eternal destiny that an all-knowing God oversees. On both counts—sexuality being exclusively defined by the union of male and female in marriage, and procreation resulting in the creation of a being with an immortal soul—Christianity could not be more opposed to Epicurean materialism.

Therefore, in contrast to Epicurean relativism, permanent monogamy is the natural, moral standard by which all other sexual practices and marriage customs are judged. The variety of sexual practices and marriage customs one happens to find, rather than being explained in terms of the accidents of place and time, are understood to be caused by moral defect, a falling away from the intended natural goal. Deviations, however useful or pleasurable they might be, are condemned as wrong. Christianity, in defining only one goal as the natural, divinely intended end for sexuality, rejected all expressions of sexuality outside of heterosexual marriage as immoral. Hence, masturbation, fornication (sex outside of marriage), adultery, homosexuality, pederasty and bestiality were all condemned as violations of the natural order.

As we see in later chapters, these radically different approaches to sexuality and marriage, the Epicurean and Christian, define our current moral debates, a point that should be obvious already. What is absolutely essential for us to realize is that the contemporary moral disagreements in regard to sexuality and marriage are not disagreements among friends about matters over which good people can disagree, for what is meant by "morality" and "good" are fundamentally opposed; that is, the opposition results from fundamentally antithetical, irreconcilable views of nature and human nature. *There is no common ground.*

And so, if we are really the result of the blind workings of chance, then basing one's moral arguments on Christian natural law would be foolish. If Epicurean materialism is right, then there is no other rational way to understand sexuality, nor any more cogent or humane way to define society's sexual customs and laws.

But if we really are designed, then our sexuality is part of that design, and therefore will be properly expressed only within heterosexual marriage. If Christianity is right, and we are so designed, then there is no other rational way to understand sexuality, nor any more cogent or humane way to define society's sexual customs and laws.

Inevitably, a society that contains a significant number of materialists and Christians will be locked in bitter and irreconcilable moral controversy in regard to sexuality and marriage. Both sides begin from fundamentally irreconcilable views of nature and human nature, and so what it means to be reasonable is completely different. The debate concerns two rival cosmologies, two mutually exclusive accounts of the universe, which yield utterly irreconcilable arguments about sexuality. It might seem to the reader as if there could be some middle ground, some way for compromise, in contemporary society, but as I make clear in the last chapters, these views must remain utterly opposed, and all compromises are merely ephemeral.

We may now move to another moral topic that is still very much with us, abortion. Neither Epicurus nor Lucretius said anything directly about abortion. However, we may safely infer the Epicurean position from its principles. First, since Epicureanism understands the conception of a child to be a kind of secondary effect which, by chance, has been associated with sexual pleasure, procreation must be judged as distinct from sexual pleasure: one kind of sexual pleasure happens to lead to procreation, but heterosexual intercourse is one species of the genus, sexual pleasure. As a consequence, the question Is childbearing good? is ultimately reducible to Is childbearing pleasurable or useful?

Societies certainly have found childbearing to be useful, and hence have shrouded it in encouraging customs. But at a different stage, particular societies may find that childbearing is no longer useful (perhaps because of perceived overpopulation) or the difficulties involved in pregnancy and childrearing, so that when it is put on the scales of pleasure and pain, the pains outweigh any pleasure or utility gained. Since nature has accidentally linked sexual pleasure to procreation, and the pleasure of intercourse does not seem to go out of style, pregnancy will still occur. Therefore, abortion would be a logical extension of Epicurean moral principles.

In regard to the practice of abortion during the times of Epicurus and Lucretius, the Greek and Roman world had a startling variety of measures available and sanctioned to prevent or end pregnancy. Our modern distinction between contraception and abortion did not really pertain; rather, all was seen on a continuum. All that was important was that pregnancy not occur, or if it did occur, to stop it either during pregnancy (with abortion) or after (with infanticide). So we find a stunning and amusing variety of modes of prevention and cure for pregnancy in antiquity: sponges or wads of wool or cotton inserted into the cervical opening before intercourse; crocodile dung, honey and natron, acacia tips and honey, or alum smeared in the vagina; or the attempt to lessen sexual desire by ingesting a mixture of snail excrement, oil and wine; the use of certain positions or motions during intercourse that supposedly prevented pregnancy; the vigorous washing of the vaginal cavity; or simply the practice of coitus interruptus. Failing all of this, one could ingest a number of poisons to induce abortion, or engage in exhausting exercise to bring on miscarriage. Finally, there was always infanticide as the ultimate solution.

In rehearsing all this, we must make clear that the recourse to abortion and infanticide was not due solely to Epicureanism. We find both in almost all ancient cultures. Epicureanism did not cause their availability or use; rather, Epicureanism was compatible with their use, and indeed, may provide the firmest foundation. In any case, as we shall see, it is the foundation of the modern reembracing of abortion and infanticide.

As for Christianity, in one of the earliest non-New Testament documents which has survived, the *Didache* or *The Teaching of the Twelve Apostles*, we find the following prohibitions:

> You shall not kill. You shall not commit adultery. You shall not corrupt boys. You shall not commit fornication. You shall not steal. You shall not use magic. You shall not administer drugs.[13] You shall not slaughter a child in abortion *[ou phoneuseis teknon en phthora]* nor slay a begotten one *[oude gennēthenta apokteneis]*. You shall not desire the goods of others.[14]

---

[13]The Greek *ou pharmakeuseis*, which, because it occurs right before mention of abortion, may well refer to those who mixed contraceptives/abortifacients. It is the same word used by Paul in Gal 5:20.

[14]Philip Schaff, *Teaching of the Twelve Apostles* (New York: Funk & Wagnalls, 1885), 2.2, pp. 168-69. My translation from the Greek.

The Greek *phthora*, "abortion," has interesting overtones: it means corruption not only in the sense of killing someone, but also in the sense of moral corruption, a double entendre meant to underline the hideousness of the crime of abortion. The slaying of a begotten one, infanticide, speaks for itself. Equally of note is that the *Didache* was an initiation manual for converts, telling them what Christian holiness demanded, and consequently, what they must leave behind from the pagan culture. Its first words are, "There are two ways [or roads], one of life and one of death, but there is a great difference between the two ways."[15]

Obviously, the prohibition of murder is rooted in the Genesis account of human beings being made in the image of God, and therefore the presence of the immortal soul defines the act of murder as murder. This comes out clearly, oddly enough, in a false distinction Christians shared with the ancient world, that the developing fetus was suddenly infused with an immortal soul, "quickened," at about forty days after intercourse. As a consequence, the Christian penitential manuals made distinctions between the seriousness of abortion before and after "quickening," a distinction which was not cleared up until the nineteenth century when the continuum of fetal development was much more fully understood (which of course brought the charge of murder back to the point of conception).

All this helps to make even more clear a fundamental difference between Epicurean materialism and Christianity in regard to abortion. On materialist grounds, the development of the human being inside the womb is simply the aggregation of an ever larger mass of material atoms. While the atoms themselves are indestructible, the aggregate is put together accidentally, and nature does not intend to invest the aggregate with some special moral status. The dissolution of a human being, whether naturally or by violence, is simply the release of the originally independent atoms from their accidental relationships. What we call "murder" is like a windstorm blowing away a pile of sand, a violent force from without that disrupts the pile.

While it may be true that, on Epicurean terms, prohibitions against "murder" (one human being causing the dissolution of the atoms of another without his consent) would certainly be useful, the utility is not grounded in nature, for nature itself is amoral. But how murder is defined could very eas-

---

[15]Ibid., 1.1, p. 162-63, my translation.

ily change in regard to what might be found useful at any particular time, and many societies, including the one into which Christianity was born, found abortion to be very useful. Epicureanism, since it regards nature as amoral and bids us to follow utility and the current customs, provides the most thoroughgoing foundation allowing abortion.

In contrast, Christianity assumes that an immaterial, immortal soul is part of the very constitution of human nature, and is what distinguishes us from other animals. Human beings do not differ *materially* from other animals. The basic *bodily* constitution of human beings and animals does not differ radically enough to cause such a fundamental moral distinction as that entailed in prohibitions against murder. It is not, then, from having or not having opposable thumbs or standing upright that prohibitions of murder arise for Christians. It is the belief that we differ *formally* from other animals—that is, insofar as human beings are made in the image of God spiritually—that prohibitions against murder arise in Christianity. As a consequence, killing an animal is fundamentally different from killing a human being, just as eating an animal is fundamentally different from eating a human being.

For these reasons, in the current debate about abortion, everything ultimately depends on whether one thinks that human beings do or do not have an immortal soul, that is, on whether one is adopting the argument of the Christian or the Epicurean. There is no common ground. If the Epicurean is right about nature, then the Christian is a fool, and a pernicious, meddling one at that, for treating a mass of cells no bigger than a pencil point as a divinely informed sacred life. But if the Christian is right about nature, then the Epicurean is promoting and engaging in mass murder on a scale dwarfing the wickedness of all other ages combined.

The historical mixture of Epicurean materialism (in the form of moral Darwinism) and Christianity is, as we shall see, the very cause of there being a debate about abortion in our society. If we were now, as a society, purely Darwinian, then there would not be *any* debate about abortion. Abortion would simply cease being an issue, and become for everyone merely a surgical remedy ensuring the maximization of sexual pleasure by removing unwanted side effects. If we were purely Christian, as the West had been prior to the Renaissance, then abortion would be just one more species of murder prohibited by the law. Abortion would not be an issue, any more than cannibalism is today (at least for the time being), because there would only be one side. That we have a debate at all is a certain sign that we live in a society that is a historical mixture of these two rival, irreconcilable views of nature and human nature.

We may now move on to the issue of suicide. Interestingly enough, Epicurus himself discouraged suicide because of his claim that what was painful, was easy to endure. The "wise man" then "neither rejects life nor fears death" for "he is utterly small-minded for whom there are many plausible reasons for committing suicide."[16] The difficulty with this admonition, however, is that many pains are long lasting and severe, a possibility which, as we have seen, Epicurus seems somehow to have missed. Two centuries after his death, as Cicero reliably reported, Epicureans had rejected their master's assessment of pain, and embraced suicide as a legitimate option. As the Epicurean interlocutor Torquatus in Cicero's dialogue *De Finibus Bonorum et Malorum* states,

> We [Epicureans] are masters of moderate pains, so that if they're tolerable, we bear them; if not, with a calm soul we exit from life, as if from the theater, when life isn't pleasing to us. . . . [Therefore, an Epicurean] doesn't hesitate, if it would be better, to depart from life.[17]

It is also important to note that Christianity stands almost alone in its condemnation of suicide. Even the ancient Stoics, who were common allies against the Epicureans, allowed the taking of one's own life. The foundation of the Christian prohibition against suicide is twofold. First, it is a kind of murder, the murder of oneself. Second, it is an act of despair, which is a mortal sin contrary to the theological virtue of hope. Over and above these things, the centrality of Christ's passion made the bearing of severe suffering the very model of redemption. Christians were commanded to take up their cross and, as Christ did, bear their suffering to the bitter end, for bearing such suffering in imitation of Christ was taken to be the path to holiness and eternal life. The only confusion in the prohibition was whether one could commit suicide to avoid being forced to engage in a mortal sin, a question which St. Augustine clarified: if we are forced to do something against our

---

[16] DL "Epicurus" 10.126; Epicurus *Maxim* 38.

[17] Cicero *De Finibus Bonorum et Malorum* 1.49, 62, my translation (with thanks to my cotranslator, Dr. Joyce Penniston).

will, it is not a sin, so we should never commit suicide, which would be an act of *our* will, in order to avoid being forced to do something against our will.[18]

When we compare Epicureanism and Christianity in regard to suicide, we find once again that there is no common ground. If Epicurus and Lucretius are right, and this is our only life and bodily existence is our only existence, then to try to bear unbearable suffering is unintelligible, for extreme pain *is* something to us, whereas "Death is nothing to us." For the Christian, however, the absolute prohibition against suicide is backed up by the fear of hell, for death brings judgment, not extinction, and furthermore, the Christian is admonished to follow Christ in his suffering. That ancient, great abyss between the Epicurean's and the Christian's moral reasoning about suicide is the very abyss that has opened up again in the contemporary debates about euthanasia and the right to die; and again, the two sides share nothing in common.

Although we could examine a number of other particular moral issues, the above issues should suffice to show how the cosmological views of Epicureanism and Christianity directly clashed from the very beginning, and more important, prepare us to understand the origin of the intractable moral issues that so divide our society today. We now turn to a historical overview of how both Christianity and Epicurean materialism were not only ancient antagonists, but historically came to define our contemporary intellectual and moral debates. The next chapter focuses on the historical eclipse of Epicurean materialism during the fall of the Roman Empire, and its rediscovery in the Renaissance.

---

[18]See Augustine *City of God* 1.18, 19.4.

The Fall and Rise
of Epicureanism

Now that we have seen the complete theoretical opposition between Christianity and Epicurean materialism, we must view the historical opposition that followed upon it, for such historical opposition was inevitable, even though the twists and turns, victories and defeats—the bumps and turns of the actual historical path—were not predictable in advance.[1] Since the path ultimately leads to us in the present day, illuminating that path will shed great light on our contemporary situation.

Epicureanism blossomed in Rome in the first century before Christ. The Roman Republic, which prior to the second century B.C. had been more concerned with war, and with building and maintaining its expanding hold on the Mediterranean region, had not been concerned with philosophical matters. But coming into contact with the culturally superior Greeks during the second century B.C. resulted in a flow of Greek culture into Rome. Philosophy was one of the imports, and Epicureanism was one of the philosophies.

By the heyday of Cicero in the middle of the first century B.C., the great Roman philosopher, statesman and orator could say with alarm that the Epi-

---

[1]For a more thorough account of the history of Epicureanism see Howard Jones, *The Epicurean Tradition* (New York: Routledge, 1989) and George Hadzsits, *Lucretius and His Influence* (New York: Cooper Square, 1963).

cureans, like an invading force, "occupied all of Italy."[2] Allowing for Cicero's
characteristic hyperbole, it is fair to say that Epicureanism flourished in, and
perhaps even dominated, Rome in the last century before Christ.

But the seeds of Epicureanism's historical downfall—or at least its temporary reversal—were present during the reign of Augustus Caesar (31 B.C-
A.D. 14). As the Roman Republic crumbled from internal decay, and the two
Caesars, Julius and then Augustus, substituted imperial for republican rule,
the new empire championed the philosophy of the Stoics, which seemed to
answer far better to the required virtues of duty and self-sacrifice for the
common good than did the apolitical and pleasure-based morality of Epicureanism. In the three centuries of philosophical debate between the death of
Aristotle (322 B.C.) and the reign of Augustus Caesar, the Stoic and Epicurean schools existed in a state of continual antagonism, for Stoicism
asserted that virtue, not pleasure, was the highest good, and dutiful sacrifice
for the state was the highest virtue. In addition, while Stoicism argued that
the natural order was divinely ordained and the gods watched over human
affairs, Epicureanism (as we have seen) denied any relation of the gods
either to nature or human affairs—and moreover had the malodorous reputation of being either openly or secretly atheistic. As they looked back, it
seemed to the Romans in the first century A.D. that the Epicurean focus on
pleasure and the withdrawal from the political realm, coupled with the disregard for the gods of Rome, were all part of the very disease that had mortally
wounded the old republic. They chose Stoicism as the cure.

But Stoicism was not the only implacable foe of Epicureanism. As Christianity, born during the reign of Augustus, spread out in its evangelization
over the very roads built by the Romans to maintain their empire, contact with
Epicureanism immediately and inevitably turned into irreconcilable conflict.
From what we saw in the last chapter, this was a highly predictable result.

As the Roman Empire, due to internal corruption and external invasion,
began its now famous fall during the fourth and fifth centuries A.D., Christianity had sufficiently established itself during its first three centuries,
thereby enabling it to remain a moral, political and theological force even
while the empire in the West crumbled into rubble. By the time of Augustine (A.D. 354-430), Epicureanism was effectively dead, or to be more

---

[2]Cicero *Tusculan Disputations* 4.7.

accurate in light of what was to come, Epicureanism was in hibernation.

But during the first four centuries of Christianity, Epicureanism was a living rival, strong enough and pervasive enough to be an object of worry, and hence an object of scorn, both in regard to its focus on pleasure and the denial of the soul's immortality, and its alleged atheism. The Christian patristic literature during these centuries is sprinkled with uniform derision directed at Epicurus himself or his followers, and the church fathers took Epicureans to task on every point of conflict between the two rival doctrines. Athenagoras (second century), Lactantius (c. 240-c. 320), Clement (c. 150-c. 215), Minucius Felix (c. second–third century), Athanasius (c. 296-373), Gregory of Nyssa (c. 330-395), Basil (c. 330-379), Hilary (c. 315-367), Augustine (354-430), Tertullian (c. 160-225), Arnobius (died c. 330), Justin Martyr (c. 100-165), Jerome (c. 342-420), Theophilus (d. 412), Ambrose (c. 339-397), Peter Chrysologus (c. 400-450)—all contribute to the river of criticism by which Christians attempted to drown Epicurus and Epicureanism for good. And it worked (at least temporarily). By the time of St. Augustine, Epicureanism was no longer an active, living rival.

As the West moved into the second five hundred years of Christianity, Epicurus passed from being a serious rival, whose philosophical positions were considered necessary to answer point by point, to a kind of hedonist straw man, who played the stock role of atheist-voluptuary. While true philosophic Epicureanism slumbered, the term *Epicureanism* simply became an epithet for the twin evils of hedonism and atheism.

Two things must be said about this transformation. First, the characterization of Epicurus as a shameless hedonist, guilty of every imaginable sensual vice and crime, and as an atheist, was false; he was, as we have seen, ascetic and pious (after his own fashion). Since Christians after the fall of the Roman Empire did not generally have available (or if available, did not read) the actual writings of Epicurus or Lucretius, the knowledge of Epicureanism was based more on rumor, as it were, and the rumors were not flattering. But second, there was a good bit of truth in the rumors, for even when the writings of Epicurus and Lucretius were readily available and thoroughly read between the first century B.C. and the fifth century A.D., Epicureanism still had the labels of hedonism and atheism firmly attached to it. The reasons it always suffered such infamy arise from the very defects of Epicurus's own arguments, defects that Lucretius repeats rather than cures.

As we have seen, Epicurus certainly equated goodness with pleasure. He further affirmed that, having done so, it was necessary that he condemn *no* pleasure as intrinsically evil (for then there would be a higher good against which pleasure itself would be measured). The only restraints on sensual pleasure were three: (1) sensual excess leads to bodily pain, and so excess should be avoided, (2) the greatest pleasure is the absence of pain, so there is no need to go beyond "barley cakes and water" to experience any greater pleasure and (3) "forbidden" pleasure, that is, pleasures forbidden by one's society, should be avoided because indulging in them will bring painful retribution. The restraints proved to be insufficient, and their weakness guaranteed that much of the reputation of hedonism that Epicureanism received was earned by later Epicureans. For while some followed the ascetic teachings of the master, others disregarded the restraints on pleasure offered by Epicurus—and with good reason. Not all sensual pleasure leads to pain, and indeed, carefully controlled excess generally does not. Second, very few sane human beings—and hence, very few Epicureans—believe that the greatest pleasure is the absence of pain. Hence, Epicureans began to cultivate the positive pleasures, leaving behind the mere absence of pain as unworthy of attention as the highest good. Finally, given that Epicurus himself argued that moral codes were merely conventional, and that there was no afterlife where one might be punished, there was no longer any reason *not* to engage in forbidden pleasures, as long as one was either secret enough or powerful enough to escape any sanctions by society.

As for the charge of atheism, regardless of Epicurus's apparently sincere piety, his account of nature as completely self-contained made the gods idle concepts. They could be dropped out completely without damaging the materialist account of nature in the least. Their only functions, we recall, were first, to provide a paradigm of tranquillity—which Epicurus himself could do just as well—and second, to fulfill the theoretical demand of *isonomia* (so the number of mortals would be matched by the number of immortals), a demand that was idiosyncratic at best. Furthermore, the proof for their existence, based on the ubiquity of the belief in the gods and on Epicurus's peculiar epistemology, was fatally weakened under attack by philosophic rivals to Epicureanism. Who could blame the later Epicureans for dropping belief in the existence of the gods, and embracing atheism?

The defects in Epicurean asceticism and piety ensured that Epicureanism could not remain as its founder had intended. Consequently, much of the bad reputation of his followers was undoubtedly well earned, especially as they became both more numerous and historically more distant from their master. As we shall see in later chapters, modern Epicureanism followed the same pattern as Epicureanism had in antiquity. Generally speaking, it started out in ascetic and pious conformity to its master, but soon enough the intrinsic defects gave rise to hedonism and atheism. By the time of Darwin, this transformation had been at least theoretically completed.

Thus, while the Dark and Middle Ages may not have attended carefully to the writings of Epicurus, relying on the reputation of Epicureans was not altogether out of place. In any case, that reputation was about all the West had to go on from the fifth to the fourteenth centuries. During the period from the fall of Rome in the fifth century, to the Viking, Islamic and Magyar raids of the ninth and tenth centuries, much of the energy of the Christian West was expended in mere survival and in the slow, difficult Christianizing of Europe. There was little time for serious study of primary texts, especially those that had such unsavory reputations.

As Christianity slowly spread out across Europe, the Christian moral arguments gradually displaced the varieties of pagan views with which they came into contact. The result was that the moral arguments of Christianity (which were at first developed in the elaboration of biblical texts, in the decisions by individual bishops, in the penitential manuals and which were enforced within the church) eventually permeated the customs of society and became enforced by civil law. This Christianization of Europe assured, historically, that both natural law arguments based on Christianity's intelligent design approach to nature, as well as specifically theological arguments, would be woven tightly into the social and legal fabric of the West. The Christian opposition to abortion, infanticide, divorce, adultery, homosexuality, pedophilia, bestiality and suicide were therefore embodied in both custom and law, and the Christian cosmology served as the foundation for these moral prohibitions.

Given this, the following point cannot be overemphasized: *The only reason that our society today has its now-familiar and interminable battles in regard to these moral issues, the only reason they are issues at all is that we are the historical heirs to this long process of Christianization which took place between the fifth and eleventh centuries, the so-called Dark Ages.* Had Christianity not succeeded in taking hold of Europe and displacing the variety of pagan customs during this period, its characteristic moral arguments would have dissolved into the stream of history, never to be heard from again. For Christians, divine providence would never have allowed this. For those who oppose these moral arguments, Christianity's successful struggle is an unpleasant and long-standing accident of history. In either case, no one can deny this time period as pivotal.

To focus on a particular moral example, if we look at human history as a whole and scan all the diverse peoples in diverse times, we shall find that abortion and infanticide are extremely common and quite acceptable. The Christianized West stands out a prominent exception, not the rule. The laws against abortion and infanticide in the West are only intelligible as the result of its earlier Christianization, and the repeal of those same laws is only intelligible in light of its de-Christianization. Thus, that abortion is currently sliding into infanticide is not evidence that the world is sliding into some unheard of age of barbarism, but rather evidence that it is simply returning from being Christianized to being paganized. It is returning, we might say, to the state in which Christianity found it. As we shall see, the reemergence of Epicurean materialism began this "undoing" of history, and moral Darwinism is its completion.

To return to our historical overview, in the eleventh to the fourteenth centuries the intellectual focus became the restoration of classical learning within the context of the development of the universities as assimilated to Christianity's theological goals. With political order stabilizing during this period, classical texts began to flow into the West in the twelfth and thirteenth centuries, mainly through contacts with Islam. While the two main sources of Epicurean doctrine existed (Diogenes Laertius's *Lives of the Eminent Philosophers* [the tenth book of which focused on Epicurus] and Lucretius's *De Rerum Natura*), they were either little known or generally disregarded. Even though some of the major extant manuscripts of these two date from this period, the level of interest was low. The reasons for the general disregard are obvious. Christianity was either concerned about the more practical exigencies of survival, or the more elevated task of building itself up intellectually. As a consequence, its attention was either turned away from the more elevated plane, or was turned toward those classical authors, such as Plato, Aristotle and Cicero, who were compatible with

Christianity's cosmological and moral commitments.

We must pause to focus on one of these pre-Christian philosophers.[3] The thirteenth-century incorporation of Aristotle as the pagan philosopher most compatible with Christianity deserves our special attention for several reasons. First, it was Aristotle's account of nature, as taken up by Christianity, that formed the intellectual foundation of scholasticism; as a result scholasticism was the reigning intellectual approach going into the Renaissance.

Second, much of the success in reintroducing Epicurean materialism on friendly terms into the West depended on a general discontent with the excessive dry formalism into which scholasticism had (unfortunately) fallen by the Renaissance. Christians, at least some of them, were therefore ready to use one pagan philosophy (Epicureanism) to uproot another (Aristotelianism), so that, oddly enough, Aristotle came to be portrayed as the source of the intellectual contamination of Christianity, and Epicureanism as the cure.

Third, because of the excesses of some who were enamored with Aristotle and neglected or downplayed Scripture as a source of truth (the so-called radical Aristotelians), other Christians (the so-called radical Augustinians) came to see Aristotle's thought as a kind of spiritual contamination and tried to destroy its influence. The theology they used to combat Aristotelianism, called nominalism, inadvertently paved the way for Epicureanism.

Finally, and without going into too much detail, Aristotle's account of nature was itself partially forged against the atomism of Democritus (both Epicurus and Lucretius lived after Aristotle), and Epicurus and Lucretius borrowed heavily from Democritus. Since, as we shall see, Darwinism is simply a modern form of Epicureanism, it turns out that Aristotle's account of nature is directly opposed to Darwinism as well. We can often learn much about something by viewing its opposite, and that is especially the case with the opposition between Aristotelianism and Epicureanism. It will be particularly fruitful to discuss the historical period in which Aristotle was adopted by Christianity, for that is where his arguments really became influential in the West.

Aristotle has often been called the philosopher of common sense because he, above all other philosophers in the West, took it as his task to explain the

---

[3]For a fuller account of the influx of Aristotelian texts in the West, see David Knowles, *The Evolution of Medieval Thought*, 2nd ed. (New York: Longman, 1988), pp. 167-74, 201-12.

way we naturally experience things, rather than to explain away what we experience. We experience things in nature as complex, distinct wholes. We think and speak as if a dog really is a dog, and a cat, a cat; that is, we suppose the visible form something presents actually represents what it really is, its essential nature. For Aristotle, then, the matter (the physical "stuff" out of which something is made) is subordinate to the form (the unified whole). The form determines that matter, and consequently, the whole really is more than the sum of its parts, especially if it is an organic whole.

But Epicurus, as we recall, took the opposite view. As a materialist, he held that the visible wholes are brought about by the accidental relationships of the invisible material entities, atoms. "Dog" is what we happen to call a particular configuration of such atoms, but that is only because of our perspective. The shape we call dog is like the shape of a dog we see in the clouds: in the same way that there really is not a dog in the sky (for if we could lift ourselves up into the midst of the cloud we would see only water vapor), so also if we could shrink to the atomic level, the "dog" would disappear and the real conglomeration of atoms would appear, and we would see a dog for what it really is. For Epicurus, then, the matter out of which a thing is made is real, while the visible form or shape it takes is ultimately not real, but instead an insubstantial appearance like the dog in the cloud. With Epicurus the whole is actually less than the sum of its parts, because it is only the parts, the atoms, which are truly real.

Perhaps the best way to illustrate the difference is with an architectural example, an example that will make clear why Aristotle would lend support to the Christian view of the creator as intelligent designer. A house looked at from the Aristotelian perspective exists first in the mind of the architect as a complex whole. The form of the house—its complex unity—determines what material will be used, how much of it, and where. The material follows upon the form in the designer's mind; or to put it another way, the goal or end (in Greek, *telos*) in the mind of the architect determines the material constituents of a house. In just this way, Aristotle argued, natural things are determined by their particular goal or end. The goal of any natural being is simply the perfection of its form. A dog (or any natural being) comes to be what it is according to its predetermined end. An acorn grows into an oak tree because the form of the oak tree was there directing the growth from the very beginning. A dog in the very first stages of its generation will only become a dog because its form determines the way that it grows materially. Aristotle's account of nature is teleological—from the Greek *telos*—because nature always acts for an end, the completeness of particular forms. Obviously this account of nature fits well with a view of Genesis where God designs things in nature, and things act according to his design.

But from the Epicurean perspective (as was especially clear in Lucretius's presentation of Epicureanism), although it *looks* as if things in nature are designed like houses, with the complex whole guiding the material constituents, we are falsely assuming nature works like a human artisan. The complex wholes that appear to be designed are really the result of chance combined with the particular properties of atoms. Nature does not, like an artisan, intend anything; the complex wholes are accidents of very simple material constituents. The visible forms of our experience are not intended by nature at all. Nature is goal-less, end-less; it has nothing in mind, because it is not directed by a mind. Hence, Epicurean materialism is non-teleological. A dog is the byproduct of the endless combining and recombining of atomic reality.

Especially as compared to Epicureanism, Aristotelianism was considered compatible with Christianity. The thirteenth century witnessed Christianity's incorporation of Aristotle, an intellectual task brought to consummation by Thomas Aquinas (c. 1225-1274). We should stress, however, that this incorporation was not without controversy. In his efforts to provide Christianity with a natural philosophy to undergird its revealed view of nature, Thomas stood as a mean between two extreme tendencies. On the one extreme, there was radical Aristotelianism, which was so enamored with the pagan philosopher that it seemed to reject Christianity for paganism, elevating natural truth above revealed truth. This extreme alarmed some of the orthodox Christians, who, rejecting Aristotle, embraced radical Augustinianism, which took revelation to be all that was needed, and considered any pagan philosophy whatsoever to be a horrible contagion infecting revealed truth. Radical Augustinians tended to assert, against radical Aristotelians, that sin had so destroyed our natural capacities that natural reason, either in regard to natural or moral science, was dysfunctional. Revelation was the only light by which one could see; sin had extinguished the natural light of reason.

We can see here, in the Middle Ages, the outlines of the two views of

Christianity to which I referred in chapter three, the one compatible with an intelligent design approach (Thomism), and the one incompatible (radical Augustinianism). Christians who believe that the goodness of the natural intellect was only wounded by sin will find themselves attracted by Aristotle, Aquinas and intelligent design theory. Christians who believe that the goodness of the natural intellect was wholly corrupted by sin will find themselves attracted to radical Augustinianism, especially if they believe that Aristotelianism and Thomism (or their combination in scholasticism), have forgotten the wounds of sin completely and have elevated natural reason above revelation (as did the radical Aristotelians in the Middle Ages). This strain of radical Augustinianism was given intellectual authority and historical influence at the end of the Middle Ages by the famous Catholic theologian, William of Occam (or Ockham), who lived just after Aquinas, from about 1285 to 1347.

One of history's great ironies is that the effort to defend Christian orthodoxy against the perceived contamination of Aristotelianism in the middle ages would yield a theological-philosophical system compatible with Epicureanism, a far more dangerous foe to Christianity. That theological-philosophical system is called nominalism, and William of Occam was its most powerful proponent.

William thought that the way to undermine Aristotelianism was to destroy its attempt to give a rational account of the world, human nature and human action, for the truth of Aristotle's purely natural account seemed to eclipse the truth revealed in Scripture. For the sake of Christian orthodoxy, William believed that reason, without revelation, must be shown to be impotent. He attacked the power of reason by arguing that the human mind, using only its own natural power, does not truly grasp universals (e.g., "dog," "cat," "justice"); indeed, argued William, there are no universals for the mind to grasp. All nature is made of *particular* things, which are ultimately unrelated. Thus, when we use the word *dog* there really is no universal entity, essence or "dog-ness" which we perceive. *Dog* is merely a *name* we apply to particular things that we happen to think look alike. Hence, the name of his system, nominalism, for the Latin, *nomen*, "name."

Since all things really are only particular and have no essential connection, then all merely human attempts at classifying things by human reason are groundless. It follows, asserted William, that the only source of truth left was revelation. That, he thought, should take care of the Aristotelians and pave the way for Christianity to be based on revelation alone.

What William could not see, however, was that while nominalism destroyed Aristotelianism (a clear and present danger to William), it invited a later alliance with Epicurean materialism that would prove much more corrosive to Christianity. By asserting that only particular things were real, and that universals or species names had no reality, nominalism was inadvertently siding with Epicurean materialism's denial of the reality of form/species distinctions. For Epicurean materialism, we recall, only individual atoms are real. The forms or shapes these atoms happen to make are ultimately unreal, and the names we apply to them ("dog," "cat," etc.) are merely conventional.

Furthermore, in denying any real correlation between our abstract names and the particular beings of nature, nominalism destroyed any and all possibility of natural theology or a natural proof of God's existence. For William, this removed any attempt by Aristotelians to claim natural knowledge of God, and ensured that we could know God by revealed theology alone. But again, this nominalist victory would fit all too well with the Epicurean disdain for intelligent design-type arguments, for it would mean that our natural reason could not detect evidence of the agency of a creative God in nature.

The nominalist revolution was also carried into the ethical sphere where, again, it would provide inadvertent support for Epicureanism when it arose again in the Renaissance. For William, it seemed that the Aristotelians of his day were affirming the possibility of both knowing and doing the human good by our natural capacities alone. This seemed to displace the need for Jesus Christ and his grace to become good. William sought to undermine the possibility of natural goodness in two related ways. First, in accord with nominalism, he declared that there was no reality corresponding to such names as "justice," "good," "virtue" and so on, so that claims to understand ethics on the natural level were deluded. Indeed, just as all beings were ultimately and only particular, so were all actions. But William was not finished. He argued that not only were all actions utterly particular but actions were good and evil simply because God happened to designate them as either good or evil. Since God is all-powerful, he could command anything he wanted, completely unrestrained by all merely human conceptions of good and evil. So radical was William's claim for God's omnipotence in this regard that he even asserted that God could change the first commandment:

> Every will can conform to the divine precepts; but God can command the cre-
> ated will to hate him, and the created will can do this (thereby refusing its own
> happiness and ultimate end). Furthermore, any act that is righteous in this
> world can also be righteous in the next, the fatherland; just as hatred of God
> can be a good act in this world, so can it be in the next.[4]

In this, William's nominalism created a complete relativism of ethics—
nothing was naturally good or just, but the goodness or justice depended
completely on God's will, which could change at any time. Again, little did
William know that this attempt to affirm God's omnipotence would lend
backhand theological support to the ethical relativism of Epicureanism when
it came back on the historical stage.

Finally, radical Augustinianism affirmed the plurality of worlds, even a
plurality of inhabited worlds other than the earth. Again, this inadvertent
support for an Epicurean position was the result of the rejection of Aristotle, in particular the rejection of Aristotle's argument (rooted in his
rather complicated doctrine of natural place) that there could only be one
world.

To the radical Augustinians, such an assertion appeared to be a limit on
God's power over nature. Even prior to the birth of William, the proposition
that the "first cause cannot make more than one world" was condemned in
1277 at Paris by the bishop Etienne Tempier in the famous 219 Propositions
issued against the radical Aristotelians (which also affected the more moder-
ate users of Aristotle, the Thomists, as well).[5] Following this, William not
only affirmed that God could create a multitude of worlds, but "could make
another world better than this one," which could contain perfect human
beings who could neither sin nor wish to sin, and who would therefore constitute a different species.[6]

William's influence passed into Christian universities alongside scholasti-

---

[4]Quoted in Servais Pinckaers, *The Sources of Christian Ethics,* trans. Mary Thomas Noble (Washington, D.C.: Catholic University of America Press, 1995), p. 247.

[5]The 219 Propositions are translated in Ralph Lerner and Muhsin Mahdi, eds., *Medieval Political
Philosophy: A Sourcebook* (Ithaca, N.Y.: Cornell University Press, 1978), pp. 335-54. The proposition quoted is proposition 27.

[6]See Steven J. Dick, *Plurality of Worlds: The Origins of the Extraterrestrial Life Debate from Democritus to Kant* (New York: Cambridge University Press, 1982), p. 33.

cism, and found many capable spokespersons, including a young Augustinian monk, Martin Luther, who brought criticisms of scholasticism in general, and Aristotelianism in particular, full force into the controversies of the Reformation. Thus, both Catholicism and Protestantism historically contain views of revelation and reason incompatible with intelligent design, and (ironically) compatible with Epicurean materialism. For our purposes, the importance of this cannot be overstressed, for Epicureanism was able to gain a foothold in the Renaissance, as we shall see, in no small part through the efforts of those Christians who used it as a weapon against and an antidote to Aristotelianism and hence scholasticism (or whose nominalism inadvertently supported Epicureanism). Before any of this could happen, however, Epicureanism had to be rediscovered.

In the spring of 1417 Epicureanism was awakened from its deep slumber. Poggio Bracciolini, infected with the characteristic Renaissance desire to recover ancient manuscripts, happened upon a copy of Lucretius's *De Rerum Natura*. In 1430 Ambrogio Traversari published a Latin version of Diogenes Laertius's *Lives of the Eminent Philosophers*, which contained not only a biography of Epicurus (and Democritus as well), but Epicurus's three famous letters explaining his doctrines in outline and a collection of Epicurean maxims as well. The works of Epicurus, along with those of his poetic spokesman Lucretius, became once again available. Not only do we have evidence of already existing interest in Epicurean doctrines from this period, but the publishing history of both attests to the spread of interest in Epicureanism all over Europe during the fifteenth and sixteenth centuries, and the firm reestablishing of Epicurean materialism by the seventeenth century.[7]

Whether editions of Lucretius and Diogenes Laertius appeared with a condemnation-as-commentary attached, or with guarded praise, the simple

---

[7] Although there were copies of *De Rerum Natura* floating around Italy in the middle years of the fifteenth century, the *editio princeps* of the poem was not published until 1473. Following this, we find a number of editions of Lucretius published throughout the rest of the fifteenth century and scattered over the sixteenth, first in Italy, then in France, Switzerland, the Netherlands, and then England. The Renaissance was also introduced to Epicurus directly through the Latin translation of Diogenes Laertius, first published in Rome in 1431, then in Venice in 1475 and in Nuremberg in 1476. The original Greek text was first printed at Basel in 1533. The tenth book on Epicurus was printed in Antwerp in 1566; in 1570 Stephanus published a two-volume edition in Paris; and in 1615 an edition appeared in Geneva.

truth was that Epicurean materialism was made available again to an ever-larger reading public. Especially in regard to Lucretius, the power of his poetic art guaranteed its success, not only in establishing itself as a literary classic, but also as a kind of intellectual time bomb waiting to go off. One need only read the popular French author Montaigne (1533-1592), whose *Essais* was peppered with references to Lucretius, to see how far *De Rerum Natura* had penetrated European culture by the mid-sixteenth century.

We should not overlook an important aspect of the reintroduction of Epicureanism which lies in what might be called the sociological realm. At this time, reviving any aspect of Epicurus's doctrines or even showing appreciation for Lucretius as a poet ran the risk of condemnation as an accomplice, and that meant being charged with the secret or open rejection of divine providence, with the denial of the immortality of the soul and the afterlife, with touting pleasure as the highest good or even with being an atheist. Epicurus's hallmark philosophical positions stood opposed to almost every line of the creed, and had been repeatedly condemned, directly or indirectly. How then could Epicurus be revived in an almost completely Christianized culture, in which the holding of any of Epicurus's positions would certainly lead to persecution, imprisonment or even death?

First, there was the not-such-a-bad-guy approach of simple restoration without advocacy, where the author or translator simply re-presented the original pious, ascetic Epicurus, as opposed to the voluptuary-atheist of rumor. Even while there was no advocacy of Epicurus's doctrines—in fact, such efforts were often accompanied with strident denunciations of the elements unsavory to Christianity—the effect, intended or not, was to circulate the original Epicurus with a good bit of the opprobrium dusted off. Such was the approach of Francesco Filelfo, Cristoforo Landino and Leornardo Bruni in the fifteenth century.

Second, there was the honey-on-the-rim-of-bitter-poison approach of introducing Epicureanism inadvertently through an appreciation of Lucretius the poet. We recall that Lucretius himself had asserted that the poetic aspect of his presentation of Epicurean materialism was the honey on the rim of the bitter medicine of his philosophy—bitter to the masses, and those not used to it, but ultimately salutary in curing us of the disturbances caused to our souls by religion. The Renaissance admirers of Lucretius's poetry agreed with the assessment of his poetic art as honeyed, but publicly denounced the philosophic content as poisonous rather than medicinal. But again, as loud and long as their denunciations were, Lucretius the philosopher could not help but be delivered with Lucretius the poet. Typical of this approach was Denys Lambin whose acclaimed critical edition of *De Rerum Natura*, published in Paris in 1563, was filled with the very highest praise for Lucretius the poet, carefully counterbalanced with condemnation for Lucretius the philosopher.

A third way attempted to subordinate the materialism of Epicureanism to Christianity, creating a Christianized hybrid of two utterly irreconcilable views of the universe. A typical approach was to make the atomism acceptable by declaring that God was the creator of the atoms, and furthermore, the one who put them in motion, so that only God was eternal, and the atoms were governed by divine intelligence—at least originally. In regard to morality, pleasure could still be considered the highest good, if only we regard union with God in the next life as the greatest possible pleasure. Such a reformulation somehow entailed reinserting the immaterial soul, but given that such an insertion was alien to the materialism, this approach inevitably created a kind of dualism.

We must also note that any examination of the Epicurean revival, even in its early stages, runs into the difficulty of assessing the motives and real opinions of Epicurus's new advocates. Precisely because Christianity had such a firm cultural hold in the fifteenth through the mid-sixteenth centuries, real Epicureans had to be careful. Thus, it is often difficult to ferret out what those who reintroduced Epicureanism actually believed from what they believed they had to say to protect themselves from persecution. Lorenzo Valla, who attempted to introduce Epicureanism using a variation of the third way just mentioned, is a case in point.

Valla's dialogue *De Voluptate* (*On Pleasure*), was first published in 1431. The dialogue takes place between a Stoic, an Epicurean and a Christian. Valla announced that his strategy in the dialogue was merely to use Epicureanism to combat the influence of pagan Stoicism, which apparently he thought was drawing adherents away from Christianity. The difficulty with the ostensive goal was that the Epicurean spokesman receives far too much attention and praise in the dialogue, and the Christian moral goal ends up being pleasure (albeit, the pleasure of heaven). Ever since its publication, the assessments of Valla's dialogue have been divided, some seeing him as a pious Christian, others a half-out-of-the-closet Epicurean. Even if he were, underneath it all, an orthodox Christian with the purest of motives, those who read it were being introduced to Epicurean materialism on very friendly, rather than antagonistic, terms. The same difficulty is inherent in any of the other modes of introduction. Was the translator merely trying to set the record straight, separating the real Epicurus from the straw man, or did he find a way to wedge Epicureanism back into competition with Christianity? Was the praise of the Lucretius's poetic artisanship and the denunciation of the philosophic content sincere, or did a secret admiration of the philosophy enter wrapped in the praises of the poetry? This same difficulty in assessing motives is present during the following centuries, as long as Christianity maintained its cultural hold.

Having traced the eclipse and reappearance of Epicureanism in the period from the birth of Christ to the Renaissance, we may now turn to the famous scientific revolution of the seventeenth and eighteenth centuries. This revolution made Epicurean materialism once again victorious, a victory won in the midst of a still Christianized culture. As one might expect, the presence of these two rival cosmologies at the same time could avoid conflict only by some subtle reengineering of both Epicureanism and Christianity.

Newtonianism

The New Face of Epicurean Materialism

As we go from the Renaissance to the Enlightenment, the atomism of Epicurus and Lucretius moved from being an alien smuggled into Christianized culture in the fifteenth and sixteenth centuries to being the only tenable theoretical view of natural philosophy during the seventeenth and eighteenth centuries.[1] The time period may be conveniently marked by the contiguous lives of Galileo Galilei (1564-1642) and Isaac Newton (1642-1727).

If I were writing a book twice as long, there would be space in this chapter to cover all the various figures who contributed to the victory of materialist atomism in science during this period, chief among them, Giordano Bruno (1548-1600), Pierre Gassendi (1592-1655) and Robert Boyle (1627-1691). These three are extraordinarily interesting because they combined atomism with fervent Christianity. The link that allowed this new combination was a common hatred of Aristotelianism, so that the use of Epicurus and Lucretius was felt to be a cure for what they considered to be the scholasticism ailing Christianity. Bruno was the martyr for the cause, burned at the stake as

---

[1]Of course, the atomism of Democritus, the intellectual father of Epicurus, was available through Diogenes Laertius as well, but since it was the foundation taken by Epicurus (and hence Lucretius), there is no need to bring up the influence of Democritus as an independent force during this period. Suffice it to say that Democritus's atomism implied the larger cosmological and moral claims made by Epicurus, and that Epicurus and Lucretius presented the more complete accounts.

a heretic on February 17, 1600. We will discuss him further below. As for
Gassendi, no one did more than this Catholic priest to reintroduce Epicurus
to the Christian world on the friendliest and most thorough terms. His *De
Vita et Moribus Epicuri* (1647) and *Animadversiones in Decimum Librum
Diogenis Laertii* (1649) were very detailed presentations of Epicurean doc-
trine, in which he sought to remove the sources of historical animosity to
Christianity by giving Epicurus the most sympathetic reading possible. Gassendi was engaged in ongoing conversations with the most famous philosophers and scientists of the day—Kepler, Galileo, Mersenne and Thomas
Hobbes—and his books enjoyed a wide and enthusiastic readership. Finally,
Boyle was the great advocate of taking atomism from the theoretical realm
of the physicists to the very practical realm of the chemists so that real work
could be done in the arena closest to the as-yet hypothetical atoms. That,
sadly enough, is about all we can say about them, because room must be left
for the two giants of the materialist-based scientific revolution, Galileo and
Newton, for there is much that we must say of these two.[2]

If we may provide the briefest statement that characterizes the Galilean-
Newtonian revolution, we might call it the vindication of atomism through
the victory of mathematics. A quick victory it was too. For at the beginning of
the seventeenth century Galileo was questioned by the Inquisition and put
under house arrest, and by the dawn of the eighteenth century Newton was
considered a demigod who had unlocked every secret of nature, a mortal
whose thoughts were identical with God's. With the complete theoretical victory of Epicurean materialism, all the essential elements of Epicurus's system—the eternal and indestructible atoms, the infinite universe with the
unlimited number of worlds, the banishment of the creator God, the rejection
of miracles, the displacement of design in nature by chance and material
necessity, and the elimination of the immaterial soul—fell into place during
the eighteenth and nineteenth centuries.

---

[2]Readers interested in a more detailed analysis, covering not only Galileo and Newton but also the
other figures mentioned (and even more whom I didn't mention), should consult the following
works. To begin, readers should study the brilliant works of Alexandre Koyré, *Galileo Studies*
(Atlantic Highlands, N.J.: Humanities Press, 1978), and *Newtonian Studies* (Cambridge, Mass.:
Harvard University Press, 1965); see also Andrew G. Van Melsen, *From Atomos to Atom* (New
York: Harper, 1960); E. A. Burtt, *The Metaphysical Foundations of Modern Science* (New York:
Doubleday, 1932); and the more recent Bernard Pullman, *The Atom in the History of Human
Thought* (Oxford: Oxford University Press, 1998).

In charting the ascendancy of materialist atomism during this period, we must avoid confusion concerning what is really at issue. At stake is not whether there exist material constituents smaller than the naked eye could see. Everyone, materialist and nonmaterialist alike, has always held that such subvisible constituents exist. The question was and is, Are these elements of such a nature that they form a closed material system of nature that excludes both divine action and the existence of the immaterial soul? In other words, are the fundamental constituents of the universe really as Epicurus and Lucretius described them?

In this regard, we must realize that, ironically, the complete theoretical victory of ancient atomism in the seventeenth century was not the result of having *seen* an atom, nor of providing any experiment that proved decisively that atoms, as described by Democritus, Epicurus and Lucretius, existed. The fields of victory were actually in the visible heavens (by astronomy), and to a lesser extent in the earthly sciences of mechanics and ballistics, but these victories were applied to the invisible, microscopic realm in the sense in which one applies capital made in one area to debts contracted in another.

To clarify, while the microscopic world (where such atoms as Epicurus described might exist) was invisible, there were analogies to atomism in the sky and on the visible earth. Planets, stars and comets, from our distant perspective, could be taken to act like points of matter moving through the void of the sky. Looking into the heavens, then, could have the same effect as suddenly being shrunken to the microscopic world to witness the whirling of the atoms through the void. The same could be said of the earthly study of inert projectiles in ballistics: a cannonball could be treated like a greatly magnified atom. If such objects could be successfully described using Epicurus's principles, then, it seemed, one could infer that actual microscopic atoms existed.

As we shall see, by such intellectual borrowing, the successes of Galileo and Newton seemed to vindicate the fundamental principles of Epicurus. Furthermore, it was the (apparently) complete victory of Newtonian atomism that allowed—nay, demanded—that Epicureanism as an entire system, both theoretical and moral, be firmly planted in modern soil. For those living in the two centuries between Newton's *Principia* and the dawn of the twentieth century, the world was as Newton had described it, and that world was almost exactly as Epicurus had planned it. To understand that moral Epicureanism followed necessarily upon the adoption of theoretical Epicureanism, and that moral Darwinism is the culmination of moral Epicureanism, is to understand the modern world. Regardless of the original intentions of those involved in the so-called scientific revolution on the theoretical level, the only moral universe possible was the one that fit the natural universe that had been accepted. Recalling one-half of our most fundamental law, "Every distinct view of the universe, every theory about nature, necessarily entails a view of morality."

I stress "regardless of the original intentions," for both Galileo and Newton seem either to have been oblivious to the connection between their theoretical atomism and the complete doctrines of Epicurus (although such is hard to imagine, given the long-standing animosity of Christianity to the entire system of Epicurus and the widespread availability of the writings of Epicurus and Lucretius in the seventeenth century), or thought that they could extract the materialist doctrine safely from the Epicureanism. In either case, historically the great law of uniformity prevailed because the Epicurean universe is a unified universe. If one part is accepted, the others necessarily follow. That necessity explains precisely why a complete moral revolution and the secularization of Western society followed directly upon the seventeenth century scientific revolution. Epicurus had seen clearly the kind of universe needed to accomplish his moral goals—taking "moral" in the broadest sense—and designed his account of nature accordingly. Taking hold of the account of nature *first*, even though it was coming at Epicureanism from the other end, resulted in the acceptance of the Epicurean moral goals that were the source of the theoretical design of the materialist account in the first place. There is a historical lesson here to be learned for contemporary scientists. You cannot have two universes, one which science describes and one in which an utterly alien morality resides. Defining reality according to the tenets of scientific materialism will mean that morality will soon enough be compelled to follow suit.

Having said all this, we now turn to the revolution in the heavens at the beginning of this period, for here the challenge to both Christianity and Aristotelianism was most serious and most damaging (although as it turns out, the challenge could be met). In regard to Christianity, if we read Genesis, we find God placing a firmament, a kind of dome in the heavens, above the earth to separate the waters above from the waters below. If we read

Aristotle, we find a similar cosmology insofar as he argues that we live in a finite universe with a distinct, incorruptible heaven surrounding the corruptible earth at the center. This geocentric universe, that is, a universe with the earth at the center and a finite heaven bounding it, was further confirmed in the second century A.D. by the ingenuity and descriptive power of Claudius Ptolemaeus's systematic astronomical account. Thus, by a combination of the authority of Scripture, Ptolemy and Aristotle, the geocentric universe was deeply etched in the Western scientific mind prior to Copernicus. Here, a picture may be helpful. If we have seen one of the many diagrams of the pre-Copernican universe, we have seen the system of concentric spheres, the earth at the very center, then (moving outward) the moon, Mercury, Venus, the sun, Mars, Jupiter, Saturn, the Firmament, the Chrystaline Sphere, the Primum Mobile and finally, surrounding it all, the *Empireum Habitaculum Dei*, the abode of God himself.

We should point out (now that we have this picture in mind) that contrary to the commonplace assertion that the medievals put the earth at the center of the universe out of some kind of anthropocentric hubris, the earth was at the center because it was considered the lowest, least divine-like place in the cosmos. For as one rose from earth toward the heavens, one left the gross world of dust and decay, and entered the world of eternal beauty and divine blessedness. Placing the earth at the center of the universe, then, was an act of profound humility.

In regard to the revival of Epicurean materialism, the arguments of Nicolas Copernicus (1473-1543) in his *De Revolutionibus Orbium Coelestum* (1543), which placed the sun at the center of the universe and not the earth, were not nearly as important as the publication by Galileo of his *Siderius Nuncius* (*The Starry Messenger*) in 1610. Galileo was a lens grinder, brilliant mathematician, powerful rhetorician, implacable foe of Aristotelianism and guarded advocate of materialist atomism. The message that he bore from the stars, "made with the aid of a new spyglass [the original name of the telescope],"[3] shattered both the belief that the heavens were more perfect than the earth, and that the heavens themselves were finite, thereby opening the way for the acceptance of the Epicurean doctrines of the homogeneity of

---

[3]Galileo Galilei, *The Starry Messenger,* in *Discoveries and Opinions of Galileo,* trans. Stillman Drake (Garden City, N.Y.: Doubleday, 1957), p. 27.

the constituents of the universe and the Epicurean assertions concerning the infinite universe with unlimited worlds.

Galileo devoted the first part of *The Starry Messenger* to a detailed description of the actual imperfections of the moon, imperfections previously hidden to the naked eye. The moon, rather than being perfectly smooth and round like a fine jewel in the heavens, was "full of cavities and prominences," "precipitous crags" and "jagged peaks." By the wondrous artifice of the spyglass, Galileo trumpeted, "one may learn with all the certainty of sense evidence that the Moon is not robed in a smooth and polished surface but is in fact rough and uneven, covered everywhere, just like the Earth's surface, with huge prominences, deep valleys, and chasms."[4] To find that one of the heavenly bodies was made of dirt, just like the earth, was a great preparation for the acceptance of Epicureanism, for it meant the eradication of the notion that the heavens were made of some unearthly substance, and therefore paved the way for acceptance of the Epicurean assertion that the universe was homogeneous, made everywhere of one quite humble substance—the lifeless, inglorious atom.

We who are so accustomed to the knowledge that the moon is made of quite earthy elements, cannot fully appreciate the shock caused by Galileo's reduction of the heavens to the humility of the earth—and doing it not by argument (the only weapon of Epicurus) but by the senses with the aid of a new man-made device. If the moon were mere dust, then also, it seemed, were the rest of the heavenly bodies—all the way up to God's abode. It appeared that the very throne of God was being shaken. Needless to say, to those already enamored by the arguments of Epicurus, the sudden humiliation of the heavens was a magnificent and unexpected vindication by the senses of Epicurus's merely theoretical speculations. Consequently, those already taken with Epicurus's arguments were taken that much further.

But Galileo bore a second message from the stars. The spyglass revealed that, in contrast to what the naked eye reported, the number of stars was "so numerous as almost to surpass belief."[5] When one peered into the heavens, the cosmos appeared far larger and far more populated by hitherto unseen bodies. On top of that, the stars were actually smaller than they appeared to

[4]Ibid., p. 28.
[5]Ibid., p. 47.

the unadorned eye. The spyglass, having removed "their adventitious and accidental rays," revealed that the stars were farther away than had been previously thought.[6] The spyglass seemed to open up an infinite universe, filled with uncountable stars at unfathomable distances, yet a universe made of the same humble material constituents as humble earth.

Galileo was very careful about directly asserting the infinity of the universe—an understandable caution on his part given the fate of Giordano Bruno, to which we now briefly turn. Bruno, who was openly indebted to Lucretius, preached the infinity of the universe with evangelical zeal, and wrote the famous Italian dialogue *De l'infinito universo e mondi,* which combined the radical Augustinian affirmation of God's omnipotence with Epicurean arguments about the infinite universe and the plurality of worlds. Subsequently, he was burned at the stake on February 17, 1600. But Bruno's fate and Galileo's caution aside, there was no doubt that the spyglass revealed a universe far more immense than had previously been suspected, and the step to infinity was (paradoxically) a small one.[7] This amazing instrument promised to settle with "ocular certainty . . . all the disputes which have vexed philosophers through so many ages,"[8] and it seemed to be settling things on the side of Epicurean materialism.

Galileo's discoveries also seemed to support other Epicurean positions. If the universe was unlimited, and it was filled with countless stars, and everywhere the universe was made of the same basic elements, could there not also be an unlimited number of worlds just as Epicurus had conjectured? As we have seen, the thought was already well established (ironically) among the Christians who were nominalists for over three centuries prior to the publication of Galileo's *Starry Messenger.* As the title of Bruno's dialogue makes clear, he certainly thought that an infinite universe entailed an infinite number of worlds, and took both to be a cause for celebrating God's creative power. In Bruno's words, "Thus is the excellence of God magnified and the greatness of his kingdom made manifest: he is glorified not in one, but in countless suns; not in a single earth, but in a thousand, I say, in an infinity of worlds."[9]

[6]Ibid., p. 46.

[7]On these developments, see especially Alexandre Koyré, *From a Closed World to the Infinite Universe* (Baltimore, Md.: Johns Hopkins Press, 1957), pp. 28-57.

[8]Galileo, *Starry Messenger,* p. 49.

[9]Quoted in Koyré, *From a Closed World,* p. 42.

While Galileo avoided such direct pronouncements, he delivered another message from the heavens which appeared to support the infinity of worlds. For him, "the matter which in my opinion deserves to be considered the most important of all . . . [is] the disclosure of four PLANETS never seen from the creation of the world up to our own time."[10] Even though these were actually moons of Jupiter, the implications were obvious: if we have found four planets, might we not find a multitude of others with ever more powerful spyglasses? And if the universe is without limit, what limit can be placed on the number of other worlds?

We are not surprised, then, that the belief in the "infinity of worlds" blossomed with the spread of materialist atomism. Not only had nominalism paved the way for the acceptance of the infinity of worlds, but every improvement of the spyglass fertilized the tendencies toward the acceptance of the existence of extraterrestrial life. Astronomer Johannes Kepler (1571-1630) implied that extraterrestrial life must inevitably exist. Philosopher and mathematician René Descartes (1596-1650) hinted that the unlimited universe compelled one to entertain the possibility of intelligent life elsewhere. As atomism took firmer and firmer hold of the seventeenth-century mind, the possibility of other inhabited worlds soon became a probability and finally a necessity, culminating in Bernard le Bouier de Fontenelle's publication in 1686 of *Entretiens sur la pluralité des mondes (Conversations on the Plurality of Worlds)*, a popularized (and hence quite popular) form of the plurality-of-worlds argument based on the new cosmology. While Fontenelle was very careful not to step on the toes of Christianity directly—he argued that other intelligent creatures were not the descendants of Adam and hence their presence in the universe did not contradict the importance of the incarnation for humanity—the result of popularizing the argument was ultimately Epicurean.

We recall that the original reason Epicurus had asserted an unlimited number of worlds was that an unlimited number of atoms swirling in infinite space would, by sheer probability, "create" purely by accident an unlimited number of worlds, so the presence of intelligent human life on earth should not be a cause for wonder. Once the basic outlines of the plurality-of-worlds argument were followed, even when they came from Christians themselves,

---

[10]Galileo, *Starry Messenger*, pp. 50-51.

the credibility of Christianity, in which God sacrificed his very Son for the sake of *one* type of creature on *one* planet, dwindled accordingly. The effect was Epicurean regardless of the original intentions of those who reintroduced it.

All of the above tended to support the reintroduction of Epicurean atomism as a viable scientific hypothesis, but—and it is impossible to exaggerate the importance of this irony—there was no "spyglass" at this time that could perform the same magic of peering into the microscopic world, the very world that contained the foundational principles of Epicurean materialism. Therefore, whereas Galileo thought he could settle with "ocular certainty" philosophic disputes that had vexed philosophers since they had scanned the heavens, he could not do so in regard to the subvisible world beneath his very feet. The closest he could come to that world (as evidenced in his *Two New Sciences*) was in the sciences of ballistics and mechanics. But while cannonballs hurtling through the air might appear to be like enlarged atoms, such was only indirect evidence for the existence of atomic particles.

Since direct empirical evidence could not clinch the Epicurean account of nature in the seventeenth century,[11] what did secure such atomism as the reigning view of science during this scientific revolution? Ironically, it was the analogy based on the effectiveness of geometry as applied to heavenly objects understood as points in astronomy, and gross earthly objects (projectiles) treated as points in ballistics. Witness the following famous statement of Galileo:

> Natural philosophy is written in a great Book, which holds itself at all times open before our eyes—I mean, the universe itself. But no one can understand it unless to begin with he sets himself to master the language, and recognize the characters, in which it is written. It is written in mathematical language, and the characters are triangles, circles, and other geometrical figures.[12]

As historian of science Stephen Toulmin rightly points out, in contrast to

---

[11]Contrary to popular belief, at least popular among science historians, Robert Boyle's famous law, that the volume of gas is inversely proportional to the pressure, did not clinch the case for atomism, as Edme Mariotte (1620-1684) independently achieved the same results via the deductive method of Descartes. On this important point see Stephen Toulmin and June Goodfield. *The Architecture of Matter* (New York: Harper & Row, 1962), p. 178. Even more important and more obvious, Boyle's was only indirect evidence and certainly did not establish that atoms were eternal, nor that "Boyle's Law" was the result of indestructable and solid atoms differing only in size, shape and position.

[12]Quoted in ibid., p. 174.

the original form of atomism in Democritus, Epicurus and Lucretius, Galileo "treated the atoms as the physical counterparts of the infinitesimal units of geometry."[13] This advance on ancient atomism via the identification of atomic points with geometric points actually made Epicureanism theoretically stronger in modernity than it had been in antiquity because atomism could now borrow its legitimacy, rigor and eternality from mathematics, with the result that the successful application of mathematics to nature on the macroscopic level seemed to "prove" the existence of atoms on the microscopic level even if Galileo had no such magical spyglass to provide "ocular certainty."

We remind ourselves again what is at stake. Just as the question is not whether there existed material constituents smaller than the naked eye can see (since, as we have said, materialist and nonmaterialist alike agree that such subvisible constituents exist), so also the question in regard to the use of mathematics in physics is not whether mathematics can be applied to nature, for both materialist and nonmaterialist alike have thought it could. At issue is how mathematics applies and what can be inferred from it. Because of the very effectiveness of this geometrization of the universe in firmly establishing Epicurean materialism (and consequently, in displacing both intelligent design theory in general and Christianity in particular), we must reflect carefully and at some length on what this transformation actually entailed.

First and foremost, the successful application of mathematics to nature is not essentially and exclusively Epicurean. That is, there is no essential link between a mathematical approach to nature and a materialist approach to nature. The ancient philosopher and mathematician Pythagoras (c. 582-500 B.C.), one of the greatest mathematicians of all time, was no materialist, and his disciples thought that number and measure were the principles of the natural order. Indeed, we have the famous story, handed down from antiquity, that Pythagoras responded to his discovery that the square on the hypotenuse of a right triangle equals the sum of the squares on the other two sides, by offering a sacrifice of oxen.[14] The crux of the story is this: the existence of an underlying order to things, which the elegance of mathematics captures, is an occasion for awe and wonder, supporting the belief that the

---

[13] Ibid., p. 175.
[14] DL "Pythagoras" 8.12.

universe is intelligently designed. Of course, this essentially religious response of Pythagoras, this natural reaction of awe and wonder, was anathema to Epicurus because it so easily slips into a recognition that such intricate, intelligible order must be the result of intelligent design, and *that* would link the divine to nature as a cause.[15]

In fact, when Euclid's *Elements*, the greatest book on mathematics in the ancient world, was rediscovered in the Renaissance, the original reaction was Pythagorean, or more exactly, Platonic.[16] By this I mean that the response to the profundity of Euclid was a kind of semi-religious awe, and the successful application of his geometry to practical matters was likewise an incitement to wonder in regard to the underlying order of created things. As claimed above, this response, following the Pythagorean spirit, was purely natural, and indeed seems to have been the inspiration behind Galileo's use of mathematics; that is, in spirit, Galileo might well be considered a Pythagorean.

But even if such is the case, by completely identifying the Euclidean point with the Epicurean atom, Galileo prepared the way for the Epicurean revolution in science, and consequently, for the ultimate quenching of the Pythagorean approach to mathematics.[17] The reason is simple: the complete identity of the geometric point and the atom entailed the acceptance of the reductionism inherent in such atomism, by stripping nature of all but the simplest mathematical properties of the point (now considered by Galileo to be a real atomic object). To grasp both how and why, we must understand this reductionism more clearly.

For Epicurus and Lucretius, since material atoms were the fundamental reality, all other aspects of our everyday experience were ultimately reducible to the shape, position and relations of these invisible material building blocks. The complex appearance of things—their forms, colors, textures, smells,

---

[15]For an interesting contemporary appreciation of this point see Eugene P. Wigner, "The Unreasonable Effectiveness of Mathematics in the Natural Sciences," *Communications on Pure and Applied Mathematics* XIII (1960): 2. See also the essay by Walter Bradley, "The 'Just So' Universe: The Fine-Tuning of Constants & Conditions in the Cosmos," *Touchstone: A Journal of Mere Christianity* (July/August 1999): 70-75.

[16]The first printed edition, a Latin translation, appeared in 1482, and many other editions followed. The first edition of the original Greek was published in 1533 and again many others soon followed. Translations into Italian began in 1543, into German in 1558, French in 1564, Dutch in 1606, English in 1570 and Spanish in 1576.

[17]There were, however, notable exceptions, such as Kepler.

sounds and so on—must be broken down into its atomic constituents, and these constituents, the atoms, have none of the qualities that we experience. To use an illustration, a dog *appears* to have a definite form by which it is distinguished from other animals as a species; it has a definite color, a definite smell, a definite texture and so on. But at the atomic level, the level of reality (and not mere appearance), we find that the definite form which we thought was so real is merely an accident of the relations of atomic shapes having fitted together in a certain way. If these shapes had come together, by chance, in another pattern, we might have had an ostrich, a tree or a rock. Likewise with the color. The atoms themselves are colorless; their shapes, positions and relations cause the appearance of color to us. Had the atoms been configured differently, the colorless atoms would, on the level of appearance, present a different color. Nor do these atoms have any smell or taste, but both are the effect that their shapes have on our senses. The atomic world, the real world, is therefore completely different from the everyday world of the senses.

If points are real (i.e., if atoms can simply function as actual, geometrical points in space), then it follows that the real world, the atomic world, is purely geometrical. That means, of course, that the goal of science comes to be the reduction of the rich world of everyday experience—the world of colors, smells, tastes and so on—to the invisible world of geometrical, atomic reality. Ultimately, then, the visible form (or species, such as "dog"), the color, the taste, the smell and even the sound can all be reduced to mathematical relationships. It is clear from his polemical treatise *Il Saggiatore* (*The Assayer*, 1623) that Galileo did accept the reductionism of atomism and incorporated it into his goal of geometrizing nature.

> Hence I think that tastes, odors, colors, and so on are no more than mere names so far as the object in which we place them is concerned, and that they reside only in the consciousness [of the perceiver]. Hence if the living creature were removed [who senses such qualities], all these qualities would be wiped away and annihilated. But since we have imposed upon them special names, distinct from those of the other and real qualities mentioned previously [of shape, position, and relation], we wish to believe that they really exist as actually different from those.[18]

---

[18]Galileo Galilei, "The Assayer," in *Discoveries and Opinions of Galileo,* trans. Stillman Drake (Garden City, N.Y.: Doubleday, 1957), p. 274.

Just as Galileo's identification of Euclidean points with atomic points reinforced the Epicurean notion that everything in nature could be reduced to material points, so also (whether Galileo intended it or not) his identification of geometric and atomic points reinforced the Epicurean assertion that nature was self-contained and governed by internal necessity with which the divine could not interfere. To illustrate, there is no need to invoke any outside principles or causes when we add 5 + 7. In and of themselves, without any divine aid, the numbers added together equal 12, and this operation works universally and eternally. Over and above this, it seems that not even divine power could make it false. Mathematical relationships seem to be independent of, and imperturbable by, divine power. The same is true of course for geometrical figures and relationships. Simply because of the intrinsic necessity of two points making a line, and the joining of three straight lines to each other to form a triangle, the three interior angles of the triangle thus formed must, in and of themselves, without divine aid and in seeming defiance of divine power, equal two right angles.

If the fundamental constituent of nature, the atom, is really identical with the Euclidean point, then the inner necessity of geometry can be directly applied to nature, and nature will therefore exist as completely self-contained, governed by its own internal geometrical-physical relationships that need no divine source or guidance and that admit no divine influence. On this account, atomic points moving in straight lines will express necessary geometrical relationships. As a result, the laws of geometry will have their exact counterpart in the laws of nature. Indeed, the laws of geometry will be the laws of nature. Euclidean points will no longer exist only in the imagination.

Thus, the very notion of laws of nature in the modern sense had its source precisely in this assumption of the identity of the geometrical point with the atomic point. But this identity had an obvious Epicurean effect beyond the intention of Galileo: it allowed nature to be considered a closed system that locked divine interference out of nature. Just as God, it would seem, cannot make 5 + 7 not equal 12, nor can he make a triangle's interior angles not equal to two right angles, so also he cannot disrupt the natural necessity expressed in the relationship of atomic points. God becomes just like the gods of Epicurus, utterly powerless to interfere with nature, for the inner laws of mathematics and geometry are eternal and unbreakable.

With Sir Isaac Newton (1642-1727), what Galileo had begun was brought to its consummation, so that all the essentials of Epicurean materialism fell into place, brought into a grand synthesis by the power and authority of mathematics. Newton's *Philosophiae Naturalis Principia Mathematica* (*Mathematical Principles of Natural Philosophy*, 1687) and *Optics* (1704) became the bibles of the age. Of course, Newton himself did not refer directly to Epicurus, nor was the spirit that animated his application of mathematics to nature Epicurean in its goal. Rather, Newton's goal was to put forth a purely mathematical account of nature conformable to ancient atomism (with some important reformulations). But as history would show, despite Newton's intentions, the entire Epicurean cosmology is an indivisible package, so that the reintroduction of ancient atomism meant the reintroduction of the whole Epicurean account.

The *Principia* was directed to an explanation of "celestial phenomena" and terrestrial tides, but Newton intended the application of his principles to all of nature, and given that these principles presupposed the identity of Euclidean points with atomic points, that could only mean nature as understood by Democritus, Epicurus and Lucretius. Thus, while the *Principia* focused on the "motions of the planets, the comets, the moon, and the sea," Newton clearly expressed his "wish" that

> we could derive the rest of the phenomena of Nature by the same kind of rea-
> soning from mechanical principles, for I am induced by many reasons to sus-
> pect that they may all depend upon certain forces by which the particles of
> bodies, by some causes hitherto unknown, are either mutually impelled
> towards one another, and cohere in regular figures, or are repelled and recede
> from one another.[19]

Precisely because Newton's ultimate aim was universal, his famous Definitions and Axioms (or, laws of motion) were not limited to particular kinds of natural objects or particular kinds of motion. They were meant to apply universally. It should also not escape our notice that the entire *Principia* was set up with Euclid's *Elements* as the direct model, moving from definition to axiom (law) and then to demonstration. The effect of this mode of demonstration was twofold: first, it treated the assumptions as if they were already

---

[19]Isaac Newton, *Mathematical Principles of Natural Philosophy*, trans. Andrew Motte, revised by Florian Cajori (Berkeley: University of California Press, 1934), 1.xviii.

proven, that is, it assumed that nature already had been reduced to geometrical entities; and second, it treated science as if it were a deductive process from these already proven first principles. What most needed to be proved—that Epicurean atomic points existed and that all the complexity of nature could be reduced to these points—was thereby taken for granted.

The reductionism inherent to materialism is evident in the way Newton applied his Definitions and Laws to *all* bodies. In Definition III, Newton asserted that "the *vis insita*, or innate force of matter, is a power of resisting, by which every body, as much as in it lies, continues in its present state, whether it be of rest, or of moving uniformly forwards in a right line." In the next Definition, Newton proclaimed that the source of motion of any body is always external: "An impressed force is an action exerted upon a body, in order to change its state, either of rest, or of uniform motion in a right line." These allowed for the famous Law I: "Every body continues in its state of rest, or of uniform motion in a right line, unless it is compelled to change that state by forces impressed upon it"; Law II: "The change of motion is proportional to the motive force impressed; and is made in the direction of the right line in which that force is impressed"; and Law III: "To every action there is always opposed an equal reaction: or, the mutual actions of two bodies upon each other are always equal, and directed to contrary parts."

Although these Definitions and Laws were only applied to, or illustrated by, particular phenomena in the *Principia*, they were stated as if they applied to *every* body, whether non-living (a cannonball, a billiard ball, a comet or a planet) or living (a plant, a cat, a dog or a human being). Such universal application would only be possible *if* all bodies and their motions could be reduced to one kind of body, a homogeneous body that was itself inert, that is, a body without its own power of motion, which only moves if another body acts upon it. That homogeneous, inert body is the atomic point. Only by this double reduction—of both body and motion—could the universality of mathematics be applied to nature in the way Newton intended.

As a consequence, all apparently complex motion of seemingly complex bodies must be reduced to the simple motion of the simplest of all bodies, the atom, for if the laws are truly to be binding and universal, then no apparent complexity can be beyond their explanatory binding force. Whether it is the growth of a crystal or the growth of a cat, whether it is a cat's sudden desire to chase a mouse or the mouse's sudden desire to run and hide, whether it is the rage of Achilles or the desire of Homer to write about Achilles, all alike must be reducible to the kind of simple motion and the kind of bodies that Laws I, II and III can cover. Whether or not it was Newton's intention to set forth such universal reductionism—nothing in his laws of motion forbids it, and he did express the desire to "derive the rest of the phenomena of Nature by the same kind of reasoning from mechanical principles"—the followers of Newton in the two centuries after the publication of the *Principia* were surely animated by the desire to reduce all apparent complexity to homogeneous uniformity, even and especially the complexity of organic beings, from plants to people.

Given this urge, it is also important to see that Newton's Definitions, as ingenious as they and the rest of his work are, are by fiat: he did not demonstrate empirically that every body is composed of inert matter; rather the assertion was the *presupposition* that allowed for the desired universality, and for the application of geometry to all motions. The laws themselves, to be laws, must apply universally, and in order for them to apply with the universality of geometry, "every body" must be ultimately reducible to the point, and all motion to the "right line." Again, just as with Galileo, the borrowing of the inner necessity of mathematics performed an Epicurean function quite beyond the intention of Newton. In the decades after his death, the laws at first restricted, then ultimately denied, divine intervention. But such was inherent in Newton's original formulation, for if every body can ultimately be reduced to Euclidean points in space, then nature is a closed system where the laws of motion not only describe completely every possible motion, but lock out any possible intervention.

Yet it is quite clear that Newton did not intend to lock the divine out of his systematic account of nature; indeed, he believed that his account glorified God. But despite his intentions, the way that Newton reinserted the deity into his account of nature actually created the famous "god-of-the-gaps" dilemma, where every advance in the mechanical principles caused the necessity of invoking God to be less and less compelling, until there was no necessity at all, and God disappeared. Because of the historical importance of the god-of-the-gaps dilemma, we must examine it very carefully.

Contrary to what present-day materialists maintain, a god-of-the-gaps dilemma arises *only* where there is a "gap" in an already closed system of nature; that is, there must be a gap, or intellectual space, not yet filled in between the accepted foundational principles and the phenomena already taken to be fully explained by those principles. That is why the classic examples of this dilemma are found in Newton. As we have seen, Newton accepted a closed system of nature, a system originally designed by Epicurus to exclude any necessity for, or interference of, the divine. Against the grain of the system, Newton injected God in at three points: first, to create atoms; second, to order or position atoms in intricate relationships; and third, to readjust the arrangements as over time they became perturbed. But since Newton had defined reality by purely material principles, it followed that the gaps were likewise defined by purely material causation. Therefore, "God" would necessarily have to mean the same thing as "I don't know what the material cause is yet." Consequently, all three of these reasons were ripe for dismissal.

Let us begin with the third place where Newton injected God into his system, for the nature of this gap and its closing demonstrate most clearly what the dilemma is. Newton asserted that the universe was a delicately balanced machine. Because all bodies have mass and exert gravitational attraction accordingly, the regular motions that planets, stars, and moons describe are caused by their exact position in relationship to each other. Disturbing gravitational forces, such as erratic comets, would thereby introduce slight perturbations, throwing off the delicate balance of mass and motion in the heavens, thereby leading to eventual chaos and collapse. Over time, Newton claimed, the "inconsiderable irregularities . . . which have risen from the mutual actions of comets and planets upon one another . . . will be apt to increase, till this system wants a reformation."[20] What the system wants, so it seemed to Newton, was a divine mechanic. Oddly enough, then, from an apparent imperfection of the system, Newton provided a proof for the necessity of direct divine influence in nature. Or so it seemed.

But as it turned out, what the system really wanted was a better, or at least more advanced, mathematician using more accurate observations. Instead of a deity, the Newtonian world needed a Laplace, Pierre Simon de Laplace (1749-1827). While Newton believed that God had to step in and

---

[20]Isaac Newton, *Optics*, Great Books of the Western World (Chicago: Encyclopaedia Britannica, 1952), 32:542.

readjust the system of the world because of the recorded inconsistencies between the visible heavenly bodies and the exact paths they should trace, as well as because of the effects that comets should have had but somehow did not, Laplace was able to sweep up the difficulties and perceived anomalies by applying Newtonianism more thoroughly. The gaps in Newton's system did not require a deity for readjustment after all, but ever more exact observations and calculations that showed that the system really was entirely stabile and completely self-contained. This snapping shut of a perceived gap in Newton's account, for which Newton himself believed he needed to invoke God, defined thereafter any attempt to assert God or an intelligent designer as committing the so-called god-of-the-gaps fallacy.

As a result, the mere mention of the phrase "god-of-the-gaps" by materialists today works like a mysteriously powerful bludgeon against legitimate dissent from materialist orthodoxy. Person X says that such-and-such is impossible to explain on materialist terms, and seems to call for an intelligent designer; person Y merely intones "god-of-the-gaps"; person X, embarrassed to silence, blushes and retreats. Every such invocation of god-of-the-gaps by materialists against intelligent design theorists since then is simply a variation of Laplace's famous reply to Napoleon. When asked by Napoleon where God was in Laplace's *Traité de la méchanique céleste*, Laplace triumphantly proclaimed, "Sire, I have no need of that hypothesis." Even when the very principles of Laplace's *System of the World* were destroyed by the advance of more powerful instruments and more powerful minds, the confidence gained by Laplace's provisional victory remained; that is, even when the Epicurean foundation of eternal atomic points was swept away at the end of the nineteenth century, the habit of mind remained (and remains). As a consequence, materialists still believe that Laplace's remark is sufficient to parry any attempt to reintroduce intelligent design, even though its original and only power lay in a quite peculiar situation: the acceptance of the eternality of matter, the motion of which was inert and which followed the lawlike confines of geometry, coupled with the attempt to inject God, as an alien element, into this closed system.

It is of no small interest to the present work that the most amazing vindication of the Laplacian spirit came in the mid-nineteenth century, just prior to Darwin. In 1781 William Herschel discovered by observation another planet, Uranus. But over the next sixty years, no matter how astronomers and mathematicians fiddled with the calculations, the actual orbit of the planet would not coincide with the calculations. But two immensely clever mathematicians, the Englishman John Adams and the Frenchman Urbain J. J. Leverreir, independently predicted by mathematics alone that given the actual perturbations of the orbit of Uranus, there must be another planet at a particular place. Using Leverrier's predictions, Johann Galle, at the Urania Observatory in Berlin, trained his telescope on that very section of the night sky on September 23, 1846. There he found, as mathematically required and predicted, another planet, now called Neptune.

No greater boost could have come to the already supremely confident nineteenth-century materialist mind. The unaided power of the human mind showed its new-found omniscience by predicting what *must* exist. By pure thought alone and according to materialist principles, the human mind could reach any corner of the cosmos, just as Lucretius said it could. The discovery of Neptune appeared to prove that the inner necessity of mathematics pertained directly and universally to nature, thereby demonstrating conclusively that nature was a closed, law-governed system. That could only mean that the Epicurean dream of a system of nature completely closed to the divine and completely comprehensible to the human intellect had been perfected. Not only was mathematics perfectly descriptive, but it was perfectly predictive, shedding light on every dark corner of the universe where it was previously thought the divine might hide. The capital gained by this victory seemed inexhaustible, for now every difficulty that materialist science encountered was considered to be solvable given time, more powerful instruments and more powerful mathematics.

Let us now turn to another place Newton injected God into his system. Newton also unwittingly helped the Epicurean cause by inserting God as the creator of atoms. We recall that Epicurus had insisted that atoms were eternal, for if they were eternal then nature had no need of any external creative power. Newton tried to fit God into the Epicurean system by asserting that the atomic points were only quasi-eternal. Ironically, it was the "quasi" that made Newtonianism so effective a medium for the reintroduction of full-fledged Epicurean materialism, for Newton argued:

> All these things being considered, it seems probable to me that God in the beginning formed matter in solid, massy, hard, impenetrable, moveable particles, of such sizes and figures, and with such other properties, and in such pro-

portion to space, as most conduced to the end for which he formed them; and
that these primitive particles being solids, are incomparably harder than any
porous bodies compounded of them, even so very hard as never to wear or
break in pieces; no ordinary power being able to divide what God himself made
one in the first creation.[21]

The assertion that God created the atoms "as never to wear or break in
pieces"—just shy of being eternal—made it easier for Christians, against
the centuries-long animosity towards Epicureanism, to embrace that very
materialism designed by Epicurus to remove all divine action from nature,
and consequently from human affairs. Such a compromise—a Christian God
creating Epicurean atoms—ended, of course, in the eventual squeezing out
of the divine by the materialism, thereby attesting to Epicurus's genius in
designing a deity-proof view of nature. For once the atoms were accepted as
quasi-eternal, it soon became an established habit of mind to think of them
as eternal, and it therefore became unclear why they needed a cause for their
existence. Again, it seemed as if a gap opened by Newton had been closed,
and that science no longer "had need of that hypothesis either."

This habit of mind was so strong that it remained even after scientists
discovered, at the end of the nineteenth century, that atoms were not "solid,
massy, hard, impenetrable, moveable particles" that were "incomparably
harder than any porous bodies compounded of them, even so very hard as
never to wear or break in pieces." That is, even after it had been discovered
that atoms were not eternal, and therefore that nature cannot be its own
cause, the materialist habit of mind remained. As a consequence, materialists kept right on thinking that nature must be self-caused even when the
destruction of the eternality of the atom demanded the opposite conclusion.
For if atoms are not eternal, then it is impossible that they have always
existed. But physical reality does exist. Therefore, it must have come into
being at some time. Yet, as even Epicurus was compelled to admit, nothing
cannot cause something. Therefore, there must have been an eternal cause
other than nature that brought nature into being. In Aquinas's words—for
this is simply one of his proofs of God's existence—that cause is what we call
God. The logic is inescapable, if only human beings were not able to be
escapists in regard to logic.

_____

[21]Ibid., 32:541.

Finally, we may examine Newton's insertion of a divine designer into a system originally designed by Epicurus to exclude gods as designers. Newton allowed God this other function in addition to mechanic and creator, but this also ran directly against the grain of the fundamentally Epicurean system. As a result, the function of designer was likewise eliminated within a very short time. But for Newton, God was indeed the grand designer, and this position was explicitly set against the Lucretian argument that the world could be the result of chance.

> Now . . . all material things seem to have been composed of the hard and solid particles above mentioned, variously associated in the first creation by the counsel of an intelligent agent. For it became Him who created them to set them in order. And if He did so, it's unphilosophical to seek for any other origin of the world, or to pretend that it might arise out of a chaos by the mere laws of Nature; though, being once formed, it may continue by those laws for many ages.[22]

We might even infer from this passage that Newton was well aware of the danger of his position, and was at pains to make clear that (contrary to the well-known position of Epicurus and Lucretius) the atoms alone, moving by necessary laws, could not create order without divine aid. Whether of the "wonderful uniformity in the planetary system" or the "uniformity in the bodies of animals" or the "contrivance" of the complex parts of animals or "the instinct of brutes and insects"—all, declared Newton, must "be the effect of nothing else than the wisdom and skill of a powerful, ever-living agent."[23]

Given his position, it would appear as if Newton were an intelligent design theorist of the first order, and, indeed, he certainly seems to have taken himself to be such. But if we look more closely, we find in Newton a mixture of incongruous elements from rival cosmologies. In fact, Newton's putting them together greatly facilitated the revival of full-fledged Epicurean cosmology, for (again) it removed the scruples of Christians in accepting the materialism they had been taught to fear. Contrary to Newton's insistence, if the laws arise from the very nature of the atom acting as a physical, geometrical point, then it is difficult to see why it is "unphilo-

---

[22]Ibid., 32:542.
[23]Ibid.

sophical" to assert that the "origin of the world . . . might arise out of a chaos by the mere laws of Nature," especially since Lucretius had already provided an argument, based on Epicurean principles, that the random motion of purposeless atoms could create, over time, the order in nature that we experience.

As before, here again there was a gap just waiting to be closed. Newton himself had already provided the laws of motion whereby all nature was described, and these laws could just as well be applied, via the forces of attraction and repulsion, to the construction of ever larger bodies from the original "hard and solid particles." Since Lucretius was already well known in the seventeenth century, and the universe seemed infinite and full of an endless supply of these particles, all that was needed to reinstate the evolutionary argument of Lucretius was a far greater age of the universe. This was provided by Charles Lyell in his *Principles of Geology* (1830).

Given this historical preparation, it is no surprise that the divine design element of Newtonianism, ill-fitted as it was to the larger Epicurean cosmology, was historically displaced by an evolutionary account that claimed that design was only apparent, not real. The advent of Darwin's *The Origin of Species* in 1859 was simply the result of the complete Epicurean system falling into place, causing the ejection of the alien element of divine design inserted by Newton. The mere laws of motion seemed more than enough, given an infinite universe and an unlimited amount of time, to create the natural order.

This accounts, by the way, for the quick acceptance of Darwin's arguments, despite the fact that Darwin had not proven that evolution by chance mutation actually occurred. To those who already believed in the existence of eternal atoms moving through infinite space during an unlimited time according to purely natural laws of motion, it seemed, by sheer probability, that evolution *must* explain the apparent complexity of nature. The probability soon became a certainty. By the time of Darwin, given the amazing explanatory and predictive power of the Newtonian system, the materialist mind had complete faith that the fundamental principles had already been fully vindicated, and that Newton's dream of deriving "the rest of the phenomena of Nature by the same kind of reasoning from mechanical principles" had been realized. The war had already been won, so to speak, and the appearance of Darwin's *Origin* was simply the last piece of the machine falling into place with a satisfying "snap."

And so, as we shall see even more clearly in chapter eight, Darwin's theories were neither revolutionary in origin nor conclusive in argument. The materialist evolutionary account had existed as part of Epicurean materialism for almost two millennia, and the goal of its design was to eliminate the divine. The modern acceptance of all the essentials of Epicurean materialism necessarily led to the acceptance of the entire theoretical construct, of which evolution was a necessary part. Thus, even though Darwin's arguments were far from conclusive, they acted to reinforce the notion that the God that Newton thought necessary to explain design had rightly been ejected from the gap closed by science.

We conclude, then, that the famous god-of-the-gaps dilemma, rather than being a universal difficulty, arose in a particular set of circumstances: when a materialist edifice, designed to reject the divine, had the divine attached to it in contradiction to its principles. Unfortunately, well-intentioned theologians were largely to blame for the perpetuation of the fallacy (and Newton himself was a well-intentioned amateur theologian). For given the success of Newtonianism, many theologians in the eighteenth and nineteenth centuries, moved by desperation or good intentions, kept inserting God into this or that nook or cranny of the Newtonian cosmology. But there was no room in such a closed system for a deity, as Newton's own attempts to inject one attest. Materialists, watching each such attempt, could hardly be blamed in one sense for developing a jaundiced eye. But in another regard, they were to blame, for generally such materialists only countenanced those theologians who accepted the principles of science as defined by materialism. Small wonder that they only encountered bungled attempts to reinstate a divinity.

In our analysis of the god-of-the-gaps dilemma created by Newton, two important further effects of the acceptance of materialist atomism have no doubt occurred to the reader. If nature is governed by the iron laws of geometrically defined physics, then both God's activity and human activity become difficult, if not impossible, to fit in. The laws of nature seem opposed to both God's ability to interfere in natural events (and hence, miracles become impossible), and the human ability to think and act freely.

We have seen that, while Newton did allow for God's intervention in nature, the source of the intervention was a defect in the cosmological machine, a defect that Newton thought necessitated divine intervention to rectify. As a consequence, through the efforts of Laplace and others the necessity for divine intervention disappeared. As the necessity of God's intervention was eliminated, the very possibility of divine intervention disappeared with it. The very laws of motion, which it would seem were freely given by God, became the manacles binding both his creative power and his powers of intervention. This occurred precisely because the elements of nature used by Newton were Epicurean in origin, and Newton's application of mathematics only served to strengthen Epicurus's original design. The laws of motion—which were simply the laws of geometry as applied to Epicurean atoms—were defined by an inner necessity which excluded outside interference. This necessity, in a very short time, crept back and shackled the divine author of the laws. And so it came to be believed that not only was it necessary that God use these laws to create, but he could not interfere with them once he created the atoms and set them in motion according to the laws.

This, of course, was an impossibly contradictory belief. For if God was powerful enough to create a universe and the very laws by which it runs, then how could he not have sufficient power to manipulate it at will? The more general source of the contradiction was, of course, the attempt to attach a divinity to a system designed to exclude the divine. The more particular source of this contradiction was Newton's own Definitions and Laws. This is a bit difficult to understand, but its importance is overwhelming for the entire history of the relationship of science to theology thereafter.

In order to subject nature to mathematical analysis, Newton had to reject any source of nonmathematical complexity and any contingency (that is, any indeterminacy or spontaneity), and reduce all such complexity and contingency in nature to the homogeneity of the inert, lifeless, Euclidean atomic points. Note how difficult it would be, in geometry, if the points had minds of their own, and kept leaping about the diagrams erratically, or constructing lines or solids that were, by some magic, more than the sum of their parts. For this very reason modern scientific Epicureanism had to reject Epicurus's own device, the "swerve," which allowed for erratic motion, and hence contingency and free will.

In the modern elimination any source of contingency, and hence any source of unpredictable motion, the atoms could then act as lifeless points that only moved when struck by an outside force. These inert bodies carried forth only as much motion as they had received from other inert bodies. Like a billiard ball, an atom remained in position until hit by another. The force that caused the ball to move was simply another inert object in motion whose velocity and bulk ("quantity of matter") caused the body in a state of rest to move. According to Newton's Definition IV, the "impressed force" was not some power latent in the cause that produced the result, but "consists in the action only, and remains no longer in the body when the action is over."[24] To use the example of billiard balls again, when the cue ball hits the eight ball head on, the cue ball stops, and the entire force of the cue ball is now in the eight ball as it careens about the table. The cue ball does not have the ability suddenly to leap up, of its own accord, and hit another billiard ball, nor would the eight ball have moved at all unless struck by the cue ball. It followed, then, that if "every body" is made up of just such atomic billiard balls, then every motion is reducible to such inert, billiard ball motion.

The definition of *cause* therefore suffered a severe reduction. In Newton's system, cause was reduced to "impressed force" and there was nothing in the cause other than the force that could be inferred from the effect. The ramifications for divine *and* human action were immense. The power to act, as a cause, had been reduced to the power to transmit rectilinear motion. On this account, we know of a cause, *any* cause, that it transmitted its entire power to the effect, for its power, or force, was only the combined moving power of its velocity and quantity of matter. With this reduced notion of cause, God could only be a kind of divine billiard player, who racked up the atoms to begin with, took the opening shot, but then had to let the atomic billiard balls act and react according to the laws of motion. God had only enough power to take the opening shot.

With the victory of Newton's system, the habit of mind created by the above suppositions became the source of the supposedly devastating criticism of all possible proofs of God's existence made by philosopher David Hume (1711-1776). Speaking in the person of Epicurus, Hume uttered this famous dictum: "When we infer any particular cause from an effect, we must proportion the one to the other, and can never be allowed to ascribe to the cause any qualities, but what are exactly sufficient to produce the

---

[24]See also Law III, "To every action there is always supposed an equal reaction," and the corollary, "The quantity of motion . . . suffers no change from the action of bodies among themselves." Both of these also helped the Newtonian universe to stay self-contained because there was no entropic loss of motion.

effect." Hence, according to Newton's definition of cause, "you have no ground to ascribe to him [i.e., God] any qualities, but what you see he has actually exerted and displayed in his productions."[25]

The double effect of this dictum was as follows. First, one could infer no other power in God beyond what produced the laws of nature; therefore, God does not have the power to override nature. We cannot infer, then, from God's power to create the universe, any residual power to manipulate it afterwards. Second, God's power became redundant to nature, for the laws of motion worked by the very nature of the atoms themselves—and why invoke a redundant explanation? What could God add to a self-contained, self-perpetuating system?

An obvious result, which again ran counter to Newton's original intentions, was the absolute denial of the power of God to perform miracles. If God could perform miracles, then Newton's Laws would be merely particular expressions of his creative power. Not only could he have created the universe with different laws, but he could override the particular regularities of this universe whenever he pleased. But now that geometry and physical reality had been identified, that would be tantamount to assertion that the rules of geometry were merely particular expressions of God's creative power, which he could have made differently, and could override at will.

But Newton's reduction of nature, and the consequent reduction of cause, not only restricted what God could do, but also and quite obviously what human beings could do. Human beings, as part of that same nature that bound God, bound themselves. This is a corollary of that most binding of universal laws: "Every distinct view of the universe, every theory about nature necessarily entails a view of morality; every distinct view of morality, every theory about human nature necessarily entails a cosmology to support it." The corollary derives from the universality of claims about nature: "Anything we assert about ourselves, we assert about nature; anything we assert about nature, we assert about ourselves." If we construct nature so that divine action becomes impossible, it thereby follows that human action becomes impossible. Any system of nature which restricts, or makes impossible or unintelligible divine action in regard to nature, restricts, or makes impossible

---

[25]David Hume, *An Enquiry Concerning Human Understanding* (Indianapolis: Hackett, 1977), section xi, pp. 93-95.

or unintelligible human action. We might even state it in another form, as the *Law of Gravitas*, since it concerns the most weighty of questions: "The force with which we cast a stone at the heavens, is the force with which it falls back upon our heads."

Ironically, the victory of Newtonianism spelled the defeat of humanity, for now human action (both the action of thinking and of doing) had to be reduced to the motion of inert forces completely described by laws of motion. This reduction occurred on both the theoretical and moral levels. We shall take the theoretical first, since it is both most surprising and most often overlooked.

The glory of Newtonianism theoretically was that in reducing the universe to Euclidean points in motion, and eliminating all contingency, it provided human beings with a new-found omniscience. Since we know geometry thoroughly, and the universe is thoroughly geometric, then it follows that we know the universe thoroughly. As a result, Newton very soon came to be seen as a semi-divinity, worthy of the kind of praise one normally only associates with God.

Indeed, the great astronomer Edmund Halley (1656-1742) wrote an ode to Newton that captured well the adulation felt by the age, felt for a man who seemed to have penetrated the inmost secrets of the universe.[26] One cannot read it without being reminded of the praise heaped upon Epicurus by his disciple Lucretius, for both Epicurus and Newton were praised for the same thing: godlike omniscience.

Halley therefore praised Newton for his "reckonings divine" whereby the "inmost places of the heavens, now gained, / Break into view, nor longer hidden is / The force that turns the farthest orb." As a result—and here, again, we strike some of the same notes as in Epicurus and Lucretius—the portents in the heavens, previously thought to be signs of divine communication or anger, were harnessed to the Laws: "Now we know / The sharply veering ways of comets, once / A source of dread, nor longer do we quail / Beneath appearances of bearded stars." Furthermore, mere philosophical controversy has now been eliminated by scientific omniscience, and sterile metaphysical speculation has been replaced by hard-nosed, rigorous physics:

---

[26]The entire poem is in Isaac Newton, *Mathematical Principles of Natural Philosophy*, trans. Leon J. Richardson (Berkeley: University of California Press, 1934), pp. xiii-xv.

Matters that vexed the minds of ancient seers,
And for our learned doctors often led
To loud and vain contention, now are seen
In reason's light, the clouds of ignorance
Dispelled at last by science.

Through the genius of Newton, we too, by knowing the laws of motion, have that very omniscience. By reducing all the complexity of the universe to a few simple laws, Newton made omniscience, through science, public property within the reach of all.

But now, behold,
Admitted to the banquets of the gods,
We contemplate the polities of heaven;
And spelling out the secrets of the earth,
Discern the changeless order of the world
And all the aeons of its history.

While this last line may seem like an awfully heady thing to say, Halley realized that since the laws of motion always pertained, they could be applied retroactively and progressively; that is, all time had been opened up, all that could have happened, all that does happen and all that will happen. All alike are determined by those laws.

Halley ended with these immortalizing lines, which celebrated the genius of Newton in the highest possible terms, as the one mortal who truly deserved to be divinized.

Then ye who now on heavenly nectar fare,
Come celebrate with me in song the name
Of Newton, to the Muses dear; for he
Unlocked the hidden treasuries of Truth:
So richly through his mind had Pheobus cast
The radiance of his own divinity.
Nearer the gods no mortal may approach.

Unlike Lucretius, however, Halley did, albeit briefly, defer to God as the author of the laws that Newton discovered: "Here ponder too the Laws which God, / Framing the universe, set not aside / But made the fixed foundations of his work." But by comparison the praise of Newton's genius received far more attention than the apparent author of the Laws. The proportion was apt, for it reflected the new position that God was given (at least for a time) in the new cosmology. There was not much one could say about him but that he set up the Laws to begin with. His omniscience was no longer a source of wonder; his wisdom no longer dwarfed mere human intelligence. For human intelligence, by its own unaided efforts, had now achieved that same omniscience. Small wonder the age was giddy with praise for Newton.

But in the victory the seeds of defeat lay hidden. It certainly did not take long for the laws of motion to be applied to the human mind as well. As materialism took greater and greater hold, fairly soon the belief arose that human thought must be the result of material forces working on inert matter; that is, our minds, as physical entities, must originally be blank (i.e., inert masses waiting to be acted upon), and be set in motion and written upon by the sum total of material forces which have affected us. Our thoughts must be reducible to the simplicity of the laws of motion; therefore, no matter how elevated or complex our thoughts appear to be, ultimately they are merely the sum total of the external forces acting upon our material intellects according to the Laws. As a result, human thought would be neither true nor false, but rather, the result of external stimuli that happen to have triggered particular responses in us.

This extension of Newtonianism to the human mind ultimately served an Epicurean goal quite well by supplanting the intellectual, immaterial soul with the material brain set in motion by external stimuli as the cause of thought. We will focus on the materialist elimination of the soul in later chapters, but let us at this point note the irony that such reductionism has this interesting effect: it eliminates the very possibility of science, an effect not only in contradiction to Newton's intentions but to most later modern materialists' intentions as well. The reduction of physical nature to law-governed atomic points, and the human mind to atoms, created a modern version of the Cretan paradox.[27] If a man from Crete says, "All Cretans are liars," then he is either lying (and the statement is false) or he is telling the truth (and the statement is false). Rather than name the modern form after Newton (who would certainly have recoiled in horror from the honor), I

---

[27]On this point see Phillip Johnson, *Reason in the Balance* (Downers Grove, Ill.: InterVarsity Press, 1995), pp. 59-66.

would like to name it after a physicist of our own time, Stephen Hawking, whose aspirations for constructing universal laws are as strong as Newton's were, and who is the Lucasian Professor of Mathematics at Cambridge University, a post previously held by Newton himself. I call this peculiarly modern form of the Cretan paradox "Hawking's Dilemma," for it is he who most elegantly and exactly states the difficulty.

> Now, if you believe that the universe is not arbitrary, but is governed by definite laws, you ultimately have to combine the partial theories [in physics] into a complete unified theory [of physics] that will describe everything in the universe. But there is a fundamental paradox in the search for such a complete unified theory. The ideas about scientific theories outlined above assume we are rational beings who are free to observe the universe as we want and to draw logical deductions from what we see. In such a scheme it is reasonable to suppose that we might progress ever closer toward the laws that govern our universe. Yet if there really is a complete unified theory, it would also presumably determine our actions. And so the theory itself would determine the outcome of our search for it! And why should it determine that we come to the right conclusions from the evidence? Might it not equally well determine that we draw the wrong conclusion? Or no conclusion at all?[28]

But Hawking misses the real paradox: the materialist view of science, contrary to its very claim, makes the activity of science both unintelligible and impossible. The complete silliness of Hawking's response to his own dilemma serves to underscore its lethal bite, and the ridiculous lengths that materialism will go to avoid undermining its own presuppositions.

> The only answer that I can give to this problem is based on Darwin's principle of natural selection. The idea is that in any population of self-reproducing organisms, there will be variations in the genetic material and upbringing that different individuals have. These differences will mean that some individuals are better able than others to draw the right conclusions about the world around them and to act accordingly. These individuals will be more likely to survive and reproduce and so their pattern of behavior and thought will come to dominate. It has certainly been true in the past that what we call intelligence and scientific discovery has conveyed a survival advantage. . . . Provided the universe has evolved in a regular way, we might expect that the reasoning

---

[28]Stephen Hawking, *A Brief History of Time* (Toronto: Bantam, 1988), p. 12.

abilities that natural selection has given us would be valid also in our search for a complete unified theory, and so would not lead us to the wrong conclusions.[29]

Hawking's answer is, of course, utter nonsense. Such binding universal laws would not only create all intellects, but determine what they think no matter how intelligent we might deem them. Furthermore, successful sexual reproduction would be better served by polygamy and the rudest animism that would support it, than by the most abstract attempts at scientific theorizing (as the reproduction rates of tribal chieftains as compared with contemporary theoretical physicists like Hawking make readily apparent).

As Hawking's Dilemma amply illustrates, the human claim to omniscience, whether in the form of Newton's universal Laws or Hawking's unified theory, has the effect of destroying human knowledge. Why? Because the elimination of the immaterial soul means that the intellect must be utterly material itself, and that means that it would be completely determined by the laws of nature. By destroying the immaterial soul, the materialist view of science ultimately destroys the very possibility of science.

In just the same way, and for the same reasons, despite Newton's intentions, the materialist view of nature that he did so much to craft, destroyed the very possibility of human moral action. If we, who are certainly bodily, are subsumed under Newton's first Law ("Every body continues in its state of rest, or uniform motion in a right line, unless it is compelled to change that state by forces impressed upon it"), then human action must be—no matter how complex it appears to be, no matter how much we feel as if we are acting freely in making choices between good and evil—reducible to our reactions to the external forces that impress us. Indeed, in regard to the human sciences, nearly all modern moral and political theorizing (in the broadest sense of moral and political) can be described accurately as so many successive attempts to achieve, in the human sciences, the same success Newtonianism enjoyed in physics. Modern political science, sociology, anthropology, psychology, economics—all came to be largely defined by the search in human action for variations of the laws of motion as found in Newton. All alike wear themselves out in the enterprise of searching for the law of human behavior, the real cause of the apparently complex and diverse

---

[29]Ibid., pp. 12-13.

human "motions," and do so by reducing all the complexity and diversity to some simple and original material cause. In the following chapters we shall take a closer look at this transformation.

Now that we have gotten an overview in this chapter of the theoretical shift that enshrined the Epicurean materialist principles of nature in modern science, we must attend to the complementary moral aspects of Epicurus's cosmology, for there was an Epicurean moral revolution going on at the same time. In contrast to the scientific aspects of the revolution, which reinforced but did not fundamentally alter the theoretical aspects of Epicurus's arguments, the modern form of moral Epicureanism was changed from the original asceticism of Epicurus himself, to a new kind of Epicurean hedonism. Another contrast will arise as well. As we have seen, the modern scientific reintroduction of atomism was largely innocent of Epicurean motives— innocent in the worst sense, perhaps. Galileo and Newton (as well as Bruno, Gassendi and Boyle) truly thought that they could set science on a firmer foundation with a revived form of ancient atomism, and just as truly seemed to believed that they could avoid the original intentions of Epicurus's materialism. But in regard to the modern revival of the moral aspects of Epicureanism, there seems to be, as we shall soon see, much more reason to be suspicious of the motives of these modern champions of Epicurus.

The Moral Revolution
of Materialism

We must now attend carefully to the modern transformation of ancient Epicurean materialism that occurred in the moral realm. This new form of moral Epicureanism was built both out of the defects of ancient Epicureanism and by a logical extension of its fundamental principles. Over and above this—and I cannot stress this enough—it was consciously defined *against* Christianity. Furthermore, whereas the figures in the last two chapters seem to have had non-Epicurean motives and apparently thought that they could divorce the theoretical aspects of Epicureanism from the moral aspects, there is no doubt that those who transformed moral Epicureanism knew what they were about. They consciously defined their arguments not only against Aristotelianism (as Galileo and Newton had done), but against natural law reasoning and against the doctrines of Christianity as well.

But as we should expect, in conformity with the great law of uniformity, this revolution in regard to the moral aspects of Epicureanism had to rely on the cosmic revolution. The theoretical aspects of Epicurean materialism embraced by Galileo, Newton and hence the entire scientific revolution, could not remain separated from the moral aspects. Not only did the theoretical revolution usher in the moral revolution, but the moral revolution co-opted the scientific revolution. Thus, the attempt by Newton and others to detach materialist atomism from full-blown Epicureanism did not succeed. Indeed, it could not succeed, for not only was the modern form of moral Epicureanism more powerful than the original ancient form (and hence, more irresistible in its pull), but materialist atomism of its own nature was only at home in a fully Epicurean universe. To understand these points in full, we must turn to our analysis of the modern form of moral Epicureanism.

There are three major points of transformation in the modern reembrace of moral Epicureanism. First, Epicureanism became Machiavellian in strategy because it arose at a time when Christianity was powerful and able to persecute its detractors. Epicureanism therefore had to present a benign public face to the more powerful Christians, even while it chipped away at the foundations of Christianity. Epicurus himself had little to fear from religion in ancient Athens because religion was, for the most part, not organized but eclectic. There was no inquisitional tribunal, no index of forbidden books and no doctrinally well-defined religious view that thoroughly permeated the entire populace. By contrast, modern Epicureanism had the characteristic animosity toward religion so evident in Lucretius, but it had to deal with all the formidable obstacles presented by Christianity. Obviously, the best place to understand this Machiavellianism is its source, Machiavelli himself.

Second, modern Epicurean materialism shifted from the original asceticism and embraced hedonism instead. We recall that Epicurus identified the good with pleasure and denied any natural justice beyond mere utility. At the same time, however, he asserted that nature limits our pursuit of pleasure because our bodies and souls are so materially constituted that indulgence causes direct physical pain (recalling, in regard to the soul, that wishing for immortality was considered a kind of indulgence) or, failing that, indulgence at least incurs the pain of societal reprobation. But the moderns rejected even these limits. Cannot Epicurus be accused of a kind of timidity? modern Epicureans asked. May we not push the material limits of nature, or better, reconstruct these material boundaries, so that we, and not chance, determine the limits of pleasure? And so, rather than turn our powers towards ourselves in an effort to control our desires, as Epicurus had counseled, modern Epicureanism bids us to turn our powers against nature itself in an effort to control it, and remake it according to our desires. By setting its goal to be the progressive removal of these natural limits through technology, modern Epicureanism shed asceticism and embraced hedonism. Here, our main focus will be on Francis Bacon.

Third, Epicurean materialism became political rather than remaining apolitical, as it had been originally. This move followed upon the second transformation, the mastering of nature and the consequent releasing of desire from its natural limits. Why? It should be obvious from our analysis of Epicurus's original doctrines that the practice of Epicurean asceticism could never become widespread. "Barley Cakes and Water" makes for an unpopular political platform. Furthermore, the focus of Epicurus's ethics was *individual* tranquillity, and that necessitated a withdrawal from political society. Against this, the moderns believed that a new politics could be built directly upon an Epicurean foundation—not ascetic Epicureanism, but hedonistic Epicureanism. Society could then be built on a rational foundation—rational defined in terms of that materialism, that is. One of the most important inventions of this new science, as we shall see, will be modern natural rights, an invention designed to replace natural law, a vestige of the old view of cosmology that Galilean-Newtonian atomism was in the process of displacing during the seventeenth and eighteenth centuries. In this section, we shall have to look at more than one thinker, for there are several important aspects of the political part of modern moral Epicureanism. In our analysis of this political transformation we shall include Thomas Hobbes, John Locke and Jean-Jacques Rousseau.

In what follows I will focus only on the most influential thinkers whom I have mentioned who best represent the transformation. The many followers always make sense in light of the few leaders. Further, the treatment will minimize redundancy. Each thinker I will cover contributed in his own way to the transformation, even though there was also a fair amount of overlap, given that they were all involved in the same project.[1] Finally, the scientific revolution and the moral revolution occur simultaneously, giving us a kind of chicken-or-the-egg dilemma: for example, which came first, the atomism of Galileo or the moral atomism of Hobbes, the atomism of Newton or the moral atomism of Locke? In general, we can say the scientific revolution paved the way for the acceptance of the moral revolution, but the finer details of that argument are beyond the scope of the present

---

[1]For a more thorough analysis of these figures one should read Leo Strauss, *Natural Right and History* (Chicago: University of Chicago Press, 1953); and Leo Strauss and Joseph Cropsey, eds., *History of Political Philosophy*, 2nd ed. (Chicago: University of Chicago Press, 1972).

work. Since the whole Epicurean universe is all of a piece, and Epicureanism had been circulating from the late fifteenth century on, the lines of
influence can become quite murky; our time will be better spent just ana-
lyzing the revolution itself. Let us begin with Machiavelli.

Niccolo Machiavelli (1469-1527) is rightly held by many to be the father of
modernity. As he himself stated, "I depart from the orders of others,"[2] meaning that he was going to give the world something new. While Machiavelli was
not, as such, a natural philosopher, but a political philosopher, his new view of
human nature was later applied to nature as such. Although it is unclear, one
suspects that such was his ultimate intention. And while we would not call
Machiavelli an explicit Epicurean materialist, he was an essential part of the
modern transformation of Epicurean materialism. But we should note some
important resemblances. As with Epicureanism, Machiavelli's new view of
human nature was completely (and purposely) at odds with both Christianity
and Aristotelianism. Furthermore, his rejection of any end for human nature,
his implicit atheism and his rejection of the immaterial, immortal soul, all
make him an excellent fit for Epicurus's account of nature and human nature.

Machiavelli's name has become synonymous with duplicity and the ruthless use of force. And with good reason. In his most famous work *The Prince*,
he openly taught the art of duplicity and the ruthless use of force. He was, at
least from the Christian perspective, a teacher of evil; nevertheless, he was a
profound teacher of evil. He took his intellectual lights from the ancients,
which is to say, the non-Christian world, but he added some things that were
new, and to understand his effect on the renewal of Epicurean materialism,
we must comprehend both the ancient and the new.

Machiavelli was a teacher of an ancient kind of duplicity, expressed in its
most famous and influential form in Polybius (c. 200-c. 118 B.C.), the Greek
historian of the Roman Republic's rise in the Mediterranean. For Polybius,
one of the great secrets to Rome's success in conquering, including its conquering of Greece, was its political use of *deisidaimonia*, a Greek word that
means literally "godfearingness" (but has the connotation of "superstition"
as well). Polybius argued that Rome was superior to Greece because it had
the intelligence to *use* religion "for the sake of the many," that is, to control

---

[2]Niccolo Machiavelli, *The Prince*, trans. Harvey Mansfield Jr. (Chicago: University of Chicago Press,
1985), chap. xv.

the foolish masses. Since the masses of people are not wise, but instead trivial, "full of unreasoned passion, irrational desire, and violent spirit," the
Roman elite realized that the only way to control them was by "invisible terrors." Hence they introduced notions concerning the gods and the terrors of
Hades—and, Polybius adds, current leaders are "now rash and irrational to
banish these things."[3] From Polybius, Machiavelli accepted both the assertion that politics will forever need religion to control the ignorant and passion-driven masses, and that those in power (who know the religion in hand
to be false) wisely consider it useful for ruling the masses nonetheless.

But Machiavelli also added something new, something that fit Epicureanism, but departed from the counsels of Epicurus. We recall that Epicurus
realized that his materialism entailed the affirmation of nature as amoral
and the denial that any act was intrinsically wrong. Ultimately, then, our
actions must be governed by utility. However, Epicurus warned his disciples
to keep within the moral confines drawn by whatever society within which
they happen to find themselves. Otherwise, they would incur the painful
punishments meted out by public guardians of morality. But Machiavelli's
words were directed to princes, not reclusive and timid philosophers, and his
frank advice on the use of ruthless force makes it quite clear to all but the
dullest reader, that while he agreed with the Epicurean assertion that there
are no intrinsically evil actions, he departed from Epicurus in counseling a
combination of bold action and artful duplicity.

A prince, if he is to be an effective ruler, argued Machiavelli, must learn
the art of duplicity, presenting a moral and religious exterior, but, in regard
to his true beliefs and actions, must do whatever is most useful for him to
found or conquer principalities, and maintain them once they are his. He
must not shy away from doing actions contrary to accepted morality, as Epicurus warned his adherents to do, for "it is necessary to a prince, if he wants
to maintain himself, to learn . . . not to be good, and to use this and not use
it according to necessity."[4] Rather than refraining from actions out of fear of
being caught, an effective prince must "know well how . . . to be a great pre-
tender and dissembler." And so, it is not necessary for a prince to have the
qualities of being merciful, faithful, humane, honest and religious,

---

[3] Polybius, *The Histories*, vi.56. My translation.
[4] Machiavelli, *The Prince*, chap. xv.

but it is indeed necessary to appear to have them. Nay, I dare say this, that by having them and always observing them, they are harmful; and by appearing to have them, they are useful. . . . This has to be understood: that a prince, and especially a new prince, cannot observe all those things for which men are held good, since he is often under a necessity, to maintain his state, of acting against faith, against charity, against humanity, against religion. . . . A prince should thus take great care that . . . he should appear all mercy, all faith, all honesty, all humanity, all religion. And nothing is more necessary to appear to have than this last quality.[5]

Obviously, if religion is reduced to the merely useful, then Machiavelli must have held that it is not true. Such is clear not only from the above counsels, but also in the intricate display of carefully crafted blasphemies with which he seasoned his texts.[6] It is just as obvious that Machiavelli's counsel of duplicity, especially in regard to religion, was not directed to ancient princes who dealt with the foolishness of pagan religions, but to modern princes who, inhabiting Christian lands, dealt with the foolishness of the cross. Such advice also meant that if Christianity were to prove useful, it would have to be tamed and transformed into a tool of the state, otherwise Christianity could not hold the subordinate place that other religions had in the ancient world.[7] A great part of his goal as a political philosopher was to restore the Polybian relationship of religion as subordinate to the state.

I can imagine that by this time, our own contemporary materialists, if they should be reading the present work, are howling in protest that I would trace their ancestry to Machiavelli, thereby creating the implicit charge that contemporary materialists agree with Machiavelli on these points. Allow me to be blunt and make the charge explicit.

---

[5]Ibid., chap. xviii.

[6]For example, he asserted that Moses was a prince who realized the essential Machiavellian teaching that ruthless force, well-applied, is always at the heart of any ruler's success, especially the success of a prince who is founding a new principality. After all, the first act of Moses was the slaying of an Egyptian. The clear lesson of history, in regard to Moses and others, is that "all the armed prophets conquered and the unarmed ones were ruined." Moses was, then, for Machiavelli primarily a military leader who used religion to found his principality. Moses, being an armed prophet, died old. By implication, Jesus Christ, an unarmed prophet, came to ruin as a young man (ibid., chap. vi, and Niccolo Machiavelli, *Discourses on Livy*, trans. Harvey C. Mansfield and Nathan Tarcov [Chicago: University of Chicago Press, 1996], 1.9 and 3.30).

[7]The problem with Christianity, for Machiavelli, was that it had risen above the political realm and controlled the state rather than being subordinate to the state as Greek and Roman religion had been. See especially Machiavelli, *Discourses on Livy*, 1.11-13.

If we focus, not on the use of ruthless force, but on the necessity for duplicity in regard to religion, then it becomes clear why contemporary materialists (i.e., Darwinians) would need to be (and indeed are) Machiavellian in strategy. Machiavelli considered Christianity, in its received form, to be an obstacle to progress. The prince, to be effective, must shed any qualms concerning the received morality of Christianity, as well as the received doctrine of hell that was its safeguard. But this advice, as we have pointed out, was offered in the midst of the thoroughly Christianized culture of Western Europe. Duplicity was a political necessity.

Today, almost five hundred years later, Christianity still informs enough lives that strict materialists often find themselves having to follow Machiavelli, taking what Phillip Johnson calls the "two-platoon strategy," denying God's existence and asserting that human beings are the result of the purposeless swirl of matter and energy, until "objectors are too numerous or influential to be ignored," and then backing off with soothing messages of the happy co-existence of materialist science and theology (as long as the theology is innocuous and subservient to their goal).[8]

An interesting, quite recent form of superbly done Machiavellianism occurred in the seven-part series *Evolution* aired on PBS in September 2001. It was designed as an extended propaganda campaign on behalf of evolution, ready to ship afterward in video form with teacher packets to every school in the nation. The soothing message: evolution and religion can co-exist happily (as long as religion behaves and does not question the doctrines of evolution). Materialists Richard Dawkins and Daniel Dennett both appear in this series, neither breathing a word of their true beliefs about the effect of Darwinism on religion—that, of course, would have caused a strong public reaction against the doctrine of evolution. Dawkins, of course, believes that the doctrine of evolution leads directly (and happily) to atheism, so that "Darwin made it possible to be an intellectually fulfilled atheist."[9] As mentioned previously, Dennett celebrates Darwinism as a "universal acid" which "eats through just about every traditional concept," with the happy result that religion is on the way to becoming a mere cultural artifact, to be preserved as long as it remains toothless.[10] Their

---

[8]Phillip E. Johnson, *The Wedge of Truth* (Downers Grove, Ill.: InterVarsity Press, 2000), pp. 87-89.
[9]Richard Dawkins, *The Blind Watchmaker: Why the Evidence of Evolution Reveals a Universe Without Design*, rev. ed. (New York: W. W. Norton, 1996), p. 6.

contrived silence on PBS's documentary was pure Machiavellianism. (Alas, when the World Trade Center and the Pentagon were attacked by terrorists on September 11—just prior to the airing of the series—Dawkins could not contain himself, and railed against the "faith-heads," each equipped, thanks to religion, with an "afterlife-obsessed suicidal brain," manifesting the true evil of all religion "of the Abrahamic kind" that "teaches the dangerous nonsense that death is not the end." The world will only be safe, asserted Dawkins, when everyone is a materialist, rejecting any notion of an afterlife.[11] This was a rather embarrassing public relations slip for PBS, but it shows us the Machiavellian two-platoon strategy quite clearly.)

The same is true in regard to morality. Outspoken materialist Stephen Pinker is a case in point. In a now-famous article "Why They Kill Their Newborns," published in the *New York Times* (November 2, 1997), Pinker quite clearly and logically argued that from the materialist evolutionary perspective—the only perspective that is rational, according to Pinker—one cannot condemn infanticide because "a capacity for neonaticide is built into the biological design of our parental emotions," allowing parents, if a "newborn is sickly, or if its survival is not promising, . . . [to] cut their losses and favor the healthiest in the litter or try again later on." Indeed, Pinker pointed out, "Many cultural practices are designed to distance people's emotions from a newborn until its survival seems probable." The flow of the article leads to one conclusion, or better, one conclusion with two parts: infanticide is not only natural, it is culturally acceptable on a wide scale (explicit conclusion), and our culture, formed by the Christian moral prohibition of infanticide and abortion, is unnatural and the annoying exception to a more human general rule (implicit conclusion). That Pinker was being Machiavellian—appearing to be "all mercy, all faith, all honesty, all humanity, all religion," but holding another view in his heart—was clear from his vague and incongruous assertion that "Killing a baby is an immoral act," set side by side with his assertion that moral philosophers do not now count neonates as having significant human traits. (Pinker also appeared in PBS's *Evolution*, but for obvious rea-

[10]Daniel Dennett, *Darwin's Dangerous Idea: Evolution and the Meanings of Life* (New York: Simon & Schuster, 1995), pp. 63, 519-20.

[11]Richard Dawkins, "Religion's Misguided Missiles," *Guardian Unlimited*, September 15, 2001 <www.guardian.co.uk/Archive/Article/0,4273,4257777,00.html>.

sons did not mention his support of infanticide.)

And so, to call contemporary materialists "Machiavellian," then, is merely to say that they exist in the same condition as Machiavelli: they want to push ahead with projects that are, on almost every point, antagonistic to Christianity both theologically and morally, and they find Christianity an annoying and still-powerful obstacle. For a contemporary materialist, as for Machiavelli, to be inhibited by Christianity is every bit as irrational as to be inhibited by worshipers of Marduk, Baal, Zeus or Jupiter, but this obstacle must nonetheless be removed. What cannot be broken to dust by force, if even by the force of argument, can be worn smooth and harmless with patience, and made subordinate to their materialist goals. And so they must maintain a public face that seems benign to Christians, even while they chip away at the Christian rock. Machiavelli was merely the first in a long line of modern thinkers who realized the necessity of speaking out of both sides of his mouth, as it were, setting forth the bold and new, even while seeming to be pious, or at least seeming not to offend piety.

What contemporary materialists do not share with Machiavelli, however, is the Polybian belief that religion is necessary to rule the masses. The reason for this lies further on in the transformation of Epicurean materialism in modernity, when modern Epicureans assert that the comforts and pleasures provided by the technological mastery of nature are sufficient to quiet any desires for a life beyond the grave. This transformation, oddly enough, has its roots in Machiavelli as well, specifically in his call for the use of force against nature to master it, an argument to which we now turn.

Machiavelli was not only a teacher of duplicity, but as said above, also a teacher of the ruthless use of force. Essential to his project was the redefinition of virtue, from meaning "the perfection of moral goodness" to meaning the "manly use of force." (He took his cue partly from the etymology of virtue in Latin: the root is *vir*, "man.") He regarded the former view of virtue—the Aristotelian, Thomistic-Christian view—as a disastrous feminization of the original, and so his revolutionary advice in the practical sphere was in direct contradiction to Christianity.

However, Machiavelli had a fundamental disagreement with Epicurus, a disagreement that would help bring about a transformation of Epicurean asceticism to Epicurean hedonism. For Machiavelli the problem with any form of asceticism, Epicurean or otherwise, was that it accepted the limits

that *chance*—Machiavelli preferred *fortuna*, to evoke its feminine quality—
imposed on us. Instead of accepting these limits, we should use our manly
strength to overcome them. In regard to being an effective prince (and for
Machiavelli, the only good prince *is* an effective prince), one must do all in
one's power to reduce the effects of *fortuna* on one's political ambitions.
What inhibits princes is, in great part, the belief that these limits are
imposed on us from above, either by God or by nature (or both). A true
prince must, in a manly way, courageously break the shackles of these
beliefs, and master *fortuna*. And so, in a remarkable passage, Machiavelli
argued that

> it is better to be impetuous than cautious, because fortune is a woman; and it
> is necessary, if one wants to hold her down, to beat her and strike her down.
> And one sees that she lets herself be won more by the impetuous than by those
> who proceed coldly. And so always, like a woman, she is the friend of the
> young, because they are less cautious, more ferocious, and command her with
> more audacity.[12]

Such is why Machiavelli counseled the reader concerning "cruelties badly
used or well used," and praised those that were well-used, and those men
who were great precisely because of their "inhuman cruelty."[13] The capacity
to use cruelty effectively, uninhibited by any moral limits, will bring success
to the prince. When the prince sees that those limits can be transgressed
without any punishment from above, he will be all the more eager to transgress these limits again. Thus, *fortuna* may be successively conquered.

Even in this brief overview of Machiavelli's thought, there are some obvious points of contact with Epicurean materialism. No man could say what
Machiavelli said and be worried about the fate of his soul, because no prince
could act according to his counsels and have any fear of eternal damnation.
Machiavelli thereby signaled to the reader what manly courage ultimately
meant: the rejection of the existence of the soul, the afterlife and God. If the
prince is to have success in this world, he must therefore reject the existence
of all three. We have, then, a parallel in regard to these fundamental aspects
between Machiavelli and Epicureanism.

Further, as we have just seen, Machiavelli introduced a fundamentally

---

[12]Machiavelli, *The Prince*, chap. xxv.
[13]Ibid., chaps. viii, xvii.

new aspect into political philosophy, the reduction of chance, *fortuna*, in human affairs by the prudent use of force unrestricted by "feminized" views of virtue. This same approach will be extended to all of nature to break those natural limits on our actions which caused Epicurus to be ascetic. Yet, as we shall see, the overcoming of the limits of nature by force will contain the important Epicurean goal, to turn human beings away from seeking satisfactions in the next life, by providing them with ever-growing material comforts in this life. Technological hedonism may then achieve quite effectively what Epicurean asceticism had ineffectively sought: this-worldly tranquillity undisturbed by anxiety about the next. To understand this aspect of the modern transformation of Epicureanism, we must turn to Francis Bacon.

Francis Bacon (1561-1626) was, unlike Machiavelli, directly concerned with natural philosophy. He allied himself with the atomism of Democritus and Epicurus early in his career, praising them openly in his *Cogitationes de Natura Rerum, De Principiis atque Originibus* and *Essays*.[14] His early support did much to enhance the status of atomism in England in the first half of the seventeenth century, even though he later withdrew some of his enthusiasm—not from materialism, but from a simple revival of Epicureanism. In short, he remained a materialist, even while asserting that the details of atomism should be the result of a full inquisition into nature, rather than a hypothesis that prematurely restricted research. Our focus, however, is the new way Bacon opened up in the natural sciences by applying Machiavelli's arguments in political philosophy to natural philosophy, and it was this new approach that most directly transformed ancient Epicurean asceticism into modern Epicurean hedonism.

As with Machiavelli, Bacon signaled to the reader that his approach was indeed new: "a way must be opened for the human understanding entirely different from any hitherto known."[15] This new way was necessary, he argued, because all previous philosophers' speculations were based on nature as it presented itself to us, but, Bacon warned the reader, nature is coy, like a woman who hides her true thoughts. To the "eye of the human understanding," asserted Bacon, nature is "framed like a labyrinth," full of

---

[14]See Howard Jones, *The Epicurean Tradition* (New York: Routledge, 1989), pp. 193-94.

[15]Francis Bacon, *The Great Instauration*, "Preface,' in *The New Organon and Related Writings*, ed. Fulton H. Anderson (New York: Macmillan, 1960), p. 7.

"deceitful resemblances of objects and signs."[16] An "inquisition" of nature was required (with all of the implied connotations), for we cannot learn from her "free and at large"; rather we can learn from nature only "under constraint and vexed; that is to say, when by art and the hands of man she is forced out of her natural state, and squeezed and moulded." For "the nature of things betrays itself more readily under the vexations of art than in its natural freedom."[17]

In this passage, clearly modeled on the above-quoted passage from Machiavelli, Bacon substituted "nature" for *fortuna*, but she was treated no less roughly. The substitution was, however, more of an identification of nature and fortune (or chance), for we recall that for Epicurean materialism, the ultimate cause of things in nature was chance. Thus, in an important sense, nature and chance can be identified.

It is clear that Bacon realized the implications of his call for an inquisition of nature, for he begged the reader not to "think that the inquisition of nature is in any part interdicted or forbidden." Why should it be forbidden? If we thought that the way nature presented itself was designed by God, we might be less inclined to try to force it out of its natural state. But Bacon tried to overcome the readers' worries in this regard by appealing to a new form of charity. In an almost comic prayer, worthy of Machiavelli himself, Bacon implored the Holy Trinity to "vouchsafe through my hands to endow the human family with new mercies," a prayer that sounds odd when compared to his ending admonition, that "in behalf of the business which is in hand I entreat men to believe that it is not an opinion to be held, but a work to be done; and to be well assured that I am laboring to lay the foundation, not of any sect or doctrine, but of human utility and power."[18]

Bacon therefore promised his readers that he would open a new way to salvation, offering a new kind of charity, relief from the burdens and imperfections of nature. In short, he promised a new Eden, a real this-worldly Eden, as opposed to a mythological Eden at the dawn of time or an otherworldly paradise in the next life. In Bacon's view labor, rather than being the punishment for sin as Genesis presented it, would become the very means of salvation. In regard to Epicurean materialism, Bacon's answer to Lucre-

---

[16]Ibid., p. 12.
[17]Ibid., pp. 18, 25.
[18]Ibid., pp. 14-16.

tius's lament about the imperfections of nature was simply "get to work!" for work shall be our salvation.

As a consequence, the scientific question shifted from, What is true about nature? to What do we desire from nature? According to Bacon, "All industry in experimenting has begun with proposing to itself certain definite works to be accomplished, and has pursued them with premature and unseasonable eagerness; it has sought, I say, experiments of fruit, not experiments of light, *not* imitating the divine procedure."[19] Bacon did not follow the "divine procedure," because his goal was to effect our salvation by a human remedy (technological works) rather than a divine remedy (grace). Thus, Bacon substituted a human hope directed to a physical amelioration of our ills, for theological hope directed to eternal salvation: "Let us hope . . . there may spring helps to man, and a line and race of inventions that may in some degree subdue and overcome the necessities and miseries of humanity."[20]

To summarize, with Bacon modern Epicureanism moved from being passive in regard to the limits of nature (as it had been in Epicurus), to being active; that is, it moved from being ascetic to hedonistic. The hedonism was based on the desire to remove the obstacles to desire, and sets up a kind of circular, self-perpetuating motion. Our desires cause us to test and overcome the limits of nature, and as the limits and imperfections are progressively removed, our desires will be progressively released, only to demand that further limits be removed (thereby duplicating the spiraling confidence of Machiavelli's bold prince). As a result, in modernity the very notion of "progress" will become indistinguishable from the progressive mastery of nature.

Since these natural limits were also the limits of the natural law, it followed that the progressive moving of natural boundaries included the moving of moral boundaries as well. As a consequence, the advance of modern Epicurean materialism will in large part occur through technological means. The merely theoretical disagreement between Epicureanism and Christian natural law will be increasingly settled in the laboratory, for as the boundaries of natural law are removed, it will become clear that they

---

[19]Ibid., pp. 11-12, emphasis added.
[20]Ibid., pp. 23.

were in no way permanent; their newly found impermanence will help in the effort to displace the Christian notion that moral boundaries were created by God and manifested in the eternally mandated natural law. Therefore, the final conflict, so to speak, between modern Epicurean materialism and Christianity in the area of morality will be one in which the Christian recoils in horror, saying, "But you *can't* do that!" and the Epicurean shall reply, "Oh, but we *can!*"

As a consequence, whether in regard to the harvesting of living flesh from live abortions, the manipulation of our genes, the artificial impregnating of a lesbian couple or the cloning of human beings, the moral battle will shift from the arena of mere words to works. This was precisely Bacon's goal. For he believed that those who provide such mercies for this world will eventually prevail in the public realm over those who promise mercies only in the next. The miracles of science thus understood will always trump the alleged miracles of prophets and priests. Or to put it another way, in the ongoing battle between Epicureanism and religion (especially Christianity), Bacon ushered in a new phase, one in which the contemporary, visible, no-moral-strings-attached miracles of the scientist will eclipse the merely reported miracles of Christ (miracles handed down in stories told by prescientific people, miracles that require faith to believe and that come firmly attached to demands for moral purity).

Ironically, the seeds of the Baconian transformation were present in Epicurus. We recall his statement: "If the things which produce the pleasures of profligate men dissolved the intellect's fears about phenomena of the heavens and about death and pains . . . then we would not have reason to criticize them, since they would be filled with pleasures from every source and would contain no feeling of pain or distress from any source—and that is what is bad." Epicureanism became hedonistic in modernity because its modern proponents believed that if the pleasures of this world were increased, the worries about, and belief in, the next world would dissolve. The pleasures of the body, so they thought, would dispel the belief in the soul.

We turn now to an analysis of Thomas Hobbes (1588-1679), who carried the transformed Epicureanism into the political arena. Hobbes was enamored with atomism, not only the ancient atomism of Democritus, Epicurus and Lucretius, but the modern atomism of Galileo and the "Newcastle circle," a group of royalist émigrés from England under the patronage of William Cavendish, Marquis of Newcastle.[21] Hobbes also made his allegiance to atomism clear in his autobiographical poem written in Latin.[22]

But Hobbes was also enamored with the deductive precision of Euclidean geometry, and it was his dream to introduce a new science of politics based on Epicurean materialism, as reformed by Galileo, and constructed on the same deductive model as Euclidean geometry. Hobbes provided a thoroughgoing materialist account of human nature, beginning from its smallest constituents—atoms in motion—and building to its largest sphere of human action, the political realm. Essential to this project would be the "rebuilding" of human nature from these atoms, so that everything from our most elevated desires to our actual thoughts could be explained in terms of a complete materialist account. In this, Hobbes was the father of modern psychology, which almost invariably, insofar as it is really modern, takes as its unargued starting point that all aspects of human nature that previously were thought to be caused by the immaterial soul are reducible to purely material actions and reactions. Hobbes presented the blueprint for such reductionism, a reductionism that, of course, fit right into the ancient Epicurean desire to eliminate the belief in the immaterial soul.

But why would Hobbes want to do such a thing? To remove the pernicious effects of religion. As with Lucretius, he believed that people were controlled by superstition, "the use of exorcism, of crosses, of holy water, and other such inventions of ghostly men." But in contrast to Lucretius, Hobbes's main concern was not individual tranquillity, but *social* tranquillity. "If this superstitious fear of spirits were taken away . . . by which crafty ambitious persons abuse the simple people, men would be much more fitted than they are for civil obedience."[23] The cure was a world without spirits, that is, a purely material world.

To effect this cure Hobbes had to redefine what was real and unreal. We must focus on the redefining, because Hobbes's materialist reconstruction of reality was not based on scientific proof, but was achieved largely through defi-

---

[21]Jones, *Epicurean Tradition*, pp. 196-97.

[22]*"Is Democratia ostendit mihi quam sit inepta, / Et quantum coetu plus sapit unus homo."* Included in Thomas Hobbes, *Metaphysical Writings*, ed. Mary Whiton Calkins (La Salle, Ill.: Open Court, 1989), p. ix. As should be clear, I disagree with Strauss's attempt to disengage Hobbes's political philosophy from the new materialism. Leo Strauss, *The Political Philosophy of Hobbes: Its Basis and Its Genesis*, trans. Elsa M. Sinclair (Chicago: University of Chicago Press, 1984).

[23]Thomas Hobbes, *Leviathan*, ed. Michael Oakeshott (New York: Collier, 1962), 1.2, p. 27.

nitional fiat of what counts as an object of science. By such fiat Hobbes declared what could be included in science and what, by contrast, was nonsense.

> The world, (I mean not the earth only, that denominates the lovers of it *worldly men*, but the *universe*, that is, the whole mass of all things that are), is corporeal, that is to say, body; and hath the dimensions of magnitude, namely, length, breadth, and depth: also every part of body, is likewise body, and hath the like dimensions; and consequently every part of the universe, is body, and that which is not body, is no part of the universe: and because the universe is all, that which is no part of it, is *nothing*; and consequently *nowhere*.[24]

He could hardly have been more blunt or more Epicurean, for he, like Epicurus and Lucretius both, claimed universal knowledge simply by declaring what could and could not be in the universe. Needless to say, Hobbes had not examined the entire universe, either the macrocosm or the microcosm. His confidence that materialism was universally applicable came from his appreciation of Galileo. That is why Hobbes began with a restatement of the Galilean law of inertia as applied to human action.

> That when a thing lies still, unless somewhat else stir it, it will lie still for ever, is a truth that no man doubts of. But that when a thing is in motion, it will eternally be in motion, unless somewhat else stay it, though the reason be the same, namely that nothing can change itself, is not so easily assented to.[25]

Whether or not Galileo meant to apply the principle of inertia universally, Hobbes extended it to human nature, for human nature was just one more collection of atoms. This allowed for a materialist physics of human action that was simply a duplication, on a larger level, of atomic motion. Atoms themselves remain still until disturbed; when disturbed they react; sometimes they simply recoil; sometimes, upon hitting together, they stick. In the same way, human beings are, as a conglomeration of atoms, inert. When something external strikes the senses, they either recoil or attach themselves

---

[24]Ibid., 4.46, p. 483.

[25]Ibid., 1.2, p. 23. For a more thorough analysis of this point and Hobbes's indebtedness to the new science of materialism in general, see Thomas Spragens, *The Politics of Motion: The World of Thomas Hobbes* (Lexington: University of Kentucky Press, 1973); and Frithiof Brandt, *Thomas Hobbes' Mechanical Conception of Nature* (Copenhagen: Levin & Munksgaard, 1928).

to it. When the thing that hits us causes pleasure, we move toward it (attraction); when it causes pain, we move away from it (repulsion). In Hobbes's words, our motion, "when it is toward something which causes it, is called *appetite, or desire*" and when it is away from "something, it is generally called *aversion*."[26] Such are the physics of human motion.

This action and reaction, attraction and repulsion, formed the basis of Hobbes's entire mechanistic psychology. Thus, love and hate were reducible to desire and aversion, which were ultimately reducible to pleasure and pain. Good and evil were likewise reduced to pleasure and pain, for "whatsoever is the object of any man's appetite or desire, that is it which he for his part calleth good; and the object of his hate and aversion, evil."[27] As with Epicurus, nature itself was amoral, and morality was derived from the pleasure and pain of the perceiving subject.

But Hobbes added something at this point that enabled him to go far beyond Epicurus (and buttressed Bacon's call to remold the limits of nature). We recall that for Epicurus, the moral boundaries were rooted in natural limitations, and the natural limitations were taken to be permanent and general. Even though nature was amoral, the limitations present in the human species guaranteed a kind of universality and solidity to his asceticism. But Hobbes wiped those boundaries away completely by applying perpetual atomic motion to the human constitution itself. "And because the constitution of a man's body is in continual mutation, it is impossible that all the same things should always cause in him the same appetites, and aversions: much less can all men consent, in the desire of almost any one and the same object."[28]

It followed, that since the good is identical to pleasure, and evil is to pain, and since our desires and aversions are as mutable as our bodily constitution, "these words of good [and] evil . . . are ever used with relation to the person that useth them: there being nothing simply and absolutely so; nor any common rule of good and evil, to be taken from the nature of the objects themselves."[29] Hobbes was thereby able to provide a *complete* denial of any natural

---

[26]Hobbes *Leviathan* 1.6, pp. 47-48. I have substituted italics for the more jarring capitals of the text.

[27]Ibid., 1.6, p. 48.

[28]Ibid.

[29]Ibid., 1.6, pp. 48-49.

justice or injustice, a denial even more radical than that of Epicurus.[30]

Given that Hobbes so baldly and blatantly removed morality from nature, would not the result be, if he were right, chaos? Indeed, it was the affirmation that our natural state was naturally chaotic that allowed Hobbes to create one of the great political fictions of all time, the "state of nature," a fiction that was a strangely transformed version of Lucretius's Epicurean Edenic state. And out of this Epicurean state Hobbes fashioned an even greater fiction, modern natural right, the very fiction which has become the foundation of modern jurisprudence and moral discourse.

In examining what Hobbes had to say about the state of nature, we must constantly hold in mind that (like the atom itself), the state of nature (being so far in the past) was something for which he could not possibly have had any direct evidence, but which was necessary for the overall project of eliminating disturbance from the divine and bringing Epicurean tranquillity to earth. For Lucretius, we recall, the account of the primitive state was actually a projection of the Epicurean ascetic back into the origins of humanity. For Hobbes the only difference was that, rather than projecting an Epicurean ascetic, he projected a modern Epicurean hedonist instead. Further, since Hobbes (unlike Lucretius) was confronting a rival account of human origins, that found in Genesis, his state of nature was also fashioned, in part, as a foundational myth specifically meant to displace the Genesis account.

In both Lucretius's and Hobbes's versions, the primitive state is amoral, apolitical and areligious. In this condition, like a homogeneous collection of

---

[30]Ibid., 1.13. As a consequence, Hobbes became the founder of the modern fact-value, science-morality split. Because nature was declared to be purposeless, and hence amoral, morality itself became one more "phenomenon" which needed to be explained in terms of the foundational commitment to materialism. Thus, a *fact* will be defined as that which is material, the atomic elements and their motions; a *value* will merely be the declaration that such and such an atomic motion pleases or displeases a particular person. Morality will thereby be reduced to "valuing," which is merely a description of someone's peculiar preferences at a particular time, based on what happened to bring pleasure or pain. "This is good," will come to mean "I value this," which in turn merely means "This pleases me." This shift of morality from the object in nature (human nature itself and its natural perfection) to the subject (the particular human will), will cause morality to become completely subjective, that is, a matter of descriptions of the will of a particular subject. Whatever happens to please someone, he values; therefore his "value system" is a more or less coherent description of what pleases and displeases him. The result, of course, is that since no one can be wrong about what happens to please him—for to the assertion "This feels good," one cannot reply "No it does not"—then no one can be wrong about what he "values."

atoms, all human beings are equal. But in contrast to Lucretius's ascetic account, Hobbes's hedonistic account presented human beings as originally filled to overflowing with a multitude of desires. In parallel to the original atomic state, human motion is purposeless, that is, absolutely nonteleological, or endless. Human action has no goal, for "there is no such *finis ultimus*, utmost aim, nor *summum bonum*, greatest good, as is spoken of in the books of the old moral philosophers." Because we have no natural end for our purposeless, desire-driven motion, each individual has for his greatest desire only to "assure for ever, the way of his future desire." Consequently, Hobbes "put for a general inclination of all mankind, a perpetual and restless desire of power after power, that ceaseth only in death."[31] The perpetual motion of atomic individuals perfectly matched the perpetual and restless motion of atoms moving through the void.

Precisely because he attributed such frantic, random, desire-driven motion to the first human beings, Hobbes's "state of nature" was neither a peaceful Christian Eden nor a bucolic, carefree Epicurean paradise, but a "state of war" in which "the life of man [was] solitary, poor, nasty, brutish, and short." In such "a war of every man, against every man, this also is consequent; that nothing can be unjust. The notions of right and wrong, justice and injustice have there no place." To make sure we see the incompatibility with the Christian Edenic account, Hobbes stated bluntly, "The desires, and other passions of man, are in themselves no sin. No more are the actions, that proceed from those passions."[32]

We must note another difference between the account of Lucretius and Hobbes. According to Lucretius, in the original free state of nature the Epicurean individual was unencumbered by the family, happily unentangled by the web of customs and laws. This carefree, presocial condition was the ideal Epicurean existence, and the development of society was a kind of falling away from that primitive carefree state where our desires were at the "barley cakes and water" level. So, although nature itself is neither good nor evil, the original unencumbered condition, where the passions were at a natural minimum, was the peak of our tranquillity—recalling, especially, that the snares of religion had not been invented yet.

---

[31]Ibid., 1.11, p. 80.
[32]Ibid., 1.13, pp. 100-101.

Hobbes radicalized Epicureanism by rejecting any goodness in nature at all, even the goodness of the original condition. As a result of substituting Epicurean hedonism for Epicurean asceticism, Hobbes's original human beings were already whipped into a passion-driven frenzy. Their only salvation lay in society. Hobbes cut off the possibility of natural, presocial tranquillity, so that the only source of tranquillity was purely human-made. By this move, politics becomes the means to our salvation from nature, so that our progress would then be measured by how far we have come from our natural, presocial, chaotic state.

Obviously, Hobbes's account was completely at odds with the Christian natural law account, just as Galilean mechanics (insofar as it was based on materialist atomism) was ultimately incompatible with the Christian and Aristotelian views of nature. Hobbes realized that with the destruction of natural law, and hence the elimination of all natural impediments to our action, Epicurean materialism must have a substitute moral system to preserve order in society. Epicurus's own asceticism would not do, for the restless motion of atoms continues within our very bodies. Therefore Hobbes invented "modern natural rights," which are, as philosopher Alasdair MacIntyre has argued, complete and utter fictions.[33] It is only by viewing the genesis of these natural rights in Hobbes that we will see how indebted we are to him, and how completely we have been defined by his moral fiction.

First, rights in the modern sense presuppose the above myth of the Hobbesian presocial state of nature and its attendant amoral chaos.

> And because the condition of man . . . is a condition of war of every one against every one; in which case every one is governed by his own reason; and there is nothing he can make use of, that may not be a help unto him, in preserving his life against his enemies; it followeth, that in such a condition, every man has a *right* to every thing; even to one another's body.[34]

Just in case readers might not think Hobbes serious about declaring our natural state to be completely amoral, he ended with the natural right to cannibalism. Rights, according to Hobbes, were simply the name we give to our amoral desires, desires that, we recall, are in and of themselves no sin.

---

[33]Alasdair MacIntyre, *After Virtue,* 2nd ed. (Notre Dame, Ind.: University of Notre Dame Press, 1984), p. 69.
[34]Hobbes, *Leviathan* 1.14, p. 103, emphasis added.

The only escape from this naturally chaotic condition, according to Hobbes, was a "law of nature," a law which replaced the natural law. Hobbes's law of nature was a counterpart to the preservation of motion in the new materialist physics. If the atomic individual wanted to avoid fatal collisions with other atomic individuals, he must "lay down this right to all things; and be contented with so much liberty against other men, as he would allow other men against himself."[35] This mutual laying down of one's rights, and investing a sovereign with the power to keep order among the individuals, was the origin of society, and it occurred not by nature but by contract, that is, by mere human agreement.[36] While those who entered the contract laid down their absolute right to everything, the sovereign alone retained the natural right to do whatever he wills.[37] Since there was no longer any natural law that could bind his actions, his will is law.

We must note several important implications of the acceptance of Hobbes's argument in modernity. First, Hobbes's natural right theory inverted the relationship between rights and law. For natural law theory, since it was built on nature and nature was created by a wise and good God, the natural law is primary, and the rights that we can legitimately claim follow after, *for no one can have a right to do anything against nature*. But for Hobbes's modern natural rights theory, since nature is ultimately ordered not by intelligence but chance, rights precede laws, and all laws are merely conventional, having as their *only* purpose balancing claims of rights.

Second, while Hobbes preferred an absolute monarch as the sovereign, the same argument could allow an oligarchy (as Locke preferred) or a democracy (as Rousseau preferred) as the locus of absolute sovereignty. The important point is this: while in natural law theory, nature (and consequently God) limited the sovereign's actions, in natural rights theory, since it was based in the Epicurean materialist rejection of nature as intrinsically ordered and God as the orderer, there was nothing above the human-made law to which one could appeal. Whether the sovereign was one person or many, that is, whether we might live in an absolute monarchy or an absolute democracy, there was no law above the human law.

Third, the mythical state of nature, where individuals are utterly antago-

---

[35]Ibid., 1.14, p. 104.
[36]Ibid., 1.14.
[37]Ibid., 1.18.

nistic, clashes directly with the natural unity of the family. Indeed, we might well ask, after reading Hobbes's account of the state of nature: How *could* it have been that way? Isn't the family natural? Hobbes anticipated the question, and his answer was a modified form of that of Lucretius: one of the violent passions, which is of itself no sin, is the sexual passion. We are originally asocial, and the family is an accident of our original sexual passion. His proof was vaguely anthropological. He pointed to the existence of "the savage people in many places in America" where "the concord whereof dependeth on natural lust," and who therefore "live at this day in the brutish manner."[38] This mode of proof—used ever after by Epicureans from Rousseau to Margaret Mead—became standard procedure for modern Epicurean materialism. The atomistic individualism that Hobbes's account promoted must continually view the natural family as a side effect of sexual desire. As a consequence of this myth, modern Epicurean hedonism will continually strive to liberate sexual desire from its unintended side effect, procreation. Another important hallmark of Epicurean hedonism will follow upon this: as opposed to the natural law argument that the family is the foundation of society, modern Epicureanism will make the individual—the presocial unit, as it were—the foundation of society.

Fourth, it should become clear how indebted much of contemporary jurisprudence and nearly all contemporary moral debate are to the Hobbesian myth that society begins when the individual *"lay*[s] *down this right to all things; and* [remains] *contented with so much liberty against other men, as he would allow other men against himself."*[39] The foundation of this myth, as we have seen, was the belief that our natural, original condition was one of the complete freedom to express our desires as asocial, atomic individuals. This mythical state was designed to be an exact reflection of the freely moving atoms prior to their accidental assembly into larger units. The word "right" was merely the name Hobbes applied to the desire to continue one's motion in the moral void, and liberty comes to mean simply the absence of impediments to one's amoral, original desires. "The *right of nature* . . . is the liberty each man hath, to use his own power, as he will himself, for the preservation of his own nature; that is to say, of his own life; and consequently, of doing

---

[38]Ibid., 1.13, p. 101.
[39]Ibid., 1.14, p. 104.

any thing, which in his own judgment, and reason, he shall conceive to be the aptest means thereunto."[40] Thus Hobbes gave us the modern definition of liberty: "By *liberty*, is understood, according to the proper signification of the word, the absence of external impediments."[41]

As followers of Hobbes, we too consider the condition of unimpeded liberty to do as we desire to be the optimization of our right to preserve our motion toward the objects we find pleasing and away from the objects we find painful. That is why everyone claims the right to so many discordant things: there simply are no intrinsic limits to modern natural rights. Indeed, the most radical statement of Hobbesian rights actually came from the Supreme Court. Witness the following statement from the Supreme Court's decision in *Planned Parenthood v. Casey*: "At the heart of liberty is the right to define one's own concept of existence, of meaning, of the universe, and of the mystery of human life."

From a natural law perspective, this is the most absurd statement ever uttered by a human being, let alone a Supreme Court judge, for natural law presumes that God, as creator, has already defined existence, meaning, the universe and the mystery of human life. From a Hobbesian perspective, however, it makes perfect sense if we simply substitute *desire* for *right*, because *right* only means "desire." It also makes sense that this statement was fashioned by the court to support the right to abortion, for only by the complete displacement of natural law reasoning by modern natural right reasoning could any one claim a right to abortion. The "choice" in "pro-choice" could only come from Hobbes's definition of *liberty* as "the absence of external impediments" within a moral void, for what other view of the universe would claim a right for each individual to decide whether a particular act was murder or not? Moreover, the presocial relationship of the mother to the unborn child duplicates Hobbes's presocial state of nature, for in such "a condition of war of every one against every one," that is, the mother against the invading fetus, "every man [and here we must add "every woman"] has a right to every thing; even to one another's body [here, the life of the fetus]."

To conclude our analysis of Hobbes, it should be clear that Richard Dawkins's statement that "the universe we observe has precisely the proper-

---

[40]Ibid., 1.14, p. 103.
[41]Ibid.

ties we should expect if there is at bottom no design, no purpose, no evil and no good, nothing but pointless indifference"[42] is merely a restatement of the assumptions underlying the Epicurean materialism of Hobbes, and Dawkins rightly draws the same conclusion. Since the universe is the purely material result of chance, it is amoral, a conclusion ultimately drawn from the belief that the universe is not designed (and therefore has no intrinsic moral order) and has no designer (and therefore no extrinsic moral orderer). Given such a universe, it is not difficult to see that the most we could hope for is the maximization of our desire and the minimization of pain, and that translates, in the political realm, to the maximization of our rights to pursue our desires with the minimum of impediments. The language of rights has become the lingua franca of moral discourse because that is the only language possible in a universe where "there is at bottom no design, no purpose, no evil and no good, nothing but pointless indifference."

We must mention, albeit briefly, two other influential modern political philosophers, John Locke and Jean-Jacques Rousseau, for they also made significant contributions to the march of modern moral Epicureanism. Although it is impossible to do them justice in so small a space, we may at least sketch how they fit in with the modern transformation of Epicureanism.

John Locke (1632-1704) made the startling and blatantly materialist arguments of Hobbes palatable by "sugarcoating" them, and it is doubtful that Hobbes's arguments would ever have been so influential had Locke not put them in a more palatable form. This sugarcoating, reminiscent of the honey-on-the-rim-of-the-cup approach of Lucretius, was not achieved through poetry, but by an astutely Machiavellian presentation of Hobbes's arguments. The publication of Hobbes's *Leviathan* was met with charges of complete materialism, Epicureanism and atheism. In contrast to Hobbes, Locke knew that to be effective meant to be more veiled.[43]

---

[42]G. Easterbrook, "Science and God: A Warming Trend" *Science* 277 (1997): 890-93, quoted in Michael Behe, William Dembski and Stephen Myer, *Science and Evidence for Design in the Universe* (San Francisco: Ignatius, 2000), p. 104.

[43]Although Strauss is, I would argue, ultimately wrong in his characterization of the relationship of reason to revelation, his analysis of modern thinkers is without parallel in its acuity. In regard to Locke, Strauss is surely right in seeing through the veneer of Locke's supposed natural law arguments to the real teaching, the natural rights argument of Hobbes. See Leo Strauss, *Natural Right and History* (Chicago: University of Chicago Press, 1953), chap. 5, and *What Is Political Philosophy?* (Chicago: University of Chicago Press, 1988), chap. 8.

That Locke was an atomist is clear from his enormously influential *An Essay Concerning Human Understanding* (1690).[44] Because Locke was so careful in his presentation not to upset the sensibilities of Christians who were still very much alive to the implications of Epicurean materialism, it is often very unclear what he actually held. Did Locke really prove that we have an immaterial soul that exists (somehow) as united to the collection of atoms that is our body, or was he really showing that the very notion of immaterial substance was hopelessly confused?[45] Did he prove the existence of God, or did he prove the opposite, that we merely have "the *idea* of a most perfect being" and that "having the idea of anything in our mind, no more proves the existence of that thing, than the picture of a man evidences his being in the world, or the visions of a dream make thereby a true history."[46] Did he uphold the status of Christian revelation as being above reason, or did he implicitly consign revelation to the realm of irrational nonsense, for "if anything shall be thought [to be] revelation which is contrary to the plain principles of reason, and the evident knowledge the mind has of its own clear and distinct ideas; there reason must be hearkened to, as to a matter within its province."[47]

But the ambiguity in Locke's arguments is instructive. How could he not understand that his materialism directly contradicted his pious assertions about the existence of the soul, God and the traditional status of revelation as above reason? How could he be unaware of both the centuries of antagonism between Christianity and Epicurean materialism that existed prior to the Renaissance and of the continual charges of impiety against the modern revivers of atomism from the Renaissance down to his own time? Such naiveté seems unlikely, especially since he borrowed so heavily from Hobbes, and Hobbes came under such intense criticism. It seems more likely that the ambiguity was a sign that Locke was acutely aware of this antagonism, and

---

[44]A more manageable, abridged version can be found in Richard Taylor, *The Empiricists* (New York: Routledge, 1961). Note his restatement of the law of inertia as applied to human action (2.21.29), the Hobbesian definition of liberty (2.21.8, 12), the focus on pleasure and pain as the sources of human motion (2.7.1-3; 2.21.73) and pleasure and pain as defining our goals (4.11.3, 8), the very ambiguous way he dealt with "spiritual substances" (2.23.1-37), and, of course, his affirmation of the basic tenets of atomism (2.8.7-10, 14-18; 2.23.11; 4.3.11-16).

[45]Locke, *An Essay Concerning Human Understanding*, 2.23.2-37.

[46]Ibid., 4.10.7; 4.11.1.

[47]Ibid., 4.18.5, 8, 10-11, 14.

such ambiguity was the result of his "two platoon strategy" of presenting a materialist argument with a patronizing quasi-Christian veneer, thereby advancing the materialism under cover of Christianity. Again, Locke was a more astute student of Machiavelli than Hobbes.

Nowhere is this two-platoon strategy more evident than in his *Second Treatise of Civil Government*,[48] a modern natural rights account of politics and morality straight from Hobbes's *Leviathan*, which contained, however, many more soothing words about God and the natural law. The importance of Locke's account for understanding our own moral and political heritage could not be overestimated: Hobbes's arguments came to America smuggled on the ship built by John Locke, and many of the founders applied his arguments to the founding of our regime as if they were natural law arguments rooted in Christian tradition, when actually they were modern natural right arguments rooted in revived and transformed modern Epicurean materialism. Most debates about the beliefs and moral caliber of the founders miss this essential point: whether the founders were religious and zealous supporters of Christian morality or not, insofar as they used the arguments of Locke to craft the American government, they were setting up the American people for another revolution, where the latent Epicurean materialism would eventually surface and manifest full control.

As for Locke's arguments in the *Treatise*, I will not belabor the reader by going over all the ways Locke duplicated Hobbes's arguments (anymore than we needed to repeat the areas of agreement wherein Lucretius followed Epicurus). But it is essential to understand at least one place where Locke extended modern Epicurean hedonism politically. For Hobbes the fear of violent death was the strongest passion, the one that forced atomic individuals to enter the artificial confines of civil society. Instead of wielding a stick, Locke thought it better to dangle a carrot, and relied on the positive desire for pleasure to lure atomic individuals from the state of nature and reconcile them to the now much lighter artificial chains of civil society. The goal of civil society, for Locke the only goal, was the promotion and protection of wealth.

In the central chapter of his *Treatise*, entitled "Of Property," we find a subtle but radical transformation of the Christian account of origins, a rewriting

---

[48]John Locke, *Two Treatises on Government,* ed. Thomas Cook (New York: Hafner, 1947).

of Genesis so that it will seem to promote Locke's political hedonism but a more prudent rewriting than that of Hobbes. Locke began with the pious assertion that "God, who hath given the world to men in common, hath also given them reason to make use of it to the best advantage of life and convenience. The earth and all that is therein is given to men for the support and comfort of their being."[49] Even here, as innocuous as this sounds, we notice a careful shift to an emphasis on material comfort.

But missing from Locke's account was any mention of Eden, the first sin, the fall and especially the punishment of man for rebellion that we find in the biblical account: "Cursed is the ground because of you; in toil you shall eat of it all the days of your life; thorns and thistles it shall bring forth to you; and you shall eat the plants of the field. In the sweat of your face you shall eat bread till you return to the ground, for out of it you were taken; you are dust, and to dust you shall return" (Gen 3:17-19). Instead Locke simply declared that nature itself was naturally barren, and it was human labor that made it good, a move that fit Bacon's desire to vex nature for the sake of "human utility and power."

> It is labour indeed that put the difference of value on everything; and let any one consider what the difference is between an acre of land planted with tobacco or sugar, sown with wheat or barley, and an acre of the same land lying in common, without any husbandry upon it, and he will find that the improvement of labour makes the far greater part of the value. I think it will be but a very modest computation to say that, of the products of the earth useful to the life of man, nine-tenths are the effects of labour; nay, if we will rightly estimate things as they come to our use and cast up the several expenses about them, what in them is purely owing to nature, and what to labour, we shall find that in most of them ninety-nine hundredths are wholly to be put on the account of labour.[50]

In a reversal of the Genesis account, nature was not originally good, but human labor made it so. Locke thereby followed Bacon in designating human labor as salvific, as that which remakes nature in accordance with our desires, removing from it the natural imperfections.

Furthermore, echoing the account in Hobbes, Locke released our desires

---

[49]Locke, *The Second Treatise of Civil Government*, 5.26.
[50]Ibid., 5.40.

from any boundaries, natural or moral, extending our natural right to self-preservation to the unlimited pursuit of wealth. While he seemed to provide a natural boundary—we should not accumulate any more natural goods, such as acorns and apples, than we can actually use before they rot—this "natural" boundary was soon wiped away by the assertion that we have a right to pursue and procure an unlimited amount of precious metals, for they never rot and are always useful. The hoarding of wealth, then, cannot be wrong:

> It is plain that men have agreed to a disproportionate and unequal possession of the earth, they having, by a tacit and voluntary consent, found out a way how a man may fairly possess more land than he himself can use the product of, by receiving in exchange for the overplus gold and silver which may be hoarded up without injury to any one, these metals not spoiling or decaying in the hands of the possessor. This partage of things in an inequality of private possessions men have made practicable out of the bounds of society and with-out compact, only by putting a value on gold and silver, and tacitly agreeing in the use of money.[51]

But the natural right to the unlimited pursuit of wealth—which is a restatement of Hobbes's assertion that we have a naturally unlimited desire for pleasure, for wealth is the universal means to satisfy any desire—soon causes the state of nature to become chaotic, so that "the enjoyment of the property he has in this state is very unsafe, very unsecure." And so, the presocial, atomic individual must leave the state of complete freedom and join with others in society "for the mutual preservation of their lives, liberties, and estates, which I call by the general name property." Thus, the "great and chief end, therefore, of men's uniting into commonwealths and putting themselves under government is the preservation of their property."[52]

By this maneuver, politics became completely defined by economics, which is to say that the hedonism inherent in the modern transformation of Epicureanism came to define the political realm completely. With Hobbes, Epicurean hedonism became political, but with Locke, the political realm became the complete servant of Epicurean hedonism. Any higher goal for political

---

[51]Ibid., 5.50.
[52]Ibid., 9.123-24.

life, such as the cultivation of virtue (as in Aristotle) or the cultivation of our souls for the sake of eternal life (as in Aquinas) was thereby removed; the only goal for our common life, and for the laws that define and direct our common life, will be economic. This was a subtle but far-reaching redefinition of human nature and human society. To redefine our political goal as purely economic amounted to redefining our highest pursuit as material pleasure, rather than spiritual perfection. Locke, not Marx, was the first to redefine human beings as *homo faber*, "man, the worker," or more accurately, as *homo oeconomicus*, economic man—man, who by his labor, lives for the accumulation of material goods as the highest good. That is, of course, quite distinct from designating us as *homo sapiens*, for this older designation presumed that there was *sapientia*, "wisdom" about heavenly things, things higher than material things. But Locke, following Hobbes (who was following Epicurus), called philosophy down from the heavens, as it were, and focused our efforts on the only real world, the material world, so that our efforts might remake it, our labor redeem it, and the pursuit of wealth might provide a new plenty that would turn the earth into a *real*, not mythical, land of plenty. The recent political phrase "It's the economy, stupid," used by former President Clinton to remind his followers of the true goal of politics, was merely a restatement of Locke's reduction of the political goal to the pursuit and expansion of material gratification.

When Hobbes's doctrine of modern natural rights and Locke's redefinition of the sole aim of government as economic are coupled, the result was a government that pursues no other aim than promoting a strong economy, which means in turn that its citizens must have equally strong (seemingly endless) desires for material gratification. The fundamentally amoral nature of desire allows for almost infinite expansion of gratification. As should be obvious, the spiraling of such desire serves a very Epicurean goal, turning our souls to the complete service of the pleasures and comforts of our bodies.

It might be objected, at this point, that there are other strains of thought in modernity that reacted against the hedonism defined by Hobbes and Locke and fueled by the devices of Bacon. But, if we examine the father of these movements, Jean-Jacques Rousseau, we find him to be indebted to Epicurus as well.

Jean-Jacques Rousseau (1712-1778) attempted a turn from Epicurean hedonism back to Epicurean asceticism. While it may appear, from all his praise of virtue, that he was embracing ancient Stoicism—for he continually appealed to the rugged virtues of the ancient Romans in his diatribe against the burgeoning hedonism of eighteenth-century Europe—if we are at all familiar with ancient Epicureanism, we see that he merely reproduced the arguments of Lucretius, and his appeal to virtue was actually an appeal to Lucretian asceticism. The reason Rousseau felt compelled to embrace Lucretius rather than the Stoics was simple: Isaac Newton's *Principia Mathematica*, published in 1687, had by the mid-1700s become gospel, and mechanistic atomism had thereby become the reigning scientific view. Rousseau was handed Newton's universe, and within the confines of atomism the only reform possible was a return to ascetic Epicureanism.

Rousseau's *Discourse on the Origin and Foundations of Inequality Among Men* (1755) presented the core of his revived Lucretian Epicureanism. In it, he chastised the hedonists Hobbes and Locke for pretending to take us back to the state of nature, but instead merely describing the inflamed passions of the "civilized" Epicurean hedonist. We must go all the way back, Rousseau cried, back to the original Epicurean Adam, who was completely asocial, amoral, and areligious, and whose desires were at a bare minimum, the "barley cakes and water" level of Lucretius's Epicurean Adam.

Rousseau began his imaginary journey back to the origins of humanity by declaring that such a journey *was* imaginary.

> Let us therefore begin by setting all the facts aside, for they do not affect the question. The researches which can be undertaken concerning this subject must not be taken for historical truths, but only for hypothetical and conditional reasonings better suited to clarify the nature of things than to show their true origin, like those our physicists make every day concerning the formation of the world.[53]

Such reasonings were hypothetical in this strict sense: given the Newtonian description of the world, Rousseau proceeded to reason about what must have been the condition of the original humans. The materialist assumption was taken to be an unquestionable fact, and his Epicurean anthropology followed on it.

---

[53]Jean-Jacques Rousseau, *Discourse on the Origin and Foundations of Inequality Among Men,* in *The First and Second Discourses,* trans. Roger Masters and Judith Masters (New York: St. Martin's, 1964), p. 103.

But there was another reason for Rousseau to call such reasonings "hypothetical and conditional"—that of Machiavelli. As Rousseau noted, "Religion commands us to believe that . . . God Himself took men out of the state of nature immediately after the creation." In order to avoid persecution, Rousseau was compelled to present his Epicurean account as merely hypothetical, for religion "commanded us" what to believe. Yet, Rousseau hastily added, religion "does not forbid us to form conjectures, drawn solely from the nature of man and the beings surrounding him, about what the human race might have become if it had remained abandoned to itself."[54] But such, of course, was a ruse. It is quite clear, as Rousseau's analysis proceeds, that he considered Lucretius to be the true authority on human origins, not the Bible, for he soon dropped any pretense of offering a hypothetical account.

Even more important, Rousseau followed Lucretius in presenting an evolutionary account of the rise of the human species, a short and vague account in the text of the *Discourse*, but a very precise and detailed account in his footnote to the text, using comparative anatomy to illustrate how human beings must have slowly moved from being quadrupeds to being bipeds.[55] It is clear from the kind of detail in the footnote that Rousseau had thought about evolution extensively, and he was merely giving readers a taste of a private, far greater hidden treasure—and this, almost a full century before Darwin.

The Epicurean Adam whom Rousseau claimed to see—once that Adam had gotten up off all fours—was little more than an animal among other animals, strong of arm but (happily) weak of mind, solitary by nature, without any fear of death (and hence without religion) and without morality (because he was solitary and had only the simplest desires). No analysis on my part can be more clear than Rousseau's own portrait.

> In the primitive state, having neither houses, nor huts, nor property of any kind, everyone took up his lodging by chance and often for only one night. Males and females united fortuitously, depending on encounter, occasion, and desire, without speech being a very necessary interpreter of the things they had to say to each other; they left each other with the same ease. The mother nursed her children at first for her own need [i.e., because the breasts, being filled with milk, were painful]; then, habit having endeared them to her, she

---

[54]Ibid., p. 103.
[55]Ibid., pp. 104-5, 183-86.

nourished them afterward for their need. As soon as they had the strength to seek their food, they did not delay in leaving the mother herself; and as there was practically no other way to find one another again [because of the density of the primitive forests] than not to lose sight of each other, they were soon at a point of not even recognizing one another.[56]

Life in the state of nature was not "solitary, poor, nasty, brutish, and short" as the Epicurean hedonist Hobbes would have it, but solitary and tranquil, as Lucretius had described it, a condition in which our desires were at a bare minimum, and sexual desire was fortuitously aroused and easily satisfied without any of the disturbing entanglements of love, the family, or society, or any of the worrisome burdens of morality, for "men in that state, not having among themselves any kind of moral relationship or known duties, could be neither good nor evil, and had neither vices nor virtues."[57]

As with both Hobbes and Locke, Rousseau provided an Epicurean counter-myth of human origins to displace the Genesis story, an account not based on evidence, but simply on the requirements of materialism devoid of divine design. Rousseau's Epicurean Adam was barely distinguishable from the other animals, and lived only for the day, blissfully unperturbed by any thoughts beyond his immediate existence. As with Epicurus and Lucretius, our natural state was amoral and asocial, and the single, most important theoretical move that allows this assertion is the severing of sexual desire from the desire for a family.

For Rousseau, the desire for sex was a blind inclination, devoid of any sentiment of the heart, produced only a purely animal act. This need satisfied, the two sexes no longer recognized each other, and even the child no longer meant anything to his mother as soon as he could do without her.[58] For natural law, by contrast, sexual intercourse was the most social of acts: the desire of the male and the female to unite was at the same time a desire for the pleasure of sexual union and a desire for children, and the family was therefore the natural origin of society. But because human beings, as opposed to other animals, can distinguish the desire for sexual pleasure from the desire for children, and freely chose to enjoy sexual pleasure for its own sake, sexual intercourse is at the same time a moral act.

---

[56]Ibid., pp. 120-21.
[57]Ibid., p. 128.
[58]Ibid., p. 142.

In Lucretius's, Hobbes's and Rousseau's accounts, by contrast, since the goal was only immediate pleasure and the release from the pain of pent-up passions, masturbation, homosexuality, pedophilia or bestiality would achieve the same result. Heterosexual intercourse would only be one option among many to achieve the desired goal. To put it in a slightly different perspective, if society should follow Rousseau, and define what is natural by his Lucretian analysis of human origins, then that society would come to view heterosexual intercourse as one option among many for releasing sexual tension and enjoying sexual pleasure. No option would have any precedence over any other, for no option would be any more natural than any other.

To return to our analysis of Rousseau, it is clear that society would not be natural; that is, human beings are naturally asocial, and society was one more accident brought about in the slow meandering of human evolution. How did it come about? According to Rousseau, the desire of man to relieve himself of the pain of exposure to the elements brought him to build crude shelters, the first great "revolution" in the "almost imperceptible progress from beginnings," where the "habit of living together gave rise to the sweetest sentiments known to men: conjugal love and paternal love." Oddly enough, it was only then "that the first difference was established in the way of life of the two sexes, which until this time had had but one."[59]

Not only were conjugal and paternal love not natural—however sweet they may be—but the distinction of the sexes was for the most part artificial. Rousseau thereby radicalized the homogeneity of the atomic presocial individuals: the original condition of human beings was nearly genderless, that is, with little or no distinction between the sexes. (Or to offer the same assertion in a contemporary form, male and female are naturally equal, but society has artificially created distinctions, or exaggerated distinctions, between them.)

It followed that love and marriage, whatever pleasures may come from them, were strictly speaking unnatural, and their development was deleterious. In this assertion, Rousseau duplicated Lucretius's argument exactly. In the state of nature, there was *only* sexual desire: "Everyone [male and female alike] peaceably waits for the impulsion of nature, yields to it without choice with more pleasure than frenzy; and the need satisfied, all desire is extinguished." Falling away from this natural state created all the anxiety

---

[59]Ibid., pp. 146-47.

and passion of romance, and our natural tranquillity was thereby lost. "It is therefore incontestable that love itself, like all the other passions, has acquired only in society that impetuous ardor which so often makes it fatal for men."[60] Jealousy was unknown to the purely natural human being; "free love" is our natural condition. The 1960s was not the origin of the free love movement; it was simply the popular flowering of a seed planted before the birth of Christ and revivified by Rousseau.

Such free love obviously entailed, for Rousseau, the deprecation of marriage as an artificial, and even pernicious restriction of unrestricted, amoral sexual expression: "The moral element of love is an artificial sentiment born of the usage of society, and extolled with much skill and care by women in order to establish their ascendancy and make dominant the sex that ought to obey." For a man—a *natural* man—ties to any particular female were unthinkable: "Any woman is good for him."[61] It is hard not to catch a whiff of misogyny in these assertions: Rousseau was implying that women, for some reason, were the cause of the loss of our natural sexual freedom, a loss felt most keenly by men in the insistence of women that men be faithful and exclusive in their sexual desire.

It followed, then, if we should like to return to this blissful state, women would have to be convinced that such free love was natural, or to be more exact, that women would have to be convinced that they should return to the state of equality and express the same indiscriminate sexuality that men seem naturally to desire. Or, to come at the same point differently, Rousseau (mimicking the Genesis account) made women the cause of the fall from our natural state. Perhaps, in no small way, such Rousseauean men, two centuries after their master, were in large part responsible for evangelizing women to liberate themselves.

But marriage had even more pernicious results. By it we not only lost our natural sexual freedom, but in binding sexuality with artificial chains, it created the occasion for vice when before there simply were no boundaries to transgress, for "the obligation to eternal fidelity serves only to create adulterers; and . . . the laws of continence and honor necessarily spread debauchery and multiply abortions."[62] There would be no laws against adultery if there

---

[60]Ibid., pp. 135-36.
[61]Ibid., p. 135.
[62]Ibid., p. 137.

were no marriages but only free love; there would be no abortions if the artificial distinction of marriage did not separate sexuality outside of or before marriage from sexuality within marriage. Can we imagine an argument more at odds with the natural law reasoning of Christianity? Or more at home among our contemporary progressives?

Certainly, insofar as our society follows Rousseau, it must try to approximate the natural, original state of nature in regard to sexuality; that is, it must sever sexual desire (which is purely natural) from marriage (marriage and the family being purely artificial, since children would be an accidental and unintended side-effect of sexual desire). But given that it is no longer possible for us to return to our presocial natural state, the best we can do is recreate its original amoral conditions. The only ways to achieve this now would be to remove the privileged status of marriage as the proper locus of sexuality and sever the connection between sexual desire and children (or turn sexuality where the unintended effect cannot naturally occur, as with homosexuality, pedophilia, masturbation and bestiality). As we shall see, the late nineteenth century and the entire twentieth century witnessed the successful championing of all these options.

Enough has been said for the reader to see that many of the moral disagreements that rend today's political fabric have their roots in the modern Epicurean redefinition of human being and human action. The actual lines of influence are more complex, and extend to many more thinkers than those we have covered. (For example, we have not covered the inadvertent support given to modern moral Epicureanism by the continuing influence of the radical Augustinian strains of Christian theology.) We have at least hit the major revolutionaries who transformed ancient Epicureanism into modern Epicureanism. It should also be quite clear that the moral world of the modern Epicurean hedonist is even more directly opposed to the world of the Christian than ancient Epicureanism—in part, because of its hedonism; in part, because it was formed directly against Christianity. But if the West was still formed by the theological and moral tenets of Christianity, how did the West come to accept Epicurean hedonism? As it turns out, in great part by the direct weakening of the authority of Christianity. For if Christianity had not been undermined, then Christian moral arguments would likely still dominate our society. In the next chapter we examine just how that weakening occurred.

The Taming
of Christianity,
or Scripture Declawed

Given the intellectual and moral transformation described in the previous chapters, it is not difficult to grasp that the effect of enshrining Epicurean materialism would be the secularization of the West. The present work cannot inch through the four centuries of secularization, from the 1500s to the 1800s, during which Christianity as the defining force of Western culture was replaced by modern Epicurean materialism. But we must understand the major causes of this transformation, as well as its contours. The main obstacle to this process was the Bible. Indeed, the materialist revolution of the nineteenth century could not have taken place without undermining the authority of Scripture, a process that began in the seventeenth century, spread in the eighteenth and became a kind of scholarly discipline in the nineteenth. Because of the enormous importance of this concerted effort to undermine the authority of Scripture, and the continuing influence of modern scriptural scholarship in supporting the Epicurean cause, we shall spend the rest of this chapter examining this transformation. Of course, many contributed to this transformation, but I will concentrate on Thomas Hobbes, Benedict de Spinoza and D. F. Strauss. Hobbes gave us the first Epicurean-friendly interpretation of the Bible, stripped of all miracles and spirits, and focused on this-worldly happiness and peace. Spinoza not only duplicated

Hobbes's efforts, but bequeathed to modernity the great fiction of Christ the merely moral man, the harmless messiah for the nonscientific masses. Strauss completed the work of both Hobbes and Spinoza, excising all elements of the Bible that did not fit into the Newtonian universe, and providing the model and method that defined modern scriptural scholarship thereafter.

The undermining of Scripture began with Thomas Hobbes. As should be clear from the last chapter, Hobbes was bent on an Epicurean revolution—and that makes it all the more interesting that he is the father of modern biblical scholarship. Hobbes did not simply reject the Bible, as do many contemporary materialists. If he had, things would have gone much better for Christianity (and probably much worse for Hobbes). Instead he did something much more devious. He devised a new method of interpreting Scripture so that the Bible actually supported Epicurean materialism.

That might seem like an absurd claim. Surely, given that Christianity and Epicurean materialism were ancient and obvious enemies, he would have been caught. But the reader must keep his historical perspective. Hobbes's scriptural exegesis, built on the premises of materialism, certainly shocked people in the mid-1600s, but by the 1700s the victory of Newtonianism made it seem inevitable to many that Christianity, to survive, had to reform itself in accordance with the tenets of materialism. And second, as we shall see, there were others after Hobbes who delivered his Epicurean exegesis in more attractive (or at least less startling) forms, or delivered it to a later audience well on its way to being secularized. We shall attend to these other figures below, but we must begin with Hobbes and give the father his due.

As we are already familiar with Hobbes from the last chapter, there is no need to belabor his obvious adherence to Epicurean materialism. We recall that the defining goal of Epicurus's cosmology was the removal of all obstacles to this-worldly material tranquillity. Belief in the gods as interfering forces, belief in the immaterial soul which would live on after death, belief in the rewards of heaven and the punishments of hell, all had to be eliminated so that we would not be disturbed. Hobbes simply incorporated all these elements into his scriptural exegesis, so that Holy Writ would conform to the dictates of Epicureanism.

At the same time, however, Hobbes (as we recall) added a political dimension to Epicureanism. The goal of Epicurus's tranquillity was private. It was focused on the individual who withdrew from society for the sake of this tranquillity, for Epicurus believed, as we have seen, that the entanglements of politics were almost as disturbing as the entanglements of religion. But Hobbes rejected Epicurus's preference for private tranquillity and substituted public tranquillity as the defining goal, so that modern Epicureanism became political. By becoming political, it could not avoid clashing all the more with established Christianity. Therefore, Hobbes's great Epicurean political treatise, *Leviathan*, was at the same time his great treatise on the reformulation of Christianity. At the heart of *Leviathan*, moreover, was Hobbes's reformulation of the "proper" mode of scriptural interpretation.

As Hobbes made clear on the very last page, his writing of *Leviathan* was "occasioned by the disorders of the present time." (Note the parallel to Lucretius, whose *De Rerum Natura* began with a lament of the ravages of the civil wars in Rome.) A quick look at those disorders in Hobbes's time will allow us to see the Epicurean goals more clearly. *Leviathan* was published in 1651. Hobbes had witnessed the horrors of the Thirty Years War (1618-1648), a Europe-wide war involving both secular (Habsburg vs. Bourbon) and religious (Protestant vs. Catholic) animosities. England itself had also suffered from civil wars (1642-1648), likewise involving both secular (royalists vs. parliamentarians) and religious (Catholics vs. Anglicans vs. Puritans) animosities. Hobbes thought that the only cure was a political science built on Galilean atomism, which gave absolute power to the sovereign, and this must include the complete power to define and control religious doctrine. Only such a shift in power could establish political tranquillity.

Duplicating Lucretius's complaint that religion was the real cause of our loss of tranquillity, Hobbes set as the sources of all political troubles the belief in miracles, in the existence of the immaterial soul, and in the rewards and terrors of the afterlife. Why? Because all of these not only disturbed our earthly tranquillity, as Epicurus had complained, but were at the very heart of the "fanaticism" that led to religious wars—for who will obey a ruler if they think that Scripture tells them otherwise or if they think that hell holds greater terrors and heaven greater rewards than the sovereign can mete out. And who will obey a civil ruler if he thinks that a priest or pope has power over his eternal destiny and furthermore can excommunicate a ruler (thereby releasing his or her subjects from obedience)?

Why, then, did Hobbes not simply call for the elimination of Christianity? Again, in a culture still dominated by Christians, such would be to invite martyrdom (and for an Epicurean, martyrdom has no rewards). But on a deeper level than saving his own life, Hobbes thought that the "natural seeds" of religion "can never be so abolished out of human nature, but that new religions may again be made to spring out of them."[1] Eradication was therefore impossible. But even more important, Hobbes (following Machiavelli) desired the Polybian use of Christianity as a tool for civil power to maintain political tranquillity. Thus, while this "seed of religion" may not be eliminable, it could certainly prove to be useful, for "some of those that have observed it, have been inclined thereby to nourish, dress, and form it into laws; and to add to it of their own invention, . . . by which they thought they should best be able to govern others, and make unto themselves to greatest use of their powers."[2] Of course, that was exactly what Hobbes intended for Christianity. This dual purpose—the championing of Epicurean materialism and the Polybian desire to use Christianity to buttress this-worldly political tranquillity—accounts for the strange character of Hobbes's scriptural exegesis.[3]

True to his Epicureanism, Hobbes had first to prove that the Bible supported his thoroughgoing materialism. However, three obvious difficulties stood in the way. The Bible is full of references to the human soul, to God's immateriality, and to the existence of demons and angels.

To rid Christianity from the belief in the immaterial, immortal soul, Hobbes asserted that the immaterial soul was a pagan idea, smuggled in from Aristotle, which had corrupted Christianity. Even worse, such belief in "separated essences," that is, immaterial souls existing apart from the body after death, which is "built on the vain philosophy of Aristotle," is used to frighten subjects "from obeying the laws of their country, with empty names; as men fright birds from the corn with an empty doublet, a hat, and a crooked stick. For it is on this ground, that when a man is dead and buried, they say his soul, that is, his life, can walk separated from his body and is seen by night amongst the graves.[4]

And so, playing on the anti-Aristotelianism of Galileo and Protestantism

---

[1]Thomas Hobbes, *Leviathan*, ed. Michael Oakeshott (New York: Collier, 1962), 1.12, pp. 94-95.
[2]Ibid., 1.11, p. 86. See also 1.12, pp. 93-94.
[3]Hobbes himself, in a letter to Francis Godophin, admitted as much about *Leviathan*: "That which perhaps may most offend, are certain texts of Holy Scripture, alleged by me to other purpose than ordinarily they use to be by others. But I have done it with due submission, and also, in order to my subject, necessarily; for they [that is, the passages in Scripture] are the outworks of the enemy, from whence they impugn civil power." Contained in Hobbes, *Leviathan*, p. 5.
[4]Ibid., 4.46, p. 485. I have generally ignored the copious and distracting use of capitals and italics in the Oakeshott edition except where used by Hobbes for quotation. The rest of the quote is interest-

as well, Hobbes thought he had found a way to eliminate the immaterial soul by portraying it as a pagan import. Of course, the truth was that the immaterial soul did not fit into his entirely material universe. For materialism, the soul is not necessary, for (in Hobbes's words) "life is but a motion of limbs," and all motion is mechanical. "For what is the heart, but a spring; and the nerves but so many springs; and the joints, but so many wheels, giving motion to the whole body." Obviously a soul would be redundant to an already working mechanism, and does not fit into a universe in which "there is no real part thereof that is not also a body."[5]

What about God? Scripture certainly seemed to be affirming unambiguously that God was pure Spirit. But Hobbes had to prove otherwise. To accomplish this feat, Hobbes engaged in exegetical acrobatics, worthy of our note because they give us a taste of the relationship of Hobbes's goal to his method of interpretation. If we truly understood Scripture (and were not contaminated by the pagan ideas of immateriality), we would see that the "Spirit of God" never really referred in the Bible to God as a spirit. Sometimes, asserted Hobbes, it meant "wind" or "breath," as in Genesis 1:2, where "the Spirit of God moved upon the face of the waters," which actually referred to God's action through the work of wind upon the waters.[6] At other times the "Spirit of God" simply meant a fit of extraordinary understanding, such as in Exodus (28:3; 31:3-6; 35:31). This was even true in the passage in Isaiah 11:2-3, "where the prophet speaking of the Messiah, saith, *the Spirit of the Lord shall abide upon him, the spirit of wisdom and understanding, the spirit of counsel and fortitude, and the spirit of the fear of the Lord.*

---

ing as well, for it shows Hobbes's particular hatred of Catholicism and Anglicanism. "Upon the same ground they say, that the figure, and colour, and taste of a piece of bread, has a being, there, where they say there is no bread [in the doctrine of the real presence in the Eucharist]. And upon the same ground they say, that faith, and wisdom, and other virtues, are sometimes poured into a man, sometimes blown into him from Heaven, as if the virtuous and their virtues could be asunder; and a great many other things that serve to lessen the dependence of subjects on the sovereign power of their country. For who will endeavour to obey the laws, if he expect obedience to be poured or blown into him? Or who will not obey a priest, that can make God [by the words of consecration of bread and wine at mass], rather than his sovereign, nay than God himself? Or who, that is in fear of ghosts, will not bear great respect to those that can make the holy water, that drives them from him? And this shall suffice for an example of the errors, which are brought into the Church, from the entities and essences of Aristotle: which it may be he knew to be false philosophy; but writ it as a thing consonant to, and corroborative of their religion; and fearing the fate of Socrates."
[5]Ibid., p. 19, and 3.34, p. 286.
[6]Ibid., 3.34, p. 288.

Where manifestly is meant, not so many ghosts, but so many eminent graces that God would give him."[7] (Of course, Hobbes failed to mention that this last passage was taken by Christians to prefigure Christ's baptism, thereby leaving the reader to wonder whether the Holy Spirit was really a spirit.) Or, Hobbes argued, the "Spirit of God" meant only "extraordinary affections" such as "extraordinary zeal and courage" as in Judges 3:10, 6:34 and 11:29. Or the "Spirit of God" may simply have been another name for "life" (which for Hobbes, as we have seen, was defined in terms of mechanical motion). And so in Genesis 2:7, where God breathed life into the dust to make man, "There the breath of life inspired by God, signifies no more, but that God gave him life" and "Not that any ghost or incorporeal substance entered into, and possessed his body."[8]

Now one might think that Hobbes would have had difficulty applying this mechanistic filter when he moved to the New Testament, but such was not the case. When Paul said in Romans 8:9 that "if any man have not the Spirit of Christ, he is none of his," he did not mean "thereby the ghost of Christ, but a submission to his doctrine." What about 1 John 4:2? By *"Hereby you shall know the Spirit of God: every spirit that confesseth that Jesus Christ is come in the flesh, is of God . . .* is meant the spirit of unfeigned Christianity, or submission to that main article of Christian faith, that Jesus is the Christ; which cannot be interpreted of a ghost."[9] And Christ himself? "Likewise these words" in Luke 4:1: *"And Jesus full of the Holy Ghost . . .* may be understood, for zeal to do the work for which he was sent by God the Father: but to interpret it of a ghost, is to say, that God himself, for so our Saviour was, was filled with God" which would be "very improper."[10] Thus by an appeal to piety, was piety undone.

But Hobbes's work was not done. Unfortunately, the Bible was so full of angels and demons, especially in the "New Testament, and [in] our Savior's own words" that their existence could not be finessed.[11] Instead of declaring them nonexistent, Hobbes asserted that demons and angels were really "spirits *corporeal*, though subtle and invisible [emphasis added]." That is, he made

---

[7]Ibid.
[8]Ibid., pp. 288-89.
[9]Ibid., p. 290.
[10]Ibid.
[11]Ibid., p. 294.

angels and demons into Epicurean deities, which, we recall, were merely extra-subtle material entities. This move allowed Hobbes to override the alleged power of the priest in exorcism, for since demons are "spirits corporeal," and two bodies cannot inhabit the same place, it is impossible that "any man's body was possessed or inhabited by them." Hobbes then traced the false belief in demonic possession to those in the time of Christ who, out of their ignorance of natural causes, attributed the effects of natural diseases to demons.[12] Furthermore, this false belief was not original to Judaism or Christianity, but (as with the philosophy of Aristotle) an alien infiltration from paganism.[13]

How did this contamination by paganism occur? Because of Greek "colonies and conquests," these false beliefs were spread throughout the Mediterranean region, including the Holy Land. "And by that means the contagion was derived also to the Jews." As a result, the Jews of Jesus' time "called demoniacs, that is possessed by the devil, such as we call madmen or lunatics; or such as had the falling sickness, or that spoke anything which they, for want of understanding, thought absurd."[14]

Here, of course, it would seem that Hobbes painted himself into a corner, for there are too many instances in the New Testament where Jesus Christ himself treated demons as real and as capable of possessing a human being. But Hobbes was nothing if not ingenious. First of all, Hobbes argued, Jesus did not deny that spirits have bodies, for we can see on the authority of Paul, who tells us that "we shall rise spiritual bodies" (1 Cor 15:44), that Christ must also have believed demons were "bodily spirits." So why did Jesus continually rebuke evil spirits, as if two bodies, possessor and possessed, could inhabit the same place?

> I answer, that the addressing of our Saviour's command to the madness, or
> lunacy he cureth, is no more improper than was his rebuking of the fever, or of
> the wind and sea; for neither do these hear; or than was the command of God,
> to the light, to the firmament, to the sun, and stars, when he commanded

---

[12]Ibid., 4.45, pp. 464-65.

[13]Hobbes did note, however, that the false pagan belief in incorpoeal beings was put to good use by crafty "governors of the heathen commonwealths to regulate" their subjects through the fear of demons, thereby "establishing . . . demonology" for the Polybian ends of securing "the public peace" and "the obedience of subjects necessary thereunto." To help establish demonology, "the poets, as principal priests of the heathen religion, were specially employed" (ibid., p. 461). The pagan belief in demons was therefore propagated by Polybian rulers bent on manipulating the ignorant masses.

[14]Ibid., pp. 461-62.

them to be; for they could not hear before they had a being. But those speeches are not improper, because they signify the power of God's word; no more therefore is it improper, to command madness, or lunacy, under the appellation of devils by which they were then commonly understood, to depart out of a man's body.[15]

Hobbes's answer was simple. Jesus Christ did not believe in demons, but condescended to the ignorance of his audience. The little matter of Christ's temptation by Satan in the wilderness, then, must be purely metaphorical, meaning only that Jesus "went of himself into the wilderness; and that this carrying of him up and down from the wilderness to the city, and from thence to the mountain, was a vision." Satan entering into Judas Iscariot in Luke 22:3-4? Of course, "by the entering of Satan, that is the enemy, into him, is meant, the hostile and traitorous intention of selling his Lord and Master . . . so that by the entering of Satan may be understood the wicked cogitations, and designs of the adversaries of Christ and his disciples."[16]

Even after all this, Hobbes felt the unease of his readers: "But if there be no immaterial spirit, or any possession of men's bodies by any spirit corporeal, it may again be asked why our Saviour and his apostles did not teach the people so; and in such clear words, as they might no more doubt thereof."[17] Hobbes's answer was (or better, would become) a classic dodge for those rewriting the Bible to conform to materialist doctrines. We may even give it a name: the "True Holiness Shuffle." Such questions, Hobbes maintained, "are more curious, than necessary for a Christian man's salvation." Rather than answer the difficulty, Hobbes deflected it by an appeal to Christian piety. We should not let such questions distress us, for

> our Saviour, in conducting us toward his heavenly kingdom, did not destroy all the difficulties of natural questions; but left them to exercise our industry, and reason; the scope of his preaching, being only to show us this plain and direct way to salvation, namely, the belief of this article, *that he was the Christ, the Son of the living God, sent into the world to sacrifice himself for our sins, and at his coming again, gloriously to reign over his elect, and to save them from their enemies eternally.*[18]

---

[15]Ibid., p. 462.
[16]Ibid., p. 463.
[17]Ibid., pp. 463-64.
[18]Ibid., p. 464.

But the Polybian use of Christianity faced an even more interesting obstacle. To control the ignorant masses, clever rulers needed to have recourse to the doctrines of heaven and hell. But the keys to heaven and hell seemed to be with the church and its ministers, not the state. Furthermore, the doctrines of heaven and hell seemed to presuppose the existence of an immaterial soul that lives on after death, and that struck directly against Hobbes's Epicureanism. Hobbes's solution was so ingenious we almost want to applaud.

As before, the ultimate Epicurean origins defining the contour of his argument are made clear. If we are to have this-worldly tranquillity, then we must remove the pernicious effects of religion that disturb that tranquillity. But that cannot happen if heaven holds greater joys, and hell greater torments than civil rulers have at their disposal.

> The maintenance of civil society depending on justice, and justice on the power of life and death, and other less rewards and punishments, . . . it is impossible a commonwealth should stand, where any other than the sovereign hath a power of giving greater rewards than life, and of inflicting greater punishments than death. Now seeing eternal life is a greater reward than the life present; and eternal torment a greater punishment than the death of nature; it is a thing worthy to be well considered of all men that desire, by obeying authority, to avoid the calamities of confusion and civil war, what is meant in Holy Scripture, by life eternal, and torment eternal; and for what offences, and against whom committed, men are to be eternally tormented; and for what actions they are to obtain eternal life.[19]

To fulfill Hobbes's goal, the keys both to the gates of heaven and of hell had to be given to the civil ruler, and further, the eternal rewards and punishments had to be diminished so as not to eclipse the rewards and punishments that a temporal ruler could give. Since the doctrines occur in Scripture, Scripture itself had to be delicately finessed so as to support Hobbes's Epicurean-Polybian goal.

Obviously, from a purely materialist view, heaven simply cannot exist. Not only do we not have an immortal soul that could enjoy an afterlife, but as Epicurus made clear, such pleasures beyond this life would destroy our this-worldly tranquillity by diverting us from real, material pleasures to imagi-

---

[19]Ibid., 3.38, p. 325.

nary, immaterial pleasures, and by focusing our efforts on a world to come, entry into which meant continually placating the gods. Even worse, the existence of hell would make us even more beholden to religion. But how could one eliminate the soul and the afterlife from Scripture without simply declaring oneself an atheist?

Rather than eliminating heaven, Hobbes materialized it; that is, he attempted to show that, contrary to centuries of interpretation, "Concerning the place wherein men shall enjoy that eternal life which Christ hath obtained for them, the texts [in Scripture] . . . seem to make it on earth." In the Old Testament, argued Hobbes, the kingdom of God was always an earthly kingdom, as exemplified in the rule of God through Moses, "which was a political government of the Jews on earth." Since the New Testament is based on the Old, reasoned Hobbes, all the New Testament references to the kingdom of God must be earthly as well. Hobbes admitted, "This doctrine, though proved out of places of Scripture not few nor obscure, will appear to most men a novelty,"[20] yet he confessed his inability to find any other way of interpreting Scripture.

> That the place wherein men are to live eternally, after the resurrection, is the heavens, (meaning by heaven, those parts of the world, which are the most remote from earth, as where the stars are, or above the stars, in another higher heaven, called *cœlum empyreum*, whereof there is no mention in Scripture, nor ground in reason), is not easily to be drawn from any text that I can find.[21]

And so, by the "kingdom of Heaven," Scripture can only mean "the kingdom of the King that dwelleth in heaven," so called, that is, "because our king shall then be God, whose throne is heaven: without any necessity evident in Scripture, that man shall ascend to his happiness any higher than God's footstool the earth."[22]

Even more surprising than his claim that the kingdom of God shall be an earthly kingdom, Hobbes asserted that Scripture does not mean that our enjoyment of this kingdom will necessitate having an immortal soul, for such "is a doctrine not apparent in Scripture."[23] How then can we enjoy this new-

---

[20]Ibid., pp. 326-27.

[21]Ibid., p. 327.

[22]Ibid., pp. 327-28.

[23]Ibid. Hobbes allowed that Enoch and Elias were taken up by God as a special act of God, not as an indication that human beings had any natural immortal aspect.

found kingdom of God on earth? By a new doctrine of the resurrection: "The immortal life . . . beginneth not in man, till the resurrection and day of judgment."[24] Thus, to avoid allowing for an immaterial, immortal soul (which after all was a pagan contamination), Hobbes invented the notion that we are extinguished at death and recreated at the moment of judgment.

What of hell? Here Hobbes was in top form. All the references to "hell fire" in Scripture, Hobbes found, were actually "spoken metaphorically." While Scripture speaks of everlasting fire in hell, each such reference "signifieth not any certain kind or place of torment; but is to be taken indefinitely, for destruction."[25] While the fire itself might be everlasting, "it cannot thence be inferred, that he who shall [be] cast into that fire, or be tormented with those torments, shall endure and resist them so as to be eternally burnt and tortured, and yet never be destroyed, nor die."[26] *That* would be far worse punishment than any civil ruler could mete out. In Hobbes's new version of hell, the damned, rather than being tormented eternally, are snuffed out immediately in a "second death."[27] A single moment of agony, and then they are no more. Earthly sovereigns, with the power of torture at their disposal, can then easily trump such a quick and nearly painless extinction.

What about all those references to demons torturing the damned souls eternally? After careful analysis, Hobbes concluded that the names "Satan" and the "Devil" were not actually proper names of individual, existing beings, but simply abstract names referring only to "an office, or quality," and mean literally "enemy" (Satan) and "accuser" (Devil). Thus such names only mean "the enemy of them that shall be in the kingdom of God," and since the kingdom is an earthly kingdom, both "the Enemy and his kingdom must be on earth also. . . . Consequently by Satan, is meant any earthly enemy of the Church."[28]

That last statement was even more devious than it may appear, for Hobbes, in his Polybian aspect, argued that the civil ruler was the head of the church, so that "Satan" meant any enemy of the civil ruler. If we look at the Old Testament, Hobbes argued, we find that "the civil and ecclesiastical power were

---

[24]Ibid., p. 329.
[25]Ibid., p. 331.
[26]Ibid., pp. 333-34.
[27]Ibid., 4.44, pp. 452-53.
[28]Ibid., 3.38, pp. 332-33.

both joined together in one and the same person," such as with Moses.[29] All Christian kings are heirs to Moses and hence unite in their person both king and priest. Since the kingdom of God of which Christ is the king shall not begin until the resurrection, the heirs to Moses maintain their absolute power over both civil and ecclesiastical matters until then. Even if the king is pagan, Hobbes asserted, we still owe him absolute obedience because Christ's own words command us to give Caesar his due.[30]

Hobbes's Christian ruler was truly absolute. Defining "the attributes of God" himself was the task of the ruler, for a commonwealth ought "to exhibit to God but one worship."[31] The ruler also had to have complete authority over revelation. It was he (or she) who should decide which books of the Bible were canonical.[32] He also defined whether or not there shall be sacraments, and what they were.[33] He, as chief pastor or priest, should appoint all subordinate pastors or priests, who would be his civil servants, and in his capacity as chief, he had no need of the imposition of hands by a bishop to receive the power to administer sacraments (should he *choose* to have sacraments).[34] As heir to Moses, and hence *the* messenger of God, it was he who defined doctrine, and therefore he could never be excommunicated. Consequently, the only meaning of *heresy* was "a private opinion obstinately maintained, contrary to the opinion which the public person [i.e., the ruler] hath commanded to be taught."[35] Finally, no alleged miracles (ancient or modern) could ever be used as signs against the ruler's power, nor could any alleged prophets (ancient or modern) speak against him. The whole purpose of miracles, if we truly understand Scripture, was obedience to legitimate religious authority, which for Hobbes simply meant the ruler.[36] As with his other claims, Hobbes attempted to substantiate all of the above by appeals to Scripture, as understood through the filter of Epicurean materialism. By such means, Hobbes was able to transform Christianity into a tool of the state, which is to say, a tool of the Polybian ruler—and since his politics were

---

[29]Ibid., 3.40, p. 347.
[30]Ibid., 3.41, pp. 354-55.
[31]Ibid., 2.31, pp. 268-69.
[32]Ibid., 3.33, p. 276; 3.42, pp. 426-27; 3.43, pp. 426-27; 4.46, p. 491.
[33]Ibid., 3.37, p. 323.
[34]Ibid., 3.39, pp. 340-41; 3.42, pp. 393-94; 3.43, pp. 426-27.
[35]Ibid., 3.40, pp. 342-51; 3.42, p. 420.
[36]Ibid., 3.37, p. 319; 3.32, pp. 273-75.

rooted in Epicurean materialism, Christianity was made the tool of a secular state.

Suffice it to say that Hobbes's Epicureanism (described in a previous chapter) and his consequent attempt to transform Christianity through a new mode of scriptural interpretation (described in this chapter) were far too obvious to win acceptance in the mid-seventeenth century. At that time, fifty years prior to the victory of Newtonianism, the cosmos had not yet been transformed. Needless to say, upon publication of *Leviathan*, Hobbes was immediately accused of being a materialist and atheist, out to warp the true doctrines of Christianity for ignoble ends. In other words, people of the time saw right through the rather thin disguise, and since they were still working within the confines of the ancient animosity of Epicureanism and Christianity, they immediately equated such materialism with atheism. But that only meant that Hobbes's time had not come. His mode of scriptural interpretation would soon enough gain the upper hand.

The other founder of modern scriptural interpretation was also born slightly before his time, but that did not keep his method of exegesis from eventually reforming the mainstream of the modern approach to Scripture either. Benedict de Spinoza (1634-1677) was given the famous celebratory epithet by the German Romantic poet Novalis[37] (1772-1801) of *der Gottvertrunkene Mann*, the meaning of which comes through quite nicely given the dependence of English on its German roots, the "God-drunken Man," or perhaps in a more elevated form, the "God-intoxicated Man." The difficulty with this curious praise is that those of Spinoza's own time considered him to be (like Hobbes) an arch-heretic. The cause of this disparity is not hard to discover. By the time of Novalis, Christianity had been transformed, at least among the intelligentsia, by the kind of doctrines that Spinoza advocated, and therefore, looking back, he seemed to be a prophet unfairly prosecuted by the unenlightened.

Spinoza could be considered *Gottvertrunkene* because he identified God with nature, and was intoxicated with praise for the new closed materialist system of nature. It might seem in his writings that he was exalting God by finding him everywhere and by continually praising his majesty in creation. But Spinoza was a disciple of Bacon, Hobbes and Descartes—and, I would

---

[37]His real name was Friedrich Leopold Freiherr von Hardenberg.

argue, of Machiavelli.[38] By collapsing God into nature, and defining nature as a completely closed, law-governed materialist system, Spinoza was essentially making God redundant to nature, and hence his system produced every effect desired by Epicurean materialism, even while Spinoza appeared (at least later) to be pious.[39]

Even more important for our present purposes, Spinoza's famous *Tractatus Theologico-Politicus* (published anonymously in 1670) provided an Epicurean filter for scriptural exegesis, a filter even more thorough than that of Hobbes. Using this exegetical screen Spinoza was able to separate the "real" message of the Bible from the inconsequential detritus. In the detritus we find the belief in the exclusive election of the Jews, miracles, the truth of prophecy and all purely theological doctrines. What is left? The purely *moral* message. Spinoza therefore stood at the head of a long line of scriptural exegetes as the creator of the great modern fiction: Christ as the merely human moral teacher.

How did Spinoza achieve such a transformation? Spinoza declared clearly and boldly that the "chief aim" of his *Tractatus* was "to separate faith from philosophy,"[40] and this goal defined his entire approach to Scripture. Philosophy and theology must be separated because—and here Spinoza was wonderfully frank—there are smart people and stupid people. Smart people seek the truth, which is found out by reason in nature (as defined by material-

---

[38]On this point and the interpretation of Spinoza in general, see Leo Strauss, *Liberalism Ancient and Modern* (Ithaca, N.Y.: Cornell University Press, 1968, 1989), chap. 9, and *Persecution and the Art of Writing* (Chicago: University of Chicago Press, 1952, 1988), chap. 5.

[39]The collapse occurred in the following way. With the moderns Spinoza reduced everything in nature to the purest material-geometrical element, *extension*. This he identified with *thought*, a move that makes sense given the identity of reality with geometrical entities, for if what is real is geometrical (that is, pure material extension without qualities, a.k.a., the humble atom), and the mind both is part of that reality and truly thinks only when it thinks geometrically, then thought and material extension are the same things. Further, if we look at the whole universe and consider God the creator of it, and God's wisdom and power are defined by and limited to this creation, then God's thought is identified with materialist extension as well. Indeed, since there is nothing else in God other than his thought, *he* is the same as the sum of materialist creation. Therefore, God and creation are identical. Spinoza was therefore able to rid modern Epicureanism of the embarrassing contradiction of trying to unite the Christian understanding of God as Creator with the Epicurean project of denying divine intervention in nature, by simply identifying God *with* nature, and proclaiming (piously) that God is eternal and does not contradict himself, therefore the laws of nature are eternal, and are never contradicted by another power outside of them. By this philosophical shell game Spinoza was able to make nature all-powerful and God utterly impotent.

[40]Benedict de Spinoza, *A Theologico-Political Treatise and A Political Treatise*, trans. R. H. M. Elwes (New York: Dover, 1951), sect. 2, p. 42; sect. 14, p. 183; sect. 16, p. 200.

ism), and hence philosophy is sufficient to guide them. Stupid people have no access to the truth, nor any desire to seek it, but are at least able to follow the moral exhortations found in Scripture. For Spinoza, it was impossible that all people could be ruled by reason, for the capacity to reason well is "not often met with." Since reason was rare, "it follows, that if anyone wishes to teach a doctrine to a whole nation (not to speak of the whole human race)," he would be forced "to suit his reasonings and the definitions of his doctrines as far as possible to the understanding of the common people, who form the majority of mankind." Therefore, since Scripture was written "for an entire people, and secondarily for the whole human race . . . its contents must necessarily be adapted as far as possible to the understanding of the masses."[41] Simply put, Scripture was for stupid people.

Here we have a parallel to Hobbes. Precisely because Spinoza considered the division between the philosophic few and the unphilosophic many to be ineradicable, he did not want to reject Scripture (as did many later materialists, such as Marx). On the contrary, Spinoza declared, "I consider the utility and the need for Holy Scripture or Revelation to be very great," for it would be "folly to refuse to accept . . . what has proved such a comfort to those whose reason is comparatively weak, and [what is] such a benefit to the state. . . . All are able to obey, whereas there are but very few, compared with the aggregate of humanity, who can acquire the habit of virtue under the unaided guidance of reason."[42]

According to Spinoza, as long as we do not look to Scripture for truth, but realize that its sole function is instilling morality into the masses, we shall not err: "It is not true doctrines which are expressly required by the Bible, so much as doctrines of obedience, and to confirm in our hearts the love of our neighbour." The happy result, considered from the viewpoint of modern Epicureans viewing the religious wars of the seventeenth century, was that no more theological controversies could disturb the tranquillity of the political realm, for all such merely theological quibbles arising from Scripture could be boiled away as inessential, leaving only the Bible's moral core. And, exulted Spinoza with an Epicurean-Polybian flourish, "How salutary and necessary this doctrine is for a state, in order that men may dwell together

---

[41]Ibid., sect. 5, p. 77.
[42]Ibid., sect. 15, pp. 197-99.

in peace and concord; and how many and how great causes of disturbance and crime are thereby cut off, I leave everyone to judge for himself!" Spinoza thought that he had found an answer to Lucretius's acidic complaint that religion was the cause of every ill—simply declaw religion!

The declawing of Christianity was achieved by cordoning theology, making its claims and purview utterly distinct from those of science. According to this dualism, "between faith or theology, and philosophy [i.e., materialist science], there is no connection, nor affinity. . . . [For] philosophy has no end in view save truth: faith, as we have abundantly proved, looks for nothing but obedience and piety."[43] Therefore, "Revelation and Philosophy stand on totally different footings."[44]

Before we examine how Spinoza "abundantly proved" this, we should note the effect of having accepted his argument. This absolute divide between philosophy (understood as the materialist views undergirding science) and theology constructed by Spinoza has been accepted as gospel both by materialists who desire not to upset Christians, and by theists who desire not to upset materialists. The notion is that science and religion cannot conflict because they deal with different realms of reality: science deals with truth (the examination of nature as a closed, materialist system), and religion deals with other "stuff"—feelings, meaning, morality and suchlike ungrounded subjectivities, which of course are neither true nor false (for science examines what is capable of being true and false), but are nonetheless salutary for those who, out of weakness or an intractable poetic bent, cannot do without them. But if "Revelation and Philosophy stand on totally different footings," then Philosophy, that is materialist philosophy, the foundation of modern science, has *its* foot on *solid* ground, and Revelation, that is, religion, has it foot dangling in thin air, and is supported, in its infirm suspension, as a vestigial limb.

If contemporary theists cannot see that they are being simultaneously used, mocked and rendered harmless as Spinoza's system is applied to them, so much the worse for contemporary theists. But at least some of the fog surrounding contemporary debates about the relationship of science to theology might be cleared up by realizing that the "two realities doctrine"

---

[43]Ibid., sect. 14, pp. 186-89.
[44]Ibid., p. 9.

was invented by a man who believed that there was really only one reality, for (as we shall soon find out) philosophy understands morality perfectly well without Scripture, and furthermore, the moral reality it grasps is that of Hobbes.

How did Spinoza prove what seems to be most contrary to Scripture, that the Bible is not concerned with truth, but has only a moral aim? Worse yet, and on a deeper level, the Bible itself seems to root its moral claims *in* nature, nature as explicitly designed by God—not a God who *is* nature, not a God incapable of breaking the laws of nature, but a God outside and above nature, able to manipulate it at will. The "proof" would have to run contrary to the Bible itself. So it did. Spinoza's proof came from applying an exegetical filter to Scripture that removed all the objectionable elements, so that Spinoza's version of the Bible not only made no truth claims but actually supported the moral aims of Epicureanism. Spinoza was nothing if not bold.

Spinoza began his scriptural analysis by echoing the complaints of Lucretius and Hobbes about the evils caused by religion. The contemporary, fierce controversies that rocked both church and state brought Spinoza, so he claimed, "to examine the Bible afresh in a careful, impartial, and unfettered spirit, making no assumptions concerning it, and attributing to it no doctrines, which I do not find clearly therein set down." And so, he announced, "I constructed a method of Scriptural interpretation."[45] It will soon become clear, however, that his method was far from neutral, for it resulted in eliminating most of Scripture on grounds that only the most strained exegesis could procure.

First and foremost, Spinoza eliminated miracles. As we have seen, the new science could not allow miracles, for miracles disrupted the closed mathematical system. God outside of nature, in complete control of nature and able to disrupt it at will—such notions were heretical for Epicureanism. Spinoza's argument for the elimination of miracles fit right into the intellectual current flowing from Galileo to Newton. By identifying God with nature, and then praising the laws of nature as if they were divine, Spinoza

---

[45]Ibid., p. 8. To be accurate, Spinoza argued that the incorporation of Platonism and Aristotelianism into Christian reasoning was the source of all the "fierce controversies . . . raging in the Church and State." That is, with Hobbes, it was the nonmaterialist philosophic foundations adopted by Christianity that caused the problem. Of course, others would argue that Platonism and Aristotelianism were adopted precisely because they were compatible with Christianity—certainly far more compatible than Epicurean materialism.

was able to assert that those who claim that miracles can happen are actually the ones guilty of impiety, for they are claiming that God can contradict himself, and consequently "belief in it [a miracle] would throw doubt upon everything, and lead to Atheism."

> Now as nothing is necessarily true save only by Divine decree, it is plain that the universal laws of nature are decrees of God following from the necessity and perfection of the Divine nature. Hence, any event happening in nature which contravened nature's universal laws, would necessarily also contravene the Divine decree, nature, and understanding; or if anyone asserted that God acts in contravention to the laws of nature, he, *ipso facto*, would be compelled to assert that God acted against His own nature—an evident absurdity.[46]

And so, Spinoza concluded, "A miracle, whether in contravention to, or beyond, nature, is a mere absurdity; and, therefore, . . . what is meant in Scripture by a miracle can only be a work of nature, which surpasses, or is believed to surpass, human comprehension."[47]

We must pause to note several things about Spinoza's argument. To begin with the obvious, Spinoza violated his initial assertion that his method of scriptural interpretation was founded only on what was "clearly therein set down." To cite the number of miracles in the Old and New Testament would result in citing a good deal of the Bible (or, to remove the miracles would result in throwing out much of the Bible). His explicit reasons for rejecting miracles came not from Scripture but from his argument concerning the identity of God with nature. Spinoza's philosophical view is directly at odds with the Bible, as is made clear from the beginning of Genesis where God is most emphatically *other than* creation, and made even clearer in the divine commands against idolatry (worshiping any created thing as if it were the creator).

Second, the laws that Spinoza took to be universal and unbreakable were not yet even clearly formulated—such would have to wait until Newton. Their universal and unbreakable character was rather rooted in Spinoza's desire to construct an airtight deductive mathematical-physical system along the lines of Euclid's geometry.

To return, if for Spinoza miracles were impossible, then the source of the

---

[46]Ibid., sect. 6, p. 83.
[47]Ibid., p. 87.

alleged miracles in Scripture had to be something other than their actual occurrence. The goal of exegesis, then, became the search for the cause of the false opinions of the actors and authors of the Bible. The cause was ignorance of the laws of nature, so that "miracle" really means an event "of which the natural cause cannot be explained by a reference to any ordinary occurrence, either by us, or at any rate, by the writer and narrator of the miracle."[48] Scripture was meant for the unlearned, and so it does not explain things "by their natural causes, but only what appeals to the popular imagination . . . in the manner best calculated to excite wonder, and consequently to impress the minds of the masses with devotion."[49] But since not only the audience was ignorant, but also the authors of, and actors in, the Bible, then the authors and actors were all part of a confederacy of dunces. Scripture was written by the ignorant, for the ignorant, reporting what the ignorant said and did. Happily, for Spinoza, ignorance at least leads to devotion, and devotion leads to moral obedience.

But Spinoza did not leave this happy circle of ignorance alone. Rather than merely remarking on it in Polybian fashion and leaving it to rulers to decide what to do with the information, he instead asserted that it was time for the human race to shed its ignorance and remove what did not accord with the new science of biblical interpretation.

> We may, then, be absolutely certain that every event which is truly described in Scripture necessarily happened, like everything else, according to natural laws; and if anything is there set down which can be proved in set terms to contravene the order of nature, or not to be deducible therefrom, we must believe it to have been foisted into the sacred writings by irreligious hands; for whatsoever is contrary to nature is also contrary to reason, and whatsoever is contrary to reason is absurd, and, *ipso facto*, to be rejected.[50]

According to Spinoza's method, the modern exegete must begin by shifting his focus from the events described in Scripture (many of which are miraculous), to "the opinions of those who first related them, and . . . recorded them for us in writing," for this will allow the exegete to see that "many things are narrated in Scripture as real, and were believed to be real,

---

[48]Ibid., p. 84.
[49]Ibid., p. 90.
[50]Ibid., p. 92.

which were in fact only symbolical and imaginary," merely "adapted to the opinions of those who have handed them down to us as they were represented to them, namely, as real." Such, for example, were God coming down from heaven in Exodus and Mount Sinai smoking because God descended on it, or Elijah ascending to heaven in a chariot of fire. Spinoza, a fallen-away Jew, assured his Christian audience that if they too were "familiar with Jewish phrases and metaphors," they would realize many seemingly miraculous events were merely "Jewish expressions," and "anyone who did not make sufficient allowance for these, would be continually seeing miracles in Scripture where nothing of the kind is intended by the writer." And in line with Spinoza's earlier assertion that Scripture, while not true, was useful to instill obedience, he informed the Christians ignorant of the peculiar customs of the Jews that "Jews employed such phrases not only rhetorically, but also, and indeed chiefly, from devotional motives." For example, when it was said that God caused water to flow from the rocks in the desert, the "words merely mean that the Jews, like other people, found springs in the desert, at which they quenched their thirst." We note, however, that although Spinoza was addressing a Christian audience, he was curiously silent at this point about all the miracles in the New Testament. The reader was left to infer, then, that in both the Old *and* New Testaments, "miracles only appear as something new because of man's ignorance,"[51] either ignorance on the part of the actors (who did not understand the laws of nature) or on the part of the audience (who did not understand the Jewish penchant for hyperbole).

Spinoza bequeathed this mode of analysis to modernity, a mode which shifts from a focus on the truth of Scripture to the opinions of the authors, actors and original audience of Scripture, that is, which shifts from the truth of what is said to the cause of what is said. "We are at work," Spinoza said candidly, "not on the truth of passages, but solely on their meaning."[52] Since much of what biblical characters said could not be true—they, of course, had no access to the laws of nature discovered centuries and centuries after they lived and wrote—then we must turn from what they said, to why they said it. Scriptural analysis must therefore move from being doctrinal to being historical, searching for the historical reasons for the opinions of the actors,

---

[51]Ibid., pp. 93-95.
[52]Ibid., p. 101.

authors and original audience of Scripture. Spinoza thereby became one of the founders of modern historicism, the belief that what someone wrote can be reduced to the environment in which he lived ("the occasion, the time, the age, in which each book was written, and to what nation it was addressed") and his own personal character and history ("the life, the conduct, and the pursuits of [the] author" and "his genius and temperament").[53]

Modern historicism, therefore, is in great part rooted in this attempt by Spinoza to remove from Scripture anything that contradicted the premises and goals of Epicurean materialism. Indeed, such historicism is rooted not just in the Epicurean desire to remove divine influence from human life, but in the very system of nature that Epicurus designed to remove it. Since all nature, including the human intellect, has been reduced to the inert reactions of lifeless atoms, thought is, like everything else, caused by the sum total of material forces acting upon the particular individual's senses. Thus, a people's thought is not true, but reducible to the external forces that have impinged on their senses, and consequently, on their intellects. The motion of their thinking, as a *reaction*, is the result of the actions of their environment, the culture of their time, the reigning opinions, the particular wars and other events occurring at the time, their parents, their internal material constitution (including their own peculiar fears and desires) and so on. Historicism is merely materialist determinism applied to the intellect. The irony, of course, is that each materialist, including Spinoza himself, believes that he or she somehow stands above the material process determining everyone *else*'s intellectual endeavors, and the discovery and application of materialist principles are both somehow exempt from the process.

Whether or not this irony was lost on Spinoza, he certainly wasted no time in applying the historicist method to Scripture. The method allowed him to dispense very quickly with the prophets, who "were endowed with unusually vivid imaginations, and not with unusually perfect minds." Such men were "less fitted for abstract reasoning," as opposed to modern thinkers who "keep their imagination more restrained and controlled, holding it in subjection, so to speak, lest it should usurp the place of reason." As a consequence, "to suppose that knowledge of natural and spiritual phenomena can be gained from the prophetic books, is an utter mistake."[54]

---

[53]Ibid., p. 103.

The revelation of God to the prophets turns out to be, according to Spinoza, merely the revelation of the character of the prophet himself, projecting his own character upon God.

> If a prophet was cheerful, victories, peace, and events which make men glad, were revealed to him; in that he was naturally more likely to imagine such things. If, on the contrary, he was melancholy, wars, massacres, and calamities were revealed; and so, according as a prophet was merciful, gentle, quick to anger, or severe, he was more fitted for one kind of revelation than another. It varied according to the temper of imagination in this way: if a prophet was cultivated he perceived the mind of God in a cultivated way, if he was confused he perceived it confusedly. And so with revelations perceived through visions. If a prophet was a countryman he saw visions of oxen, cows, and the like; if he was a soldier, he saw generals and armies; if a courtier, a royal throne, and so on.[55]

Even more important, Spinoza argued, "The prophecies varied according to the opinions previously embraced by the prophets, and . . . the prophets held diverse and even contrary opinions and prejudices."[56] Since prejudices are not rational, and contradictions cancel each other out, there was not much left of the prophets.

What was the cause of Scripture passing on such ignorance? "God adapted revelations to the understanding and opinions of the prophets," and once we realize this, we know that, oddly enough, God must not have intended that we "go to the prophets for knowledge, either of natural or of spiritual phenomena." What is left of the Old Testament prophets? Only a *moral* message. And does this apply to the New Testament? Indeed. "We come to no different conclusion with respect to the reasonings of Christ" for "He adapted them to each man's opinions and principles." The words of Christ, then, are not true, but (like everything else in Scripture) merely concerned with teaching us "to lead the true life."[57] Spinoza then proceeded to remove from Christ's words anything that contradicted the tenets of Epicurean materialism.

For instance, when He said to the Pharisees (Matt.xii. 26), "And if Satan cast

---

[54]Ibid., sect. 2, p. 27.
[55]Ibid., p. 30.
[56]Ibid., p. 33.
[57]Ibid., p. 41.

out devils, his house is divided against itself, how then shall his kingdom stand?" He only wished to convince the Pharisees according to their own principles, not to teach that there were devils, or any kingdom of devils. So, too, when He said to His disciples (Matt. Viii. 10), "See that ye despise not one of these little ones, for I say unto you that their angels," &c., He merely desired to warn them against pride and despising any of their fellows, not to insist on the actual reason given, which was simply adopted in order to persuade them more easily.[58]

Rather than tax the reader's patience by multiplying examples, he exhorted the "curious reader" to "consider others by himself," Spinoza pausing only to remind the reader that the "end in view" of the entire argument was "the separation of Philosophy from Theology."[59]

Again, all that was left for theology when such separation occurs was the moral core. Christianity was therefore transformed from being doctrinally true to being merely a morally edifying story for the masses. The glorious hymn to Christ at the beginning of John's Gospel was replaced with this rather tepid jingle: "Christ . . . was sent into the world . . . solely to teach the universal moral law. . . . His sole care was to teach moral doctrines."[60]

Now all this might seem at least *morally* inspiring, but the moral doctrines to which Spinoza actually referred were not rooted in Christianity, but came from Epicurean materialism. Spinoza's version of Christ the merely moral teacher turns out to be a fiction, a lifeless fleece thrown over the Epicurean doctrines as a disguise, for when we lift it, we find none other than Thomas Hobbes underneath.

If Spinoza had really intended to salvage the "merely moral" part of Scripture, we would expect to find that he followed the major contours of the moral arguments in the Bible, such as, for example, that there is a natural good and evil that human beings transgress and that such transgressions are sins. Indeed, we might think that the first and greatest sin would be the desire to define good and evil as if we were gods. But, following Hobbes, we find that not only is this desire to define good and evil not the first and worst sin, but it is actually a natural right. Why? Since for Spinoza God is identical to nature, nothing that has happened can contradict him. Thus, we can-

---

[58]Ibid.
[59]Ibid., p. 42.
[60]Ibid., sect. 5, p. 71.

not "conceive sin to exist in the state of nature, nor imagine God as a judge punishing man's transgressions," because "all things happen according to the general laws of universal nature."[61] And "inasmuch as the power of nature is simply the aggregate of the powers of all her individual components, it follows that every individual has sovereign right to do all he can; in other words, the rights of an individual extend to the utmost limits of his power. . . . [Therefore] so long as men are considered of as living under the sway of nature, there is no sin."[62]

Two things are obvious in this move: first, the assertion directly contradicts the scriptural account in Genesis of the very origin of sin; and second, and even more ironic, Spinoza has taken the side of the serpent. This occurred, however, not because Spinoza believed in the devil and was consciously following him, but because Epicurean materialism's view of nature is amoral.

Echoing Hobbes, Spinoza asserted that there is no good or evil, just or unjust, until we yield our right to civil rulers who will define what is good and evil, just and unjust, and enforce their definition with the power of the sword. "The possessor of sovereign power, whether he be one, or many, or the whole body politic, has the sovereign right of imposing any commands he pleases."[63] And just so we are not confused about the extent of this absolute right, Spinoza reminded the reader, "When I said that the possessors of sovereign power have rights over everything, and that all rights are dependent on their decree, I did not merely mean temporal rights, but also spiritual rights; of the latter, no less than the former, they ought to be the interpreters and the champions." How can this be so? Because "religion acquires its force as law solely from the decrees of the sovereign. God has no special kingdom among men except in so far as He reigns through temporal rulers."[64]

As we would expect, in accordance with the Polybian designs of modern Epicurean materialism, the earthly ruler was *the* head of the church, and the only meaning to Spinoza's appeals to charity and the moral message of Christ turns out to be that "it is . . . the function of the sovereign only to

[61]Ibid., sect. 19, p. 246.
[62]Ibid., sect. 16, pp. 200-201.
[63]Ibid., p. 207.
[64]Ibid., sect. 19, p. 245.

decide the limits of our duty towards our neighbour—in other words, to
determine how we should obey God." As a consequence, "no one can rightly
practice piety or obedience to God, unless he obey the sovereign power's
command in all things." [65] These views are pure Hobbes.

It is historically important that Spinoza advocated that the many be sovereign rather than, as with Hobbes, the one.[66] He chose democracy rather
than monarchy because the former allowed the most extensive expression of
natural rights within a civil society; that is, democracy, since it depended on
the will of the majority, allowed for the least inhibited expression of the pre-
civil, unlimited, amoral desires—desires that, in and of themselves, were not
sinful. It followed that moral doctrines were best defined, not by nature
(since nature is amoral), nor by explicit commands and prohibitions of
Scripture (since the ruler interprets these, and the original commands and
prohibitions can always be attributed to the prejudices and opinions of the
ancient Hebrews or early Christians), nor from any authoritative moral tradition. Moral doctrines were properly defined solely by popular desire, and if
such desire changed, then moral doctrines must follow. The omnipresence of
this view today is obvious.

So we see, at the very origin of modern scriptural scholarship, that both
the method and the goal were designed by those from outside the Christian
citadel, who wished to transform Christianity into a useful tool of a worldly
philosophy designed to make religion innocuous. It only remained for those
well-intentioned Christians within the citadel to embrace these alien methods as a way of "saving" Christianity from irrelevance.

As with Hobbes, the arguments of Spinoza were not immediately
embraced. Indeed, just the opposite. The manipulation of Scripture according to views entirely alien to Scripture and Christianity was so glaringly
obvious to Christians of the time, that Spinoza was immediately branded as
an atheist bent on the destruction of Christianity. But after Newton's great
victory, less than a quarter century after Spinoza's arguments were first
published, it really did seem that nature was defined by materialist atomism,
the arguments of both Hobbes and Spinoza appeared much more inviting—
although it was not Hobbes and Spinoza themselves, but John Locke's

---

[65]Ibid., pp. 249-50.
[66]Ibid., sect. 16, p. 207.

honey-coated version of their arguments that won the most adherents.

With his *The Reasonableness of Christianity* (1695), Locke became the prophet of the transformed Christianity, Deism, which swept both Europe and America in the eighteenth century. Deists were never quite clear whether they were actually *the* true Christians, the ones who held to the true and universal religion at the core of Christianity (once it had been unburdened of its superstitious historical accretions), or whether Deism was a new religion that arose purely from reason, and in complete animosity to all religions based on revelation (such as Judaism, Christianity and Islam). That ambiguity was inherent in the arguments of Hobbes and Spinoza, and was retained, though muted, in Locke.

As with Hobbes and Spinoza, Locke transformed Christianity into a religion useful for teaching moral truths to the masses, for

> 'tis too hard a task for unassisted reason, to establish morality, in all its parts, upon its true foundations, with a clear and convincing light. And 'tis at least a surer and shorter way, to the apprehensions of the vulgar, and mass of mankind, that one manifestly sent from God, and coming with visible authority from him, should, as a King and law-maker, tell them their duties, and require their obedience, than leave it to the long, and sometimes intricate deductions of reason, to be made out to them: such strains of reasonings the greatest part of mankind have neither leisure to weigh, nor, for want of education and use, skill to judge of. We see how unsuccessful in this, the attempts of philosophers were, before Our Saviour's time.[67]

Shedding his characteristic circumspection momentarily, Locke expressed his exasperation with those who thought that, with the advent of the new science, religion could be completely dispensed with.

> And you may as soon hope to have all the day-labourers and tradesmen, the spinsters and dairy-maids, perfect mathematicians, as to have them perfect in ethics this way: hearing plain commands is the sure and only course to bring them to obedience and practice. *The greatest part cannot know, and therefore they must believe.*[68]

---

[67]John Locke, *The Reasonableness of Christianity with a Discourse of Miracles and Part of a Third Letter Concerning Toleration*, ed. I. T. Ramsey (Stanford, Calif.: Stanford University Press, 1958), sect. 241.

[68]Ibid., sect. 243, emphasis added.

As for miracles, Locke displayed his characteristic circumspection in *A Discourse of Miracles* (1702), arguing that miracles were necessary to validate Christ's mission as divine, but declaring, oddly enough, that "the truth of his mission will stand firm and unquestionable, till any one rising up in opposition to him shall do greater miracles than he and his apostles did."[69] One suspects that Locke was making an indirect reference to the Baconian project of mastering nature, a mastery that would allow the miracles of science to replace the alleged miracles in Scripture.

Whatever we might draw from the judicious and circumspect Locke, his followers drew what they took to be the natural conclusions, and these conclusions matched those of Hobbes and Spinoza. One such ardent Lockean, John Toland, published his *Christianity Not Mysterious, Or a Treatise Shewing, That There Is nothing in the Gospel Contrary to Reason, nor ABOVE it* in 1696. The title alone—almost a mini-treatise in itself—is sufficient to let us know his position. By 1699, Toland had cast serious doubts on the authenticity of the New Testament in his *Amyntor*; in 1720 he published *Tetradymus*, which provided natural explanations for all the New Testament miracles; and in the same year he published *Pantheisticon*, expounding pantheism as a substitute for Christianity. But the influence of Locke (and hence of Hobbes and Spinoza) was most prominently and influentially displayed in Matthew Tindal's *Christianity as old as the Creation, or the Gospel a Republication of the Religion of Nature* (1730), which acted as the bible for the spread of Deism all across Europe and America.

But, of course, the single most important cause of the rise and spread of Deism was the victory of Newtonianism. Newton himself was anti-trinitarian, and his anti-trinitarian views lent immense authority to the anti-trinitarianism of Deism. For how could the one man who had gained by "reckonings Divine," the "inmost places of the heavens," and who had dispelled at last all "the clouds of ignorance" and "unlocked the hidden treasures of Truth," be wrong in his theological reckonings? If "nearer the gods no mortal may approach," then surely Newton could not have failed when mapping the heavens to have mapped the nature of the Divinity. And if Newton, in knowing the laws of nature, knew the very mind of God, certainly he would know whether God were triune or not.

---

[69]Locke, *Discourse of Miracles*, p. 83.

The ultimate rejection of miracles also reinforced the Deist rejection of the divinity of Christ. If there are laws of motion that cannot be broken, then there can be no miracles, and miracles were *the* sign by which Christ demonstrated his divinity. Newton himself, ironically, did allow for miracles, but that exception was a gap exactly like the gap caused by his perceived necessity for God to readjust the spinning planets. As a consequence, the Deists soon slammed shut the window for the miraculous—and this, because of the very success of Newtonianism. Since miracles were the way by which Christ had manifested his divinity, he could have not been divine. Since he was not divine, then he must have been human. The same logic which denied that God, who created the universe and its laws, was powerless to interfere with his own creation, soon enough declared that the incarnation was impossible because it would be the most radical intrusion of the divine into the closed system of nature.

In Deism, then, the living Logos was replaced by the laws of motion as that which defined the order of existence: all things were made through the laws, and without them was not anything made that was made. The second person of the Trinity, who previously had been considered the one through whom "all things were made," became redundant, for the impersonal laws accomplished all. Furthermore, Newton himself, in cracking the divine code, had plumbed the depths of divine wisdom. Wisdom was not a divine person, but a law, and the law was no longer mysterious.

Deism therefore became the religion of the new view of nature; that is, it was the religion that a closed system of nature would allow. As with Epicurus, the Divine was both distant and impotent to interfere with nature. The characteristic animosity of Deism toward Christianity, seen especially (but not exclusively) in the French Enlightenment figures such as Voltaire and Diderot, was rooted in the Epicurean animosity to an interfering, miracle-performing deity. Simply put, Deism was the form religion had to take in a Newtonian cosmos; and one sign that God did not ultimately belong in the system was the all too easy slide of Deism in the eighteenth century into materialist atheism in the nineteenth.

It is no accident, therefore, that the battle cry so often raised by Enlightenment intellectuals in their war with Christianity came from Lucretius's *De Rerum Natura*: "*tantum religio potuit suadere malorum* [only religion was able to persuade men of such evil things]." While many of the Enlightenment *philosophes* quoted the Stoics (as more evidence of the superiority of paganism of Christianity), the true source of their paganism was Epicurean materialism. Why? The triumph of Newtonian mechanics, the view of nature that grounded Deism, meant the triumph of Democritus, Epicurus and Lucretius, not Zeno the Stoic. Consequently, Deists did not appeal to the natural philosophy of the Stoics (where fire is the basic element, and the providence of God directs all things to their natural ends), or if they did, it was only insofar as the materialism of the Stoics matched the materialism of the Epicureans. Rather, it was the moral arguments of the Stoics that enamored Deists, but again, such appeals to virtue could fit just as well with the original asceticism of Epicurus. Even so, Deists soon shifted to a kind of utilitarianism based on pleasure and pain, a view directly antagonistic both to Christianity and Stoicism, but quite at home with the new Epicurean hedonism.

But again, since our focus in this chapter is the reformulation of Christianity through the reinterpretation of Scripture, perhaps the best way to end our discussion of the Enlightenment, is a portrait—or snapshot, really—of Thomas Jefferson, the great American Deist. Picture the following, which actually did occur: Jefferson sitting quietly in the evening, cutting up copies of the New Testament, pasting some of the passages back together again in a different order, and throwing away the larger number of "unusable" passages that did not fit his Deism. The result was Jefferson's *The Life and Morals of Jesus of Nazareth*, where (in his own words) he succeeded in "abstracting what is really his [i.e., Jesus'] from the rubbish in which it is buried, easily distinguished by its luster from the dross of his biographers, and as separable from that as the diamond from the dung hill."[70] We are not surprised to find that the "diamond" was the moral message of Christianity, while on the dunghill were unceremoniously piled the virgin birth, the prologue to the Gospel of John, Jesus' assertions of divinity, all the miracles and finally the resurrection. Jefferson completed his New (and improved) Testament in 1816, and had his own copy bound in red morocco. He did not allow it to be published during his lifetime, however, fearing further charges of atheism (which plagued him throughout his life).

---

[70]Thomas Jefferson, quoted in Jaroslav Pelikan, *Jesus Through the Centuries* (New Haven, Conn.: Yale University Press, 1985), p. 190.

Jefferson was not an atheist. He was, however, an adamant anti-trinitarian, and his approach to Christianity, and to the Bible in particular, manifests well the entire current of eighteenth-century thought. Such is not a surprise when we find out that privately Jefferson considered himself an Epicurean and studied Epicurus in Greek.[71] As for "Jefferson's Bible," as it came to be called, it was not a scholarly work as much as a personal revelation of Jefferson's Deism, and it did not influence many beyond the shores of his home country. To find the true bearers of the "good news" according to Hobbes and Spinoza into the nineteenth century, the century of Darwin, we must go to Germany, for it was especially there that scriptural scholarship as a distinct discipline flourished. Rather than follow the whole line of such scholarship from beginning to end, we shall focus on one of its first, most famous and most influential proponents, D. F. Strauss.

David Friedrich Strauss (1808-1874) was, by all accounts, one of the most important and influential—if not the most important and influential—of modern scriptural scholars. Although Strauss's work occurred about a century and a half after Hobbes's and Spinoza's, he completed what they had begun, but did so with the following difference. Hobbes's and Spinoza's efforts on behalf of Epicureanism were undertaken from outside the citadel of Christianity, and were designed with the hope that a new mathematical-materialist science would soon reign supreme. Strauss, living long after the victory of Newtonianism, and neither a scientist nor a philosopher, was working from within Christianity trying to salvage what he could in a universe already defined by Epicurean materialism. Typical of a whole line of German and English scriptural scholars of the nineteenth century, he gave up doctrine after doctrine in a frantic effort to save the faith from irrelevancy, and then having given everything away, he himself became a materialist denying Christianity altogether. He ended, therefore, where Hobbes and Spinoza had begun. Epicurus finally took his soul. The historical lesson is simple, and allows for Strauss to stand as a kind of nineteenth-century type: having adopted Epicurean means, Strauss could not help but achieve Epicurean ends, not only in his work as a scriptural exegete, but in himself.

In the first half of the nineteenth century, it certainly seemed to nearly everyone that the universe was as Newton had described it, and that uni-

---

[71]See George Panichas, *Epicurus* (New York: Twayne, 1967), p. 147.

verse was the universe of Epicurus and Lucretius. Strauss, at least when he wrote his most influential works, was piously attempting to salvage Christianity in a materialist cosmos. This is clear right from the very beginning of his most influential work *Das Leben Jesu kritisch bearbeitet* (1835-1836), later translated into English as *The Life of Jesus Critically Examined* (1848). The title itself is instructive, for it was the life of Jesus the man, not Christ the divine Messiah. Echoing Hobbes and especially Spinoza, Strauss focused on Jesus the moral man, and relegated Christ the divine Messiah to the realm of myth. This approach, so characteristic of the nineteenth and twentieth centuries and taken to be truly novel, was simply the inevitable echo of Epicurus's words as applied to Scripture: "Just be sure the myths are kept out of it!"

Thus the introductory chapter of his *Life of Jesus* was entitled "Development of the Mythical Point of View in Relation to the Gospel Histories."[72] The title betrays the Spinozan presupposition that what is not in conformity with the laws of nature as defined by the tenets of materialism cannot have happened, and must therefore have its source not in the facts of history, but in the fancy either of the followers of Jesus or the writers of the New Testament. That is, such things must have "been foisted into the sacred writings," to use Spinoza's words. At the head of the criteria defining how we separate historical fact from mythical fiction, Strauss provided the following negative rule. An "account is not historical" and hence "the matter related could not have taken place in the manner described is evident" when

> the narration is irreconcilable with the known and universal laws which govern the course of events. Now according to these laws, agreeing with all just philosophical conceptions and all credible experience, *the absolute cause never disturbs the chain of secondary causes by single arbitrary actions of interposition* [emphasis added]. . . . When therefore we meet with an account of certain phenomena or events of which it is either expressly stated or implied that they were produced immediately by God himself (divine apparitions—voices from heaven and the like), or by human beings possessed of supernatural powers (miracles, prophecies), such an account, is *in so far* to be considered as not historical. And inasmuch as, in general, the intermingling of the spiritual world with the human is found only in unauthentic records, and is irreconcilable with all just

---

[72]All quotes from Strauss translated from the fourth German edition in *The Life of Jesus Critically Examined,* ed. Peter C. Hodgson (Philadelphia: Fortress, 1972).

conceptions; so narratives of angels and of devils, of their appearing in human shape and interfering with human concerns, cannot possibly be received as historical.[73]

According to Strauss, materialism was right in denying the possibility of miracles, immaterial entities and the divinity of Jesus, but wrong in denying the kernel of "truth" contained as edifying myths, that is, stories told to capture the *meaning* of an event or person. Strauss thereby duplicated and slightly modified Spinoza's distinction between *meaning* and *truth* in Scripture, and with Spinoza directed the exegetical energies to the recovery of the original meaning of the actors and authors of Scripture. For example, Jesus could not have been born of the virgin Mary, miraculously conceived by the Holy Spirit, as Christian orthodoxy maintained, for "such a conception would be a most remarkable deviation from all natural laws."[74] What should be done? Uncover the meaning behind the myth.

If we peel back the historical layers in the Bible, Strauss asserted, we find how later Jews had taken literally and prophetically what was originally meant by earlier Jews only metaphorically. "In the world of mythology many great men had extraordinary births, and were sons of the gods. Jesus himself spoke of his heavenly origin, and called God his father; besides, his title as Messiah was—Son of God." Although this was originally meant as a kind of honorific metaphor, later Jews began to take it literally, and so the "belief prevailed that Jesus, as the Messiah, should be born of a virgin by means of divine agency; . . . and thus originated a philosophical (dogmatical) mythus concerning the birth of Jesus." But, Strauss hastened to add, "according to historical truth, Jesus was the offspring of an ordinary marriage, between Joseph and Mary."[75] We may then explain the virgin birth and the purported divine origin of Jesus historically, as a gradual shift in the minds of the Jews, whereby what was originally meant metaphorically was taken literally, for "it was a daily occurrence, especially among the later Jews, to attach a sensible signification to that which originally had merely a spiritual or figurative meaning."[76]

The same pattern occurred in Strauss's analysis of the entire life of Jesus

---

[73]Ibid., introduction to sect. 16, pp. 87-88.
[74]Ibid., 1.3.26, p. 130.
[75]Ibid., 1.3.29, p. 140.
[76]Ibid., p. 142.

Christ, right up to the very end. In regard to the death and resurrection, he argued that the "proposition" that "a dead man has returned to life, is composed of two . . . contradictory elements. If he has really returned to life, it is natural to conclude that he was not wholly dead; if he was really dead, it is difficult to believe that he has really become living."[77]

Interestingly enough, Strauss did not reject the existence of the soul, but exactly like Epicurus and Lucretius, denied its immortality (and implicitly, its immateriality). The body and soul must be conceived "at once in their identity, the soul as the interior of the body, the body as the exterior of the soul," and since the soul is "the governing center which holds in combination the powers and operations of the body, . . . the soul as such ceases in the same moment with its dominion and activity." Any "restoration of the lifeless bodily organs" then, would be "an immediate interposition of God in the regular course of nature, *irreconcilable with enlightened ideas of the relation of God to the world.*"[78]

"Hence," Strauss asserted, "the cultivated intellect of the present day has very decidedly stated the following dilemma: either Jesus was not really dead, or he did not really rise again."[79] Strauss claimed that he truly died and was not resurrected, but the *myth* of his resurrection can be explained—that is, we can explain how it came to be believed—and therefore, recognize it, not as an intended falsehood, but the expression of a salutary and comforting story. In the minds of the disciples, what began as metaphorical and poetic became historical. The followers of Jesus, "after the first shock was past," began to reflect on all the messianic passages in the Old Testament that predicted the suffering and death of the Messiah, such as Isaiah 53 and Psalm 22. A new light was thereby shed on the sorrowful death of Jesus.

> How could they, when their mind was opened to the hitherto hidden doctrine of a dying Messiah contained in the scriptures, and when in moments of unwonted inspiration their *hearts burned within them* (Luke xxiv.32),—how could they avoid conceiving this to be an influence shed on them by their glorified Christ, an opening of their understanding by him (v.45), nay, an actual conversing with him? Lastly, how conceivable is it that in individuals, espe-

---

[77] Ibid., 3.4.140, pp. 735-36.
[78] Ibid., p. 736, emphasis added.
[79] Ibid.

cially women, these impressions were heightened, in a purely subjective manner, into actual vision; that on others, even on whole assemblies, something or
other of an objective nature, visible or audible, sometimes perhaps the sight of
an unknown person, created the impression of a revelation or appearance of
Jesus: a height of pious enthusiasm which is wont to appear elsewhere in religious societies peculiarly oppressed and persecuted.[80]

The empty tomb? As it turns out, Strauss reasoned, the disciples immediately dispersed after the crucifixion "to their home in Galilee" and, no longer
fearing the wrath of the Jews of Jerusalem, "gradually began to breathe
freely." In Galilee, "where no body lay in the grave to contradict bold suppositions," the disciples gradually formed "the idea of the resurrection of Jesus,"
the idea so invigorating them that "they ventured to proclaim it in the
metropolis" where, of course, "it was no longer possible by the sight of the
body of Jesus either to convict themselves, or to be convicted by others."[81]

Once Strauss emptied all the elements of Christianity that could not fit
the Procrustean bed of materialism, what was left of Jesus himself? Very little. At best, Jesus exhibited a powerful "God-consciousness," which
amounted, in the end, to a vague grasp by a man who lived in the reign of
Caesar Augustus and Tiberius, of the Baconian project of mastering nature
as transformed and rarified by the German philosopher Georg Wilhelm
Friedrich Hegel (1770-1831). According to Strauss, Jesus manifested the
idea of spirit conquering nature, of the divine-like power of the human mind
mastering, intellectually and technologically, brute matter. The notions of
miracles and the resurrection, which had no reality in the historical Jesus,
had at least a reality as a mythical adumbration of the modern power of
humankind over nature. Even so, these two—the particular individual,
Jesus, and the general historical progress of humanity—must be kept distinct, for only the latter is the bearer of truth, only the latter really happens.
"Though I may see the human mind in its unity with the divine, in the
course of the world's history, more and more completely establish itself as
the power which subdues nature; this is quite another thing, than to conceive
a single man endowed with such power, for individual, voluntary acts."[82]

For Strauss, the *real* good news had come about centuries after the life of

---

[80]Ibid., p. 742.
[81]Ibid., p. 743.
[82]Ibid., "Concluding Dissertation," sect. 151, p. 779.

Jesus, when science discovered the long-hidden laws of nature (and hence achieved divine wisdom), and by its increasing power over nature, gave evidence of actual miracles, real scientific miracles to replace the mythical miracles of the old gospel. As for the historical Jesus, "shall we interest ourselves more in the cure of some sick people in Galilee, than in the miracles of intellectual and moral life belonging to the history of the world—in the increasing, the almost incredible dominion of man over nature—in the irresistible force of ideas, to which no unintelligent matter, whatever its magnitude, can oppose any enduring resistance?"[83] Apparently not.

Strauss, at least at this point in his life, could not bring himself to jettison Christianity entirely. He retained Christianity by transforming its central doctrines, focused on the person of Christ, to the idea of progress in the mastery of nature, a central tenet of the transformed version of Epicureanism we found in Bacon. Strauss retained the Scriptures as a palimpsest upon which he overwrote materialist doctrines designed as antithetical to Christianity. As with Spinoza, the particulars of Scripture were ultimately unimportant for those enlightened by the philosophic truth toward which the ancient writers fumbled. "When the mind has thus gone beyond the sensible history," Strauss declared, "and entered into the domain of the absolute, the former ceases to be essential; it takes a subordinate place, above which the spiritual truths suggested by the history stand self-supported; it becomes as the faint image of a dream which belongs to the past, and does not, like the idea, share the permanence of the spirit which is absolutely present to itself."[84] Christianity, the faint image of a dream, had all but dissipated for Strauss.

As if to pour all of his pent-up religious fervor into the transformation of Christianity—the religious fervor that, given the materialism he accepted, could find no real object—Strauss waxed mystical upon the new doctrines of humanity divinized, raised by its own efforts to a new power that ancient Christians had mistakenly assumed belonged to God alone. The apostle of materialism provided a new creed.

> In an individual, a God-man, the properties and functions which the church
> ascribes to Christ contradict themselves; in the idea of the race, they perfectly

---

[83] Ibid., p. 781.
[84] Ibid.

agree. Humanity is the union of the two natures—God become man, the infinite manifesting itself in the finite, and the finite spirit remembering its infinitude; it is the child of the visible Mother and the invisible Father, Nature and
Spirit; it is the worker of miracles, in so far as in the course of human history
the spirit more and more completely subjugates nature, both within and
around man, until it lies before him as the inert matter on which he exercises
his active power; it is the sinless existence, for the course of its development is
a blameless one, pollution cleaves to the individual only, and does not touch
the race or its history. It is Humanity that dies, rises, and ascends to heaven,
for from the negation of its phenomenal life there ever proceeds a higher spiritual life; from the suppression of its mortality as a personal, national, and terrestrial spirit, arises its union with the infinite spirit of the heavens. By faith
in this Christ, especially in his death and resurrection, man is justified before
God; that is, by the kindling within him of the idea of Humanity, the individual man participates in the divinely human life of the species.[85]

We pause to note the supreme irony (or, to be less charitable and more
exact, the contradiction) in this approach. Strauss argued at one and the
same time that (1) miracles cannot occur because, as we all know, the laws of
motion directing matter are inviolable, therefore, God cannot have done miracles in the New Testament; and (2) we are to understand all christological
doctrines as pertaining to the human race because human beings apparently
can contradict the laws of nature, both in their individual freedom to act and
in their miraculous mastering of nature itself (for in a closed system any
acts contrary to the laws of nature must be considered miraculous). What
Strauss denied to God, he affirmed in humankind.

To return, Strauss realized that the enlightened theologian preaching the
new gospel would face an uphill battle, for the masses would still cling fool-
ishly to their unphilosophic literalism and to their belief that the central doctrines of Christianity, oddly enough, attached only to the person of Jesus
Christ. For the sake of the poor masses, Strauss maintained that the enlightened theologian must engage in a kind of Machiavellian duplicity in the pul-
pit, speaking as if he believed in the old-fashioned literal account, while at the
same time patiently pushing the sheep through the gates of materialism. The
mode of preaching and teaching Strauss recommended is enlightening on its
own account, for it was taken over by many modern seminaries, and hence, by

---

[85]Ibid., p. 780.

a multitude of priests, ministers, deacons and religious educators.

> In his discourses to the church he [i.e., the enlightened theologian] will indeed
> adhere to the forms of the popular conception, but on every opportunity he will
> exhibit their spiritual significance, which to him constitutes their whole truth,
> and thus prepare—though such a result is only to be thought of as an unend-
> ing progress—the resolution of those forms into their original ideas in the
> consciousness of the church also. Thus . . . at the festival of Easter, he will
> indeed set out from the sensible fact of the resurrection of Christ, but he will
> dwell chiefly on the being buried and rising again with Christ, which the Apos-
> tle himself has strenuously inculcated.[86]

In offering this variation of the "two platoon strategy," Strauss realized
the danger in such intellectual *noblesse oblige*, that the preacher will end up
"a hypocrite."[87] Alas, that is just what happened to Strauss himself. No
longer able to fool himself by appeals to a Christology which was irritatingly
redundant to a self-contained materialist system, Strauss at last shed the
last vestiges of Christianity, and became a pure advocate for materialism.
His last work, *Der alte und der neue Glaube*, published in 1872 (and in its
English version, *The Old Faith and the New,* a year later), simply rejected
Christianity as the old faith, and openly embraced scientific materialism as
the new faith. Strauss had become Epicurus, preparing the way for Darwin
by weakening Christianity, the long-standing foe of Epicurean materialism.

Before we turn to an analysis of Darwin, we end by repeating this essential point. If Christianity had not been weakened by the undermining of its
authority, then the Epicurean revolution would either not have taken place
or, what is more likely, would have been severely blunted. Insofar as Christianity remains under the sway of the exegetical principles founded by Hobbes and Spinoza, and baptized by the likes of Strauss, Christianity will
remain in the weakened and subservient condition to which it was reduced
by the injection of alien elements as interpretive principles. A much longer,
more detailed history of the ruination of scriptural scholarship needs to be
written (such a task is far beyond the scope of the present work), but this
chapter at least provides the proper starting point for such a history. We
may now focus our attention on the arguments of Charles Darwin.

---

[86]Ibid., sect. 152, p. 783.
[87]Ibid., p. 784.

Epicureanism
Becomes Darwinism

We have at last reached Darwin himself. Perhaps it is best to begin this chapter by clarifying what we will not cover. I will not be providing a minute analysis either of Charles Darwin's life or his arguments. Nor will I be entering directly into the debate going on today between advocates of Darwinism and advocates of intelligent design. Instead, I will focus on Darwin's arguments as the culmination of the West's reembrace of Epicurean materialism. Looked at in this aspect, Darwin's arguments may be seen on a far larger scale than they appear in his written works. But that, of course, is the point of this entire book—Darwinism in its most fundamental sense is not merely biological, but truly cosmological in scope. Indeed, the biology was deduced from the cosmology. Of course, by this I do not mean that Charles Darwin sat down at his desk after reading Epicurus and Lucretius, and churned out *The Origin of Species*. Rather, *The Origin of Species* was the result of the permeation of Western intellectual culture by the materialist tenets of Epicureanism. The new cosmology, as we have seen, was Epicurean in origin, and modified through the efforts of Machiavelli, Bacon, Galileo, Hobbes, Newton, Locke and other moderns. Biology becomes the historical focus in Darwin because biology was the last part of the cosmos not fully subdued by modern Epicurean materialism prior to the nineteenth century.

Seen in this way, the usual historical account of Darwin's theory of evolution as revolutionary is a distortion. Far from being revolutionary, it was inevitable. As many have pointed out, evolutionary theory itself was already in the air prior to the nineteenth century, and this is a strong indication that it was not novel, but simply part of the entire Epicurean framework which had existed for over 2000 years. Indeed, the pieces of evolutionary theory had already been picked up many times prior to Darwin, by Beniot de Maillet (1656-1738); Jean-Jacques Rousseau (1712-1778); the Comte de Buffon (1707-1788); Darwin's grandfather and correspondent with Rousseau, Erasmus Darwin (1731-1802); Jean Lamarck (1744-1829); William Wells (1757-1817); Patrick Matthew (1790-1874); Robert Chambers (1802-1871); Geoffroy Saint-Hilaire (1772-1844); Alfred Wallace (1823-1913); and many lesser figures mentioned by Darwin himself in his "Historical Sketch" at the beginning of the *Origin*. Thus, if Darwin was putting together the pieces of a puzzle, it was a puzzle that had been constructed by Epicurus and Lucretius, taken apart and cast aside by Christianity, recovered in the Renaissance, and slowly reconstructed between the sixteenth and eighteenth centuries. The last pieces were waiting to be fit together in the nineteenth century, and if Darwin had not written the *Origin*, someone else almost certainly would have written something very much like it.

It is therefore quite easy to account for evolution being in the air for so long prior to Darwin. As should be obvious by now, evolution was an essential part of the Epicurean framework right from the beginning, and Epicurean materialism could not be revived without its eventually reasserting its rightful place. This can be seen quite clearly from two related angles, as a deduction from Galilean-Newtonian atomism, and even more simply, from the evolutionary account in Lucretius that had been circulating widely for over three centuries prior to Darwin.

Perhaps the best way to see how Darwinism necessarily followed on the acceptance of materialist atomism is to focus on the most important word, *species,* in the title of Darwin's most famous work, *The Origin of Species.* To remind ourselves of what is at issue, we may review Aristotle's account of species, for it is the most directly opposed to Darwin's, both philosophically and (recalling the anti-Aristotelianism of the moderns) historically.

Aristotle had argued that the visible complex unity of each living thing was the result of two principles, the immaterial form (the organizing cause) and the matter (the material to be unified into a complex whole). The form made each thing a recognizable, complex, living unified being of a certain kind, that is, a certain *species*; the matter provided the individual particularity appropriate to the species. On this account, we call a dog a "dog" because of the form, the principle of unity that allows us to classify it as a species; we call this dog "Fido" because of the individuating matter that makes up its particular physical characteristics and abilities. All dogs, as dogs, share the common form, that is, they are members of the same species, otherwise they could not be classed as dogs. Each dog, however, has its peculiarities—a particular color, hair type, length, height, length of ears, characteristic habits and temperament, and so on—because of the matter. The permanence, then, is caused by the form (the origin of species), and the mutability and particularity are caused by the matter.[1]

For Epicurean materialism, we recall, it is quite the reverse. Matter is the only reality, and by its random motion and cohesion, it creates the *appearance* of form (i.e., species). The complex unity, then, is the accidental result of the random variations of simple material constituents. The origin of species, therefore, is the random mutation of matter on the atomic level. Nothing can be said to have an integrated "design," because its complex unity is the unintended result of unintelligent matter "constructing" similar forms accidentally. We call "species" those accidentally created organisms that resemble each other (or more properly, resemble each other by proximity of common descent, such mechanism being that by which similarity is perpetuated). But since the motion of atoms is perpetual on the atomic level, continual transformation of the forms (species) is likewise perpetual. The Aristotelian belief that forms (species) are permanent, then, is the result of where we are standing, as it were, on the time-line of continual mutation: we invest a "snapshot" of a transforming species with permanence, when if we could step back and view the transformation on a greater time scale, it would look like a "motion picture." In Darwin's words,

---

[1]We can see that Aristotle's argument (or better, a modified version of it) could easily take into account the kind of variation within species that Darwin took to be explicable only by a materialist account. The individuating matter would allow for a broad range of variations, but variations within a determinate form. The capacity to vary would simply be part of the potentiality of matter. That variation is not utterly random, but occurs within the confines of a determinate form, would explain both why we do not find one kind of thing changing into another kind of thing. and why all variation occurs in a well-orchestrated shift of many well-defined, interdependent parts.

I look at the term species as one arbitrarily given, for the sake of convenience, to a set of individuals closely resembling each other, and that it does not essentially differ from the term variety, which is given to less distinct and more fluctuating forms. The term variety, again, in comparison with mere individual differences, is also applied arbitrarily, for convenience's sake.[2]

When modernity embraced Epicurean materialism, it not only became anti-Aristotelian philosophically (taking into account that often it happened in the reverse, bad scholasticism led many to seek an alternative to Aristotle), but had ultimately to reject the reality of species as a manifestation of immaterial form. The result, of course, was the acceptance of the materialist account of form, or species, as an accident of matter, where "the term species" is "arbitrarily given."

That does not mean, of course, that individual moderns all understood that the acceptance of the materialist cosmology necessarily entailed the materialist reduction of species to mere epiphenomena of matter in motion. Newtonianism is a good case in point, as a glance back to the eighteenth century verifies, for Newtonianism seemed to breed a spate of design-type arguments during the 1700s. But as we have seen above, the intelligent design aspect of Newtonian physics—as long as it lasted—was an unsuccessful hybrid between divine causation and a self-contained materialist physics, and this was as true in regard to accounting for the regularity of heavenly motions as it was in accounting for the apparent design of living beings. And so, Newton did invoke God to explain "the uniformity in the bodies of animals" and the "contrivance of . . . [the] parts of animals, the eyes, ears, brain, muscles, heart, lungs, midriff, glands, larynx, hands, wings, swimming bladders . . . and other organs of sense and motion," and insisted that "the instinct of brutes and insects can be the effect of nothing else than the wisdom and skill of a powerful, ever-living agent."[3] But in the preface to his *Principia* he identified himself, and rightly so, as one of the "moderns, rejecting substantial forms and occult qualities" in order "to subject the phenomena of nature to the laws of mathematics."[4] This rejection of form left a vacuum, as it were, in

---

[2]Charles Darwin, *The Origin of Species* (New York: Mentor, 1958), chap. 2, "Doubtful Species," p. 68.

[3]Isaac Newton, *Optics,* Great Books of the Western World, vol. 32 (Chicago: Encyclopaedia Britannica, 1952), 3.1, p. 542.

[4]Isaac Newton, *Mathematical Principles of Natural Philosophy*, trans. Andrew Motte, rev. Florian Cajori (Berkeley: University of California Press, 1962), p. xvii.

regard to the cause of species. Newton seemed to think God was somehow necessary to cause brute matter to be brought together in complex biological beings, but the laws that governed all motion soon seemed quite sufficient to his followers to explain the source of species. Since the laws were self-sufficient, Newton's appeal to God, however pious, was redundant. Darwin simply extended Laplace's argument that we "have no need of that hypothesis," from physics to biology. Therefore, because Newtonianism, true to its Epicurean roots, ultimately undermined any account of form, or species, other than as the result of the random variations of material constituents, evolution was simply a deduction from the Epicurean physics established by Newtonianism in the eighteenth century: if Newton; then Darwin.

But even aside from the inevitability of evolutionary arguments given the materialist foundation of Newtonianism, we must not overlook the obvious. Lucretius's great Epicurean poem, with its extended evolutionary passage, ensured that evolution would be in the air from the 1500s forward. Whether or not Darwin himself ever read Lucretius—he developed a dislike of the classics from having Greek and Latin drubbed into him as a youth—many others had, and the idea could not help but circulate widely. I quote it again, to drill into the reader how thorough this amazing passage from Lucretius is.

> Many were the portents also that the earth then tried to make, springing up with wondrous appearance and frame: the hermaphrodite, between man and woman yet neither, different from both; some without feet, others again bereft of hands; some found dumb also without a mouth, some blind without eyes, some bound fast with all their limbs adhering to their bodies, so that they could do nothing and go nowhere, could neither avoid mischief nor take what they might need. So with the rest of like monsters and portents that she made, it was all in vain; since nature banned their growth, and they could not attain the desired flower of age nor find food nor join by the ways of Venus. For we see that living beings need many things in conjunction, so that they may be able by procreation to forge out the chain of the generations. . . .
>
> And many species of animals must have perished at that time, unable by procreation to forge out the chain of posterity: for whatever you see feeding on the breath of life, either cunning or courage or at least quickness must have guarded and kept that kind from its earliest existence; many again still exist, entrusted to our protection, which remain, commended to us because of their usefulness. . . .

But those to which nature gives no such qualities, so that they could neither live by themselves at their own will, nor give us some usefulness for which we might suffer them to feed under our protection and be safe, these certainly lay at the mercy of others for prey and profit, being all hampered by their own fateful chains, until nature brought that race to destruction.[5]

We see in this passage all the fundamentals of Darwin's account: (1) random material variations that bring about modifications in the structure between generations; (2) the survival of the fittest of these variations as determined by the enhanced abilities of the animals, and by the conditions in which the animals live; and (3) the necessity of passing along the beneficial variations by heredity. The only things missing were (again) an explicit account of the transformation of one species into another, and also the Malthusian breeding beyond the level of sustenance to enhance the competition.

Now here one might object and say that, whether or not evolution was in the air, or whether or not one might deduce evolutionary theory from Newtonianism, Darwin's account was first and foremost an empirical account, arrived at by pure induction, and not deduced from a preestablished framework.

To the contrary, I shall attempt to show that in his presuppositions, his mode of argument and his conclusions Darwin displays a modern form of Epicurus's ancient materialist faith. As we have just seen, Darwin followed Epicurean materialism in eliminating species distinctions, and his account of natural selection was also an expansion of that which occurs in Lucretius. If that were the sum of similarities between Epicurean materialism and Darwinism, then we would not be justified in regarding Darwinism as the modern form of Epicureanism. But we also find many more similarities that fit the overall Epicurean pattern all too well. To begin with, Darwin manifests the same faith as Epicurus in the materialist principles that undergird his arguments even though they are undemonstrated assumptions. In particular, we see in Darwin the same faith in a simple material explanation of all natural complexity—faith in the extraordinarily simple mechanism of natural selection, rather than the Epicurean atom. In Darwin there is also the same need for and belief in infinite time to create order out of randomness,

---

[5]Lucretius *De Rerum Natura*, Loeb Classical Library vol. L 181, trans. W. H. D. Rouse, rev. Martin F. Smith (Cambridge, Mass.: Harvard University Press, 1924, 1975), 5.837.77.

the same a priori rejection of intelligence as a cause of natural complexity, the same systematic exclusion of divine action, and the same rejection (albeit implicit) of the immortal, immaterial soul and the afterlife as we have seen in Epicureanism. In the moral realm, we also find in Darwin that nature is amoral and that morality itself is relative, a mere historical product of evolution.

But that is not all. Moral Darwinism is not simply a reproduction of ancient Epicurean materialism, but Epicurean materialism as modified in modernity. Going beyond Epicurus and Lucretius, Darwin embraced the Hobbesian-Baconian assertion that human nature itself is malleable to human will, and the Machiavellian-Baconian assertion that fortune/nature may be conquered and reformed. Since, for Darwin, our nature is the result of random natural selection, human nature has been formed, in great part, by chance. Darwinism becomes moral Darwinism precisely in advocating that we take evolution into our own hands and remold our nature according to our will. Moral Darwinism calls us to leave chance and merely natural selection behind, and by *artificial* selection remold human nature. In this, Darwin is the founder of the modern eugenics movement in all its later myriad forms, whether it is expressed through calls to weed out the unfit, breed more of the fit, abort the undesirable and deformed or manipulate our nature genetically through technology. Let us take up each point in turn, beginning with Darwin's materialist habit of mind, that is, his materialist faith.

As we recall, Epicurus sought to establish a *habit* of thinking, where meditation on materialist principles established a way of approaching nature that excluded the divine. The materialist habit of mind was supposed to sustain his disciples even and especially when materialist explanations faltered. Epicurus urged his followers never to lose heart even when the theoretical materialism seemed to fail in explaining natural phenomena: "We must not accustom ourselves to hold that our study of these matters has failed to achieve a degree of accuracy which contributes to our undisturbed and blessed state." In the often convoluted and conflicting "just so" stories that Darwin (and his followers down to the present day) offered to explain how natural selection had brought about this or that animal, complex structure or intricate instinct, we seem to hear a modern version of that ancient Epicurean battle cry, "Evolution can produce biological complexity in several different ways—just be sure the myths are kept out of it!" Such stories are not evidence, however. They are mere hypotheses that serve to reinforce the Darwinian habit of mind.

That, of course, is a serious charge on my part, so I had better make good by providing significant evidence. First, we must establish that Darwin's confidence in his theory was not the result of its having been demonstrated conclusively, but was rooted in his *faith* that his theory would be vindicated in the future. To begin with, Darwin himself admitted that his account was hypothetical. His position was not that all the difficulties with his theory had been answered, but that "it can hardly be supposed that a false theory would explain, in so satisfactory a manner as does the theory of natural selection, the several large classes of facts . . . specified." That is, Darwin appealed to the explanatory power of his theory over its rivals (or to be more exact, over its rival, what Darwin often called "the theory of independent acts of creation," or simply, the "theory of Creation"). Darwin admitted that some "objected that this is an unsafe method of arguing," but countered that "it is a method used in judging of the common events of life, and has often been used by the greatest natural philosophers."[6]

In the abstract, there is nothing wrong with this type of argument, as long as it is not confused with a strict demonstration. If we only allowed, in science and in everyday life, whatever could be deduced from indemonstrable first principles, we would have very little science and even less ability to act on the practical level. But since Darwin's arguments are often mischaracterized, it is important to establish that the *Origin* sets forth the parameters of Darwin's evolutionary hypothesis, then proceeds to present a host of particular examples that demonstrate its explanatory power. It is not a set of demonstrations. To Darwin's credit, he knew exactly what kind of an argument it was, and was honest enough at several points to explain where the argument was weak, and what evidence would overthrow it.

Furthermore, Darwin knew that the evolutionary hypothesis was questionable, and that his most serious antagonists were from the scientific community—Lord Kelvin, St. George Mivart, Fleeming Jenkin, Louis Agassiz, Richard Owen and others. In the introduction to the *Origin*, Darwin let the reader know that he was "well aware that scarcely a single point is discussed

---

[6]Darwin, *Origin of Species*, chap. 15, "Conclusion," p. 452.

in this volume on which facts cannot be adduced, often apparently leading to conclusions directly opposite to those at which I have arrived."[7] In the conclusion to the *Origin*, we see not only that Darwin realized that other scientists were his main rivals, but that his own arguments had gaps.

> Although I am fully convinced of the truth of the views given in this volume under the form of an abstract, I by no means expect to convince experienced naturalists whose minds are stocked with a multitude of facts all viewed, during a long course of years, from a point of view directly opposite to mine. . . . Any one whose disposition leads him to attach more weight to unexplained difficulties than to the explanation of a certain number of facts will certainly reject the theory.[8]

He then appealed "with confidence to the future,—to young and rising naturalists, who will be able to view both sides of the question with impartiality."[9]

It is obvious from the above quotes that, contrary to the popularized version of his theories, Darwin himself admitted that "a multitude of facts" could be "viewed . . . from a point of view directly opposite" to his, and viewed by "experienced naturalists," not unthinking fools. Because Darwin rightly considered the type of argument he was making to be inductive and hypothetical, he had to have *faith* that his hypothesis would ultimately be vindicated in the future.

Because the status of Darwin's evolutionary arguments is so important, we shall look at the character of Darwin's faith in several related areas, beginning with his faith in natural selection itself. We recall that one of the hallmarks of Epicureanism was its appeal to theoretical simplicity as an antidote to the disturbing possibility that the evident complexity of nature would require a designer. The simple atom was the hypothetical point to which all complexity could ultimately be reduced. Of course, this reduction was a promise, an object of faith, for Epicurus could not have proven the existence of this most fundamental constituent of materialism. In the same way, the whole of Darwin's argument rested on the very simple theory of natural selection, so simple that Darwin summarized it in less than a paragraph:

---

[7]Ibid., "Introduction," p. 28.
[8]Ibid., "Conclusion," p. 453.
[9]Ibid.

As many more individuals of each species are born than can possibly survive; and as, consequently, there is a frequently recurring struggle for existence, it follows that any being, if it vary however slightly in any manner profitable to itself, under the complex and sometimes varying conditions of life, will have a better chance of surviving, and thus be *naturally selected*. From the strong principle of inheritance, any selected variety will tend to propagate its new and modified form.[10]

The whole of the *Origin* was aimed at the elaboration and defense of this simple formula. And just as with Epicurus's faith in the atom, Darwin's faith in natural selection as a principle acted as a theoretical filter that brought him to collect and interpret evidence accordingly, the whole purpose of which was to show that, no matter how complex something appeared to be, the derivation of its complexity ultimately could be reduced to the simple action of natural selection. We shall see more clearly both the presence and the nature of Darwin's faith if we examine, in some detail, the following particularly important examples.

In great part, Darwin's faith in natural selection was an extrapolation from changes actually effected by breeders in artificial selection. As Darwin noted, human beings are able to breed for various traits in animals under their direct care, and can bring about, fairly rapidly, significantly different varieties of the species which they breed. In Darwin's words, "Several eminent breeders, during a single lifetime, have so largely modified some of the higher animals which propagate their kind much more slowly than most of the lower animals, that they have formed what well deserves to be called a new sub-breed."[11] Perhaps, Darwin reasoned, there simply was no limit to such change; perhaps in nature, by random variation and selection according to the most "fit" traits, all species barriers might be crossed.

> Slow though the process may be, if feeble man can do much by artificial selection, I can see no limit to the amount of change, to the beauty and complexity of the coadaptions between organic beings, one with another and with their physical conditions of life, which may have been effected in the long course of time through nature's power of selection, that is by the survival of the fittest.[12]

---

[10]Ibid., "Introduction," p. 29.
[11]Ibid., chap. 10, "On the Lapse of Time," p. 298.
[12]Ibid., chap. 4, "Circumstances Favourable," p. 111.

There were two hidden and related assumptions contained in Darwin's faith that the species barrier was no barrier at all. The first was, as we have seen, rooted in the view of nature enshrined by Newton (again, with the alien elements taken out). To make the inference from small changes within a species under the intelligent guidance of a breeder, to unlimited changes creating species, genera, families, orders and classes, Darwin must have held that the form and complex structure of all living things were reducible to variations of the configurations of atoms. Otherwise, species would not be mutable.

But nature left to itself did not reveal its essential malleability, and so Darwin resorted to a Baconian stratagem. As Darwin confessed, in nature free and at large, "we see nothing of these slow changes in progress"[13] that would lead us to believe in the impermanence of species. Even so, he was convinced that the essential malleability of species was revealed in the domestic breeding of animals, for (to quote Bacon) "the nature of things betrays itself more readily under the vexations of art than in its natural freedom."[14] We can see Darwin's confidence quite clearly in his rejection of the common experience of breeders and naturalists concerning the limits of breeding. In regard to "the ordinary belief that the amount of possible variation is a strictly limited quantity" held by breeders and naturalists, Darwin asserted that such was merely "a simple assumption."[15] This simple assumption was gotten, however, from those doing the breeding, who found that attempts to breed beyond a certain range, as well as the release of domestic breed into the wilds, resulted in reversion to "aboriginal stocks," that is, the original variety. Given the weight of evidence against the malleability of species, Darwin did admit the following:

> If it could be shown that our domestic varieties manifested a strong tendency to reversion,—that is, to lose their acquired characters, whilst kept under the same conditions, and whilst kept in a considerable body, so that free inter-crossing might check, by blending together, any slight deviations in their structure, in such case, I grant that we could deduce nothing from domestic varieties in regard to species.[16]

---

[13]Ibid., chap. 4, "Natural Selection," p. 92.
[14]Francis Bacon, *The Great Instauration*, in *The New Organon and Related Writings*, ed. Fulton H. Anderson (New York: Macmillan, 1960), pp. 18, 25.
[15]Darwin, *Origin of Species*, chap. 4, "Natural Selection," p. 92.
[16]Ibid., chap. 1, "Effects of Habit . . .," p. 37.

"But," he immediately argued, "there is not a shadow of evidence in favour of this view: to assert that we could not breed our cart- and race-horses, long and short-horned cattle, and poultry of various breeds, and esculent vegetables, for an unlimited number of generations, would be opposed to all experience." [17] Of course, this was merely a rhetorical parry. Breeding seemingly infinite variations within distinct species does not translate into breeding successfully across species barriers. Darwin's faith that such barriers did not present insurmountable obstacles came, not from breeders and naturalists whose experience he rejected, but from his assumptions that nature was constituted by purely material elements that accidentally cohered to create species, and these elements could therefore be shifted and reconfigured indefinitely to create other species.

Darwin's faith that infinite time could allow chance to produce order without divine guidance is also Epicurean in character. Even though Newtonianism provided the materialist foundation, modern evolutionary theory still needed time, and lots of it. That gift was provided by the great geologist James Hutton (1726-1797) in his *Theory of the Earth* (1788) and more directly to Darwin by Sir Charles Lyell (1797-1875) in his *Principles of Geology* (1830-1833). Both argued that the earth as we see it is the result not of instantaneous and recent activity, but rather the continual, gradual work of uniform physical forces over millions of years. Hutton and Lyell seemed, all at once, to destroy the "young earth" literal reading of Genesis and the geological "catastrophism" which seemed to support it, and to allow for the unlimited time so essential to the materialist argument that no intelligent agency was necessary to produce the myriad beings we find inhabiting the world. Whereas Galileo's spyglass had provided infinite space and an infinite supply of matter, Hutton and Lyell provided potentially infinite time.

Why was infinite time so important both for Epicureanism in general and Darwin in particular? Whenever we compare the effects of intelligence and chance, it is clear that intelligence can produce very quickly what it would take chance a very long time to produce (if it could do it at all). For example, "Darwin has seen the light" took me less than a second to produce intellectually, and only a few seconds to write down. How long would it take to generate this sentence by random variation of letters?

---

[17]Ibid.

Calculating the probability of generating the entire sentence,[18] we get a probability of 1 in 6.08 x 10^{35}. But what does that mean in terms of time? Without doing any calculating, we might think that, assuming a random-letter–producing machine working at one variation per second, a million years would be more than enough to plow through all the possibilities. But that faith is caused by our not clearly knowing how many seconds are in a million years. (As Darwin himself said, "Few of us . . . know what a million years really means."[19]) It might surprise us to find that there are only 31,557,600 seconds in a year, so that going through all the possibilities of "Darwin has seen the light" at one per second would take approximately 19,270,000,000,000,000,000,000,000,000 years. Even if our random letter-generating machine would have been around for 20 billion years, the oldest estimated age of the universe (the actual age, probably being half that), the number of years needed is still almost 1,000,000,000,000,000,000 times *longer*.[20]

Darwin himself, on his own admission, was no mathematician. Referring to his early education at Christ's College, Darwin recalled,

> I attempted mathematics . . . but got on very slowly. The work was repugnant to me, chiefly from my not being able to see any meaning in the early steps in algebra. This impatience was very foolish, and after years I have deeply regretted that I did not proceed far enough at least to understand something of the great leading principles of mathematics; for men thus endowed seem to have an extra sense.[21]

If we might be blunt here, the lack of this "extra sense" caused Darwin (and many of his followers) not to test the vague but compelling general evolutionary arguments with precise and particular mathematical analysis, allowing him to move all too easily from what seemed probable hypothetically to sweeping conclusions.

---

[18] Assuming, for example, a modified typewriter, with only the letters of the alphabet and a space bar, and discounting the difference between small and capital letters.

[19] Darwin, *Origin of Species*, chap. 10, "On the Lapse of Time," p. 298.

[20] Of course, the odds against randomly generating anything in nature are far greater, for nature (if it is truly as the materialist describes it) does not plow methodically through all the possibilities like an intelligently designed machine. (Computer simulation, one of the key mystifying techniques used by contemporary Darwinists such as Richard Dawkins to "prove" the possibility of generating complex order by random variation, rests on the confusion between what can actually happen according to true random variation, and what can happen through methodical goal-directed variation.)

[21] Quoted in Gavin de Beer, *Charles Darwin: A Scientific Biography* (New York: Doubleday, 1965), p. 28.

Indeed, two of the most damaging criticisms of Darwin's theory—criticisms that remained unanswerable to him in his lifetime—came from those who had very good abilities in mathematics and were able to rub Darwin's vague assertions against the sharp edges of numbers. Fleeming Jenkin, a brilliant Scottish engineer, showed very clearly by mathematics that beneficial variations arising in an individual would very soon be completely diluted through heredity in the population of the species. If Jenkin were right, then no amount of time would help Darwin. Lord Kelvin, arguably the greatest physicist of the nineteenth century, demonstrated mathematically that the infinite time provided by Hutton and Lyell was actually unavailable, and that the age of the earth must be reduced to mere millions of years.

As it turned out, the criticisms of Jenkin and Lord Kelvin were founded on errors, Jenkin's on the "blending" theory of inheritance (which Darwin accepted) and Lord Kelvin's on the physics of the time (wherein radiation had not been discovered yet, thereby throwing off the calculations of the earth's age which relied on subterranean temperature variation). In regard to Darwin's whole lifetime, however, these two hard-edged criticisms seemed, especially to Darwin himself, to have deflated significantly the strength of his argument. (In a letter, Darwin referred to Lord Kelvin as an "odious spectre,"[22] which gives us a flavor of the despondency Darwin must have felt being dogged by the century's most eminent physicist.)

The normal assessment of the nineteenth century criticisms of Darwin by the great scientists of the day is well illustrated in the following words of Sir Gavin de Beer, himself one of the twentieth century's great evolutionary theorists and also a biographer of Darwin.

> If Kelvin was right, it meant that so little time was available for the pageant of evolution to have taken place that it could not have been achieved by natural selection of fortuitous variations. Instead, design and direction would have to be invoked, which was exactly what Darwin had always fought against. He attached little weight to the physicists' estimates of the age of the earth because they differed so widely: "I feel a conviction that the world will be found rather older than Thomson [i.e., Lord Kelvin] makes it." Darwin's uncanny dumb sagacity was well founded, for the discovery of radioactivity has made nonsense of Kelvin's arguments and has lengthened the estimated

---

[22]Quoted in Loren Eiseley, *Darwin's Century* (New York: Anchor, 1961), p. 235.

age of the earth to over 4000 million years [i.e., 4 billion years], sufficient to allow evolution by natural selection of fortuitous variations to have done its work. There is therefore no reason to repudiate natural selection and to invoke design and direction on the score of the age of the earth.[23]

But de Beer's analysis does not address several important points. First, as we have seen in the above calculations with "Darwin has seen the light," the addition of three zeroes makes little difference when dealing with vastly improbable outcomes.

Second, de Beer misrepresents the actual time available for the evolution of complex organisms to occur. For the first half-billion years of the earth's history, no evolution would be possible, because no life was possible until the earth cooled sufficiently and a suitable climate developed. Moreover, approximately 85 percent of geologic time occurred in the Precambrian period where the comparatively few life forms fossilized were quite primitive. With the Cambrian period came the sudden appearance of a multitude of complex life forms, an "explosion" that occurred beginning, not four billion years ago, but approximately five hundred and fifty million years ago. Even more difficult to explain, the explosion itself actually did occur within a few million years, thereby reducing the evolution of all the major animal groups in biology to Kelvin's calculated time span (albeit for different reasons than Kelvin's). We note that Darwin himself agonized over the Cambrian explosion (although he did not call it that): "the difficulty of assigning any good reason for the absence of vast piles of strata rich in fossils beneath the Cambrian system is very great. . . . The case at present must remain inexplicable; and may be truly urged as a valid argument against the views here entertained."[24]

Third, the discovery of radioactivity undermined not only Lord Kelvin's calculations, but also the eternal nature of the atom itself, so that nature could no longer be considered a closed system. (I return to this point in another chapter.)

Finally, in the very quote de Beer pulled from Darwin, Darwin himself was expressing a conviction that his theory was true *despite* strong contrary evidence from the best science of the day; that is, at that point in time, hold-

---

[23]De Beer, *Charles Darwin*, pp. 173-74.
[24]Darwin, *Origin of Species*, chap. 10, "On the Sudden Appearance," pp. 316-17.

ing evolutionary theory was clearly showing itself as an act of faith.

So the point (contra de Beer and others) is not that the calculations of Jenkin and Kelvin were based on faulty science and that Darwin was ultimately right to keep his faith in evolution, but that Darwin had to have faith in evolution as a hypothesis to see him through when the best science of the day, whose principles he accepted, contradicted his hypothesis on the most fundamental level.

Turning now to the difficulty of intermediate species, we can see once again the presence of Darwin's faith despite the evidence. We recall the above principle that intelligence can do in a very short time what it takes chance an unfathomably long time to bring about. To eliminate acts of divine intelligence in the formation of complex living things, Darwin had to hold fast to the dictum *Natura non facit saltum*, "Nature does not make a leap." To put his assertion in context, intelligence does make leaps, creating vastly complex things by organizing a multitude of parts into a complex whole in a short amount of time. If we disallow intelligence as an active power, then nature is left only with unintelligent random variation. In Darwin's words:

> Why should not Nature take a sudden leap from structure to structure? On the theory of natural selection, we can clearly understand why she should not; for natural selection acts only by taking advantage of slight successive variations; she can never take a great a sudden leap, but must advance by short and sure, though slow steps.[25]

Since natural selection, being unintelligent, can only advance with "extreme slowness,"[26] and by "slight successive variations," then, concluded Darwin, there must have been "an infinite number of . . . fine transitional forms which, on our theory, have connected all the past and present species of the same group into one long and branching chain of life."[27] Indeed, "the number of intermediate and transitional links, between all living and extinct species, must have been inconceivably great. . . . But assuredly," he added with confidence, "if this theory be true, such have lived upon the earth."[28]

Unfortunately, there was a problem, one he was forced to recognize. "But,

---

[25]Ibid., chap. 6, "Special Difficulties," p. 184.
[26]Ibid., chap. 4, "Circumstances Favourable," p. 110.
[27]Ibid., chap. 10, "On the Absence," p. 311.
[28]Ibid., chap. 1, "Introduction," pp. 293, 295.

as by this theory innumerable transitional forms must have existed, why do we not find them embedded in countless numbers in the crust of the earth?"[29] Darwin's approach to this dilemma was a wonderful example of his faith in the evolutionary hypothesis—he shifted the blame to the fossil record, and took the shift as proof itself. "But I do not pretend that I should ever have suspected how poor was the record in the best preserved geological sections, had not the absence of innumerable transitional links between the species which lived at the commencement and close of each formation, pressed so hardly [sic] on my theory."[30]

In syllogistic form, if evolution is true, there must be innumerable transitional forms preserved as fossils; but the fossil evidence does not show innumerable transitional forms; therefore, the geological record must be imperfect. One must admit this to be a very clear example of Darwin's faith, and not a very good example of his logic. If the proof of a hypothesis is missing, then it is a dubious procedure at best to hold onto the hypothesis as if it had been proven so that another hypothesis based on the first may be offered as proof to explain why the original necessary proof did not appear. But Darwin did just that, arguing not only that the number of fossils collected was insufficient, but more important (somewhat against the geological uniformitarianism of Hutton and Lyell which had originally provided him with infinite time) that the geological record was permanently imperfect because the layers in which fossils were preserved accumulated only sporadically "so that vast intervals of time . . . elapsed between each formation."[31] He also offered the hypothesis that the sudden appearance in the fossil record of distinct species was not proof against the existence of innumerable transitional forms, but was caused by entire populations having migrated into an area, giving the illusion in the fossil evidence that they suddenly appeared fully formed.[32] Thus, to provide the full context of a quote used above, Darwin concluded, "We have no right to expect to find, in our geological formations, an infinite number of those fine transitional forms which, on our theory, have connected all the past and present species of the same group into one long and branching chain of life." But we do have a right, especially since Darwin

---

[29]Ibid., chap. 6, "On the Absence," p. 162.
[30]Ibid., chap. 10, "On the Absence," p. 311.
[31]Ibid., p. 301.
[32]Ibid., pp. 304-5.

offered only another hypothesis to explain why we do not find what, of necessity, should exist if the theory were true. We should not be asked to convert by faith alone.

An even greater need for faith in natural selection was necessary when Darwin confronted organs of extreme complexity. As Darwin rightly confessed, "If it could be demonstrated that any complex organ existed, which could not possibly have been formed by numerous, successive, slight modifications, my theory would absolutely break down."[33] Indeed, he was well aware that to claim that "the eye with all its inimitable contrivances for adjusting the focus to different distances, for admitting different amounts of light, and for the correction of spherical and chromatic aberration, could have been formed by natural selection, seems, I freely confess, absurd in the highest degree."[34] How, then, could a case for natural selection be made in the face of such complexity?

If chance were to create such complexity, we ought to find, for each particular species, the innumerable transitional forms leading up to the most complex. Further, there would have to a geometrically greater number of transitional forms for every advance toward greater complexity. The greater the complexity, the greater the number of transitional forms necessary to achieve the higher level. While Darwin admitted, "In searching for the gradations through which an organ in any species has been perfected, we ought to look exclusively to its lineal progenitors," he took refuge, as it were, in the imperfection of the fossil record. Because of the absence of transitional forms, "this is scarcely ever possible, and we are forced to look to other species and genera of the same group, that is to the collateral descendants from the same parent-form, in order to see what gradations are possible . . . [for] the state of the same organ in distinct classes may incidentally throw light on the steps by which it has been perfected."[35] Thus, rather than producing the required steps of development in a single species, Darwin believed that it proved his theory if he could find many distinct gradations of complexity in eyes in organisms as diverse as the starfish, lancelet, cuttle-fish and so on, up to the eagle.

At first, this type of argument might appear convincing—certainly it con-

---

[33]Ibid., chap. 6, "Modes of Transition," p. 175.
[34]Ibid., chap. 6, "Organs of Extreme Perfection ," p. 171.
[35]Ibid., p. 172.

vinced Darwin. But moving from distinct gradations of complexity in very different organisms to the necessity of such gradations in "lineal progenitors" is a weak argument. Showing the existence of eyes differing in complexity in distinct species does not demonstrate in any one of them, especially the most complex, that you have recreated the pathway by which natural selection has brought about extreme complexity. On intelligent design grounds, for example, it makes perfect sense for there to be a variety of types of eyes, more or less complex, as appropriate to each species. Therefore, the mere presence of the gradations in different species unconnected by descent is, at best, ambiguous evidence, fitting both evolution and intelligent design.

The most serious objection to Darwin's argument, however, he himself could not have known: since the time of Darwin, we have found that the magnitude of complexity of even the simplest eye is more complex than he conjectured for the vertebrate eye.[36] But even in his own lifetime, the complexity of the vertebrate eye so astonished him that he confided in a letter, "The eye to this day gives me a cold shudder."[37] If Darwin, through some miracle, could have seen the far, far greater complexity of the eye as we now know it, I contend that, given his intellectual integrity, he never would have published the *Origin*.

Faith was also necessary because of the very difficulty of trying to prove, according to the best canons of science, that evolution has actually occurred. Since it occurred in the past, and by definition always takes thousands if not millions of years to achieve any major evolutionary change, no one could do a simple experiment during Darwin's lifetime to demonstrate conclusively that evolution did indeed occur. Such is why, to return to our first point, Darwin had to put his argument together as hypothetical.

Finally, Darwin's faith manifested itself in regard to the very imperfection of the state of the sciences at his time. At the end of the *Origin*, Darwin made a very odd admission. Speaking of the serious objections brought against his theory, Darwin remarked, "I have felt these difficulties far too heavily during many years to doubt their weight. But it deserves especial notice that the more important objections related to questions on which we

---

[36]See the wonderful discussions in Michael Denton, *Evolution: A Theory in Crisis* (Bethesda, Md.: Adler & Adler, 1986), chap. 14; and Michael Behe, *Darwin's Black Box* (New York: Free Press, 1996), pp. 18-22.

[37]From a letter to Asa Gray. Quoted in Denton, *Evolution*, p. 326.

are confessedly ignorant; nor do we know how ignorant we are."[38] In other words, the very areas that science would have to know clearly in order to prove the theory of evolution, were the areas of which the science of Darwin's day was "confessedly ignorant." According to the *Origin*, scientists were ignorant of "the laws governing inheritance,"[39] and "variability is governed by many unknown laws, of which correlated growth is probably the most important";[40] furthermore, "it is unreasonable to expect a precise answer" to questions regarding the actual path of the evolution of any particular species "considering our ignorance of the past history of each species";[41] and finally, scientists were "profoundly ignorant . . . in regard to the normal and abnormal action of the reproductive system."[42] Yet, Darwin took the ignorance as a sign that science had not contradicted evolutionary arguments, so the confidence—the *faith*—in their explanatory power was warranted. But to quote Darwin against himself, "ignorance more frequently begets confidence than does knowledge," a gibe he used against those "who so positively assert that this or that problem will never be solved by science."[43]

Now that we have seen Darwin's faith, it is fair, given the thesis of the present book and the analysis so far, to ask, Was it the faith of Epicurus? Or to put it another way, Was Darwin's faith in the ultimate vindication of this theory a transformed version of the faith of Epicurean materialism? Again, by this I am not inquiring whether Darwin read Epicurus and Lucretius, and consciously wrote the *Origin* as a modern remake. I am asking, Do we find the same pattern of presuppositions and conclusions in Darwin as we have found in Epicurus and Lucretius, and in the modern champions of transformed Epicurean materialism? We may begin by examining the status of God.

The systematic exclusion of the divine in Darwin may not, at first, be as evident as it was in Epicurus and Lucretius. There is a good reason for this, one that is too often overlooked. Such evolutionary ideas were directly

---

[38]Darwin, *Origin of Species*, conclusion, p. 440-41.

[39]Ibid., chap. 1, "Effects of Habit," p. 36.

[40]Ibid., chap. 1, "Circumstances Favourable," p. 57.

[41]Ibid., chap. 7, "Miscellaneous Objections," p. 227.

[42]Ibid., chap. 9, "Fertility of Varieties," p. 285.

[43]Charles Darwin, *The Descent of Man, and Selection in Relation to Sex* (Princeton, N.J.: Princeton University Press, 1981), introduction, p. 3.

opposed to Christianity, and Christianity had considerable power in the sixteenth, seventeenth and eighteenth centuries. Even though the great success and consequent authority of Newtonianism allowed the necessary materialist foundation for evolutionary theory to be laid in the eighteenth century, the implications of this materialism for biology, and more particularly, for human nature, were muted until the nineteenth century, in no small part because of the fear of directly contradicting Christian doctrines about human nature, the incarnation and human redemption. Hence, a great part of the roundabout nature, the hinting and vague implications one finds in both the precursors of Darwin and in Darwin himself, were a direct result of the fear of persecution, rather than any difficulty with drawing the ultimate conclusions. Simply put, proponents of evolutionary theory were often Machiavellian in their presentation.

To begin, a certain amount of Machiavellianism pervades Darwin's *Origin*. As early as 1838 Darwin understood that his evolutionary theory applied directly to human beings, and entailed a radical transformation of the Christian belief in the special nature of human beings. On November 27 in his N Notebook (not written for the public eye) he wrote, "I will never allow that because there is a chasm between man . . . and animals that man has a different origin." A bit earlier, on August 16, he penned the following aphorism in his M Notebook (likewise not public): "He who understands baboon [sic] would do more toward metaphysics than Locke."[44] That is, to understand human nature, especially in regard to its rationality, we would learn more from an analysis of our simian ancestors about the mind than from any rarified attempts to construct metaphysical explanations. (Given what we have already argued about Locke, it is clear Darwin knew him only secondhand.)

But in his *Origin* itself, Darwin was careful to neither directly affirm nor deny the implications of his evolutionary account for human beings. Indeed, he simply did not mention the connection, except for one cryptic passage at the very end. "In the future I see open fields for far more important researches. Psychology will be securely based on the foundation already laid by Mr. Herbert Spencer, that of the necessary acquirement of each mental

---

[44]The quoted material is from John Bonner and Robert May's introduction to Darwin, *Descent of Man*, p. x.

power and capacity by gradation. Much light will be thrown on the origin of man and his history."[45]

It was not until *The Descent of Man*, published in 1871, that he dared elaborate, and the reason he offered at that point is quite interesting. "During many years I collected notes on the origin or descent of man, without any intention of publishing on the subject, but rather with the determination not to publish, *as I thought that I should thus only add to the prejudices against my views*" [emphasis added].[46] Simply put, Darwin feared that revealing the implications for human nature would invite animus against the larger theoretical framework. Of course, once the framework was established, those implications would necessarily follow, and Darwin went on to explain that he decided to make his arguments public in the *Descent* because at least a significant number of the "younger and rising naturalists" had already accepted "the agency of natural selection," and so, the war had been largely won.[47]

In his private correspondence, we also see (in the words of John Bonner and Robert May) "the divergence between private views and public pieties." And Darwin was quite clear in private as well about the reason for this divergence: "Let theory guide your observations, but till your reputation is well established be sparing in publishing theory. It makes persons doubt your observations." [48] The *whole* of evolutionary theory, then, was used by Darwin in his gathering, analysis and presentation of "a multitude of facts," but he was less than candid about the implications of evolution for human nature.

In regard to Christianity in particular, Darwin was even more circumspect, not only in public, because of the effect it would have on the acceptance of his arguments, but in private, because of the effect it would have on his devout wife. In regard to Darwin's own beliefs, the religious milieu that he inherited directly was at best Unitarian (from his one grandfather, Josiah Wedgwood, a disciple of Joseph Priestley), and at worst, a strong worship of nature seasoned with a very, very distant deity (from his more famous grandfather, Erasmus Darwin, a robust hedonist, who also bequeathed to Darwin much of the theory of evolution). Darwin's father, Robert Darwin,

---

[45]Darwin, *Origin of Species*, chap.15, "Conclusion," p. 458.

[46]Darwin, *Descent of Man*, chap 1, "Introduction," p. 1.

[47]Ibid., chap. 1, "Introduction," pp. 1-2.

[48]Ibid., editors' introduction, p. xiii.

was a closet freethinker who was concerned to have young Charles baptized properly in the Anglican church for the sake of public appearances, thereby wishing to avoid the odor of atheism that surrounded the name of Darwin through his father Erasmus. But Robert's wife, Susannah, took the children on Sundays to the Unitarian chapel.[49]

Unlike his grandfathers, Darwin himself remained quite circumspect, preferring to avoid controversy, especially about religion. But we do have his reply to a seventeen-year-old German student, W. Mengden, who, after reading the *Origin*, wrote to the aging Darwin himself. "Please tell me," the young man pleaded, "can one believe in Christ as described in the Bible?" Darwin's reply was to the point. "I am much engaged, an old man, and out of health, and I cannot spare time to answer your questions fully,—nor indeed can they be answered. Science has nothing to do with Christ, except insofar as the habit of scientific research makes a man cautious in admitting evidence. For myself, I do not believe that there ever has been any revelation. As for future life, every man must judge for himself between conflicting vague probabilities." Perhaps Darwin was moved to this rare and direct response by the situation of young Mengden, whose best friend had just died, and who therefore was "agitated" by the questions of "life after death and whether one should expect to meet others in [the] afterlife?"[50]

The difficulty in regard to the afterlife was, of course, rooted in the materialism originally designed to eliminate the immortal, immaterial soul. To my knowledge, Darwin explicitly took up the question of the soul only once in his two great works, *Origin* and *Descent*. In his concluding words in the latter, Darwin made the following ambiguous remarks, well worth quoting because of the importance of the elimination of the soul for Epicureanism.

He who believes in the advancement of man from some lowly-organized form, will naturally ask how does this bear on the belief in the immortality of the soul. The barbarous races of man . . . possess no clear belief of this kind; but arguments derived from the primeval beliefs of savages are . . . of little or no avail. Few persons feel any anxiety from the impossibility of determining at what precise period in the development of the individual, from the first trace

[49]See Adrian Desmond and James Moore, *Darwin: The Life of a Tormeneted Evolutionist* (New York: W. W. Norton, 1991), pp. 5-12.
[50]The material on Mengden and Darwin is quoted in Stanley Jaki, *The Savior of Science* (Grand Rapids, Mich.: Eerdmans, 2000), pp. 5-6.

of the minute germinal vesicle to the child either before or after birth, man becomes an immortal being; and there is no greater cause for anxiety because the period in the gradually ascending organic scale cannot possibly be determined.[51]

We should note several things. First, although Darwin seemed to be saying that we could draw no conclusions from primitive beliefs, much of his *Descent* used such beliefs to show that some trait or other in more civilized man was not natural and original, but the result of later natural selection. Therefore, reading between the lines, it would appear that Darwin would at least have us wonder whether the belief in the immortal soul is merely the result of rather late natural selection in the evolution of humankind.

Second, and more important, Darwin never answered the question, Is there an immortal soul? but instead dodged it by a counter-assertion, "If you do not know when a baby gets an immortal soul, then do not trouble yourself about when (or *if*) the human species received its immortal soul." Why is this a dodge? The classic definition of the soul given by Aristotle and taken up by St. Thomas was that the soul was the *form* of the body,[52] but since form, for Darwin, was caused by the random variations of matter as selected according to fitness, *form*, and hence *soul*, were useless concepts. Even if Darwin believed in the soul, the soul would have no function in his materialist account (as will become quite clear in our discussion of the *Descent* below).

We should also note that Darwin's nonanswer was founded on the prevailing belief, which had dominated Western thinking since the Roman empire, that the immortal soul was given to the baby in the womb at "quickening," that is, at about forty days when the woman might first feel the baby move. This was, of course, a biological error, but Darwin was disingenuous in referring to it because it depended on a *nonmaterialist* view of the divine ability to manipulate nature at will, a view that Darwin persistently and consistently rejected.

But even worse, the immortality and immateriality of the soul were, in Christian philosophy and theology as well as pre-Christian nonmaterialist philosophy, both predicated on the presence of rationality as distinct to

---

[51] Darwin, *Descent of Man*, 1.21, p. 395.
[52] Aristotle *On the Soul* 412a3-413a11.

human beings alone. Immortality and immateriality were deduced from the immaterial and eternal nature of the reasoning power itself. In the words of Aquinas, "The principle of intellectual operation which we call the soul, is a principle both incorporeal and subsistent." So that, given that it is immaterial and can subsist independently, "we must assert that the intellectual principle which we call the human soul is incorruptible."[53]

Darwin, of course, recognized that "many authors have insisted that man is separated through his mental faculties by an impassable barrier from all the lower animals,"[54] but part of his self-defined task in his *Descent* was to show that "there is no fundamental difference between man and the higher mammals in their mental faculties."[55] In regard especially to the primates he concluded, "All have the same senses, intuitions and sensations—similar passions, affections, and emotions, even the more complex ones; they feel wonder and curiosity; they possess the same faculties of imitation, attention, memory, imagination, and reason, though in very different degrees."[56]

Since none of these faculties, especially reason, were peculiar to humans, one could not argue from human rationality to the immateriality or immortality of the human soul. Darwin's dodge, therefore, was an act of self-preservation on his part; that is, to preserve his theory, he had to dodge the implications. We may conclude that the soul, on Darwin's account, was an idle concept and had no place in his system. Indeed, the very titles of his two great works, the *Origin of Species* and the *Descent of Man* both imply, albeit circumspectly, that we no longer have need of the hypothesis of the soul: the *Origin of Species* placed the origin of the unified complexity (the form) in matter, and thereby eliminated the soul; the *Descent of Man* destroyed the distinct feature, reason, which nonmaterialist philosophy understood as *the* sign of the existence of an immortal and immaterial soul in man.

It is also helpful to put Darwin's assertions in the larger context of the weakening of the authority of Christianity (through a weakening of the authority of the Bible), which we detailed in the previous chapter. In contrast to Darwin's claim that "science has nothing to do with Christ," it was the materialist prohibition of miracles that provided the strongest acid in

---

[53]Aquinas *Summa Theologiae* 1.75.2 and 6.
[54]Darwin, *Descent of Man*, 1.2, p. 49.
[55]Ibid., 1.2, p. 35.
[56]Ibid., 1.2, pp. 48-49.

dissolving biblical authority, and thereby helped prepare the West for the reception of evolutionary theory as a substitute faith. Furthermore, the undermining of the authority of Christianity affected not only the explicitly Christian doctrines (such as the Trinity, God's providence, the incarnation), but the intelligent design arguments of which Christianity was the main historical bearer. *Both* were directly opposed to Darwin's evolutionary account. The exegetical efforts of Hobbes, Spinoza, Strauss and their followers not only resulted in a direct rejection of the biblical accounts of miracles, but also reduced the authors and actors of the Bible to the sum total of their historical prejudices, peculiar passions and ill-founded beliefs (so that one could provide an account of the evolution of their beliefs, but not an account of the truth of them). Christianity appeared, at least to the rising intelligentsia, as one more ancient superstition that had outlived its usefulness in an age of materialist science. Since Christianity was the bearer of intelligent design arguments, it also appeared to the rising intelligentsia that the notion of God's creative, intelligent agency was one more folk belief, like the sky being a dome, that could safely be discarded, one more vestige of prescientific culture that had arisen out of ignorance and outlived whatever usefulness or charm it may once have had.

This sheds light on another aspect of Darwin's argument, or better, his mode of argument. Darwin insisted throughout the *Origin* on defining the only rival theory to evolution as the "theory of independent acts of creation," a kind of conflation of intelligent design and a literal reading of the creation account in Genesis. For him there were only two choices, law or miracle: either the laws of nature (ultimately reducible to the laws of motion found in Newton) "created" the multiple forms of life, or God miraculously created every single species and variation of species *ex nihilo* and placed them right where naturalists happened to find them.

What caused Darwin to define the controversy as if there were only two alternatives, law or miracle? For Newtonianism, the impersonal and self-sufficient laws of nature determine all motion, and these laws are universal in time and space. They determine everything, everywhere, in the past, present and future. Since any act by God would be a violation of these laws, *any* such act would be considered miraculous, no matter how profound or how trivial. It was this presupposition, as we have seen, that allowed Spinoza and Strauss to reduce the Bible to a rather vague set of moral commands, or, to put it the other way around, to reduce all statements in the Bible concerning nature to irrelevancy. By the time of Darwin, the vanguard of the modern revolution in scriptural scholarship had already collapsed creative acts into miraculous acts, and rejected the possibility of miraculous acts because any act by God against the laws of nature would, on materialist assumptions, be a miraculous violation of the inviolable laws.

Given this intellectual atmosphere, we may understand more clearly why Darwin characterized the alternative to the materialist generation of species by random variation as "miraculous acts of creation." In the only passage in the entire *Origin* where he mentioned his materialist foundation directly, it was in the service of parodying the opposition: "But do they really believe that at innumerable periods in the Earth's history certain elemental atoms have been commanded suddenly to flash into living tissue?"[57]

What about God? At best, in Darwin, God is relegated to an original act of creation. In the famous concluding passage to the *Origin*, Darwin waxed semipoetic:

> There is grandeur in this view of life, with its several powers, having been orig-
> inally breathed by the Creator into a few forms or into one; and that, whilst
> this planet has gone cycling on according to the fixed law of gravity, from so
> simple a beginning endless forms most beautiful and most wonderful have
> been, and are being evolved.[58]

But however grand this sentiment sounds, we see immediately that on its most charitable reading, Darwin has brought back a slightly modified Epicurean deity. However, it is even weaker than Newton's God, because Darwin disallowed any interference after the original act of creation (whereas Newton, unlike later Newtonianism, thought God must at least interfere to keep the cosmic machine from going awry).

If we examine the *Descent*, we find that belief in God has been subjected to an evolutionary analysis. "There is no evidence that man was aboriginally endowed with the ennobling belief in the existence of an Omnipotent God." If we analyze our roots, we find instead that the less civilized races have merely a "belief in unseen or spiritual agencies," a belief that (following Hobbes) most likely arose, in savages, from dreams, "for savages do not readily dis-

---

[57]Darwin, *Origin of Species*, chap. 15, "Conclusion," pp. 454, 458.
[58]Ibid., p. 459.

tinguish between subjective and objective impressions." Darwin illustrated the "tendency in savages to imagine that natural objects and agencies are animated by spiritual or living essences" by a story about his dog, which growled at an umbrella lying nearby that fluttered in the breeze—the actions of the unseen wind making the dog believe that the umbrella was an animate being "on his territory." By such inferences from ignorance, "the belief in spiritual agencies would easily pass into the belief in the existence of one or more gods," the savages attributing their own thoughts and passions to those objects they believed were animated. As for feelings of religious devotion, "a dog looks on his masters as on a god," therefore, such devotion is not of very noble origin.[59] Thus, although the "belief in God has often been advanced as not only the greatest, but the most complete of all the distinctions between man and the lower animals," Darwin concluded that "it is impossible, as we have seen, to maintain that this belief is innate or instinctive in man." Rather, "the idea of a universal and beneficent Creator of the universe does not seem to arise in the mind of man, until he has been elevated by long-continued culture."[60] Of course, on evolutionary grounds to say that a trait or instinct develops later does not make it any more or less true.

In an interesting Lucretian flourish to his analysis, Darwin noted the evils of religion, from the sacrifice of human beings to witch trials, and reminded the reader "what an infinite debt of gratitude we owe to the improvement of our reason, to science, and our accumulated knowledge." By this, of course, Darwin meant reason, science and knowledge according to the tenets of materialism. Quoting Sir J. Lubbock, who seems to be tearing a page right out of Lucretius's *De Rerum Natura*, " 'It is not too much to say that the horrible dread of unknown evil hangs like a thick cloud over savage life, and embitters every pleasure.' " To which Darwin added, "These miserable and indirect consequences of our highest faculties may be compared with the incidental and occasional mistakes of the instincts of the lower animals."[61] The acceptance of evolutionary theory, and the consequent analysis of the development of religions from primitive conditions, could go a long way in removing that "thick cloud" that "embitters every pleasure."

---

[59]Darwin, *Descent of Man*, 1.2, pp. 65-68.
[60]Ibid., 2.21, pp. 394-95.
[61]Ibid., 1.2, p. 68-69.

We have now gotten an overview of the Epicurean elements in Darwin's theoretical arguments, but as we have seen from the very first chapter, Epicurus used the theoretical arguments to undergird a materialist ethics. Darwin seemed to have gone at it the other way around; that is, Darwin drew moral conclusions in the *Descent* from his theoretical assumptions in the *Origin.* In some respects, these moral conclusions may seem closer to ancient ascetic Epicureanism than to modern Epicurean hedonism. The crowning glory of evolution, in regard to morality, was the development of the Victorian set of virtues—or so Darwin thought. But as we shall see, Darwin's hopeful conclusion was at odds with his own presuppositions, and Darwin was merely artificially imposing his own preferred virtues upon an essentially amoral process. Thus, while the virtues Darwin thought that evolution had produced have faded away with Victorian culture, his presuppositions rooted in the *Origin* have not. As a result, we have inherited moral Darwinism, the moral view that is actually consistent with the presuppositions of his theoretical foundations, and moral Darwinism is, as shall become obvious, the form that modern moral Epicurean hedonism takes.

If our analysis stopped here, then Darwin could be painted as one of the many moderns who accepted the theoretical foundations of Epicurean materialism (as applied to the origin and development of species) but was innocent of its moral consequences. Indeed, that would be our impression of Darwin if we were *only* to read the *Origin,* as so many do. But when we turn to the *Descent,* Darwin's innocence dissipates rather quickly. Contrary to the oft-repeated claim that the arguments of Darwin the scientist are historically separable from the later distortions of his theory made by the so-called social Darwinists and the eugenics movement, we find that Darwin was the first social Darwinist and also the father of the modern eugenics movement—not accidentally, in the in the sense of his being an intellectual product of his time, but essentially, in that Social Darwinism and eugenics were necessary deductions from his evolutionary premises. Furthermore, in his embrace of eugenics, Darwin manifested his indebtedness to the arguments of Machiavelli, Bacon and Hobbes in regarding human nature as essentially malleable. Leaving the construction of our nature to chance and natural selection means that we are defined ultimately by chance (i.e., *fortuna*). Eugenics, the science of artificial selection as applied to human nature, allows us to take evolution into our own hands.

To begin, we have seen that for Epicurean materialism nature is essentially amoral and that the presence of morality is one more natural phenomenon to be explained via materialism. As we may have already expected, for Darwin nature was amoral, and morality was one more phenomenon to be explained by natural selection. We must always keep this in mind: for Darwin nature did not intend to create morality, any more than nature intended to create certain species; morality was just one more effect of natural selection working on the raw material of variations in the individual.

As it comes from the same Epicurean font, Darwin's account of the genesis of human morality followed the general contours of the arguments of Lucretius and Rousseau.[62] He offered, in his words, a "natural history" of morality, that is, an evolutionary account of morality.[63] In accordance with his arguments in the *Origin*, Darwin asserted that "the intellectual and moral faculties of man" were not original and inherent, but acquired (as with everything else) through natural selection. Furthermore, "These faculties are variable; and we have every reason to believe that the variations tend to be inherited."[64]

How were they acquired? For Darwin human beings were social creatures, but their social nature itself, from which all morality eventually evolved, was acquired "through natural selection, aided by inherited habit."[65] To become moral, we first had to become social. "In order that primeval men, or the ape-like progenitors of man, should have become social, they must have acquired the same instinctive feelings which impel other animals to live in a body; and they no doubt exhibited the same general disposition."[66] As with all instincts in all animals, the "social instincts" of man were the result of variations in the individual bringing some benefit for survival, and from these social instincts the familiar set of virtues evolved. Darwin imagined the selection of such beneficial traits in the following way:

---

[62] He seemingly rejected the Hobbesian notion that our original condition was one of antagonism—even though he continually referred to the "state of nature" as a "state of war" where each individual frantically scrambles to preserve itself—and argued instead that asocial traits were eliminated through natural selection. (See ibid., 1.3, pp. 84, 90, 92.) Yet the debt Darwin owed to the Hobbesian belief in nature as a state of war is clear insofar as he considered the struggle to survive as the engine of natural selection.

[63] Ibid., 1.3, p. 71.

[64] Ibid., 1.5, p. 159.

[65] Ibid., 1.5, p. 162.

[66] Ibid., 1.5, pp. 161-62.

When two tribes of primeval man, living in the same country, came into competition, if the one tribe included . . . a greater number of courageous, sympathetic, and faithful members, who were always ready to warn each other of
danger, to aid and defend each other, this tribe would without doubt succeed
best and conquer the other. Let it be borne in mind how all-important, in the
never-ceasing wars of savages, fidelity and courage must be. . . . Selfish and
contentious people will not cohere, and without coherence nothing can be
effected. A tribe possessing the above qualities in a high degree would spread
and be victorious over other tribes; but in the course of time it would, judging
from all past history, be in its turn overcome by some other and still more
highly endowed tribe. Thus the social and moral qualities would tend slowly to
advance and be diffused throughout the world.[67]

We should not overlook in this account that the endowment of human
beings with intellectual and moral capacities would never have come about
without war, for it is only through such struggle that intellectual and moral
qualities are selected as beneficial. "Had he not been subjected to natural
selection," Darwin intoned, "assuredly he would never have attained to the
rank of manhood." In conformity with his arguments in the *Origin*, the
development of the intellectual and moral qualities that human beings happen to have could not have occurred "had not the rate of increase been rapid,
and the consequent struggle for existence [been] severe to an extreme
degree."[68]

Not only the virtues, but conscience itself must be the result of natural
selection. Darwin described it as a "feeling of dissatisfaction which invariably results . . . from any unsatisfied instinct."[69] The feeling of dissatisfaction occurs when two instincts conflict. Since the "ever-enduring social
instincts" are more primitive and hence stronger than our desire to do some
action of ours that contradicts them, we feel the stronger pull of the social
instincts whenever such conflict arises. This pull of the stronger social
instincts against a weaker desire to do some action that violates them causes
the feeling of unease we call "conscience."[70]

If this were all Darwin had said, then we might be justified in thinking that

---

[67]Ibid., 1.5, pp. 162-63.
[68]Ibid., 1.5, p. 180.
[69]Ibid., 1.3, p. 72.
[70]Ibid., 1.3, p. 91.

he had shown us the evolutionary path to the development of natural law, complete with human beings defined as social animals, who have a definite set of virtues and a regulatory conscience as well. We could even imagine social conservatives latching onto Darwin as vindicating conservative accounts of morality against liberal relativism. But Darwin had to be a thorough relativist— such were the demands of his presuppositions. The task of his natural history of morality in the *Descent* was the same as the task of his evolutionary argument in the *Origin*: to explain the existence of actual species and their particular faculties and instincts. Morality was just one more thing to be explained. Since human morality arose as an accident of natural selection, it need not have arisen in just one form—evolution gives us not *a* morality but many moralities. As with finch beaks, many variations were possible, and since varieties are incipient species, and species are incipient genera, moralities may branch off in many diverse ways, and none can be judged any better or worse than any other. As Darwin himself informed the reader, "I do not wish to maintain that any strictly social animal, if its intellectual faculties were to become as active and highly developed as in man, would acquire exactly the same moral sense as ours."[71]

> If, for instance, to take an extreme case, men were reared under precisely the same conditions as hive-bees, there can hardly be a doubt that our unmarried females would, like the worker-bees, think it a sacred duty to kill their brothers, and mothers would strive to kill their fertile daughters; and no one would think of interfering. Nevertheless the bee, or any other social animal, would in our supposed case gain, as it appears to me, some feeling of right and wrong, or a conscience. For each individual would have an inward sense of possessing certain stronger or more enduring instincts, and others less strong and enduring; so that there would often be a struggle which impulse should be followed; and satisfaction or dissatisfaction would be felt. . . . In this case an inward monitor would tell the animal that it would have been better to have followed one impulse rather than the other. The one course ought to have been followed: the one would have been right and the other wrong.[72]

The same variability holds as well within the natural history of human morality as it actually evolved. So, for example, the "murder of infants has

---

[71]Ibid., 1.3, p. 73.
[72]Ibid., 1.3, pp. 73-74.

prevailed on the largest scale throughout the world, and has met with no reproach" and "infanticide, especially of females, has been thought to be good for the tribe, or at least not injurious."[73] As for suicide, in "former times" it was "not generally considered as a crime, but rather from the courage displayed as an honourable act; and it is still largely practiced by some semi-civilized nations without reproach, for the loss to a nation of a single individual is not felt."[74] In regard to both infanticide and suicide, the acts did not directly contradict the "ever-enduring social instincts" and so did not cause any "feeling of dissatisfaction which invariably results . . . from any unsatisfied instinct."

Even sympathy, which Darwin (following Rousseau as mediated through Adam Smith) considered the "all-important emotion" arising from our primitive social instincts, did not necessarily have to form a part of morality, for "animals sometimes are far from feeling any sympathy . . . for they will expel a wounded animal from the herd, or gore or worry it to death." While Darwin lamented such as "almost the blackest fact in natural history," yet he hastened to add that "their instinct or reason leads them to expel an injured companion, lest beasts of prey, including man, should be tempted to follow the troop." Natural selection, therefore, sometimes favored those animals that harry their sick and injured, for those that do not are soon weeded out by predators. And so, Darwin concluded, the conduct of such animals, even though it contradicted sympathy, made perfect sense in terms of the survival of the fittest, and "is not much worse than that of the North American Indians who leave their feeble comrades to perish on the plains, or the Feegeans [sic], who, when their parents get old or fall ill, bury them alive."[75]

But as we have hinted above, Darwin hoped to give some goal to moral evolution. In seeming contradiction to the amoral underpinnings of natural selection, he apparently could not resist asserting that "disinterested love for all living creatures" where sympathy is extended "beyond the confines of man . . . to the lower animals," is "the most noble attribute of man," and "seems to arise incidentally from our sympathies becoming more tender and more widely diffused, until they are extended to all sentient beings."[76] (Darwin even asserted

---

[73]Ibid., 1.3, p. 94.
[74]Ibid.
[75]Ibid., 1.3, pp. 76-77.
[76]Ibid., 1.3, p. 101.

that Christ's Golden Rule was reached, not by revelation, but natural selection.[77]) At the very pinnacle of moral "progress," as measured by the extension
of sympathy, are the "Western nations of Europe, who now so immeasurably
surpass their former savage progenitors and stand at the summit of civilization."[78] Darwin took his analysis as vindicating the typically nineteenth-century
view of progress, "the cheerful view that progress has been much more general
than retrogression; that man has risen, though by slow and interrupted steps,
from a lowly condition to the highest standard as yet attained by him in knowledge, morals, and religion."[79] The following words, written a little over a quarter century before World War I and three quarters of a century before World
War II, strike us, in their optimism, as both tragic and foolhardy.

> Looking to future generations, there is no cause to fear that the social
> instincts will grow weaker, and we may expect that virtuous habits will grow
> stronger, becoming perhaps fixed by inheritance. In this case the struggle
> between our higher and lower impulses will be less severe, and virtue will be
> triumphant.[80]

Darwin had in mind, of course, the kind of virtues with which he was
quite familiar, those which he believed had been reached by the "Western
nations of Europe." But hidden within these words, there was a gathering
darkness that was to envelop the supposedly superior West in the first half of
the twentieth century. To this we must now turn.

For Darwin the human intellectual and moral capacities were both variable and heritable. As a consequence, not only would different races express
different capacities, but it should be possible to breed for these capacities.
We see in animals that "in regard to mental qualities, their transmission is
manifest in our dogs, horses, and other domestic animals. Besides special
tastes and habits, general intelligence, courage, bad and good temper, &c.,
are certainly transmitted. With man we see similar facts in almost every
family."[81] As said above, Darwin concluded that "we have every reason to
believe [in regard to the intellectual and moral faculties of man] that the
variations tend to be inherited." Given all this, gradations of intellectual and

---

[77]Ibid., 1.3, p. 106; 1.5, p. 165.
[78]Ibid., 1.5, p. 178.
[79]Ibid., p. 184.
[80]Ibid., 1.3, p. 104.
[81]Ibid., 1.4, p. 110.

moral capacities would be found both between human races and also within any one race.

In regard to the different races, Darwin spent quite a bit of effort in the *Descent* trying to determine whether human *races* were actually distinct *species*. "Some of these, for instance the Negro and European, are so distinct that, if specimens had been brought to a naturalist without any further information, they would undoubtedly have been considered by him as good and true species."[82] Darwin was unsure whether to rank the races "as species or sub-species" but finally asserted that "the latter term appears the most appropriate."[83] It mattered little, for as Darwin had argued in the *Origin*, every sub-species, or variety, was an incipient species, and every species was an incipient genus, and so on, so that what we call "human being" was really a gradation in the midst of continual variation and selection. Therefore, as with all use of "species" for Darwin, "human being" as a species designation would be "arbitrarily given, for the sake of convenience."

Such reasoning allowed Darwin to rank the races. Because natural selection must be the cause of different races, and intellectual and moral capacities were inherited as part of selection, Darwin argued that different races would have different intellectual and moral characteristics. So that, for example, the "American aborigines, Negroes and Europeans differ as much from each other in mind as any three races that can be named."[84]

> The races differ also in constitution, in acclimatization, and in liability to certain diseases. Their mental characteristics are likewise very distinct; chiefly as it would appear in the emotional, but partly in their intellectual faculties. Every one who has had the opportunity of comparison, must have been struck with the contrast between the taciturn, even morose, aborigines of S. America and the lighthearted, talkative Negroes.[85]

Even more interesting, because the races are to one another like varieties, they represent the gradations of transitional, or intermediate, forms. Since Darwin insisted in the *Origin* that "natural selection is daily and hourly

---

[82]Ibid., 2.21, p. 388.

[83]Ibid., 1.7, p. 235.

[84]Ibid., p. 232. Darwin then remarked how strange it was that Fuegians and a "full-blooded Negro" whom he met were so similar to Europeans in character and mind. For natural law, since all human beings share one essence, such is not strange, but demanded.

[85]Ibid., p. 216.

scrutinizing, throughout the world, the slightest variations; rejecting those that are bad, preserving and adding up all that are good; silently and insensibly working, *whenever and wherever opportunity offers*, at the improvement of each organic being in relation to its organic and inorganic conditions of life,"[86] the races, of necessity, would have to undergo the same type of selection and extinction, in relationship to each other, that causes in all animals the extinction of intermediate forms. This argument is essential to his theoretical account of natural selection in the *Origin*:

> The forms which stand in closest competition with those undergoing modification and improvement will naturally suffer most. And . . . it is the most closely-allied forms,—varieties of the same species, and species of the same genus or of related genera,—which, from having nearly the same structure, constitution, and habits, generally come into the severest competition with each other; consequently, each new variety of species, during the progress of its formation, will generally press hardest on its nearest kindred, and tend to exterminate them.[87]

This argument—which, by the way, was part of Darwin's attempt to explain the lack of innumerable transitional species existing both in the present and in the fossil record—translated directly to his assessment of the evolutionary history of human races.

> At some future period, not very distant as measured by centuries, the civilized races of man will almost certainly exterminate and replace throughout the world the savage races. At the same time the anthropomorphous apes [that is, the ones which look most like the savages in structure] . . . will no doubt be exterminated. The break will then be rendered wider, for it will intervene between man in a more civilized state, as we may hope . . . the Caucasian, and some ape as low as a baboon, instead of as at present between the negro or Australian and the gorilla.[88]

The European race, following the inevitable laws of natural selection, will emerge as the distinct species, human being, and all the transitional forms—such as the gorilla, chimpanzee, Negro, Australian aborigine and so on—will be extinct.

---

[86]Darwin, *Origin of Species*, chap. 4, "Natural Selection," pp. 91-92.
[87]Ibid., chap. 1, "Extinction Caused," p. 112.
[88]Darwin, *Descent of Man*, 1.6, p. 201.

And we must remember that natural selection works not only between but within races. Here, following Rousseau, Darwin maintained that savage man has an advantage over civilized man. In savage man the intellectual and moral qualities are not as developed, so they have neither the benefits of modern medicine nor the strong instinctual pull of sympathy. But such lack actually works to weed out the unfit: "With savages, the weak in body or mind are soon eliminated; and those that survive commonly exhibit a vigorous state of health."[89] Unfortunately, the very development of the intellectual and moral qualities that Darwin thought served to mark the Europeans as more civilized, also worked against the principle of survival of the fittest.

> We civilized men, on the other hand, do our utmost to check the process of elimination; we build asylums for the imbecile, the maimed, and the sick; we institute poor-laws; and our medical men exert their utmost skill to save the life of every one to the last moment. There is reason to believe that vaccination has preserved thousands, who from a weak constitution would formerly have succumbed to small-pox. Thus the weak members of civilized societies propagate their kind. No one who has attended to the breeding of domestic animals will doubt that this must be highly injurious to the race of man. It is surprising how soon a want of care, or care wrongly directed, leads to the degeneration of a domestic race; but excepting in the case of man himself, hardly any one is so ignorant as to allow his worst animals to breed.[90]

Yet, however tempting it might have been for Darwin to yield to a more calculated approach to human breeding, he backed off. Why? It seemed that the evolutionary development of sympathy was worth the cost, so to speak. We could not "check our sympathy, if urged by hard reason, without deterioration in the noblest part of our nature. . . . Hence we must bear without complaining the undoubtedly bad effects of the weak surviving and propagating their kind." But, "there appears to be at least one check . . . namely the weaker and inferior members of society not marrying so freely as the sound; and this check might be indefinitely increased, though it is more to be hoped for than expected, by the weak in body or mind refraining from marriage."[91]

---

[89]Ibid., 1.5, p. 168.
[90]Ibid.
[91]Ibid., pp. 168-69.

We shall come back to that suggestion. At this point, we must note that Darwin was deadly serious about the need to take selection into our own hands. While he was optimistic about evolutionary progress—viewing with pride "the Western nations of Europe, who now so immeasurably surpass their former savage progenitors and stand at the summit of civilization"—he was by no means convinced that evolutionary development was *necessarily* progressive. If we "do not prevent the reckless, the vicious and otherwise inferior members of society from increasing at a quicker rate than the better class of men, the nation will retrograde, as has occurred too often in the history of the world." (Interesting in regard to the treatment of the Irish by the English, Darwin quoted with approval a "Mr. Greg" who complained that the "careless, squalid, unaspiring Irishman multiplies like rabbits" while "the frugal, foreseeing, self-respecting, ambitious Scot . . . marries late, and leaves few behind him.")[92] "We must remember," Darwin warned the reader, "that progress is no invariable rule. . . . We can only say that it depends on an increase in the actual number of the population, on the number of men endowed with high intellectual and moral faculties, as well as on their standard of excellence."[93]

What, then, can be done to save the European race from slipping back down the slope of evolution? The *Descent* ended with a call to arms, as it were, a call that summarized his whole moral argument. We human beings must take natural selection into our own hands. To echo both Machiavelli and Bacon, we must no longer allow chance, or *fortuna*, to govern selection. We must exercise the same care for the human species as we exercise over our domestic animals breeds. Darwin concluded the *Descent* where the *Origin* had begun, with domestic breeding. As he stated in the *Origin:*

> When a race of plants is once pretty well established, the seed-raisers do not pick out the best plants, but merely go over their seed-beds, and pull up the "rogues," as they call the plants that deviate from the proper standard. With animals this kind of selection is, in fact, likewise followed; for hardly any one is so careless as to breed from his worst animals.[94]

In the finale of the *Descent* we hear, "Man scans with scrupulous care the

---

[92]Ibid., p. 174.
[93]Ibid., p. 177.
[94]Darwin, *Origin of Species*, chap. 1, "Principles of Selection," p. 49.

character and pedigree of his horses, cattle, and dogs before he matches them; but when he comes to his own marriage he rarely, or never, takes such care." What can be done? Again, "Both sexes ought to refrain from marriage if in any marked degree inferior in body or mind; but such hopes are Utopian and will never be even partially realized until the laws of inheritance are thoroughly known." Then Darwin made a most damning remark: "All do good service who aid towards this end."[95]

But as we have noted, Darwin hesitated to override the developed characteristic of sympathy—or, if we recall his hesitation in regard to Christianity, perhaps he simply could not state his real views openly. In either case, he only hinted at a solution. Recalling the foundational principles of evolution, he reminded the reader, "Man, like every other animal, has no doubt advanced to his present high condition through a struggle for existence consequent on his rapid multiplication; and if he is to advance still higher he must remain subject to a severe struggle."

> Otherwise he would soon sink into indolence, and the more highly-gifted men would not be more successful in the battle of life than the less gifted. Hence our natural rate of increase, though leading to many and obvious evils, must not be greatly diminished by any means. There should be open competition for all men; and the most able should not be prevented by laws or customs from succeeding best and rearing the largest number of offspring.[96]

Of course, Darwin was making a veiled reference to the deleterious laws and customs that made marriage monogamous, all of which came from Christianity. Darwin married only one woman, Emma Wedgwood, but he did have ten children, not all of whom lived. The irony, however, is that Darwin himself, rather than being robust, was so sickly that he had to curtail all activities severely to ensure that he was not too taxed to squeeze out a few precious hours of research and writing each day. His children seemed to have inherited his weak constitution, one girl dying shortly after birth, another in childhood, another at age two, yet another suffering a complete breakdown at fifteen, and three of the boys being so continually sick that Darwin considered them semi-invalids.[97]

---

[95] Darwin, *Descent of Man*, 2.21, pp. 402-3.
[96] Ibid., p. 403.
[97] Gertrude Himmelfarb, *Darwin and the Darwinian Revolution* (Chicago: Ivan R. Dee, 1996), pp. 130-37.

Now that we have examined Darwin himself and established both that his theoretical arguments were rooted in the Epicurean materialism that permeated the intellectual culture of the nineteenth century, and that his moral arguments were consistently drawn from his theoretical presuppositions, we may now simply adopt the modern name for the ancient and call the whole edifice moral Darwinism. This might seem odd, given that in Darwin himself, the moral aspects were derived from the theoretical arguments. But as stated before, since Darwin's theoretical arguments were not proven, but were made by him as an act of faith, the force that kept his hypothesis about evolution from crumbling under the various attacks it suffered after first being put forward were not entirely the result of the promising nature of the evolutionary hypothesis itself. Just as with Epicurus himself, the moral implications became desirable in and of themselves, and helped to cement the theory firmly in place as if it had actually been established. This is far more true of Darwin's followers than of Darwin himself, and accounts for much of the intransigence to criticism of evolutionary theory after Darwin. That is a strong claim, and we shall wait until the next chapter to illustrate it.

How We Became Hedonists

A s we have seen, moral Darwinism is the result of the acceptance of the tenets of Epicurean materialism as modified to create modern Epicurean hedonism. Consequently, moral Darwinism is larger than "mere" Darwin-ism. The reason for this should be obvious. To refer again to the great law of uniformity, Darwin's arguments were not put forward in theoretical isolation from a larger cosmological and moral framework. Such should be obvious from looking at how easily Darwinism fit into the already strong current of materialism flowing through the nineteenth century. Further, as we have seen from our analysis of his *The Descent of Man*, Darwin himself realized that (to quote one-half of our law) "every distinct view of the universe, every theory about nature, necessarily entails a view of morality." But that is not to say that Darwin himself drew all the necessary conclusions in regard to morality—far from it. Although what he did draw in regard to eugenics was ghastly enough, we need to look at the full implications of moral Darwinism, as drawn by others, to get a full picture of what it entails. We have already seen some of these implications in Hobbes, Locke and Rousseau, all of whom were working within the framework of Epicurean materialism. This chapter examines these implications as they were manifested in the latter half of the nineteenth century and the first half of the twentieth (with one brief foray into the late twentieth century). The last chapter examines the contemporary moral scene, encompassing the last fifty years.

There are many worthy studies of philosophy and culture in the nineteenth and twentieth centuries, covering all the famous names of movements and thinkers—Immanuel Kant, Georg Wilhelm Hegel and German idealism, John Stuart Mill and utilitarianism, Marx and Marxism, Sigmund Freud, Friedrich Nietzsche and nihilism, Jean-Paul Sartre and on and on. I have spent two decades studying this era and realize as well as anyone that attempts at providing an overview of it all would be a hopeless task. All of these thinkers share the common task of making sense out of a world that has been defined by materialism, but part company in choosing the best mode of dealing with the results. Most are openly hostile to Christianity, a few try to remake Christianity from the roots up to fit the new cosmological order. For almost all, if not all, whether they regard the notions of an immortal soul and an afterlife as quaint or pernicious, the soul, heaven and hell are all considered products of immature minds, to be discarded along with geocentricism and the folk belief in the intrinsic purposefulness of nature. These common roots, immediately recognizable to the reader as Epicurean in origin, yield all manner of strange branches too complex, too tangled to sort in a mere chapter.

Instead, I have chosen to examine the lives and arguments of three less renowned but, in many respects, far more influential figures—more influential in that they directly carry the message of moral Darwinism to the masses. These figures are all the more illuminating because it is quite clear, especially in the latter two, that the way of life they desired was the force driving their use of science. That is, it is clear that they matched Epicurus's original disposition, desiring to vindicate their way of life by an appeal to materialism, especially as focused on Darwinism. It will also be quite clear that, just as with Epicureanism, their moral Darwinism was directly opposed to Christianity. The figures I have chosen—and there are more than a hundred who could have been chosen—are the great German zoologist and proponent of Darwinism, Ernst Haeckel; the social reformer and founder of Planned Parenthood, Margaret Sanger; and the eminent founder of the modern study of sex, Alfred Kinsey. Haeckel gives us moral Darwinism purified of all sentiment. Sanger and Kinsey make it quite clear how moral Darwinism yielded sexual hedonism.

The following passage should sound familiar and quite at home in moral Darwinism now that we have seen its like in the *Descent*:

> Though the great differences in the mental life and the civilization of the higher and lower races of men are generally known, they are, as a rule, under-valued, and so the value of life at different levels is falsely estimated. . . . [The] lower races (such as the Veddahs or Australian Negroes) are psychologically nearer to the mammals (apes and dogs) than to civilized Europeans; we must, therefore, assign a totally different value to their lives. . . . The gulf between [the] thoughtful mind of civilized man and the thoughtless animal soul of the savage is enormous—greater than the gulf that separates the latter from the soul of the dog.[1]

Ernst Haeckel (1834-1919), to whom this quote belongs, and whom Darwin greatly admired as is clear by the number of references made to his work in the *Descent*, was one of the most brilliant and influential zoologists of the latter half of the nineteenth century.

Haeckel was a convert to Darwinism. Darwin's *The Origin of Species* was first translated into German in 1860 and Haeckel read it that summer. In his own words, when he read Darwin the "scales fell from my eyes," for he "found in Darwin's great unified conception of nature and in his overwhelming foundation for the doctrine of evolution the solution of all the doubts which had bothered me since the beginning of my biological studies."[2] Haeckel saw evolutionary theory in its proper light, as part of an overall cosmology, and made of it a kind of materialist religion which he called "Monism," a term meant to contrast with the "Dualism" of spirit and matter. "By the Theory of Descent," Haeckel proclaimed, "we are for the first time enabled to conceive of the unity of nature" so that we may have "a mechanico-causal explanation of even the most intricate organic phenomena," the result being that "the distinction between animate and inanimate bodies does *not* exist." All natural phenomena, whether "a stone . . . thrown into the air," or "sulphur and quicksilver" uniting "in forming cinnabar," are "neither more nor less a mechanical manifestation of life than the growth

[1]Ernst Haeckel, *The Wonders of Life: A Popular Study of Biological Philosophy*, trans. Joseph McCabe (New York: Harper & Brothers, 1905), pp. 390-91. See also Daniel Gasman's excellent *The Scientific Origins of National Socialism: Social Darwinism in Ernst Haeckel and the German Monist League* (London: MacDonald, 1971), pp. 39-40.

[2]Quoted in Gasman, *Scientific Origins*, p. 6.

and flowering of plants, than the propagation of animals or the activity of their senses, than the perception or the formation of thought in man."[3]

As professor of zoology at the University of Jena, he was a tireless promoter of Darwinism, not only the descriptive biological theory, but also the proscriptive agenda in Darwin's *Descent*. An essential element of monism, as ultimately rooted in Epicurean materialism, was the acidic rejection of religion, especially Christianity. What was muted in Darwin, becomes trumpeted in Haeckel. In the first place, Haeckel believed that materialist science had completely undermined Christianity's foundations. In his *Wonders of Life* Haeckel attacked Christianity's Apostles' Creed line by line. As for "God the Father Almighty, Creator of heaven and earth," Haeckel asserted that "the modern science of evolution has shown that there never was any such creation, but that the universe is eternal and the law of substance all-ruling." Moving to the second article of the creed on Jesus Christ, Haeckel followed the likes of D. F. Strauss, arguing that "the myth of the conception and birth of Jesus Christ is mere fiction, and is at the same stage of superstition as a hundred other myths of other religions. . . . The curious adventures of Christ after his death, the descent into hell, resurrection, and ascension, are also fantastic myths due to the narrow geocentric ideas of an uneducated people." Of the final article of the creed dealing with, among other things, the resurrection, Haeckel stated that "its roots were destroyed when Copernicus refuted the geocentric theory in 1545; and athanatism [the belief in immortality] became quite untenable when Darwin shattered the dogma of anthropocentricism."[4]

To focus on this last important point, Haeckel maintained that the existence of the immortal, immaterial soul must be rejected, for the "doctrine of the *personal* immortality of man has, indeed, been absolutely refuted for more than a half a century by the great progress in our knowledge of comparative physiology and ontogeny, of comparative psychology and psychiatry." In contrast to those who still believed that "some part, at least, or our mental life" might be "traceable to the activity of an immaterial soul," Haeckel pointed out that the advance of science had shown that it is "utterly senseless now to speak of the immortality of the human person, when we know that this person,

---

[3]Ernst Haeckel, *The History of Creation*, trans. E. Ray Lankester (New York: D. Appleton, 1901), 1.23.
[4]Haeckel, *Wonders of Life,* pp. 63-64.

with all its individual qualities of body and mind, has arisen from the act of fertilization." And so Haeckel concluded that "the human person, like every other many-celled individual, is but a passing phenomenon of organic life. With its death the series of its vital activities ceases entirely, just as it began with the act of fertilization."[5]

Ironically, a great part of Haeckel's proof rested on his many famous diagrams comparing the embryos of various species to that of a human being, of which Haeckel boasted, "The facts of embryology alone would be sufficient to solve the question of man's position in nature, which is the highest of all problems."[6] But Haeckel's drawings were fraudulent; actual embryos show enormous dissimilarities, as Haeckel himself was forced to admit by his scientific colleagues.[7] Unfortunately, the confession was lost, and generations of biology students have been studying the diagrams as reproduced in biology texts for a century. But with Haeckel the materialist faith that evolution must be true, and hence that the materialism underlying it must also be true, brought him to falsify the evidence when it did not fit. And this fictitious evidence helped to convince Haeckel himself, and generations of biology students, that evolutionary theory had solved "the question of man's position in nature."

But the soul was not just a theoretical impossibility for Haeckel; it was a practical obstacle to evolutionary progress. For Haeckel and the monists, the acceptance of Christianity brought with it the erroneous belief that each individual of the human species had an immaterial soul, and that belief, in turn, brought about the protection of the biologically unfit. For Haeckel this insidious belief in an immortal soul caused the weak to be artificially selected by protecting them from the rigors of natural selection. Haeckel complained that such artificial selection "practiced in our civilized states sufficiently explains the sad fact that, in reality, weakness of the body and character are on the perpetual increase among civilized nations, and that, together with strong, healthy bodies, free and independent spirits are becoming more and more scarce."[8]

---

[5]Haeckel, *History of Creation*, 1.341-42.

[6]Ibid., 1.334. The diagrams are on the following two pages.

[7]See Elizabeth Pennisi, "Haeckel's Embryos: Fraud Rediscovered," *Science* 277 (1997): 1435, and the excellent treatment in Jonathan Wells, *Icons of Evolution* (Washington, D.C.: Regnery, 2000), chap. 5.

[8]Quoted in Gasman, *Scientific Origins*, p. 36.

But there could be beneficial artificial selection. Haeckel praised "the remarkable instance of *artificial* selection in man . . . furnished by the ancient Spartans, among whom, in obedience to a special law, all newly-born children were subject to a careful examination and selection. All those that were weak, sickly, or affected with any bodily infirmity, were killed." As a happy result, "only the perfectly healthy and strong children were allowed to live, and they alone afterwards propagated the race."[9] While such selection in regard to the body was important, Haeckel argued that the "struggle for life will ever become more and more of an intellectual struggle," for the "organ which, above all others, in man becomes more perfect by the ennobling influence of natural selection, is the *brain*."[10] Of course, that meant that one had to be ever on guard against the biological degradation of this physical instrument as well.

To those who took issue with his eugenic views, Haeckel responded, "What good does it do to humanity to maintain artificially and rear the thousands of cripples, deaf-mutes, idiots, etc., who are born every year with an hereditary burden of incurable disease?" The opposition of Christianity was not a legitimate obstacle to evolutionary eugenics. "It is no use to reply that Christianity forbids it." Criticizing Darwin indirectly for irrationally holding to the vestiges of Christianity, Haeckel asserted such opposition "is only due to sentiment and the power of conventional morality—that is to say, to the hereditary bias which is clothed in early youth with the mantle of religion, however irrational and superstitious be its foundation. Pious morality of this sort is often really the deepest immorality." Contrary to Darwin's praise of the evolution of sentiment, Haeckel declared that "sentiment should never be allowed to usurp the place of reason in these weighty ethical questions."[11]

The monists, with Haeckel at the forefront, were not only concerned about the physical and intellectual decay of the race, but also the moral decay. In agreement with Darwin, "immoral" qualities were likewise genetic malformations and could be removed by artificial selection.[12] Haeckel therefore welcomed "capital punishment . . . as an artificial process of selection."

---

[9]Haeckel, *History of Creation*, 1.175-76.
[10]Ibid., 1.178-79.
[11]Ibid., 1.119-20.
[12]Charles Darwin, *The Descent of Man, and Selection in Relation to Sex* (Princeton, N.J.: Princeton University Press, 1981), 1.3, p. 92.

In the same way as by careful rooting out of weeds ["rogues" as Darwin called them], light, air, and ground is gained for good and useful plants, in like manner, by the *indiscriminate* [emphasis added] destruction of all incorrigible criminals, not only would the struggle for life among the better portion of mankind be made easier, but also an advantageous artificial process of selection would be set in practice, since the possibility of transmitting their injurious qualities by inheritance would be taken from those degenerate outcasts.[13]

Try as we might, there is no way to divorce Haeckel's arguments either from the earlier arguments of Darwin, or from those arguments and actions later made famous in Nazi Germany. We have already seen almost the exact same arguments made by Darwin in the *Descent*, the only difference being that Haeckel seems to have been less endowed by evolution with sympathy. As for the Nazis, the trail leading back to Haeckel is too well marked to deny. Haeckel's books were enormously popular in Germany—selling hundreds of thousands—and his first-class status as a zoologist only added to the authority of his eugenic arguments in the popular mind.[14] His eugenic arguments made for the seamless acceptance of the Nazi eugenic program, and, in particular, Wilhelm Bölsche, a disciple and biographer of Haeckel, provided Hitler himself with "direct access to major ideas of Haeckelian social Darwinism"[15] with his own popularized account of Haeckel's arguments. Further, as Robert Lifton has pointed out, "Haeckel was a constantly cited authority for the *Archiv für Rassen- und Gesellschaftsbiologie* (*Archive of Racial and Social Biology*), which was published from 1904 until 1944, and became a chief organ for the dissemination of eugenics ideas and Nazi pseudo science."[16] In Daniel Gasman's words, "Hitler's views on history, politics, religion, Christianity, nature, eugenics, science, art, and evolution, however eclectic, and despite the plurality of their sources, coincide for the most part with those of Haeckel and are more than occasionally expressed in very much the same language."[17]

But Haeckel was ahead of his time in other areas of morality as well, and again, his moral positions were in harmony with Epicureanism but at com-

---

[13]Haeckel, *History of Creation*, 1.178.
[14]On the popularity of Haeckel's books in Germany see Gasman, *Scientific Origins*, p. 14.
[15]Gasman, *Scientific Origins*, p. 160.
[16]Robert Jay Lifton, *The Nazi Doctors* (New York: Basic Books, 1986), p. 441, footnote.
[17]Gasman, *Scientific Origins*, p. 161.

plete odds with Christianity. In regard to suicide and euthanasia Haeckel asserted that we are purely biological beings, who have our "personal existence" not because of "the favor of the Almighty" but simply as a consequence of "the sexual love of one's earthly parents"; thus, we may exit this life when it becomes too burdensome.

> If, then, the circumstances of life come to press too hard on the poor being who has thus developed, without any fault of his, from the fertilized ovum—if, instead of the hoped-for good, there come only care and need, sickness and misery of every kind—he has the unquestionable right to put an end to his sufferings by death. . . . The voluntary death by which a man puts an end to intolerable suffering is really an act of redemption. . . . No feeling man who has any real "Christian love of his neighbor" will grudge his suffering brother the eternal rest and the freedom from pain which he has obtained by his self-redemption.[18]

True to his larger eugenic views, Haeckel was an advocate not only of voluntary euthanasia, but involuntary euthanasia as well, expressing outrage that "hundreds and thousands of incurables—lunatics, lepers, people with cancer, etc.—are artificially kept alive . . . without the slightest profit to themselves or the general body." Again the problem was not only misguided sympathy (misguided by Christianity, that is), but also the very advance of medical science itself, for "the progress of medical science, although still little able to cure diseases, yet possesses and practices more than it used to do the art of prolonging life during lingering, chronic diseases of many years."[19]

Again, Haeckel's views were quite influential. His books not only sold hundreds of thousands of copies in Germany but were translated into twenty-five languages. In Germany, while the first public espousal of euthanasia as such came in the 1890s with Adolph Jost, it was Haeckel's Monist League journal *Das monistische Jahrhundert* that published in 1913 the first sustained arguments supporting euthanasia, and thereby helped pave the way for the even more influential euthanasia tract (using the same arguments) written by Karl Binding and Alfred Hoche, entitled "Permission for the Destruction of Life

---

[18]Haeckel, *Wonders of Life*, pp. 112-14.
[19]Quoted in Hugh Gallagher, *By Trust Betrayed: Patients, Physicians, and the License to Kill in the Third Reich*, rev. ed. (Arlington, Va.: Vandamere, 1995), p. 56.

Unworthy of Life" (1920).[20] This tract, in turn, facilitated the easy acceptance of the Nazi euthanasia program Aktion T-4, which at five locations in
Germany dispatched from 120,000 to 275,000 mental patients, physically
disabled persons, incurables and other undesirables.[21] These patients were
not killed in cold blood by sadistic members of the SS, but by a vast and complex network of very ordinary doctors and nurses, filling out minutely detailed
forms in triplicate, generally doing their best to treat patients to be eutha-
nized with the utmost concern and gentleness—all in the name of compassion. As with many of the euthanasia programs being floated today, there
were many layers of checks and double-checks, an immense bureaucracy of
careful compassion, to ensure that no one who was curable or who still had a
reasonable prospect for a pleasant existence would be inadvertently terminated.[22] But, alas, even the most careful boundaries somehow proved perme-
able to excess compassion. In 1943, for example, Hadamar, one of the five
killing stations, began to euthanize children as well, not merely the disabled
or retarded, but members of asylums, juvenile homes and orphanages as well.
Of course, troublemakers were included, as were children of mixed races, and
even those with significant childhood acne.[23]

In regard to abortion, we find Haeckel at the forefront of moral Darwinism as well. "It is said to be a great merit of canon law," Haeckel remarked
sarcastically, "that it was the first to extend legal protection to the human
embryo, and punished abortion with death as a mortal sin."[24] From canon
law, such prohibitions passed into civil law.

> But while civil law thus takes its inspiration from canon law, it overlooks the
> physiological fact that the ovum is *part of the mother's body over which she has
> full right of control* [emphasis added] and that the embryo that develops from
> it, as well as the new-born child, is quite unconscious, or is a purely "reflex
> machine," like any other vertebrate. There is no mind in it as yet; it only
> appears after the first year, when its organ, the phronema in the cortex, is dif-
> ferentiated.[25]

---

[20]Michael Burleigh, *Death and Deliverance: "Euthanasia" in Germany c. 1900-1945* (Cambridge:
Cambridge University Press, 1994), pp. 12.
[21]Gallagher, *By Trust Betrayed*, p. 86.
[22]Ibid., pp. 25-42.
[23]Ibid., p. 9.
[24]Haeckel, *Wonders of Life*, p. 325.
[25]Ibid., p. 326.

For Haeckel, since the distinguishing moral characteristic, the mind, "only develops, slowly and gradually, long after birth," human beings were indistinguishable from the mother in the womb and from other animals outside the womb. We become distinct as human beings only when "rational consciousness" reveals itself "for the first time (after the first year) at the moment when the child speaks of itself, not in the third person, but as 'I.'" Again, the "erroneous and untenable" view that a conceived individual is fully human "came mostly from the canon law of the Catholic Church," a view that Haeckel called "'extravagant' nonsense."[26] Therefore, abortion laws founded on such nonsense were obviously irrational and unscientific.

Abortion and euthanasia were, then, for Haeckel, logical extensions of eugenics. Abortion, along with infanticide, cleaned up the undesirables at the beginning of life; euthanasia eliminated those who avoided the initial biological cleansing or who developed incurable biological problems later.

Three things should be quite clear from our analysis of Haeckel. First, *everything* that Haeckel advocated has either already been accepted (as in abortion), is on the verge of being accepted (as in infanticide) or is being reintroduced in a disguised or modified form (as in the rehabilitation of the pre-World War II eugenics movement in the guise of genetic screening; abortion on demand to eliminate the deformed, the retarded and the otherwise defective or potentially defective; and now cloning to create nondefectives). Second, Haeckel's arguments came straight from Darwin and were modified in the direction of an even more coherent fit with the larger materialist cosmological framework. Finally, Haeckel's arguments reveal the ancient, implacable animosity between the moral arguments of Epicureanism and the moral arguments of Christianity. If the culture wars started in the '60s, pitting the morality of the Christians against the "new" morality, it was the 1860s not the 1960s that provided the watershed.

We now turn to the social reformer Margaret Sanger. As founder of Planned Parenthood, she was the architect of one of the most influential, powerful and well-funded international organizations for the promotion of modern Epicurean hedonism. Planned Parenthood is a multimillion-dollar agent of change, receiving millions not only from the federal government, but from corporations and individuals as well. Not only is it the largest promoter and pro-

---

[26]Ibid., pp. 323-26.

vider of abortion, but by its continual educational, legislative and judicial advocacy, it has been at the very core of the sexual and larger moral transformation of the latter half of the twentieth century.

It might seem out of place here to examine Margaret Sanger, for she is generally presented in quite a favorable light and certainly seems to have no connection to Darwin and moral Darwinism. But let her own words bear testimony:

> In the early history of the race, so-called "natural law" [i.e., natural selection] reigned undisturbed. Under its pitiless and unsympathetic iron rule, only the strongest, most courageous could live and become progenitors of the race. The weak died early or were killed. Today, however, civilization has brought sympathy, pity, tenderness and other lofty and worthy sentiments, which interfere with the law of natural selection. We are now in a state where our charities, our compensation acts, our pensions, hospitals, and even our drainage and sanitary equipment all tend to keep alive the sickly and the weak, who are allowed to propagate and in turn produce a race of degenerates. [27]

Obviously this is more than a faint echo of Darwin's words in the *Descent* and a very clear duplication of Haeckel's numerous diatribes against the unfit. Sanger, in following the stream of moral Darwinism, which was far stronger by the early twentieth century, was an avid proponent of eugenics. Eugenics was not a side issue to her, as we shall see, but *the* issue. Even more important, because it will clarify many connections in our current moral debates, her dedication to the propagation and legalization of birth control was, for her, part of an overall eugenics program that she advocated with all the zeal of a prophet.

But she did have an important difference with Haeckel. He was "conservative" in at least some of his moral views; that is, he believed that moral degeneracy—from stealing to sexual libertinism—had biological causes, and could therefore be eliminated by artificial selection. The moral traits that Haeckel and the monists wished to select were, in Gasman's words, "strongly conservative and frequently puritanical to the point of ludicrousness."[28] Not so with Margaret Sanger. While she certainly shared Haeckel's desire to cleanse humanity of a variety of physical and mental defects, the liberation of sexuality from such conservative and puritanical confines, that is, from

---

[27] Margaret Sanger, "Birth Control and Women's Health," *Birth Control Review* 1, no. 12 (1917): 7.
[28] Gasman, *Scientific Origins*, p. 92.

Christianity, defined her program from beginning to end.

In regard to the eugenic aspects of her thought, Sanger was quite as blunt as Haeckel and Darwin. Her journal *The Birth Control Review* was filled from cover to cover, in issue after issue, with the strongest and crudest arguments for eugenics,[29] and one of her favorite slogans adorning the masthead was "Birth Control: To Create a Race of Thoroughbreds." For Sanger the "lack of balance between the birth rate of the 'unfit' and the 'fit'" was "the greatest present menace to civilization," so that "the most urgent problem to-day is how to limit and discourage the over-fertility of the mentally and physically defective." In the face of such danger, Sanger warned that "possibly drastic and Spartan methods may be forced upon American society if it continues complacently to encourage the chance and chaotic breeding that has resulted from our stupid, cruel sentimentalism."[30]

As with the other eugenicists, Sanger was particularly upset by the presence of the "feeble-minded," a vague term that, for eugenicists of the day, seemed to encompass everyone from lunatics and those with nervous disorders, to those hitting low marks on the newly developed IQ tests. "There is but one practical and feasible program in handling the great problem of the feeble-minded. That is, as the best authorities are agreed, to prevent the birth of those who would transmit imbecility to their descendants." The special difficulty facing society, however, was that "feeble-mindedness . . . is invariably associated with an abnormally high rate of fertility. . . . The philosophy of Birth Control points out that as long as civilized communities encourage [such] unrestrained fecundity . . . they will be faced with the ever-increasing problem of feeble-mindedness, that fertile parent of degeneracy, crime, and pauperism."[31]

---

[29]There is no substitute for reading through issues of *The Birth Control Review*, edited by Sanger from 1917 to 1938. For those who have no access to these journals, Human Life International has culled pages upon pages of shocking quotes of all kinds from Sanger's journal; search their website for *Birth Control Review*. On Sanger's life, her espousal of eugenics and the continuation of her aims in Planned Parenthood see Robert Marshall and Charles Donovan, *Blessed Are the Barren* (San Francisco: Ignatius, 1991); George Grant, *Grand Illusions,* 4th ed. (Nashville: Cumberland House, 2000); Elasah Drogin, *Margaret Sanger: Father of Modern Society* (Coarsegold, Calif.: CUL Publications, 1980); and Rebecca Messal, "The Evolution of Genocide," *The Human Life Review* 26, no. 1 (2000): 47-75.

[30]Margaret Sanger, *The Pivot of Civilization* (1922; reprint, New York: Maxwell, 1969), p. 25.

[31]Ibid., pp. 80, 81.

Repeating the laments of Darwin and Haeckel, Sanger claimed that traditional philanthropy only succeeded in making the problem worse. "My criticism," she remarked frankly, "is not directed at the 'failure' of philanthropy, but rather at its success,"[32] for "it encourages the perpetuation of defectives, delinquents and dependents. These are the most dangerous elements in the world community, the most devastating curse on human progress and expression."[33]

True charity, by contrast, should not both coddle and perpetuate the "dead weight of human waste."[34] Instead, true charity should rely on the gospel of eugenics. For example, "Every feeble-minded girl or woman of the hereditary type, especially of the moron class, should be segregated during the reproductive years. . . . The male defectives are no less dangerous." Mere segregation may not prove sufficient. Society may need to opt for "an emergency measure" to stem the tide of the defectives, for "when we realize that each feeble-minded person is a potential source of an endless progeny of defect, we prefer the policy of immediate sterilization, of making sure that parenthood is absolutely prohibited to the feeble-minded."[35]

As mentioned above, her specific contribution to the eugenics movement was birth control. For Sanger, the problem with most eugenicists was that they relied solely on survival of the fittest to weed out the undesirables, rather than stopping the growth of weeds at its source. "Birth Control . . . is really the greatest and most truly eugenic method, and its adoption as part of the program of Eugenics would immediately give a concrete and realistic power to that science." Indeed, "Birth Control has been accepted by the most clear thinking and far seeing of the Eugenists themselves as the most constructive and necessary of the means to racial health." Sanger then listed the enlightened as including Dean Inge, Arthur Thomson, Havelock Ellis, William Bateson, Major Leonard Darwin (the son of Charles Darwin) and Norah March.[36]

Birth control was not only a negative eugenic force for Sanger but a positive force as well. Here enters Sanger's Epicurean hedonism in the form of

---

[32]Ibid., p. 108.
[33]Ibid., p. 123.
[34]Ibid., p. 112.
[35]Ibid., pp. 101-2.
[36]Ibid., p. 189.

moral Darwinism. Sexuality for her was a dynamic biological drive that could take evolution beyond mere survival of the fittest to the development of genius. For this to occur, she thought, sexuality had to be released from its traditional restraints. Sanger was aided in the liberation of sexuality from natural and religious constraints by the infamous sexual revolutionary Havelock Ellis (1859-1939). Ellis was also an advocate of eugenics and wrote the introductory essay "The Evolutionary Meaning of Birth Control" for Margaret Sanger's *Medical and Eugenic Aspects of Birth Control,* volume three of *The Sixth International Neo-Malthusian and Birth Control Conference,* published in 1926. But his greatest influence on Sanger was as a self-proclaimed "sexologist," a named coined to give the advocacy of sexual liberation a scientific aura. In this regard his seven-volume *Studies in the Psychology of Sex* (1897-1928) formed the modern foundation of the complete release of sexuality, making sexual pleasure an end in itself.[37]

Sanger's indebtedness to Ellis was immense; he provided her with a theoretical framework for liberation from the confines placed on sexuality by the natural law tradition in Christianity. But this liberation was not only theoretical. On the practical level, while Sanger and Ellis were both married, they became avid sexual partners. Ellis had often been unfaithful to his wife, but this affair with Sanger so distressed Ellis's wife that she attempted suicide. Sanger soon notified her husband of her desire for divorce and later married Three-in-One Oil magnate J. Noah Slee. She made him sign a prenuptial agreement establishing what we might call an "open marriage"; his enormous wealth provided her with the resources to carry on her revolution.

---

[37]For Ellis all modes of sexual expression were normal insofar as, he argued, all could ultimately be understood as imitations of the actions and emotions of heterosexual intercourse. From homosexuality and masturbation, to exhibitionism, urolagnia and coprolagnia, all participants were merely engaged in what Ellis called "erotic symbolism," *not* in perversion. Having removed the burden of moral judgment, Ellis merely described the variations of sexuality with the same clinically benign face as a scientist describing variations in flora. The most influential of his works, at least immediately, were his *Sexual Inversion* and *Auto-Eroticism* which argued, respectively, that homosexuality and masturbation were both widespread and natural. His mode of argument depended on the acceptance of evolution in two important ways. First, in arguing from what occurs among other animals to what is natural among human beings, Ellis was presupposing that since human beings were in an evolutionary continuum with animals, anything done by other animals could be inferred to be natural and part of human evolutionary history as well. Second, as we have seen in Darwin, because the moral codes of societies were rooted in their particular evolutionary history, the moral beliefs of cultures vary significantly, and societies could be successful with all kinds of sexual practices as long as they engaged in heterosexual intercourse as well.

In regard not only to Ellis but to all her life, Sanger treated marriage as incidental to her sexual desires. She had numerous affairs, not only with Ellis but with Hugh de Selincourt, Harold Child, H. G. Wells, her lawyer J. G. Goldstein, Angus MacDonald and Herbert Simond, among others. Sanger advised her first husband to take a mistress, and the marriage contract with her second husband provided the same freedom to both. As contemporary Mildred Dodge wrote of her, "She was the first person I ever knew who was openly an ardent propagandist for the joys of the flesh."[38]

On the theoretical level Sanger argued that the "ethical dogmas of the past, no less than the scientific, may block the way to true civilization."[39] Relying on the arguments of Ellis and others, and putting them in the context of biological and societal evolution, she asserted that "psychology is now recognizing the forces concealed in the human organism. In the long process of adaptation to social life, men have had to harness the wishes and desires born of these inner energies, the greatest and most imperative of which are Sex and Hunger."[40] While "Hunger . . . has created 'the struggle for existence,' . . . no less fundamental, no less imperative, no less ceaseless in its dynamic energy, has been the great force of Sex."[41] While hunger drives us to create cities with complex economies, sex is the evolutionary force that creates genius.

> Modern science is teaching us that genius is not some mysterious gift of the gods. . . . Nor is it . . . the result of a pathological and degenerate conditions. . . . Rather it is due to the removal of physiological and psychological inhibitions and constraints which makes possible the release and channeling of the primordial inner energies of man into full and divine expression. The removal of these inhibitions, so scientists assure us, makes possible more rapid and profound perceptions,—so rapid indeed that they seem to the ordinary human being, practically instantaneous, or intuitive.[42]

Sanger's attempt to drape her desire to release sexuality from constraint with the earnestness of evolutionary psychology is all the more laughable when we see the "scientific" data to which she was referring. According to

---

[38]Quoted in Marshall and Donovan, *Blessed Are the Barren*, p. 6.
[39]Sanger, *Pivot of Civilization*, p. 237.
[40]Ibid., p. 227.
[41]Ibid., pp. 227-28.
[42]Ibid., pp. 232-33.

Sanger, science had recently discovered the importance of the "ductless glands and their secretions," showing that "these organs, such as the thyroid, the pituitary, the suprarenal, the parathyroid and the reproductive glands, exercise an all-powerful influence upon the course of individual development or deficiency," the most important and powerful being, of course, the reproductive glands.[43] It followed, according to Sanger, that repression of sexual energy was destructive, and therefore the traditional approach to sexuality had to be replaced. Only then could the full power of biological evolution be released.

In a chapter of her *Pivot of Civilization* (which began with a long quote from Havelock Ellis) Sanger argued, "Our approach opens to us a fresh scale of values, a new and effective method of testing the merits and demerits of current policies and programs."[44] Christianity had failed humanity by attempting to suppress the font of our genius, our inherent sexual energy, thereby resulting in the stunting of evolution. But victory was just around the corner.

> Slowly but surely we are breaking down the taboos that surround sex; but we are breaking them down out of sheer necessity. The codes that have surrounded sexual behavior in the so-called Christian communities, the teachings of the churches concerning chastity and sexual purity, the prohibitions of the laws, and the hypocritical conventions of society, have all demonstrated their failure as safeguards against the chaos produced and the havoc wrought by the failure to recognize sex as a driving force in human nature,—as great as, if indeed not greater than, hunger. Its dynamic energy is indestructible. It may be transmuted, refined, directed, even sublimated, but to ignore, to neglect, to refuse to recognize this great elemental force is nothing less than foolhardy.[45]

Echoing Rousseau's argument that moral codes restricting sexuality actually cause vice, Sanger complained that "out of the unchallenged policies of continence, abstinence, 'chastity' and 'purity,' we have reaped the harvests of prostitution, venereal scourges and innumerable other evils."[46] We need, Sanger cried, to educate for a new understanding of sexuality, one that allows the dynamic release of sexual energy. The old view of sexuality,

---

[43]Ibid., pp. 234-36.
[44]Ibid., p. 243.
[45]Ibid., p. 246.
[46]Ibid.

"taught upon the basis of conventional and traditional morality and middle-class respectability, . . . is a waste of time and effort."[47] The new approach must be different.

> Instead of laying down hard and fast laws of sexual conduct, instead of attempting to inculcate rules and regulations, of pointing out the rewards of virtue and the penalties of "sin" (as is usually attempted in relation to the venereal diseases), the teacher of Birth Control seeks to meet the needs of the people. Upon the basis of their interests, their demands, their problems, Birth Control education attempts to develop their intelligence and show them how they may help themselves; how to guide and control this deep-rooted instinct.[48]

Simply put, "We are not seeking to introduce new restrictions but greater freedom."[49] This greater freedom is that of individuals over their evolution-ary destiny, for the "great principle of Birth Control offers the means whereby the individual may adapt himself to and even control the forces of environment and heredity."[50] Birth control, therefore, was "the very pivot of civilization," for it allowed us to control, in evolution, what had previously been a matter of chance. It is "really the greatest and most truly eugenic method" because it allows human beings "the power to control this great force" of sexual energy, "to use it, to direct it into channels in which it becomes the energy enhancing their lives and increasing self-expression and self-development."[51]

And so, for Margaret Sanger, the founder of Planned Parenthood, "the great central problem, and one which must be taken first is the abolition of the shame and fear of sex." The sexual revolution, she realized, must reedu-cate humanity sexually. "We must teach men the overwhelming power of this radiant force. . . . Through sex, mankind may attain the great spiritual illu-mination which will transform the world, which will light up the only path to an earthly paradise. So must we necessarily and inevitably conceive of sex-expression."[52]

This was the cry of the twentieth-century sexual revolution by one of its

---

[47]Ibid., p. 249.
[48]Ibid., p. 250.
[49]Ibid., p. 255.
[50]Ibid., p. 189.
[51]Ibid., p. 258.
[52]Ibid., p. 271.

founders, and this cry was clearly that of the Epicurean hedonist in content
and aim, and grounded by continual appeals to evolution. The release of sex
from the restrictions of Christianity will bring about, so she claimed, an
earthly paradise, one where sexually enhanced genius will flourish freed not
only from the shackles of limitations on sexual desire, but also, by eugenic
application of birth control, so that humanity may shed "the dead weight of
human waste."[53] Sanger ended her *Pivot of Civilization* with a paean to this-
worldly happiness, a happiness for which, true to Epicurus, the rejection of
the next world is essential:

> I look, therefore, into a Future when men and women will not dissipate their
> energy in the vain and fruitless search for content [sic] outside of themselves, in
> far-away places or people. Perfect masters of their own inherent powers, con-
> trolled with a fine understanding of the art of life and of love, adapting them-
> selves with pliancy and intelligence to the milieu in which they find themselves,
> they will unafraid enjoy life to the utmost. . . . Interest in the vague sentimental
> fantasies of extramundane existence, in pathological or hysterical flights from
> the realities of our earthliness, will have through atrophy disappeared, for in
> that dawn men and women will have come to the realization, already suggested,
> that there close at hand is our paradise, our everlasting abode, our Heaven and
> our eternity. Not by leaving it and our essential humanity behind us, nor by
> sighing to be anything but what we are, shall we ever become ennobled or
> immortal. Not for woman only, but for all of humanity is this the field where we
> must seek the secret of eternal life.[54]

In regard to other moral issues, we note Sanger's support of the Euthanasia Society of America, and that Alan Guttmacher, one of Planned Parenthood's most influential figures, was a member of the board of directors of the
Euthanasia Educational Council.[55] We further note the words of Norman
Haire, one of the contributors to Sanger's *Medical and Eugenic Aspects of
Birth Control*: "Infanticide is repugnant to present-day feeling, though I
think a later and wiser generation will adopt it in the case of babies who are
obviously hopelessly unfit at birth."[56] Further, one of Sanger's more famous

---

[53]Ibid., p. 116.

[54]Ibid., pp. 275-76.

[55]Marshall and Donovan, *Blessed Are the Barren*, pp. 5, 182.

[56]Margaret Sanger, *Medical and Eugenic Aspects of Birth Control*, vol. 3 of *The Sixth International
Neo-Malthusian and Birth Control Conference* (New York: The American Birth Control League,
1926), p. 89.

lovers, H. G. Wells, was one of the founders of the British Voluntary Euthanasia Society in 1935 (along with fellow luminaries George Bernard Shaw, Harold Laski and Bertrand Russell), the first organization in the world set up to campaign for euthanasia. In 1938 the Rev. Charles Potter, a Unitarian minister, founded the Euthanasia Society of America, basing it on the British model, and scores of euthanasia societies have been popping up since, both in Britain and in America. The historical lesson here is important: the support for euthanasia, as the support for eugenics as a whole, was not solely a German phenomenon, but as a thorough canvass of the literature prior to World War II clearly shows, a British, American and German phenomenon.

It is beyond the scope of this book to trace in great detail Sanger's influence as manifested in the multimillion dollar international corporation she founded. Others have documented extensively the history of Planned Parenthood after Sanger and have shown that it has remained true to it founder, not only in the promotion of eugenics (whether overtly, as she did, or in a more benign way by promoting screening for genetic defects and abortion without restrictions), but even more in the promotion of Sanger's modern Epicurean vision of sexuality freed from all restrictions.[57] A short overview, however, is necessary for the reader to see the face of moral Darwinism in Sanger's organization.

Planned Parenthood began in 1922, named originally the American Birth Control League. In 1939 it became the Birth Control Federation of America. Finally, in 1942 it received the name it bears today, the Planned Parenthood Federation of America (PPFA). As Sanger's organization, it propagated her eugenic views, and it is therefore no surprise to find a great overlap of membership (including many common board members) in the American Birth Control League and the American Eugenics Society. While the name of the organization changed twice by the 1940s, we find the same overlap in membership between PPFA and the American Eugenics Society during the 1940s through the 1960s. One prominent double member deserves special note. Alan Guttmacher, the president of PPFA from 1962 to 1974 and founder of the Alan Guttmacher Institute (the research and statistics offshoot of Planned Parenthood), was the vice president of the American Eugenics Society in 1957.

---

[57]Again, please see Marshall and Donovan, *Blessed Are the Barren;* Grant, *Grand Illusions;* and Drogin, *Margaret Sanger.*

Although PPFA began to drop explicit references to eugenics as part of its aim and purpose during World War II (because of the association of the word with the Nazis), the eugenic aim remains central to this day through its double advocacy of prenatal testing and abortion on demand. In the 1960s amniocentesis was developed, and proponents of eugenics were able to shift very forthright speech about eliminating undesirables to more subdued and clinical speech about the need for testing for disorders and defects in the womb. Not surprisingly, PPFA became a big advocate of such prenatal testing as a standard precaution for those who are at risk for having babies with birth defects. In a policy paper written in 1977, "Planned Births, the Future of the Family and the Quality of American Life: Towards a Comprehensive National Policy and Program,"[58] PPFA called for a national plan (with copious funding) that would emphasize "pregnancy testing and preventive services, prenatal diagnosis of fetal defects, genetic counseling, venereal disease prevention and other services." Obviously, given the victory in *Roe v. Wade* less than five years earlier, these "other services" would include abortion. Sanger, of course, would whole-heartedly approve. Such testing for defects has as its goal nothing other than the elimination of "defectives" by abortion.

As for sexuality itself, essential to PPFA's view of sex is the Sangerian belief that sexuality is some kind of an inner, natural drive that must be released from restrictions so that it may express itself creatively. Typical of its approach is a PPFA "White Paper," "Adolescent Sexuality,"[59] which contends in the very first line that "we are sexual from birth, and sexual expression is a basic human need throughout our lives." The notion that we are "sexual from birth" has become a commonplace of sexual revolutionaries. As we shall see, the claim has its roots in research first touted by Alfred Kinsey in his *Sexual Behavior in the Human Male* (1948), and these roots are not flattering.

Not surprisingly, Sanger's views of sexuality continue to define PPFA's extensive efforts to define the content of sexual education curricula. PPFA's educational agenda can be seen quite clearly in its recent "Human Sexuality: What Children Should Know and When They Should Know It."[60] Again following Kinsey, they claim that five-year-old children should "know that it is normal for them to touch their genitals for pleasure." And since sexual plea-

---

[58]This paper is readily available on the web under its title.
[59]Available on the Planned Parenthood website <www.plannedparenthood.org>.
[60]Ibid.

sure, not procreation, is the goal, elementary school children should "be aware that sexual identity includes sexual orientation: lesbian, gay, straight, or bisexual." Nine- to thirteen-year-old children should know that "sex is pleasurable as well as the way to make a baby" and that "sexual acts can be separated from reproductive acts." These same children, then, must be taught that "masturbation is very common, and . . . that it is normal to masturbate—but only in private." The result is that by the time they are eighteen, those educated by PPFA will not only be well-practiced in "sexual expression" but also understand that heterosexual marriage is just one of many modes of sexual expression—and by no means to be accorded privileged status. We are back in the amoral world of Epicurus but with all the limits taken away by modern Epicurean hedonism. And while Darwin certainly would not have approved personally of such sexual innovations we must recall that evolution begins from amoral nature. Evolutionary varieties, whether in regard to a particular body structure or a particular sexual desire, are neither good nor bad. One can describe them, but not censure them.

We would have an incomplete picture of the spread of moral Darwinism in the twentieth century if we did not examine the even more egregious example of Epicurean hedonism driving scientific inquiry in Alfred Kinsey (1894-1956). While Sanger was certainly a champion of sexual pleasure, she was not a scientist, and therefore her many appeals to evolution and pop psychology to support her views on sexuality had less authority. But Kinsey helped to change that by providing "scientific" proof that beneath the conventional morality on the surface, our naturally sexually uninhibited selves—seen so clearly in both Lucretius and Rousseau—lay barely hidden, just waiting to be released. Kinsey's two great works *Sexual Behavior in the Human Male* (1948, hereafter the *Male Report*) and *Sexual Behavior in the Human Female* (1953, hereafter the *Female Report*) became bestsellers[61] and—since they were riddled with numbers and charts and spoke in abstract and seemingly detached terms about sexuality—authoritative and defining scientific documents that were cited repeatedly in the scientific and legal literature dealing with sexuality.[62]

The public face of Kinsey's seemingly austere Institute for Sex Research

[61]Alfred Kinsey et al., *Sexual Behavior in the Human Male* (Philadelphia: W. B. Saunders, 1948), and *Sexual Behavior in the Human Female* (Philadelphia: W. B. Saunders, 1953).

[62]See Judith Reisman, *Kinsey: Crimes & Consequences* (Arlington, Va.: The Institute for Media Education, Inc., 1998), chap. 8.

was that of dispassionate scientists going about the workaday tasks of observation, tabulation and presentation, the very tasks that occupy all scientists. But hidden from public view was a twisted sexual drama of such proportions as would rival the Roman emperors Tiberius, Caligula and Nero, or in more modern times, the Marquis de Sade. Kinsey's sexual data, which have been—more than any other source—the scientifically authoritative foundation used by the sexual revolution in the latter half of the twentieth century, were autobiographical in origin and goal, projections of Kinsey's own dark sexual desires. Even more than was the case with Sanger, the moral Darwinism manipulated the science.

Kinsey was a driven man. As a boy he was not only an Eagle Scout but a model student, chosen as valedictorian of his high school class (1912) and dubbed by his classmates a "second Darwin," a young man destined to change the world through science. His father, Alfred Seguine Kinsey, was a staunch Calvinist, providing young Alfred with a strict moral upbringing, including the area of sexuality. But young Alfred, as much as he desired to excel in following his parents' stern moral codes, was obsessed with masturbation and his own homosexual desires. Hidden from his parents, he engaged in masochistic forms of masturbation, the masturbation releasing his sexual desire and the masochism relieving his guilt through painful punishment. As Kinsey biographer James Jones notes of Kinsey's dual life, "For a boy like Kinsey, a righteous boy whose sense of self-worth depended upon rigid self-control, nothing needed to be kept more hidden than the fact that he masturbated and that he did so with a foreign object inserted up his penis."[63] The result, however, was not penance but a lifelong, deep-seated sado-masochism that Kinsey practiced feverishly, yet kept hidden from the public behind his grave face and white lab coat.

Kinsey went on to Harvard and earned a doctorate in science (1920). His specialty was taxonomy, and as an entomologist, he was a world-class authority on the gall wasp. William Wheeler (1865-1937), the director of the Bussey Institute at Harvard where Kinsey studied, was one of the scientists most influential for Kinsey. The Bussey Institute was a major center for the New Biology (evolutionary in origin and focus), and Wheeler not only pub-

---

[63]James H. Jones, *Alfred C. Kinsey: A Public/Private Life* (New York: W. W. Norton, 1997), pp. 82-83.

lished works on evolution (such as *Emergent Evolution and the Development of Societies*) but spread eugenic views as a natural offshoot of his evolutionary work. As Jones rightly note, eugenics was the "favorite cause" of the Bussey Institute.[64]

Kinsey himself embraced both positive eugenics (where the good are encouraged to outbreed the "rogues") and negative eugenics (where the bad are either isolated or sterilized).[65] Kinsey was especially impressed by Wheeler's satirical essay entitled "The Termitodoxa, or Biology and Society," in which an imaginary termite kingdom is taken over by biologists who, as social engineers, purify it by abolishing priests and instituting tightly controlled eugenics and birth control programs. This essay was a favorite of Kinsey's; he kept it near him for years to come. From it he drank in the Darwinian dream of biologists controlling the evolutionary direction of society.[66]

But sex, and not eugenics, became Kinsey's passion; the scientific materialism he imbibed helped him to resolve the tension between the moral codes received from Christianity and his increasingly bizarre sexual desires. The materialist, evolutionary biology guided the resolution.[67] Yet, even though he had come to believe that sexuality had to be released from restrictions, he was Machiavellian enough to understand that the revolution would have to be achieved by stealth, that is, in the guise of science. In Jones's words, Kinsey's research

> sprang from a private agenda shaped by personal politics. Decades of inner turmoil had transformed Kinsey into a rebel, a man who rejected the sexual mores of his age. He meant to change the public's thinking on sexual matters. Convinced that cold, hard facts alone would persuade the public to develop more tolerant sexual attitudes, Kinsey was determined to provide that data.[68]

Kinsey therefore wore the solemn, disinterested face of the scientist in public, and the Kinsey research team orchestrated carefully staged publicity pictures of themselves, dressed in respectable coats and ties, speaking calmly to

---

[64]Ibid., pp. 129, 153.

[65]Ibid., pp. 194-95, and p. 809 n. 78.

[66]Ibid., pp. 153-54.

[67]Ibid., p. 154. In Jones's words, "Four years at Harvard had changed Kinsey. After hanging around [William] Wheeler and other godless scientists, he had grown less rigid morally and had become more skeptical of authority. . . . In short, Kinsey emerged from Harvard a changed man."

[68]Ibid., p. 513.

each other as they sifted through various data. However, the Institute for Sex Research itself was for Kinsey a microcosm of a new society, freed from all sexual restriction, that he hoped to create by his revolution.

> Within the inner circle of his senior staff members and their spouses, he endeavored to create his own sexual utopia, a scientific subculture whose members would not be bound by arbitrary and antiquated sexual taboos. . . . Unfettered sex would be the order of the day. . . . Kinsey decreed that within the inner circle men could have sex with each other, wives would be swapped freely, and wives, too, would be free to embrace whichever sexual partners they liked.[69]

Yet not even this sexual utopia was sufficient for Kinsey. "Bringing in outsiders was absolutely essential for Kinsey to achieve sexual satisfaction, as no other member of the inner circle could fulfill his masochistic or homosexual desires." One of those brought in, called Mr. Y by Jones to maintain his anonymity, describes his many visits to the Kinsey household. He not only had sex with Kinsey regularly, but "also had sex with everybody else around there [in the Institute] too." As Jones reports, "Mr. Y had fond memories of copulating with Clara [Kinsey's wife] and Martha (Pomeroy's wife) and equally warm recollections of his contacts with their husbands." Alas, Mr. Y "found Kinsey's performance as a masochist a trifle disappointing, complaining that 'he liked [for me] to beat him with a cat-o'-nine-tails but not very hard.' "[70]

Nor is that the end of Kinsey's private sexual distortions. Not only did Kinsey demand that his wife be filmed engaging in sex acts (purely for scientific reasons, of course), but Kinsey was both an avid voyeur and exhibitionist.[71] While Kinsey was primarily interested in filming homosexual acts, especially acts of sado-masochism, for the sake of science, he captured the full gamut of sexual expression.[72] Staff photographer William Dellenback "often filmed Kinsey, always from the chest down, engaged in masochistic masturbation."

Once the camera started rolling, the world's foremost expert on human sexual

---

[69]Ibid., p. 603.
[70]Ibid., pp. 603-4.
[71]Ibid., pp. 608-10.
[72]Ibid., p. 612.

behavior and a scientist who valued rationality above all other intellectual properties would insert an object into his urethra [two examples given were a toothbrush, brush end first, and a swizzle stick], tie a rope around his scrotum, and then simultaneously tug hard on the rope as he maneuvered the object deeper and deeper.[73]

Why dwell on these gory, nearly unbelievable details? What have they to do with moral Darwinism? Independent of the argument of the present work, the sordid details of Kinsey's life have remained hidden far too long; they reveal that Kinsey had put supposedly neutral science in the service of his unmentionable sexual desires. If such things were known about Kinsey in the mid-twentieth century, Kinsey and his Institute would have been shut down, and Kinsey himself stripped of his academic credentials and perhaps sent to jail. Instead, he became the "scientific giant" upon whom stood the sexual revolution in the latter half of the twentieth century.

But directly related to our argument, Kinsey's mode of argument assumed the entire framework of moral Darwinism. He assumed, to begin with, that nature was amoral, and that social codes and restrictions only arose later as merely conventional restrictions on natural sexual desires. The sexual deviation from present moral codes by certain members of society represented not moral deviation, but rather a return to the expression of the original, natural, amoral sexual passions. Kinsey's strategy, as we shall see, was to multiply examples of alleged deviation, to convince the public that society was supressing these primitive natural expressions of sexuality. Of course, we have already seen in Lucretius, and even more clearly in Rousseau, the Epicurean assertion that human beings are naturally sexually amoral. Defenders of Darwin may bristle at my calling Kinsey's pansexualism "moral Darwinism"; however, as we have seen, the Victorian virtues, sexual or otherwise, are not lying inherent in evolution, waiting to unfold. Evolution is inherently amoral. Further, disgust at Kinsey's beliefs and actions would only tell us, on Darwin's account, about the evolution of conscience in a particular individual or set of individuals, and not about whether Kinsey's beliefs and actions were right or wrong. Right and wrong, as Darwin correctly reasoned according to his premises, arise in particular societies only after the evolution of the social instincts, and

---

[73]Ibid., p. 609.

the particular mode of sociality will determine the feelings of disquiet and disgust of any particular individual.

To return, Kinsey's strategy in the *Male Report* was simple. He reported all sexual behavior as a supposedly neutral, scientific observer, not making distinctions between normal and abnormal (good and evil). Once it was shown that human beings engaged in previously unmentionable sexual activities with great frequency, and what was thought to be abnormal occurred quite frequently, then it must be inferred that such acts are natural. In this regard, Kinsey criticized previous scientific studies of sex, which "show little understanding of the range of variation in human behavior. More often the conclusions are limited by the personal experience of the author." As Kinsey's personal sexual experience was almost without limits, he obviously considered himself the best sexual judge. And so, since "many items in human sexual behavior which are labeled abnormal, or perversions, in textbooks, prove, upon statistical examination, to occur in as many as 30 or 60 or 75 per cent of certain populations. . . . It is difficult to maintain that such types of behavior are abnormal because they are rare."[74]

Furthermore, treating purely natural sexual desires as if they were unnatural was not only unscientific but harmful to otherwise healthy individuals. According to Kinsey, "Many of the socially and intellectually most significant persons in our histories, successful scientists, educators, physicians, clergymen, business men, and persons of high position in governmental affairs, have socially taboo items in their sexual histories, and among them they have accepted nearly the whole range of so-called sexual abnormalities."[75] Almost all of these individuals, reported Kinsey, were "well adjusted." Indeed, "Most of the complications which are observable in sexual histories are the result of society's reactions when it obtains knowledge of an individual's behavior, or the individual's fear of how society would react if he were discovered."[76] Repeating the now familiar conclusions of moral Darwinism, Kinsey claimed that specific moral codes of societies were variable; underneath this relativity or moral codes, nature itself was sexually amoral. Consequently, moral interpretations of sexuality are not scientific, for "there is no scientific reason for considering particular types of sexual activity as

---

[74]Kinsey et al., *Sexual Behavior in the Human Male,* pp. 199-201.

[75]Ibid., p. 201.

[76]Ibid., p. 202.

intrinsically, in their biologic origins, normal or abnormal."[77]

And so, for Kinsey, while the truly scientific approach to sexuality does distinguish different types of sexuality, it does not rank them morally.

> Viewed objectively, human sexual behavior, in spite of its diversity, is more easily comprehended than most people, even scientists, have previously realized. The six types of sexual activity, masturbation, spontaneous nocturnal emissions, petting, heterosexual intercourse, homosexual contacts, [and "contact with animals or other species"][78] may seem to fall into categories that are as far apart as right and wrong, licit and illicit, normal and abnormal, acceptable and unacceptable in our social organization. In actuality, they all prove to originate in the relatively simple mechanisms which provide for erotic response when there are sufficient physical or psychic stimuli.[79]

To recall Epicurus and especially Lucretius, good and evil are measured by pleasure and pain, and in regard to sexuality, the pleasure is experienced in the individual with a variety of "physical or psychic stimuli." Since the good is identified with pleasure, then no physical or psychic stimuli that prove "sufficient" to provoke the "relatively simple mechanisms which provide for erotic response" can be evil. By such reasoning, Kinsey hoped to usher in a society governed by the enlightened condition of pansexuality, that is, sexuality unrestricted by the confines of traditional views of sexuality.

As we have seen, Kinsey was not above molding science and scientific data to fit his moral aims. Kinsey's treatment of homosexuality provides a shocking example. Many are aware of the result of Kinsey's analysis: the claim, based on Kinsey's data, that at least 10 percent of the male population is homosexual. But all too few know of the distortions and data manipulation made by Kinsey to achieve his desired result of normalizing homosexuality.

For example, in order to inflate the percentage of homosexuals in the general population, Kinsey purposely selected interview populations with high rates of homosexuality. Approximately 25 percent of his interview pool had prison or sex offender history. Indeed, as Kinsey associate Paul Gebhard later admitted, even within the prisons there was no attempt made by Kinsey to do interviews by true random sampling of the prison populations: "We

---

[77]Ibid.

[78]Ibid., p. 157.

[79]Ibid., p. 678.

simply sought out sex offenders and, after a time, avoided the more common types of offense (e.g., statutory rape) and directed our efforts toward the rarer types. . . . The great majority of the prison group was collected omnivorously without any sampling plan—we simply interviewed all who volunteered." Kinsey "never . . . [kept] a record of refusal rates—the proportion of those who were asked for an interview but who refused."[80] For Kinsey, such an obviously biased approach to interviewing was legitimate, for he believed prior to beginning his study that everyone was actually animated by amoral sexual desires, desires that ran against the merely conventional moral codes of society. Only a few got caught and sent to jail, however. (Given this presupposition, it is no accident that Kinsey worked for the decriminalization of nearly every sex crime.)

To focus on an obvious problem in Kinsey's approach, he refused to make allowance for what social scientists call "volunteer bias," the distortion of the interviewee pool that comes from attracting those least likely to represent the population as a whole—that is, those *most* likely to have nontraditional views of sex. Abraham Maslow, who first called attention to this phenomenon, pointed the problem out directly to Kinsey, but Kinsey ignored Maslow's warnings and published the results as if they represented the entire population.[81] The inflation of the data caused by volunteer bias, especially in regard to adult homosexual males, was immense.

But that is not all. Kinsey inflated the numbers even more (again, in all categories, but especially in regard to homosexuality) by shrinking the original interview pool, taking those sex histories that best fit his predetermined goal. This can be seen clearly in the confusion of numbers presented in the *Male* and *Female Reports*. In one place in the *Male Report* the reader was led to believe that there were 21,350 interviewees; at another, only 12,214. In regard to the number of males, Kinsey was unclear, at one point claiming it to be as high as 6,200. But, using the very data provided by Kinsey in his morass of charts and graphs, W. Allen Wallis, a University of Chicago statistician and past president of the American Statistical Association, found the number to be, at the very most, 4,120.[82] Even more telling, this shrunken

---

[80]Quoted in Reisman, *Kinsey*, pp. 52-53.

[81]See Judith A. Reisman and Edward W. Eichel, *Kinsey, Sex and Fraud* (Lafayette, La.: Huntington House, 1990), pp. 20-21, 62.

[82]Reisman, *Kinsey*, pp. 53-54.

pool contained not only a high percentage of prisoners and sex offenders, as mentioned above, but to this pool (as admitted by Kinsey himself) "several hundred male prostitutes contributed their histories."[83]

Kinsey also engaged in what statisticians call the "accumulative incidence" technique of data manipulation, which treats "each case as if it were an additional case falling within each previous age group or previous experienced category." The result was that, for example, "a man who was 45 at the time of the interview would provide a case for each age group previous to that" with the result being that "if he was married at the time of interview" he would "constitute a case for the single tabulation in the years before he was married."[84] This technique falsely stacked the numbers in all previous categories in accord with Kinsey's belief that whatever is done once must have been done all along, and allowed him to inflate percentages in all age categories.

On top of all this, as Judith Reisman points out, in Kinsey's data

two totally different types of homosexual experience were added together as if they were one and the same thing. Incidental adolescent homosexual experiences of heterosexuals (the most common type of same-sex experience recorded by Kinsey) were combined with the adult experiences of true homosexuals. This created the illusion that a significant percentage of males were genuinely homosexual.[85]

Given all these modes of inflation, it is not difficult to see how Kinsey could create the "scientific" illusion that 10 percent of the male population was homosexual.

Even more disturbing than Kinsey's manipulation of data in regard to homosexuality was his treatment of pedophilia and bestiality. In both cases, we clearly see the presuppositions of Epicurean hedonism as vindicated through a Darwinian evolutionary analysis.

The main source, perhaps nearly the only source, for Kinsey's data on child sexuality came from a single man who worked for the government, one of the "well-adjusted" individuals mentioned above, who, according to Kinsey coresearcher Wardell Pomeroy, was "sixty-three years old, quiet, soft-

---

[83]Quoted in Reisman and Eichel, *Kinsey, Sex and Fraud*, p. 29.
[84]Reisman, *Kinsey*, pp. 56-57.
[85]Reisman and Eichel, *Kinsey, Sex and Fraud*, p. 186.

spoken, self-effacing—a rather unobtrusive fellow."[86] Mr. X, as he is called
by Kinsey biographer Jones, was "obsessed with sex, a walking id with poly-
morphous erotic tastes," who "had sex with his grandmother when he was
still a young child, as well as with his father. In the years that followed, the
boy had sexual relations with seventeen of the thirty-three relatives with
whom he had contact." After this illustrious beginning, as Pomeroy later
recalled, "This man had had homosexual relations with 600 preadolescent
males, heterosexual relations with 200 preadolescent females, intercourse
with countless adults of both sexes, with animals of many species, and
besides had employed elaborate techniques of masturbation." Most important for Kinsey, not only was he the perfect sexual agent freed from every
sort of social inhibition, but "he had made extensive notes on all his sexual
activities, chronicling not only his behavior and reactions but those of his
partners and victims."[87]

If we recall the Epicurean view of the original natural amorality of sexual
desire which we have seen in Lucretius and Rousseau, we can see why Kinsey regarded Mr. X as a "scientific treasure." In Jones's words:

> Privately, Kinsey had long believed that human beings in a state of nature were
> basically pansexual. Absent social constraints, he conjectured, "natural man"
> would commence sexual activities early in life, enjoy intercourse with both
> sexes, eschew fidelity, indulge in a variety of behaviors, and be much more sexu-
> ally active in general for life. To Kinsey, Mr. X was living proof of this theory.[88]

Kinsey used the "data" from Mr. X to craft the famous fifth chapter of
the *Male Report*, in which he "established" that human beings were sexual
almost from birth. Charts and diagrams, statistical means and medians, and
a canopy of scientific-sounding extrapolation all covered the simple truth
that Kinsey was using data largely derived from a man who had done physi-
cal-sexual violence to hundreds of little children. As could be expected, Kinsey believed that adult-child sex was natural, and that problems only came
about because our society happened to consider pedophilia to be evil. While
Kinsey admitted in his more frank *Sexual Behavior in the Human Female*
that "some 80% of the children had been emotionally upset or frightened by

---

[86]Jones, *Alfred C. Kinsey*, p. 508.
[87]Ibid., p. 507.
[88]Ibid., p. 512.

their contacts with adults," yet only a "small portion had been seriously disturbed; but in most instances the reported fright was nearer the level that children will show when they see insects, spiders, or other objects against which they have been adversely conditioned." For Kinsey, "It is difficult to understand why a child, except for its cultural conditioning, should be disturbed at having its genitalia touched, or disturbed at seeing the genitalia of other persons, or disturbed at even more specific sexual contacts." The problem, according to Kinsey, lay not in pedophilia itself, but in children "constantly being warned by parents and teachers against [sexual] contacts with adults." Kinsey then shifted the blame to society, warning that "the emotional reactions of the parents, police officers, and other adults who discover that the child has had such contact, may disturb the child more seriously than the sexual contacts themselves." Turning the table on those trying to enforce legal sanctions against pedophilia, Kinsey claimed that the "current hysteria over sex offenders may very well have serious effects on the ability of many of these children to work out sexual adjustments some years later in their marriage."[89]

Just as Kinsey's views on the naturalness of premarital sex and homosexuality became the scientific foundation for the transformation of sexual morality from a Christian natural law position to that of the Epicurean, so also Kinsey's views on the naturalness of pedophilia have become the foundation of the slow but sure revolution going on right now pushing adult-child sex as natural.[90] True to his belief in the naturalness of pansexuality, moreover, Kinsey not only offered a benign view of pedophilia but bestiality as well.

"To many persons it will seem almost axiomatic that two mating animals should be individuals of the same species," Kinsey began his chapter on "Animal Contacts," but such beliefs are immature. "To those who believe, *as children do* [emphasis added], that conformance should be universal, any departure from the rule becomes an immorality." But while such "immorality seems particularly gross to an individual who is unaware of the frequency with which exceptions to the supposed rule actually occur," such childlike beliefs are inappropriate to the scientist. While many scientists "have been considerably biased in their investigations" because "they too have accepted the traditions,"

---

[89]Alfred Kinsey et al., *Sexual Behavior in the Human Female*, p. 121.
[90]For the "state" of the revolution see especially Reisman and Eichel, *Kinsey, Sex and Fraud*, pp. 128-34, 205-13 and Reisman, *Kinsey*, pp. 230-36.

science has become increasingly aware of "the existence of interspecific matings," not only among plants, but among birds and higher mammals. Viewing
the many instances of attempts at interspecies breeding among animals, "one
begins to suspect that the rules about intraspecific matings [i.e., between
members of the same species] are not so universal as traditions would have it."
What is "particularly interesting" then is not that animals attempt to mate
across species lines, but "the degree of abhorrence with which intercourse
between the human and animals of other species is viewed by most persons
who have not had such experience."[91] The historical source of such taboos,
Kinsey argued, was ultimately the Old Testament; the prohibition of bestiality
and other sexual deviations, through Christianity, helped define Western cultural norms, thereby making it seem that what was abhorred was also rare.
But, claimed Kinsey, rather than sexual contact with animals being rare,

> it is certain that human contacts with animals of other species have been
> known since the dawn of history, they are known among all races of people
> today, and they are not uncommon in our own culture, as the data in the
> present chapter will show. Far from being a matter for surprise, the record
> simply substantiates our present understanding that the forces which bring
> individuals of the same species together in sexual relations, may sometimes
> serve to bring individuals of different species together in the same types of
> sexual relations.[92]

Thus, to prove his case, Kinsey followed the mode of argument, rooted in
evolutionary theory, which we noted above. First, he showed that all the animals do it, then, contrary to our expectations, a surprising number of human
beings do it as well. Since human beings are just another animal on the evolutionary spectrum, and other animals have interspecies sex, it must be natural for human beings as well. Sex with animals is simply one more outlet for
our essentially amoral sexual desire.

But surely, we think after reading Kinsey's account of the naturalness of
bestiality, no one else, at least no significant public person, has sided with
Kinsey on this issue. Enter the current holder of the Ira W. DeCamp Chair
of Bioethics at Princeton University's Center for the Study of Human Values, Dr. Peter Singer. Singer explicitly follows Darwinism's evolutionary era-

---

[91]Kinsey et al., *Human Male*, pp. 667-68.
[92]Ibid., pp. 668-69.

sure of the significance of the species boundary defining "human being," and heralds a new age of ethics rooted in compassion that crosses all species boundaries. In regard to sexuality, that means for Singer breaking down the last taboo, prohibition of bestiality. In a cheerful and positive review of Midas Dekkers book on human-animal sexual relations, *Dearest Pet: On Bestiality*, Singer notes that "not so long ago, any form of sexuality not leading to the conception of children was seen as, at best, wanton lust, or worse, a perversion. One by one, the taboos have fallen." All except for one, bestiality, which (following Kinsey's mode of argument) "is not because of its rarity."

For Singer, human-animal sex is as old as contact between human beings and animals. But where did this irrational taboo come from then? According to Singer, "Especially in the Judeo-Christian tradition . . . we have always seen ourselves as distinct from animals, and imagined that a wide, unbridgeable gulf separates us from them. Humans alone are made in the image of God. Only human beings have an immortal soul." But even when the old fiction of the immortal soul has been all but forgotten, the Hobbesian belief in *human* rights serves much the same purpose. "Today the language of human rights—rights that we attribute to all human beings but deny to all nonhuman animals—maintains that separation." Whether it has its root in the belief in the soul or in modern natural rights, maintaining the taboo against bestiality no longer makes sense, however. And so, while the "taboo on sex with animals may . . . have originated as part of a broader rejection of non-reproductive sex, . . . its persistence while other non-reproductive sexual acts have become acceptable suggests that there is another powerful force at work: our desire to differentiate ourselves, erotically and in every other way, from animals." The taboo on bestiality is, then, part of our broader sin of *speciesism*. To overcome speciesism, for Singer, is the goal of his evolutionary ethics of compassion; therefore, the taboo on bestiality must fall—provided that one does not physically harm the animals, for "sex with animals does not always involve cruelty."

Singer ends with a Machiavellian twist, clearly meant to protect him from criticism. After relating an account of a human female worker in Camp Leakey (a rehabilitation center for captured orangutans in Borneo) carried off by an amorous male orangutan, Singer notes such "sexual interest is not a cause for shock or horror" since "we are great apes" on the same evolutionary continuum. "This does not make sex across the species barrier normal, or natural, whatever those much-misused words may mean, but it does imply that it ceases to be an offence to our status and dignity as human beings."[93]

To conclude, then, the point of this chapter has been to show how it is that Darwin's principles, as the culmination of modern Epicureanism, were expanded after Darwin into full-blown Darwinism, including the hedonism which we do not find in Darwin's own account. I have purposely chosen three figures who were not among the "Who's Who" of philosophers of the hundred years after Darwin, but whose influence, in regard to their immediate impact on reforming Western culture according to the premises of moral Darwinism, has been immense. Also, I purposely chose figures whose moral conclusions were most at odds with Christianity, and who, at least in some respects, would appall both Darwin and (I hope) many later Darwinians. I do *not* mean, then, to imply that all or even most Darwinians desire the crippled and infirm to be exterminated (with Haeckel) or that the feeble-minded should be sterilized (with Sanger) or that pedophilia and bestiality should be normalized (with Kinsey). But I do mean to imply, indeed to assert, that once the amoral view of nature—intrinsic to ancient Epicureanism, revived in modernity and articulated as an essential element of evolutionary theory by Darwin—has been accepted, then there is no *theoretical* objection the Darwinist can offer to Haeckel, Sanger or Kinsey. Even more telling, since the time of Darwin, society itself has shifted ever closer to the views of Haeckel, Sanger and Kinsey, and consequently, ever further away from the moral arguments taken from natural law and transformed by Christianity. Therefore, all *practical* objections are simply being continually overridden.

This trend, this shift, is called by nearly everyone "secularization," but *secularization* simply means (as should be obvious by now) accepting the premises and conclusions of Epicurean materialism, and these premises and conclusions reached consummate expression in Darwin. Such is why Darwin is rightly considered to have been the most forceful agent of secularization. Thus, we are justified in calling this new cosmological and moral view "moral Darwinism," for it defines not only a scientific theory, but a way of life. As I make clear in the next chapter, any objections by Darwinians to being thrown in with the likes of Haeckel, Sanger and Kinsey are groundless.

---

[93]Peter Singer, "Heavy Petting," a review of Midas Dekkers, *Dearest Pet: On Bestiality* (New York: Verso, 2000). Singer's review is available on the Web by title and author, one location being at <www.nerve.com/Opinions/Singer/heavyPetting/main.asp>.

Conclusion

Undoubtedly, many self-defined materialists who have reached this point in the book are quite indignant, first of all, with my continually speaking of the materialist view of science as a kind of faith, and second, at my direct association of materialist principles with unsavory moral positions. Such scientists do not generally appreciate the presuppositions of their disciplines being called articles of faith, and few scientists of the materialist bent would want to be associated, even remotely, with the atrocities of the Third Reich, or the eugenic and sexual utopianism of Sanger, or the pansexual acrobatics of Kinsey and his coworkers. But while such indignation may be quite genuine, it affords little help or clarity in the debate. Those whose indignation is aroused should remember the following points.

In one sense, to call science a kind of faith is merely to describe something quite uncontroversial: the scientist not only *believes* that the universe is intelligible, but also *believes* that he or she holds the best theory for discovering that intelligibility. As a scientist, one can cease being a believer under two circumstances: if the universe has been completely explained so that no hypothesis is any longer needed to guide discovery, or if the scientist has simply given up believing that the universe has any intelligibility to be discovered. In the first case, science is finished, in the second, science is abandoned.

As I have shown, Epicurus knew that his view of nature was a kind of faith. I have also shown that Darwin's arguments for evolution were put forward, on Darwin's own admission, as an act of faith. But Darwin's faith was (he thought) justified not only because of the explanatory power of his evolutionary arguments but also, in the larger context of the history of science, because evolutionary theory was a part of the already victorious Newtonian materialist view of the universe. By the time of Darwin, the Newtonian account of the universe was no longer considered hypothetical. The universe had been completely explained, the laws of motion completely applied and science was finished (except for a few minor details). The successful application of Newtonianism to biological phenomena was one of those details, but one that, given the success of Newton's account of nature, seemingly could not fail.

It is one of the great ironies of history that as Darwin's hypothetical arguments began to be accepted as established fact during the latter half of the nineteenth century, and further, as the moral implications of Darwinism began to permeate Western culture, the Newtonian view of science, which had provided the ultimate theoretical justification for both, was crumbling. It would seem, recalling our many pages of analysis, that the entire edifice of Epicurean presuppositions should have crumbled as well, but oddly enough, the *habits* of materialist thinking continued even after the theoretical framework collapsed; it is the retention of such habits without the ultimate theoretical framework that I am calling the *faith* of the materialist.

Such faith has a different character than the normal faith of scientists who believe that the universe is intelligible and that they have the best theory for explanation and discovery. The materialist faith, as it now exists, is not known by materialists as *faith*; rather, contemporary materialists are still filled with the Newtonian confidence that science has already completely explained the universe according to materialist presuppositions. Therefore, insofar as science has completely established materialism, it is, as far as they are concerned, finished. The universe may be far stranger than Epicurus or Newton had imagined it, the materialist muses, but it is still the same self-contained, self-subsistent, divinity-and-soul-free universe.

Against this, I argue that, with the collapse of Newtonianism, such confidence is unjustified, and that materialist science has been thrown back into the condition of being, once again, hypothetical. If it is merely hypothetical, even if it is very promising as an hypothesis, it has been reduced to the level of possibility or probability, but not certainty. It therefore cannot rule out the possibility of an intelligent design approach to science, but must compete with it. To understand all of this, we must take a quick look at the dissolution of the Epicurean-Newtonian universe during the last half of the nineteenth century and the first half of the twentieth.

Nothing was so important for reestablishing the divinity-free universe in modernity than the rehabilitation of the eternal atom, for its very eternality eliminated the need for God the creator, and allowed nature to be self-sustained and self-contained. The brilliance of Epicurus's original strategy was made clear in modernity when all attempts (even and especially Newton's) to integrate a creator with Epicurean atomism ended with the atoms reasserting their self-subsistent eternality, thereby making the creator superfluous. Of course, since evolutionary theory has been an integral part of such materialism for almost two millennia prior to Darwin, the same divine superfluity exists in every scheme of theistic evolution that assumes the complete truth of natural selection as the sole means by which biological complexity is evolved.

But the destruction of the eternal atom occurred (if we cared to pinpoint a date) in 1897, in the Cavendish Laboratory at Cambridge, England, when J. J. Thompson identified a negatively charged particle of much less mass than hydrogen, the lightest known element. So began the unraveling of the atom into a miniature universe of subatomic particles, not only electrons, protons and neutrons, but mesons, muons and pions, and so on until tens of such subatomic particles have turned into hundreds. This was not the simple, eternal point of Epicurus, Galileo and Newton.

Added to this was the discovery of radioactivity during roughly the same period, wherein it became clear that atoms were not eternal, but could quite easily decay. Even above this, the solidity of the atom vanished as well. Not only could it be split, but it consisted mostly of empty space, as Ernest Rutherford discovered when, in 1909, he directed alpha particles at a thin metal sheet, and found that only a very small number were deflected (when they hit the positively charged nucleus), but most went right through. The radius of the atom, as it turns out, is ten thousand times greater than the radius of the nucleus—most of the atom is empty.

Nor, as we have found out, can the universe itself be put forth as an eternal rival to a deity. This Epicurean belief began to crack when in 1929 Edwin Hubble set forth the argument that the universe was expanding, an argument based on observations of the red-shift effect in the spectra of galaxies. If the universe was expanding, then its origin in time could be easily discovered by reversing the calculations and arriving, by contraction, at its birthday. Since the discovery of cosmic microwave background radiation in the 1960s, there is little or any doubt that the universe began with a big bang. Like the atom, the universe is contingent and mortal, and not a counter-deity, as Epicurus had hoped.

What about the various physical laws? Don't they ensure that the universe is self-contained? Don't they lock out divine action? To recall our analysis, the self-contained nature of physical laws in the modern sense relied on an identity of the Euclidean and atomic point, so that the inner necessity of mathematical relations really existed in nature. This mathematical necessity was the true binding force of those laws of nature that supposedly disallowed any divine interference (and, thereby, achieved an Epicurean end). Once the identity of the atom and the point was broken, that is, once the atom lost its geometrically precise and indestructible nature and revealed itself to be not only far more complex than any mathematical entity but also contingent, then the inner necessity of mathematical relationships no longer had their natural counterpart. A sign of this is the independence of nature from mathematics, or if we want to look at it the other way around, the dependence of the mathematical analysis of nature upon nature itself (seen in the frenzied attempts to stretch and invent new modes of mathematical analysis to describe the ever-stranger, ever more complex world of physics uncovered in the twentieth and twenty-first centuries). When Newtonians thought that all of nature had been captured with Euclidean geometry as modified by calculus, then it made sense to claim that nature was a self-contained system and that the laws of nature precluded any external interference. But with the fall of Newtonianism, mathematical analysis once again depends upon nature, and continues to need restructuring in order to capture the actual discovered complexity of nature. Nature itself breaks the closed circle of mathematical necessity. Of course, that does not mean that nature is lawless. Far from it. The things of nature are very regular. That is what allows for the wonderful ability to apply the regularity of mathematics to the regularity of nature. But the source of regularity is in nature, not in mathematics, and since neither the things of nature nor the universe itself are eternal, then the regularities of nature are not eternal either.

All this, one would think, would lead to a reassessment of the belief that nature is a closed system and that material processes were sufficient to explain what previously had been attributed to immaterial intelligence, but the materialist *habit* of mind has continued long after the theoretical presuppositions that undergirded it have fallen away. Materialists still act as if the Epicurean-Newtonian universe is intact, and certified free from deity and soul. But if the atom is neither eternal nor simple, and the universe is not eternal, what is left of Epicurean materialism but the original faith?

That does not, I hasten to add, mean that intelligent design has somehow won by default. Rather, it means that intelligent design is a live alternative again. Neither the universe or the atom are self-subsistent—might there be a cause of the universe other than itself? Might this cause be intelligent? The atom is far from simple. It seems to be as complex as the visible, biological phenomena its alleged simplicity was intended to replace. But if the atom is as complex as these biological phenomena of which it is part, then intelligent design certainly seems a serious alternative to the materialist belief that all visible, biological complexity can be reduced to atomic or subatomic simplicity. And this is all the more true because, since the time of Darwin, scientists have discovered that biological complexity is far more intricate than ever Epicurus or Darwin dreamed. Perhaps there is complexity all the way down to the subatomic level and all the way up to the farthest reaches of the heavens.

The more complex all layers of reality are—subatomic, atomic, cellular, biological, ecological and astronomical—the more difficult it becomes to believe that chance could replace intelligence, and the harder it becomes to hold to the faith of the materialist. Many contemporary materialists circumvent this problem by unwarranted reliance on quasi-Epicurean simplicity. I will use Richard Dawkins as an example. In his bestselling *The Blind Watchmaker* he relies on the existence of simplicity in two areas without justification: simplicity in the sub-biological world and simplicity of generating biological complexity. As to the first, his famous statement that "biology is the study of complicated things that give the appearance of having been designed for a purpose" is followed by the unwarranted assertion that "physics is the study of simple things that do not tempt us to invoke design."[1] The hidden assumption: since biological things rest, for the materialist, upon the sub-biological phenomena of physics, then because the sub-biological things are ultimately simple, biological things rest securely upon this foundation of simplicity. Thus, there is ultimately no need to invoke an intelligent cause.

The second area of alleged simplicity upon which Dawkins relies without warrant, the ease of generation of complexity, builds upon the first. It is Dawkins's "personal feeling . . . that once cumulative selection has got itself properly started, we need to postulate only a relatively small amount of luck in the subsequent evolution of life and [human] intelligence," so that (again) it is his "feeling . . . that, provided the difference between neighbouring intermediates in our series leading to [complex biological structures such as the] eye is *sufficiently small*, the necessary mutations are almost bound to be forthcoming."[2] Why the recourse to "feeling" precisely where one would need the most argument to prove his overall thesis that natural selection produces biological complexity that only appears to be designed? Mr. Dawkins has faith.

To this, I am sure, Mr. Dawkins would reply that my lack of faith that biological complexity can be caused by natural selection alone, without the aid of intelligence, is a form of the dreaded "Argument from Personal Incredulity," which he makes clear "is an extremely weak argument."[3] I reply: Are we better off, scientifically, with Dawkins's Argument from Personal Credulity, which we have just witnessed in the previous paragraph? Are we better off *believing* that natural selection can produce anything, or are we better off having *demonstrated* whether it can or cannot?

I repeat my charge that materialism has been reduced to the status of faith, and that faith is, ultimately, Epicurean in origin, rooted in the desire to keep the universe closed and locked tight so that the divine may not reenter. I call to witness contemporary materialist Richard Lewontin, candidly describing the "struggle between science and the supernatural."

We take the side of science *in spite* of the patent absurdity of some of its constructs, *in spite* of its failure to fulfill many of its extravagant promises of

---

[1] Richard Dawkins, *The Blind Watchmaker* (New York: W. W. Norton, 1996), p. 1.
[2] Ibid., pp. 146, 79.
[3] Ibid., p. 38.

health and life, *in spite* of the tolerance of the scientific community for unsubstantiated just-so stories, because we have a prior commitment, a commitment to materialism. It is not that the methods and institutions of science somehow compel us to accept a material explanation of the phenomenal world, but, on the contrary, that we are forced by our *a priori* adherence to material causes to create an apparatus of investigation and a set of concepts that produce material explanations, no matter how counterintuitive, no matter how mystifying to the uninitiated. Moreover, that materialism is absolute, for we cannot allow a divine Foot in the door. . . . To appeal to an omnipotent deity is to allow that at any moment the regularities of nature may be ruptured, that miracles may happen.[4]

Another objection could be made at this point. Granted that materialism may be a kind of faith, hasn't it proven itself to be a far more powerful scientific and intellectual tool, a far more fruitful hypothesis than any of its rivals, even and especially an intelligent design approach to science? To answer this properly, we would have to take a long detour into the history of science since the 1600s, so long, indeed, that it would make a rather large chapter in a book. To answer quickly but accurately, however, we may say that the history of the application of materialist principles to nature has been extraordinarily fruitful, insofar as it represented a half-truth, yet it has ended ultimately in undermining its own presuppositions. For example, insofar as chemical elements act *as if* atoms were actually little round indestructible balls, the atomism of John Dalton (1766-1844), the Newton of chemistry, was quite fruitful, even though many eminent chemists expressed skepticism toward chemical atomism throughout most of the nineteenth century. But it was precisely when chemists and physicists began to acknowledge areas where the Daltonian view did not apply, that chemistry and physics discovered subatomic reality at the beginning of the twentieth century, a discovery that spelled the end of Dalton's chemical system. As the history of science should make clear—whether we examine the fate of Dalton's Epicurean-like atoms or Newton's arguments—being fruitful and being true are not always identical.

Furthermore, as I have outlined above, the Epicurean premises of modern materialism were undermined during the very process by which scientists were trying to vindicate them. It was by the drive to the ultimately simple

---

[4]Richard Lewontin, "Billions and Billions of Demons," *New York Review of Books*, January 9, 1997.

atom that the incredible complexity of the atom was discovered. It was by the attempt to reduce visible biological complexity to the simplicity of the cellular level that the marvelous complexity of the cell was uncovered. Finally, as intelligent design theorists have recently been pointing out in great detail, it was in the century-long attempt to vindicate Darwinism that has shown most clearly that the same problems explaining the development of biological complexity—the gaps in the fossil record, the Cambrian explosion and so on—that plagued Darwin in his own day, still plague Darwinists today. In sum, the assiduous application of scientific materialism may have proven the most effective means for its final overthrow.

So much for intellectual indignation. What about the indignation of the materialist at my having argued that moral Darwinism yields all manner of atrocious moral results? To such moral indignation, I offer the following four points.

First of all, as I have shown, materialism has been amoral in principle from the very beginning. When modernity adopted Epicurean materialism as its scientific foundation and reality filter, it simply reinstated the ancient belief in the amorality of nature. The intrinsic purposefulness of nature, which was the foundation of moral claims according to the Christian natural law argument, was given the *coup de grâce* by Darwin. And if Darwin was right, Richard Dawkins has correctly drawn the implications: "The universe we observe has precisely the properties we should expect if there is at bottom no design, no purpose, no evil and no good, nothing but pointless indifference." Or as he asserts elsewhere, "Nature is not cruel, only pitilessly indifferent. This is one of the hardest lessons to learn. We cannot admit that things might be neither good nor evil, neither cruel nor kind, but simply callous—indifferent to all suffering, lacking all purpose."[5] If nature itself is not the result of an intelligent cause, and feelings (moral or otherwise) are likewise an unintended result of that unguided process of evolution, then even indignation merely tells us something about a person's evolutionary history, not about unmovable moral standards and prohibitions. There are no such moral standards or prohibitions in a universe defined by chance and flux.

And so, to the indignant materialist I say, it is not a question of what moral beliefs you happen to have (they may be quite laudable), but what

[5]Richard Dawkins, *River Out of Eden* (New York: Basic Books, 1995), p. 96.

moral beliefs your theoretical materialism will actually support. The answer to that last question, I hope, has been made clear in the previous chapters. If not, it will be startlingly clear by the end of this conclusion. As Hobbes especially realized, in a universe defined by purely materialist principles, moral principles must be reduced to descriptions of individual's preferences (or "values" as we now call them). And as Darwin concluded, in an evolutionary view moral sentiments must be mere descriptions of the pleasure or uneasiness that certain actions or omissions cause particular individuals at particular times.

Second, whatever a particular materialist may happen to desire morally, it is simply an incontrovertible fact that, with the increasing secularization of the West, the repugnance toward abortion, infanticide, eugenics, euthanasia and sexual libertinism, which had its theoretical and historical origin in Christianity (stretching back through Judaism), has given way to acceptance. The cause for this moral reversal is secularization, and as we have seen, the cause of secularization has been the rise of Epicurean materialism as culminating in moral Darwinism. Darwin's argument does indeed, to quote Daniel Dennett again, act like a "universal acid" that "eats through just about every traditional concept, and leaves in its wake a revolutionized world-view." It acts like an acid because it was originally designed by Epicurus to destroy belief in a creator God, the soul, the afterlife, purposefulness in nature and a permanent, natural foundation for morality independent of human opinion. The worldview that it leaves in its wake is a unified theoretical and moral account of the universe and humanity's place in it; and this revolutionized worldview is irreconcilable both theoretically and morally with any nonmaterialist view, but especially with Christianity.

Third, following on the second, I suspect that a good deal of the indignation of the materialist after reading the last chapter is due, in no small part, to vestigial moral habits of mind and feeling left over from Christianity. But these vestigial Christian moral habits, however laudable to the Christian, cannot be supported by materialist foundations. It will do no good, for example, to appeal to vague notions of "humanity" against barbarism, when materialism itself, through evolutionary theory, destroyed the very species distinction that allows one to speak of humanity as the source of permanent and definite moral distinctions. We saw in Darwin himself the contradictory nature of asserting that evolution has no goal *and* that natural selection somehow generates, as its culmination, "the disinterested love for all living creatures" as manifested in the expansion of our sentiment of sympathy. Haeckel certainly saw the contradiction, and removed it with one swipe by jettisoning the vestigial Christianity in Darwin. In doing this, Haeckel was simply forcing Darwinism to be true to its principles. As both Darwin and Haeckel pointed out, the distinction of species is a matter of scientific convenience for the materialist, a way to track momentary similarities among ever-changing material phenomena. But if the species distinction is arbitrary for the scientist, it is equally arbitrary, so Haeckel argued, for the moralist.

By contrast, for the natural law and Christianity the belief in the existence of the soul as that which causes human beings to be a distinct species, grounds all moral claims in regard to human beings. As an obvious example, "Thou shalt not kill" is a command that presupposes an absolute natural distinction between human beings and other animals. Without the soul, this distinction must inevitably be lost, and decisions about whom to kill and when will be made by the very criteria we apply to other animals: Is the animal—whether a human being, a chimpanzee or a cat—suffering or deformed, and does it contribute to the better breeding of the herd?

For those who doubt these assertions, I bring in, again, Richard Dawkins, who not only grasps the fundamental amorality of nature in Darwinism but also realizes the moral implications of eliminating the permanence of the species distinction. Dawkins argues that "it is just as well that the fossil record is poor"; a "complete fossil record would make it very difficult to classify animals into discrete nameable groups" because the existence of all the intermediate species would represent a seamless continuum to which we could not apply "discrete names."

In the midst of this argument he draws the following conclusion for morality: "It isn't just zoological classification that is saved from awkward ambiguity only by the convenient fact that most intermediates are now extinct. The same is true of human ethics and law. Our legal and moral systems are deeply species-bound. The director of a zoo is legally entitled to 'put down' a chimpanzee that is surplus to requirements, while any suggestion that he might 'put down' a redundant keeper or ticket-seller would be greeted with howls of incredulous outrage." The attempt to distinguish morally between a chimpanzee and a human being lacks any "defensible rationale at all." Indeed, "such is the breathtaking speciesism of our Christian-inspired attitudes, [that] the abortion of a single human zygote (most of them are destined to be spontaneously aborted anyway) can arouse more moral solicitude and righteous indignation than the vivisection of any number of intelligent adult chimpanzees!"

Such "speciesism" is, however, without foundation, for it results from an evolutionary accident: "the intermediates between humans and chimps are all dead." All those who believe "that there is something obvious and self-evident about human 'rights' should reflect that it is just sheer luck that these embarrassing intermediates happen not to have survived." Evolution undermines any belief in species-based distinctions. "The more our view of evolution approaches the extreme of smooth, continuous change, the more pessimistic shall we be about the very possibility of applying such words as bird or non-bird, human or non-human, to all animals that ever lived."[6]

As Dawkins realizes, if design in nature is the result of the Blind Watchmaker, that Watchmaker is also *morally* blind, and the "breathtaking speciesism of our Christian-inspired attitudes" is a historical vestige without foundation. But since Darwinism ultimately knocks the breath out of speciesism, the arbitrary moral boundaries historically imposed by Christianity should, he thinks, wither and die. Dawkins has little to worry about. The great inversion of Christian morality by moral Darwinism is already well-seated. Abortion on the developmental continuum from the zygote up to and including (with partial-birth abortion) the half-delivered baby is now permitted by law, and the passionate defense of animal rights is fast becoming a part of the curricula of accredited schools of law.

A final point about the materialist's indignation, one that flows from the last. As I shall show quite clearly below, all such feelings of indignation are transitory anyway. For some time now, Western society has been in the process of being transformed from Christian to Epicurean principles. As a parallel to the way that species for evolutionary theory only *appear* to be permanent because of our relatively ephemeral point of view, so also with moral feelings in regard to moral transformation. What one or two hundred years ago would have made even most materialists blush would not even raise an eyebrow today; what today makes many materialists cringe will

---

[6] Dawkins, *Blind Watchmaker*, pp. 262-64.

soon enough be quite acceptable. To use an obvious example, the acceptance of abortion even in extreme circumstances was almost unimaginable among wider materialist circles two hundred years ago. That, of course, was due to Christianity's influence over society, and hence over the moral feelings and imagination. But today, abortion on demand, for any reason whatsoever, is considered a fundamental right, and the popular push for infanticide is gaining steam. Any ephemeral, vestigial moral feelings which momentarily block the progress of moral Darwinism continually fall prey to the above transformation. We may call this phenomenon the law of moral compromise: what yesterday was considered barbaric and unimaginable, is today considered acceptable under extreme circumstances, and tomorrow will be considered part of the general advance of civilized society and unimaginable to live without.

But it is not just materialists who illustrate the law of moral compromise (and hence, it is not only materialists who will express indignation at my words). A significant number of Christians also illustrate this law, those who, in one way or another, have made their peace with Darwinism and have no wish to have that peace disturbed.

Some Christians have made peace by complete capitulation, accepting both Darwinism and moral Darwinism. They accept the Darwinist argument that the development of the cosmos has been entirely the result of material forces, and that nature itself (while it may somehow have been originally caused by a creator God) is completely self-contained and impregnable to divine manipulation (or, far worse, they immanentize God *as* the process of evolution, where God is equally redundant and even more impotent). This kind of Christian also accepts the moral conclusions of Darwinism, and therefore continually rewrites the moral codes of Christianity to match the process of moral secularization, so that divine charity now commands access to abortion and the gentle death of euthanasia, the acceptance of a continuum of sexual expression that includes premarital and nonheterosexual sex as equally "caring and mutually enriching," and so on. Those who have made their peace in this way are generally called "liberal Christians," a term that covers Christians of all persuasions from the mainstream, up the left bank, and beyond. Their ancestry, as I have argued, can be traced to Thomas Hobbes, Benedict de Spinoza and D. F. Strauss, and they are therefore continually at the forefront of the historical transformation from Christianity via Epicurean materialism to moral Darwinism, aiding and abetting the cause of complete secularization by smoothing out all the obstacles on the road of progress (and if they are theologians, removing the scruples of Christians by exegetical and doctrinal acrobatics almost exactly like those of Hobbes, Spinoza and Strauss). Indeed, no greater and more effective alliance has existed for the eradication of Christianity, both doctrinally and morally, than that between liberal Christianity and materialists.

But there are other Christians, those who have made peace with Darwinism, but who resist the encroachments of moral Darwinism—not realizing, in conformity to the great law of uniformity, that acceptance of the one must bring acceptance of the other. You cannot accept the theoretical foundations of Darwinism and reject the moral conclusions. A sure sign of this law in action is that the historical acceptance of Darwinism brought in its wake a great moral revolution, one which shows every sign of gaining speed, devouring beleaguered Christian moral principles as a predator picks off the weak and sickly as easy prey. Did you think the advent of abortion a bad thing thirty years ago? How soon it slipped into the acceptance of partial-birth abortion! And partial-birth abortion is now sliding into cries for compassionate infanticide. Did you dream thirty years ago that at the turn of the millennium people would be divided about *whether* we should grow human embryos for experimentation and medicinal tissue? Cloning? The great law of uniformity is relentless.

With this analysis of indignation in mind, let us look at the moral issues that divide us today—divide us because as a society we are in the midst of secularization, and therefore we are an utterly irreconcilable mix of rival views of the universe, of human nature and the human good. My point will be quite simple: there are only two extremes, moral Darwinism and Christianity. All attempts at compromise by those in between are only temporary, and one extreme—one view of the universe, our place in it, and the human good—will win out. As an illustration of the great law of uniformity, I will show that each side, each extreme, is drawing perfectly legitimate and consistent moral conclusions from its own principles. Such a mode of procedure will make manifest the ultimate importance of the debates between scientific materialists and intelligent design theorists, for the debates are about the truth and falsity of those very principles. And while intelligent design theorists are not necessarily Christian, intelligent design supports Christianity both in regard to the argument for an intelligent designer and also in regard to the intelligent design of nature that forms the basis of all natural law arguments.

Let us begin with abortion. As I have shown, Christianity was opposed to abortion right from the beginning, and has been all throughout its history— until the twentieth century, when the liberalized elements among Christians allowed materialism to transform their understanding of Christian moral doctrine. Materialism, on the other hand, has been amoral from the beginning. Even though Epicurus himself said nothing about abortion, he did argue that ultimately there was no natural justice, and the only reason we should refrain from particular acts against society's views of morality was to avoid the pain of punishment or disapproval.

If a particular society's moral views change, however, then such is no longer a problem. In regard to modern Epicureanism, Hobbes clearly stated that, since nature was amoral, we have a natural right to everything, even to one another's bodies, this being an extension of our absolute right to self-preservation. Little extrapolation is necessary to derive the right to abortion from these statements. Haeckel, following Darwin's principles, quite cogently drew abortion as a logical conclusion from Darwinism one hundred years before *Roe v. Wade*. Finally, as modern Epicurean sexual hedonism took hold, bringing with it complete freedom of sexuality, abortion became both desirable and historically inevitable. Thus, the Sangerian and Kinseyan sexual revolution, rooted firmly in moral Darwinism, could not help but destroy prohibitions against abortion, so that the presence of abortion would finally shift from being an aberration to a social necessity.

If that were not enough, abortion must be understood also as an extension of the eugenic views of Darwin. Not only did Darwin's account of species undermine the Christian prohibition of abortion by making the existence of the immortal, immaterial soul superfluous, but Darwin himself stated that if we "do not prevent the reckless, the vicious and otherwise inferior members of society from increasing at a quicker rate than the better class of men, the nation will retrograde, as has occurred too often in the history of the world." While Darwin's focus was on the breeders, little imagination was necessary to apply it to selection of those bred, as Haeckel's frank advocacy of abortion well illustrates. Abortion, then, is simply eugenics applied to the first stages of life.

In this regard, the arguments of contemporary moral Darwinist Michael Tooley for abortion and infanticide, which are supposed to represent the cutting edge of the new morality, are merely reproductions of Haeckel's reasoning. Like Haeckel, Tooley (rightly) blames Christianity for the animus against abortion and infanticide,[7] realizes that the "fiction" of the immortality of the soul is at the heart of the rejection of abortion and infanticide,[8] and denies personhood not only to the preborn but also to newborns because their capacities are identical to other animals who lack "personhood."[9] He therefore concludes—and correctly, given his materialist presuppositions, the same presuppositions held by Haeckel—that not only abortion but infanticide should be sanctioned because "new-born humans are neither persons nor even quasi-persons, and their destruction is in no way intrinsically wrong."[10]

We should not be surprised, then, that abortion is used for eugenic reasons, especially with the advent of better, more accurate prenatal screening. Indeed, its major selling point ever since *Roe v. Wade* has been as a means to eliminate the defective. It should be equally obvious that the more the genetic code is understood, the more it will be manipulated and commandeered to bring about eugenic perfection. The very day I am writing this sentence James Watson, the Nobel prize-winning scientist who helped discover the structure of the DNA double helix, has called for an end to laws prohibiting scientists from altering the genes of sperm, eggs and embryos to rid them of genetic defects. "I strongly favour controlling our children's genetic destinies. Working intelligently and wisely to see that good genes dominate as many lives as possible is the truly moral way for us to proceed."[11] Watson, of course, is perfectly illustrating Francis Bacon's call "to endow the human family with new mercies" by "laboring to lay the foundation . . . of human utility and power" over nature, conquering *fortuna* by technological mastery of nature, removing what mere chance gives us and replacing it with what we desire. For those who have qualms with manipulating human nature, Watson would certainly agree with Bacon that "the

---

[7]Michael Tooley, *Abortion and Infanticide* (Oxford: Clarendon, 1983), pp. 318-22.

[8]Ibid., pp. 329-47.

[9]Ibid., pp. 371, 397, 407.

[10]Ibid., p. 411.

[11]James Watson, "Fixing the Human Embryo is the Next Step for Science," *The Independent*, April 16, 2001 <www.independent.co.uk/story.jsp?story=66804>.

inquisition of nature" is not "in any way interdicted or forbidden" for there is no longer any Creator to forbid it.

We have uncovered another mode of eradicating moral limits used by moral Darwinists, one that is every bit as important as (and almost always works in tandem with) the law of moral compromise. We may call this expression of the susceptibility of moral limits to technological change Bacon's axiom: Whatever *can* be done, *will* be done. It is properly considered part of the moral Darwinian revolution precisely because, in Darwin's removing the species barrier and making the notion of human nature indistinct, the remaking of human nature cannot "in any way [be] interdicted or forbidden," for we are only (as contemporary physicist Stephen Hawking and many others are fond of saying) taking evolution into our own hands (and out of the hands of fortune, or chance).

Try as we might to deny it, with Darwinian ends and Baconian means, we are attempting (in Sanger's words) to breed a race of thoroughbreds by the elimination of all undesirables, and that requires (as Planned Parenthood has made known) ready access to abortion. Those in the womb who are discovered to be crippled, deformed, mentally retarded, mentally deficient, prone to serious disease or the wrong sex are already being aborted. As our technological ability to detect the unfit advances, so will our increasing desire for eugenic perfection yield ever more abortions. Whatever can be done, will be done.

We should also point out another, very Epicurean reason why abortions have become so commonplace. Given the world according to materialism, the moral Darwinist need not fear divine retribution. If a human being has no soul, and there is no God (or God is metaphysically locked out of the universe), then there is no reason to fear that procuring an abortion or engaging in infanticide will produce some dreadful effect. Once a fetus, as a biological growth dependent on the woman, has been terminated, the woman is simply relieved of a burden or pain which she was experiencing, and the fetus, as a material entity, is no more. There is no hell to fear, no spirit of the dead child to haunt the woman or doctor, no God to exact punishment. There is only relief, or in Epicurus's words, freedom from disturbance. Christians who still have some qualms may read one of the many theologians indebted to Hobbes, Spinoza and Strauss who have likewise removed both the soul and hell from Christianity and left only a benevolent Cheshire deity.

We must also note that pleas from Christians have little effect other than to irritate the moral Darwinist (as Dawkins makes clear). From the materialist's perspective it is those who oppose abortion who are truly irrational, offering groundless superstitions as reasons for making *others* suffer needlessly. The universe, if it is as the materialist believes, simply does not support any special moral status for a human being, and the same is all the more true for a biologically dependent entity growing within a woman. Placing restrictions on abortion is, then, for the moral Darwinist not only irrational but actually cruel.

But Christians do not live in that universe. Since Christians believe that human beings at the moment of conception are endowed with immortal souls, abortion is just another species of murder, an especially egregious one, since the unborn child is as innocent as a human being can get. While for the materialist, the nonhuman appearance of the fetus in its earliest stages is another sign that abortion should be allowed, for the Christian the appearance of the fetus at the early stages is inconsequential precisely because of belief that the soul, present from the very beginning, directs the continuous growth. Whether at one week or thirty-nine, the humanity of the unborn child is the same. Consequently, the hard cases (which seem so easy and obvious to the materialist), when a child is conceived by incest or rape, or the unborn child is detected in the womb as severely deformed, still do not allow for exceptions. Since full humanity is granted from conception, it is just as immoral to abort these hard cases in the womb, as it would be to kill a two-year old child who was originally conceived by rape or incest, or a two-year old severely handicapped child.

Further, for the Christian, since abortion is a species of murder, the killing of an unborn child causes even more serious ill effects to the souls of the woman and the abortionist. In contrast to the materialist, the morality of an act can never be reduced to the physical pleasure or pain it brings in this world, for the Christian believes all acts are to be judged in light of the eternal destiny of the immortal soul. Thus, a Christian must always choose the eternal good of the soul, even if it brings great pain to the body.[12] The pains of eternal damnation are far more terrifying than any pain of this world, and

---

[12]There is one exception. According to the principle of double-effect, if the life of the mother is *directly* and *immediately* endangered, abortion is permissible but regrettable.

the joys of heaven eclipse all previous pleasure and pain. Finally, the humanity of the unborn is, for the Christian, the object of charity, charity in the original sense of love. Since God so loved the world that he gave his only Son that sinners might be saved from their self-wrought destruction, every life is the object of that divine charity, every life is made in the image of that God who gave himself up to death so that human beings, regardless of whether they are convenient or deformed, might have eternal life. The ultimate worth of all human beings, born or unborn, is rooted, then, both in their origin and their goal.

Obviously, the two sides can never be reconciled over the issue of abortion, for their moral principles are based on entirely irreconcilable universes. For a materialist, the unnecessary causing of pain for the sake of a belief in imaginary entities (like souls) and imaginary worlds (like heaven and hell), is not only irrational, as we have said, but evil (defined as the causing of pain without providing significant pleasure). Whether or not any individuals wish to engage in such fantasies themselves, to impose make-believe worlds on *others* is not only absurd but pernicious. Would a Christian, if starving, want to be kept from eating meat by a Hindu who believes in reincarnation? No, for the Christian, reincarnation is pure nonsense. Why should a materialist be controlled by the likewise groundless Christian belief system left over from our prescientific history?

For a Christian, on the other hand, the rise and quick acceptance of abortion was by far the greatest evil of the twentieth century, dwarfing, by the sheer number of corpses, the atrocities of the Nazis. And the evil continues unabated today. Nothing could be more horrifying, more satanic, than that day after day, hour after hour, minute after minute, for over thirty years the systematic and routine killing of unborn children has been taking place on a scale that makes the twentieth and now the twenty-first centuries the darkest and most barbaric ages the world has ever seen.

Again, how can there be a compromise? What *one* sees as a medical benefit relieving suffering that, prior to the legalization of abortion, was denied to women (causing them untold suffering with the bearing of unwanted and undesirable children), the *other* sees as the advance of an evil so profoundly immense and pervasive as to approach apocalyptic proportions. What for one is technological progress that should be spread across the globe so as to reduce suffering, is for the other moral regress, the spread of which must be considered nothing less than demonic. Between the two moral universes there is no bridge, no possible compromise. That is precisely why the abortion debate refuses to die down, for there can be no reconciliation until either the materialist becomes a Christian (or at least a follower of the natural law), or the Christian becomes a materialist. Until then, there shall only be ceaseless battle.

The appearance of compromise is, as stated above, caused by the presence of moral Darwinists who still hold Christian moral beliefs by vestigial habit *and* of liberal Christians who are in the middle of bargaining away successive pieces of Christian moral doctrines. It is merely an appearance, because any compromise position short of either pure Christianity or pure moral Darwinism is inherently unstable: it is already moving before the ink can dry on any such compromise position, and it is moving ever more quickly toward pure moral Darwinism.

We can best understand this law of moral compromise by seeing it in action. The pattern is simple, and seen very clearly in the history of the acceptance and extension of abortion rights in the twentieth century. At the beginning, a compromise in the Christian moral argument was sought in regard to extreme cases. When proponents of abortion were attempting to change the laws of the country in mid-twentieth century, they always appealed to cases where the child was severely deformed, or the mother's life was in immediate danger, or the child was the product of rape or incest, and further, they originally designated the legitimacy of abortion to be in the first trimester only, when the fetus least resembles a human being.

But the law of moral compromise prevailed: what yesterday was considered barbaric and unimaginable is today considered acceptable under extreme circumstances, and tomorrow will be considered part of the general advance of civilized society and unimaginable to live without. No one in 1972—except the hard-core materialist (who never had any qualms) and the hard-core Christian (for whom abortion and infanticide are both species of murder)—would have imagined that legalizing abortion only for "extreme" cases in the first trimester would lead so quickly to abortion on demand for any reason throughout all nine months of pregnancy, or that we would be debating, twenty-five years after *Roe*, whether we should make partial-birth abortion illegal. Such would have been, for most, unimaginable, but the "most" to whom we are referring here are the moral Darwinists with vestigial Christian moral beliefs and liberal Christians who accepted the universe of Darwinism and molded Christianity to suit it. But today, the moral imagination of these two compromise positions has moved. Neither can now imagine a world without the full right to abortion up to and including the right to partial-birth abortion. At this point, they both *may* still find infanticide unimaginable, or find it unimaginable except in hard cases where the newborn is severely deformed, but of course, since the powers of the moral imagination follow the compromise as it shifts toward pure moral Darwinism, what is unimaginable today will soon enough be unimaginable to do without.

The eugenic continuum of moral Darwinism includes not only abortion and infanticide, but also euthanasia. If we look at the growing acceptance of euthanasia, we can see the same pattern as with abortion and infanticide. For moral Darwinism, a human being is one more animal. When other animals are severely deformed, or are infirm because of age, we human beings consider it humane to relieve them of their suffering. We do not drag it out because all the animal has is its physical existence, and when such existence becomes unbearable or undesirable, or is overly burdensome to those who are its caretakers, then we put it down. And so the moral Darwinists ask (and quite rightly, given their principles), Why on earth, since earthly existence is all we have, would we deny ourselves that same compassionate recourse to euthanasia? On moral Darwinist grounds it is not only foolish to spend the last days of one's life in pain waiting patiently to die a natural death, but it is pernicious to require someone else to do so, especially since the prohibition is based on beliefs that materialist science has entirely discredited.

For a Christian, however, the prohibition against suicide and against killing others even out of mercy, is one more part of the Christian rejection of pagan morality, and has its roots not only in a belief in the afterlife (and hence an immortal, immaterial soul), but also in the belief that Christians have been called to suffer in imitation of Jesus Christ. As Christ in the Gospels makes clear, "If any man would come after me, let him deny himself and take up his cross daily and follow me" (Lk 9:23; Mt 16:24; Mk 8:34), for "he who does not take his cross and follow me is not worthy of me" (Mt 10:38). "Whoever does not bear his own cross and come after me, cannot be my disciple" (Lk 14:27). Or in Paul's words, "If we have been united with him in a death like his, we shall certainly be united with him in a resurrection like his" (Rom 6:5), for we are "fellow heirs with Christ, provided we suffer with him in order that we may also be glorified with him" (Rom 8:17). "For as we share abundantly in Christ's sufferings, so through Christ we share abundantly in comfort too" (2 Cor 1:5). Thus, while Christians may certainly take palliative measures in reducing such pain, to stretch such measures to the direct elimination of life must be considered evil.

What compromise can there be, in regard to euthanasia, when the views of the moral Darwinist and the Christian in regard to suffering are so diametrically opposed? Again, we find that what is good according to moral Darwinism is evil for the Christian; and what is good for the Christian is considered evil by the moral Darwinist.

We are now, in regard to euthanasia, at a kind of "hinge-point"; that is, the right to doctor-assisted suicide has been accepted in extreme cases, and, therefore, according to the law of moral compromise, within a few short years, through the combined efforts of moral Darwinists and liberal Christians, we shall move inevitably toward euthanasia on demand for any reason. Soon enough "unbearable pain" in regard to decisions of euthanasia will be construed as broadly as "a woman's health" is in regard to abortion, extending from physical to psychological pain, and from pain present now to pain present only by anticipation. Further, euthanasia will be quickly extended from voluntary to involuntary cases (indeed, it already has been in the Netherlands). The reason should by now be clear. Any limit imposed on the right to die, or the right to kill someone whose life is judged to be worthless (or simply, worth less), is, according to the amoral foundation of materialism, arbitrary. Such limits are only imposed by those still faintly controlled by Christian moral habits. Today we may find it unimaginable that allowing euthanasia in extreme cases will lead to euthanizing the elderly, the infirm, the retarded and the otherwise undesirable, but as with abortion, what is unimaginable today will soon enough become a cherished right. We may find it unimaginable that we could end up doing exactly as the Nazis did, but that is to disregard the historical fact that the very same arguments about euthanasia being circulated in respectable academic circles right now circulated in Germany among equally respectable circles in the 1920s. Indeed, if we were to place our euthanasia debates alongside the translated debates of pre-World War II Germany, and take out all particular historical references, no one could tell whether the arguments came from early twentieth-century

Germany or early twenty-first-century America.

It should also be obvious that the moral Darwinist and Christian must be divided in regard to questions of cloning and using "tissue" from embryos for research and medical therapy. For a moral Darwinist, since a human being is reducible to its physical parts, and since this life is all we have, technologically manipulating modes of reproduction, whether we want to create a child for a childless couple or create a source of living tissue for research and medicinal purposes, is perfectly reasonable, and, in both the short and long run, reduces the suffering in the world. Such, as we recall, was Bacon's dream, and the moral Darwinist puts Bacon's axiom, which he takes as a self-evident truth, into the imperative: Whatever can be done, *should* be done. *If* we can clone, *then* we should clone. *If* embryonic stems cells may be harvested and used, *then* we should do it. For the Christian, however, not only is it abominable to manipulate the mode of procreation designed by the Creator, but it is even more horrid to use "tissue" from abortions for medicinal purposes, especially since it must be living tissue to be useful. Beyond all this, to grow human beings for medicinal harvesting makes the evils of Nazi Germany seem minuscule by comparison. Again, the two are irreconcilable. What one sees as a medical advance, shedding more light on this world, the other sees as precipitous moral decline, bringing an incomparably dark age upon the human race.

In matters of sexuality, we are so far beyond the original Christian moral position, and so far on the road to becoming complete Epicurean hedonists, that little remains of our culture in regard to sex that is identifiably Christian. The normalization of premarital sex, of divorce, of homosexuality and so on is nearly complete. Yet it is still worthwhile to carry out the analysis, especially since moral Darwinists may not be inclined to see themselves as contributing to the Sangerian-Kinseyan sexual revolution.

If we look at the entire modern revival of Epicurean materialism, it should be clear by now that for an Epicurean materialist, since pleasure is equated with the good and pain with evil, and since sexual pleasure, of all the pleasures of sense, is the strongest, then (as Sanger and Kinsey saw clearly) society progresses insofar as it releases sexuality from the limits imposed on it both by Christianity and by nature. The limits set on sexuality by Christianity are simply based on a belief system that has long since been overthrown, so that, for example, opposition to homosexuality is akin to Christianity's earlier opposition to Copernicus. Whatever limits to sexual expression seem to be set by nature are not there because of an intelligent designer, and hence such limits have no moral purpose but exist ultimately as products of Darwinian evolution, that is, of a combination of chance and natural selection. However beneficial these limits may have proven in the past, we are at a point where we can take evolution into our own hands by the Baconian mastery of nature. Thus, not only may sexuality be freed from any natural limit, but even the evolutionary purpose sexuality once served in regard to the perpetuation of genetic advantages can be carried on by far more efficient technological means. Since physical existence is all we have, and physical pleasure of one sort or another is our only good, then to keep harmless sexual desires from being expressed is, again, not only irrational (in regard to ourselves) but pernicious, if we insist that *others* must restrict their desires.

For the Christian, however, the heart of the natural law is the family, for the distinction of male and female is at the very origin of our divinely ordained social nature. Deviation from the ordained goal of heterosexual intercourse within marriage therefore strikes at the very heart of the natural law. Not only are biblical injunctions against homosexuality (let alone besti- ality) crystal clear, but the very design of the male and female seem, to the Christian, obvious, incontrovertible proof of the heterosexual nature of human sexuality. Releasing sexuality from heterosexual marriage, then, con- stitutes rebellion not only against nature and nature's God, but against com- mon sense as well.

As with our other issues, we find that the two rival moral universes have nothing in common. The modern Epicurean hedonist regards pleasure as the highest sexual good; the Christian confines sexual pleasure to the higher good of marriage and the family. The Epicurean hedonist focuses on the release of sexuality from conventional and natural restrictions; the Christian continually forces convention to follow natural restrictions. As a result, what is progress to one is regress to the other.

In regard to our current situation, Epicurean hedonism is far along the path to establishing Sanger's and Kinsey's sexual utopia, where the only restrictions on sexuality will reside in one's imagination. We have come to the current state by that same law of moral compromise, where acceptance of the extreme has simply meant that the extreme was normalized and extended within a short period of time. No one in the first part of the twen-

tieth century (except the pure Epicurean bent on revolution and the pure
Christian warning of anarchy) could imagine that the liberalization of
divorce laws could lead in the second part of the twentieth century to the
near acceptance of homosexual marriages. But the sons and daughters of
those very church members who out of compassion argued alongside the
Epicurean in regard to divorce laws, are now devising the marriage rites for
same-sex couples in their churches and lobbying for same-sex insurance
benefits as a fundamental human right. As with abortion, the very nature of
the principles of each side, the Epicurean and the Christian, ensures that
any compromise must inevitably shift toward the pure position of one or the
other, because neither side supports the compromise.

Homosexual marriage is a clear example. Why, on Epicurean principles,
should two men need to conform to standards of monogamous fidelity, standards that have as their bases the Christian restriction of marriage? Or, to
look at it the other way, the very nature of the monogamous fidelity for
Christians is rooted in a sexual ethic that rejects homosexuality however it is
expressed. Making it monogamous does not make it any better, any more
than a man promising to have sex with only one child would make it any less
a reprehensible act of pedophilia. The compromise position, then, could only
make sense to a materialist still nagged by subliminal, vestigial Christian
moral habits, or a Christian who has sold nearly everything in his universe to
the materialist. The notion of sanctifying homosexual unions by demanding
that they be monogamous will soon enough go the way of limiting abortions
to the first trimester. Furthermore, the push for pedophilia is now the
"extreme" which will push homosexuality out of the spotlight of public
debate and into full normality. That pedophilia is even being debated, rather
than simply rejected as unimaginably vile, means that it is likely the next
item of sexual liberation due for normalization.

To all this, the moral Darwinist may say that here, especially, I am way
off base. For while one may make a case that Epicurean hedonism might be
at the root of the Sangerian and Kinseyan view of sexuality, it certainly has
no connection to Darwin. As proof of this objection the materialist could
offer the following: While Darwin did advocate eugenics, he certainly did
not advocate sexual libertinism—quite the opposite! The necessity of successful breeding to make natural selection effective ensures that heterosexual intercourse is given pride of place in any evolutionary scheme.

I confess that I have been baiting the Darwinist throughout this section, referring mainly to Epicurean hedonism, so as to help elicit just such a response. Here is my reply. First and most obvious, while Darwin himself was a quite traditional, monogamous husband, he advocated a return to a much less restricted mode of breeding for the better stock of human beings: "The most able should not be prevented by laws or customs from succeeding best and rearing the largest number of offspring." Second, as should be clear from Darwin's "natural history" of morality in the *Descent*, many customs are compatible with a society's survival as long as they are accompanied by sufficient breeding as well. Thus, just as, for example, many societies have existed for quite long periods with a custom of infanticide of the deformed, so also the practice of homosexuality or pedophilia (say, along the ancient Greek model) does not violate the principles of natural selection as long as it does not displace heterosexual breeding (and may, according to some, promote "the disinterested love for all living creatures"). Finally, since we are on an evolutionary spectrum with other primates, any mode of sexual expression engaged in by other primates is part of our heritage as well. What is licit for them, since it is obviously natural, is licit for us. For any that doubt that we could find Kinsey's sexual utopia in our evolutionary history, the recent PBS *Evolution* series[13] made the connection quite vivid. In the fifth episode, entitled "Why Sex?" the audience was treated to extended footage of the bonobos. Bonobos are the "make love, not war" member of the primate family. Yes, males and females mate, but sex is used as a substitute for aggression and also simply for pleasure, so that they copulate continually and not just in relation to mating cycles. In addition, the females engage in frequent sessions of lesbian genito-genital rubbing, and the males have their parallel homosexual means of sexual release. Finally, older bonobos engage sexually with juveniles as well. PBS captured it all for public television. Even though, according to the series, we are more directly related to the aggressive, far less sexual chimpanzee, the narrator could not help emitting a sigh: if only our evolutionary path had been somewhat different, "we might have evolved to be a totally different, more peaceful, less violent, more sexual species." PBS's showcasing of the bonobos was undoubtedly fashioned after the research and propaganda program of primatologist Frans de Waal, C. H.

---

[13]The series first aired in September 2001.

Candler Professor of Primate Behavior at Emory University. Author of many books on the social behavior of primates, he recently collaborated with Frans Lanting, a wildlife photographer, to create *Bonobo: The Forgotten Ape*. Even a glance at this book will make it clear that Kinsey and the bonobos are kindred spirits, so to speak, and that moral Darwinists are now pushing (in de Waal's words) for "a revised view of the origins of human nature."[14]

Given the above analysis, several points should now be obvious. First, any attempt to divide the universe in two—giving the scientific "stuff" to Darwinism and the moral "stuff" to religion—is bound to fail. In full accord with the great law of uniformity, Epicurus designed a unified materialist view, both theoretical and moral. No amount of gerrymandering of reality, whether it has its roots in Polybius, or the good intentions of materialists, or the desperation of Christians, can override this most fundamental law: *there is only one universe*. And so, Stephen Jay Gould's NOMA concept (of non-overlapping magisteria in which "scientists cannot claim higher insight into moral truth from any superior knowledge of the world's empirical constitution," as long as "religion can no longer dictate the nature of factual conclusions residing properly within the magisterium of science") is doomed to failure.[15] A materialist universe necessarily yields a materialist ethics. Historically, that is just what is happening, or has all but happened. The materialist universe, the universe of Darwin, has nearly eaten and digested the Christian cosmos, and is attempting to make a last meal out of the Christian moral world as well. The culture wars are cosmological wars.

That last point is bound to be overlooked, even after working through the arguments of this entire book. When Gould demands, as a term of peace, that "religion can no longer dictate the nature of factual conclusions residing properly within the magisterium of science," he is already assuming that science means science as defined by materialism. The intelligent design movement arose to challenge those very assumptions, and to do so on scientific grounds. Gould places himself in the comfortable position, in his concordat, of treating all nonmaterialist attempts to explain the world (such as intelligent design) as violations of the treaty. He purports to keep hands off the moral realm as a concession, but as we have seen above, "factual conclu-

[14]Frans B. M. de Waal, "Bonobo Sex and Society," *Scientific American* 277 (1995): 82-88.
[15]Stephen Jay Gould, *Rocks of Ages* (New York: Ballantine, 1999), pp. 9-10.

sions" about nature entail, of necessity, that these conclusions be applied to human nature, and that means materialist science cannot and will not honor the terms of this false peace.

A second point should be equally obvious by now. In regard to the current moral conflicts that so disturb our culture, we must realize that no appeal to "rights" can resolve these conflicts. It might *seem* that we could all agree to disagree about the nature of the cosmos, and settle our differences according to agreed upon notions of rights which all human beings believe, and that may be used to adjudicate disputes. Nothing could be further from the truth, however, and it is worthwhile to examine why, for such an examination will show the real state of the crisis that now afflicts our culture.

As a previous chapter stated, Thomas Hobbes was the father of our contemporary use of the term "rights." Hobbes clearly understood that, since the universe was amoral, natural law in the traditional sense was dead. In its place, he substituted natural *right*, where "right" was merely a high-flown description of a personal desire. His assumption was the very same one which underlies the hopeful appeals to rights today: since we cannot agree on what is truly good and truly evil, each of us must *"be contented with so much liberty against other men, as he would allow other men against himself."* Even more telling, as Dawkins makes clear, evolution eliminates *all* moral claims based on species distinctions, thereby disallowing even modern rights arguments to be applied only to human beings as a distinct species.

But the very assumption that gave birth to modern natural rights belongs solely to the universe of the materialist. According to the rival view of natural law, the good has already been determined; indeed, it is written into our very nature. No one, according to the natural law, can claim the liberty to do anything against the natural law. Thus, while the materialist is trying to maximize the liberty of individuals to follow whatever they happen to desire, the Christian is attempting to reestablish the standards of goodness inherent in the natural law (or at least, forbid the most obvious transgressions).

Thus, just as Christians cannot be satisfied with Gould's NOMA, for it binds them in chains while they await eventual extermination, so also Christians cannot make peace by appealing to the supposedly neutral framework of modern natural rights. Since modern rights are rooted in an amoral view of the universe, if Christians fall into arguing as if the foundation of morality were in such rights (rather than in nature), they must always lose ground, rather than gain it, for the boundaries of claims for rights will always and only represent the extent to which society has been secularized, and will inevitably move (according to the law of compromise) toward pure Epicurean materialism. Only when a nonmaterialist account of nature is reestablished, and moral arguments are rerooted in the natural law, can rights once again reside in their proper place, as following upon and in accordance with natural law.

Moreover, arguing for Christian principles using the Hobbesian language of modern rights, is like arguing for the importance of God as an evolutionary theist: the claims to rights always trump any other supposed moral claim, in the way that materialist nontheistic evolution always makes superfluous any theistic evolutionist's theoretical claims. The reason should be clear: as we have seen in Hobbes, such rights are merely the description of desires, and since all desires are equal, and the desire to live according to Christian moral principles is just one more desire jostling for elbow room in the judicial arena, natural law is doomed to extinction by reducing it to the level of trivial descriptions of merely personal desires. A bumper sticker I once saw sums up the fate of Christian natural law: "If you don't like abortion, don't get one." Abortion is reduced to a matter of mere personal preference.

A third point should be obvious as well. The moral conflicts that divide our society today can only be resolved on the theoretical level; that is, the moral conflicts are ultimately rooted in cosmological conflicts, so that resolving the scientific debates about nature is the only way to resolve the moral conflicts about human nature. Since all compromise by the well-intentioned middle is ephemeral, and neither the pure Epicurean nor the pure Christian can accept compromise, our moral battles must be cosmological battles.

It should also be clear that moral Darwinists—those whose lives are defined by the gains won by the rise to ascendancy of the moral tenets of modern Epicureanism as culminating in Darwin—will not only fight passionately to keep those gains, but will throw their considerable cultural weight behind the materialist interpretation of science *and* the debunking and humiliation of Christianity. Advocates and beneficiaries of abortion on demand and the growth of cloned human beings for experimentation and organ harvesting must have a universe that supports their desires and their way of life, and that means they must have a universe without human souls, the afterlife or God. Advocates of euthanasia must believe, with Epicurus, that "death is nothing to us," for when we die, "we do not exist," and therefore they must have a universe in which, again, immaterial entities—the immortal soul or an avenging God—cannot exist. Death must be the final exit, beyond which there is endless nothingness. Advocates of the release of sexuality from all restrictions must also have a universe in which nature is amoral, and nature can only be amoral if it is the result of chance rather than an intelligent designer. Simply put, advocates of moral Darwinism, whether the scientist who wishes to clone, the woman who defends partial-birth abortion, the compassionate advocate of death with "dignity," or the propagandist for pansexual bliss—all alike must defend the *faith* of the materialist, and all alike must attack the faith of the Christian.

Part of this defense consists in treating intelligent design as if it were a species of uneducated biblical fundamentalism, and part consists in keeping evidence that contradicts materialism hidden from public view. Part of this attack consists in luring Christians into yielding all intellectual grounds to scientific materialism in exchange for a chair at the low end of the table in the debate, and part consists in keeping caricatures of Christians burning righteous scientists at the stake before the public eye. All these add up to a continued attempt to keep legitimate, scientifically verifiable evidence from entering the public debate, evidence that challenges the materialist faith.

As for the merely theoretical materialists, the work-a-day scientists whose minds have been so formed by the tenets of scientific materialism that to entertain the possibility of criticism of its foundations is to shake their very universe, they may or may not support moral Darwinism with their hearts. But they cannot have the luxury of two universes that contradict each other, a scientific universe defined by materialism and a moral universe defined by the natural law and Christianity. They cannot have a science that tells them that species distinctions are merely arbitrary because species are continually in flux, and have a moral position, as in natural law, that depends essentially on the reality of the species distinction "human being." They cannot be humane if humanity is not real, and it is just this distinction "human being" that allows for the moral distinction between the killing of an animal and the killing of a human being. If, then, these scientists' work supports materialism, then their work inevitably advances the cause of moral Darwinism, and that means the extinction of any rival moral view.

To return to the full-fledged moral Darwinist, we conclude that much of the resistance to intelligent design arguments is not theoretical but moral, and since (as I have argued), the materialist principles that excluded the divine from nature have been undermined by the progress of science itself, then even more of what *appears* to be purely theoretical resistance to intelligent design is actually moral in origin. If materialism is a kind of faith—that is, a hypothesis attempting to explain nature, but doing so by excluding, *a priori*, nonmaterialist explanations (a hypothesis against which there is mounting counter-evidence)—then what fuels this faith? To be quite blunt, the fervent desire that its opposite, intelligent design, *not* be true. That is what makes it, above all, Epicurean in origin.

Given these stark alternatives, I would now like to argue as an apologist for Christianity, especially to those between the extremes of pure materialism and pure Christianity. Moving from the position of a neutral observer to a Christian, I can say that the proper way to characterize the moral Darwinist who still holds to Christian moral habits of thought is someone capable of conversion. I believe that such half-hearted Darwinists still have half their hearts; that is, the materialists who cling to moral positions that their pure materialist principles undermine are demonstrating the existence and resilience of their God-given consciences. Treating a human being as yet another animal in the laboratory, and carting the elderly, the retarded or the handicapped off to be exterminated as we would take animals to the veterinarian to be put down, raise a natural repugnance within the half-hearted materialists' hearts, and the source of that repugnance is the natural recognition that human beings truly are distinct as species. This desire to treat human beings *as if* they had an immaterial, immortal soul, *as if* they were made in the image of God, is parallel to the secret desire of half-hearted materialists to wonder at nature *as if* it were designed. They have generally suppressed this latter desire, but thankfully they still have difficulty suppressing their consciences—and that is a sign of no small hope. But we must not have false hope, for history proves all too well that the conscience may become so deformed that the natural recognition of humanity is almost completely lost. For every half-hearted materialist drawing back in disgust at the thought of legalizing infanticide, there is an Ernst Haeckel or a Michael Tooley or a Peter Singer pushing the eradication of humanity to its proper materialist conclusion. Thus, the half-hearted materialists must truly search their hearts, for their hearts may be telling them something most urgently, even though the message of their consciences cannot be heard in a universe that does not support it.

And so, to the half-hearted moral Darwinists I say, Do not let your hearts be hardened all the way. Your vestigial Christian moral habits are not vestigial but natural, rooted in your humanity, for Christian morality is rooted in the natural law, and your humanity is real. Do not cut off the support for humanity by rejecting *a priori* that the universe really is ordered, not just apparently, but really ordered by an intelligence so much greater than ours that the intricate complexity of nature is unending. Because the universe is irreducibly complex—not just on one level, but on successive layers of inter-related complexity—accepting the apparent complexity as real does not eliminate science but destroys materialist reductionism so that science may be released from the desire to shrink the universe and instead may inquire ever more deeply into creation, confident that there is no end to the wonder of discovery. To increase our awe and wonder at creation is the natural effect of human science; and to increase the awe and wonder at nature increases our respect for the inviolability of human nature. The commands of God, written into our very nature, are not ultimately negative; they are our guide to true happiness. Certainly the attempt to replace the natural law with the laws of motion has not made us, in the West, any happier; we seem, instead, to have created a dreary Brave New World where scientific manipulation of our humanity is destroying our humanity. Perhaps the psalmist, singing his praises so very long ago, was correct in seeing the intricate connection between the glorious order of creation and the special status of human beings that allows "humanity" to be a true moral distinction:

> When I look at thy heavens, the work of thy fingers,
>> the moon and the stars which thou hast established;
> what is man that thou art mindful of him,
>> and the son of man that thou dost care for him?
> Yet thou hast made him little less than God,
>> and dost crown him with glory and honor. (Ps 8:3-5)

To the half-hearted Christian, we must say that the redefinition of charity, so that its object is the maximization of pleasure and minimization of pain in this world, can only end in the destruction of all charity. It can only end, according to the inevitable law of moral compromise, in the world of Epicurus, Hobbes and Darwin. Denying the pains of hell and the joys of heaven out of misplaced charity only results in creating a world in which human beings consider any pain to be infernal, and throw themselves into the pursuit of every pleasure with the same single-minded intensity as saints throw themselves into the pursuit of heavenly glory. The twentieth century should be enough of a prophetic warning that a hell on earth can quite easily be created out of the burning desire to create a heaven on earth.

I also hope that this book will bring half-hearted Christians to consider the unexamined assumptions about the history and nature of science that (through Hobbes, Spinoza and Strauss) came to define modern scriptural analysis. An entire book could be written on this very topic, but again, I believe that I have at least given enough in outline to see the general problem created by Christians accepting premises that were designed to destroy Christianity. As should be abundantly clear, there is no Christianity without Christ who is both God and man. The strange and contradictory belief that God exists but cannot manipulate his creation at will is the ultimate Epicurean source of the rejection not only of the miracles of Christ, but (since the miracles were signs of his divinity) the divinity of Christ. The rejection of the divinity of Christ, and substitution of Christ the merely moral man, has not saved Christianity from irrelevance. Indeed, just the opposite has occurred. Nothing could be more irrelevant than a superfluous example of secular humanity—we have too many present around us to need one from ancient Galilee. I pray, then, that half-hearted Christians may have the other half of their hearts awakened by the above analysis of the spoliation of Christianity by alien ideas.

I hope as well that this book will bring some clarity not only to the scientific debates between materialists and intelligent design theorists, but in the more public realm, to the moral debates which tear at the fabric of our society. In regard to the latter, the general shift in Western society from Christian to Epicurean moral principles has continued unabated—if anything, it seems to have picked up speed—as the universal acid of Darwinism eats away unceasingly at all that contradicts it. At the time of this writing, the newspapers are discussing cloning of human beings; by the time of this book's publication, it may have been done. At the time of this writing, the Dutch have just legalized euthanasia, insisting that all due precautions will be in place to ensure that it is used only in extreme cases; by the time of this book's publication, euthanasia in comparatively trivial cases will quite possibly have occurred frequently in the Netherlands and therefore become acceptable, rendering all official precautions moot.

All of this, I hope, makes the intelligent design movement far more important in the minds of the readers. Intelligent design is not just an academic or intellectual fad, but a most needed attempt to restore the human intellect to its rightful place as that which can know and take delight in the created order. Properly, that is its primary goal. As stated in the introduction, "Every distinct view of the universe, every theory about nature necessarily entails a view of morality; every distinct view of morality, every theory about human nature necessarily entails a cosmology to support it." The restoration of the proper view of nature will bring with it the restoration of the proper view of human nature. Let us hope and pray that the intelligent design revolution will not be too late.

But again, I issue this warning: the *desire* that a particular moral argument be true is not, as such, *evidence* that the universe actually supports the desired moral argument. This is a warning to both Christians and moral Darwinists. Moral aspirations on both sides must be kept from distorting or manipulating the actual evidence uncovered by science. Regardless of which side evidence supports, all evidence must be examined and none censored. The truth shall be revealed.

SUBJECT INDEX

abortion, 9, 24-25, 29-30, 85, 99-100, 150, 156, 165, 176-77, 221, 263-65, 273-74, 297, 299-309, 312, 316
  Christian vs. Epicurean, 89-93
Achilles, 126
Adam and Eve
  biblical, 81, 118
  Epicurean, 65-66, 68, 72, 172-74
Adams, John, 129
afterlife, 10, 21-22, 33, 46, 71, 81, 83, 98, 108, 150-52, 156, 180, 186, 221, 256, 272, 297, 308, 317
  and Darwin, 237
Agassiz, Louis, 222
Aktion T-4 euthanasia program, 263
Ambrose, St., 97
American Birth Control League, 273
American Eugenics Society, 273
angels, 181, 183-84, 200, 209
Aristotle/Aristotelianism, 60n. 1, 67-68, 79n. 2, 81n. 5, 85, 96, 100-104, 106-7, 111, 114-15, 143, 146, 151, 162, 171, 181, 184, 194n. 45, 216-18, 238
  radical Aristotelians, 101, 103, 106
Arnobius, 97
Athanasius, 97
Athenagoras, 97
atomism, 23, 34, 37-38, 40-44, 46-47, 49, 51, 54, 56, 61-62, 68, 70, 86, 91, 102-3, 105, 109, 111-12, 115-

16, 118-25, 127-33, 136, 139, 142, 144, 153, 157-64, 167-68, 172, 180, 198, 202, 216-17, 223-25, 229, 241
  its collapse, 291-96
  and the swerve, 53-54, 134-35
Augustine, St., 93-94, 96-97
  radical Augustinians, 101, 103, 117, 177
Augustus Caesar, 96, 211
Bacon, Francis, Baconian, 61n. 6, 145, 153-56, 159, 169, 171, 190, 204, 211-12, 215, 221, 225, 243, 252, 303-4, 310, 311
Bacon's Axiom, 304
Barbour, Ian, 12
Basil, 97
Bateson, William, 267
Beer, Gavin de, 228-30
Behe, Michael, 15n. 1
bestiality, 88, 99, 175, 177, 281, 283, 285-88, 311
Binding, Karl, 262-63
Bölsche, Wilhelm, 261
Bonobos, 313-14
Bonner, John, 236
Boyle, Robert, 111-12, 119n. 11, 142
Bradley, Walter, 121n. 15
British Voluntary Euthanasia Society, 273
Brownlee, Donald, 42
Bruni, Leonardo, 108
Bruno, Giordano, 111, 117, 142
Buffon, Comte de, 216
Caligula, 276
Cambrian period, 229
cannibalism, 93, 162
Cavendish, William (Marquis of Newcastle), 157
Chambers, Robert, 216
Chesterton, G. K., 79n. 2
Child, Harold, 269

Christianity, 22, 24-30, 41, 44-45, 57-58, 70-71, 73-74, 75-94, 96-97, 99-107, 109-10, 114-15, 117-18, 120, 130-31, 143-44, 146, 148-51, 155-56, 167-68, 177, 179-80, 183-84, 186, 189-90, 193-94, 197, 200, 202-9, 212, 214, 216, 235, 236-37, 238-40, 253, 256, 258-62, 266, 268, 270, 272, 277, 285-88, 296-321
  liberal Christianity, 300-302, 307-9
Cicero, 34n. 6; 44n. 28; 51, 54, 93, 95-96, 100
Clement, 97
Clinton, William (U.S. president), 171
cloning, 29, 156, 264, 301, 310, 316-17, 320
contraception/birth control, 90, 90n. 13, 265-67, 271-72, 277
Copernicus, Nicolas, 115, 258
Cretan paradox, 139
Dalton, John, 295
Dante Alighieri, 67
Darwin, Charles, 9, 11, 25-26, 29, 60, 60n. 1, 62-64, 66n. 13, 70, 99, 128, 132-33, 140, 173, 207, 214, 215-54, 260-61, 264, 265-67, 275-76, 279, 288, 290, 293, 296-98, 302, 312-14, 320
  eugenics in, 251-53, 312
  and God, 234-37, 241-42
  and hell, 71
  racism in, 248-50
  as related to Epicureanism, 234-42
Darwin, Emma, 253
Darwin, Erasmus, 216, 236
Darwin, Leonard, 267
Darwin, Robert, 236-37

Darwinism, 11-13, 19-21,
25-27, 58, 64, 92, 101,
149, 258, 296
    moral, 19, 24, 27, 29-30,
    59-60, 64, 75-76, 85,
    92, 100, 114, 221, 243,
    255-88, 296-319
    social, 243, 253, 261
Dawkins, Richard, 17, 57,
149-50, 165-66, 227n. 20,
293-94, 296, 298-99, 305,
315
deism, 203-7
Dekkers, Midas, 287-88
Dembski, William, 9-13, 15n.
1
Democritus, 34, 101, 107,
113, 120, 124, 153, 156,
206
demons/Satan, 84, 181, 183-
85, 188, 199-201, 209,
306-7
Dennett, Daniel, 23, 26-27,
149, 297
Denton, Michael, 15n. 1
Descartes, René, 118, 190
determinism, 53
Didache, 90-91
Diderot, Denis, 205
Diogenes Laertius, 100, 107
divorce, 87, 99, 310, 312
Dodge, Mildred, 269
economics and hedonism,
170-71
Eden
    Christian, 161, 169
    Epicurean, 69, 160, 161
    modern, 154, 161, 171,
    271-72
Ellis, Havelock, 267-70
embryonic research/manipu-
lation, 29, 310
Empedocles, 60n. 1
Epicurus, Epicureanism, 9-
11, 18-27, 30-58, 97-98,
101, 107-14, 116-18, 120-
21, 123-24, 126, 129-31,

134-35, 137, 142, 144-47,
151, 153, 155-57, 159,
164, 166, 168, 170-71,
174, 177, 179-81, 184,
186, 189-92, 194, 198-201,
205-8, 210, 214-21, 223-
24, 226, 234, 237, 241,
243-44, 254-56, 261, 264,
267, 272-73, 275, 279,
281, 283, 285, 288, 290-
96, 299-300, 302, 304,
310, 312, 314, 316-18, 320
    asceticism, 48-50, 85,
    108, 142, 144-45, 151,
    153, 155, 158-60, 162,
    171-72, 206, 243
    vs. Christianity, 78-94,
    264, 297-318
    virtues, 51-53
Etienne Tempier (bishop),
106
Eucharist, 50n. 45, 182n. 4
Euclid/Euclidean, 121, 123-
24, 126, 137, 157, 195,
292
eugenics, 29, 221, 243, 251-
53, 255, 259-61, 264-68,
271-74, 277, 289, 297,
302, 304, 308, 312
euthanasia, 9, 24-25, 94,
262-64, 272-73, 297, 300,
308-10, 317, 320-21
Euthanasia Education Council, 272
Euthanasia Society of America, 272-73
evolution, 149, 219, 240,
275, 312
    of conscience, 245-47
    in Darwin, 29, 63, 133,
    219, 222, 226, 230-36,
    238, 241-53, 279-80,
    290, 297-98
    in Dawkins, 294, 299
    of different races/species
    of human beings, 250-51
    in Ellis, 268n. 38

in Haeckel, 257-59
in Kinsey, 276-77, 279-81,
283, 286
in Lucretius, 60-64, 73,
132, 216
of morality, 64, 68-70,
243-49, 296, 311-12
of religion, 70, 72-73, 240-
42
in Rousseau, 173, 175
in Sanger, 268-72, 275
in Singer, 286-88
of society, 64, 68-70, 175
and theism, 27, 316
Filelfo, Francesco, 108
Fontenelle, Bernard le
Bouier de, 118
fossil record, 231, 250, 298
Freud, Sigmund, 12, 21-22,
256
Galilei, Galileo/Galilean, 111-
12, 114-24, 126, 142-43,
145, 156-58, 162, 180-81,
194, 215-16, 226, 291
Gasman, Daniel, 261, 265
Gassendi, Pierre, 111-12,
142
Gebhard, Paul, 281-82
geometry/mathematics
    in Galileo, 119, 121-23
    in Newton, 124-26, 128,
    134, 137
    in science, 120, 129, 292-
    93
God (gods), 9-10, 17-18, 20,
22, 26, 28, 33-34, 37-39,
43-47, 49, 57, 62, 70-72,
76-83, 87-88, 91-92, 96,
98, 103, 105-6, 109, 112,
116, 119, 123, 126-39,
144, 149, 152, 154, 156,
163, 165, 167-69, 173,
179, 181-85, 187-91, 194-
95, 197, 199-204, 206,
208-10, 212-13, 218-19,
240-42, 269, 287, 293,
295, 297, 300, 304, 311,

316-18, 319-20
God-of-the-gaps dilemma, 126-33
golden rule, 248
Gould, Stephen Jay, 27, 57, 314-15
great law of uniformity, 22, 29, 57, 64, 68, 114, 136, 143, 255, 301, 314, 321
Gregory of Nyssa, 97
Guttmacher, Alan, 272-73
Hadamar, 263
Haeckel, Ernst, 256-67, 288, 298, 302-3, 318
Haire, Norman, 272
Halley, Edmund, 137-38
Haught, John, 12, 27
Hawking, Stephen, 39, 140-41, 304
    Hawking's Dilemma, 140-41
heaven, 47, 57, 67, 83, 179, 180, 186-87, 256, 272, 306, 320
hedonism, 29, 48, 51, 66, 97-99, 142, 144, 151, 153, 155-56, 160-62, 164, 168-72, 177, 206, 243, 255-88, 288, 302, 310-14
Hegel, Georg Wilhelm Friedrich, 211, 256
hell (Hades), 33, 47, 57, 71-72, 83, 94, 147, 149, 152, 179-80, 186-88, 256, 258, 304-6, 320
Herschel, William, 128
Hilary, 97
historicism
    in Epicureanism, 198
    in modern scriptural exegesis, 197-98
Hitler, Adolf, 261
Hobbes, Thomas, 69, 112, 145, 156-66, 168-69, 171-72, 174-75, 178-92, 194, 200-204, 207-8, 214, 215, 221, 240-41, 243, 255,

287, 297, 300-302, 304, 315-16, 320
Hoche, Alfred, 262-63
Homer, 71, 126
homosexuality, 9, 24, 29, 86, 88, 99, 175, 177, 275, 278, 281-83, 285, 300, 310-13
Hubble, Edwin, 292
Hume, David, 135-36
Hunter, James Davison, 10
Hutton, James, 226, 231
infanticide, 25, 29, 90-91, 99-100, 150, 247, 264, 272, 297, 300-301, 303-4, 307-8, 313, 318
infinite time, 42, 49-50, 132, 220, 226, 228, 231
infinite universe, 41, 116-18, 132, 226
Inge, Dean, 267
Institute for Sex Research, 275-76, 278, 279
intelligent design, 11-13, 21, 24, 26, 28-30, 45, 56-57, 76-77, 85, 99, 104-5, 107, 120-21, 128, 131, 215, 218, 233, 240, 291, 293, 295, 302, 318
    movement, 15-16, 18, 21, 23, 25-26, 36, 77, 296, 314, 317-18, 321
    vs. creationism, 77-78
Islam, 45, 75-76, 100, 203
Jefferson, Thomas, 206-7
Jenkin, Fleeming, 222, 228, 230
Jerome, 97
Jesus Christ, 24, 50, 78, 82-84, 87, 93-94, 105, 110, 119, 156, 176, 183-85, 187, 189, 203-4, 208-14, 258, 306, 308, 320
    and Darwin, 237, 239, 248
    as the merely moral man, 191, 199-201, 205-6, 208, 211, 320

Johnson, Phillip, 10-11, 139n. 27, 149
Jones, James, 276-78, 284
Joseph, St., 209
Jost, Adolph, 262
Judaism, 45, 75-76, 85, 87, 184, 187, 191, 197, 202, 203, 209, 211, 287, 297
Julius Caesar, 96
Justin Martyr, 97
Kant, Immanuel, 256
Kelvin (William Thomson, Lord Kelvin), 222, 228-30
Kepler, Johannes, 112, 118
Keynes, John Maynard, 9
Kinsey, Alfred, 69, 256, 274-89, 302, 310-14
Kinsey, Clara, 278
Lactantius, 97
Lamarck, Jean, 216
Lambin, Denys, 109
Landino, Cristoforo, 108
Lanting, Frans, 314
Laplace, Pierre Simon de, 127-28, 133, 219
Laski, Harold, 273
law of *gravitas*, 137
law of inertia, 158
law of moral compromise, 300, 304, 307, 309, 311, 316, 320
laws of nature, 123, 125-26, 129, 131, 133-34, 136, 138-40, 204-5, 208-9, 219, 241, 292-93
    in D. F. Strauss, 208, 213
    in Darwin, 240-41
    in Hobbes, 163
    in Spinoza, 195-97, 201
Leverreir, Urbain, J. J., 129
Lewontin, Richard, 294-95
Lifton, Robert, 261
Locke, John, 61n. 6, 69, 145, 163, 166-72, 202-4, 215, 235, 255
Lucretius, 25, 27-28, 58-74, 100-101, 103, 107-11, 113-

14, 117, 120, 124, 129,
131-32, 137-38, 144, 154-
58, 160-61, 164, 166, 168,
172-75, 180, 193-94, 205-
8, 210, 215-16, 219-21,
234, 242, 244, 275, 279,
281, 284
  asceticism, 65-67
  vs. Christianity, 78-94
Luther, Martin, 107
Lyell, Charles, 132, 226, 231
Machiavelli, Niccolò; Machia-
vel
lianism, 144, 146-53,
155, 166, 168, 173, 181,
191, 213, 215, 221, 235,
243, 252, 277, 287
MacIntyre, Alasdair, 162
Maillet, Beniot de, 216
March, Norah, 267
Mariotte, Edme, 119n. 11
marriage, 66, 86-89, 174-77,
253, 275, 311-12
Marx, Karl, 171, 192, 256
Mary, Blessed Virgin, 209
Maslow, Abraham, 282
materialism (naturalism) as
habit of mind or faith, 34,
38-40, 54-56, 130, 132,
135, 220-34, 259, 289-95,
317-18
Matthew, Patrick, 216
May, Robert, 236
Mead, Margaret, 164
Mersenne, Marin, 112
Meyer, Stephen, 15n. 1
Mill, John Stuart, 256
Miller, Kenneth, 12, 27
Minucius Felix, 97
miracles, 78, 112, 133-36,
156, 178, 180, 189, 191,
194-97, 204-5, 208-9, 211-
13, 239-41, 295, 320
Mivart, George, 222
monism, 257-58, 260, 262
Montaigne, Michel Eyquem
de, 108
morality, 22

materialist, 10, 23-24, 46-
47, 50, 141-42, 158-59
  Christian, 81-94, 99
  in Darwin, 243-54, 297
  in Haeckel, 260-64
  in Hobbes, 158-66
  in Kinsey, 276-87
  in Locke, 203-4
  in Machiavelli, 147, 151-
54
  in Rousseau, 173-77
  in Sanger, 264-75
  in Spinoza, 192-94, 196,
199-202
Moreland, J. P., 15n. 1, 81n.
5
myth, 40, 56, 80, 164, 174,
208-11, 222, 258
Napoleon Bonaparte, 128
natural law, 28, 49, 69, 76,
82, 85, 87-88, 99, 145,
155, 162-65, 168, 174,
177, 246, 249n. 85, 268,
285, 288, 296-98, 302,
307, 311, 315, 316-17, 319
natural rights, modern, 145,
160, 162-66, 168, 170-71,
200-202, 262-63, 287, 299-
300, 302, 312, 315-16
natural selection, 62-64, 140-
41, 220-33, 236, 238, 244-
47, 249-51, 259-60, 265,
294, 298-99, 311-12
nature
  as a closed system, 34, 36-
37, 44-45, 123, 128-29,
136, 190-91, 193-95,
205, 214, 218, 229, 290,
292-93
  as contingent, 35-37, 292
  as eternal, 35-38, 44, 258,
290
Nazis, 261, 263, 274, 289,
306, 309-10
Nero, 276
Netherlands, 309, 320-21
Newcastle circle, 156-57

Newton, Isaac; Newtonian-
ism 111-12, 114, 124-43,
145, 172, 179, 190, 194-
95, 202, 204-7, 215-16,
218-20, 225-26, 235, 240-
41, 290-91, 293, 295
Nietzsche, Friedrich, 256
nominalism, 101, 104-7,
117-18
nonoverlapping magisteria
(NOMA), 314-15
Novalis (Friedrich Leopold
Freiherr von Hardenberg),
190
Odysseus, 71
Owen, Richard, 222
Paul, St., 82, 183-84, 308-9
pederasty/pedophilia, 88, 99,
175, 177, 283-85, 288,
312-13
Pennock, Robert, 12
Peter Chrysologus, 97
Pinker, Stephen, 150-51
Planned Parenthood, 256,
264, 271-75, 304
Planned Parenthood v. Casey,
165
Plato/Platonism, 67, 85, 100,
121, 194n. 45
plurality of worlds, 41-42,
106, 117-18
Poggio (Giovanni Francesco
Poggio Bracciolini), 107
Polybius/Polybian, 146-48,
151, 181, 186, 188-89,
192, 196, 201, 314
Pomeroy, Wardell, 278, 283-
84
Priestley, Joseph, 236
Ptolemy, 115
Public Broadcast System
(PBS), 149-50, 313
Pythagoras/Pythagorean-
ism, 60n. 1, 120-21
racism
  in Darwin, 248-50
  in Haeckel, 257

Reisman, Judith, 283
Roe v. Wade, 274, 302-3, 307
Rousseau, Jean-Jacques, 69,
    145, 163, 166, 171, 216,
    244, 247, 251, 255, 270,
    275, 279, 284
Ruse, Michael, 27
Russel Bertrand, 273
Rutherford, Ernest, 291
Sade, Marquis de, 276
Sagan, Carl, 35n. 10,- 39,
    42, 57
Saint-Hilaire, Geoffroy, 216
Sanger, Margaret, 256, 264-
    75, 288-89, 302, 304, 310-
    14
Sartre, Jean-Paul, 256
science as therapeutic, 32-34,
    54, 57
Scripture, 29, 36, 76, 78-84,
    178-214
as merely moral, 191-93, 199
Selincourt, Hugh de, 269
sexuality
    Christian vs. Epicurean,
        85-89
    in Epicureanism, 51
    in Genesis, 81
    in Hobbes, 164
    in Kinsey, 277-86
    in Lucretius, 65-66
    moral conflict today, 25,
        310-14
    in Planned Parenthood,
        274-75
    in Rousseau, 173-77
    in Sanger, 265, 267-72
    in Singer, 287-88
Shaw, George Bernard, 273
simplicity, 40-42, 54, 56, 70,
    125, 139, 142, 220, 223-
    24, 293-94
Singer, Peter, 286-88, 318
Slee, J. Noah, 268
Smith, Adam, 247

Socrates, 50
soul, 20-22, 33-34, 46-47,
    49, 53, 57, 66, 71-72, 74,
    80-81, 88, 91-92, 108-9,
    112-13, 139, 141, 144,
    146, 152, 156-57, 167,
    171, 179, 181-82, 186-88,
    210, 221, 256, 258-59,
    287, 290, 293, 297-98,
    303-6, 308, 316-18
    and Darwin, 237-39, 302
speciesism, 287, 299
Spencer, Herbert, 235
Spinoza, Benedict de, 178-
    79, 190-204, 207-9, 212,
    214, 240, 300-301, 304,
    320
state of nature, 160-64, 170,
    172-73, 175, 201, 284
state of war, 161
sterilization, forced, 267
Stoics/Stoicism, 85, 93, 96,
    109-10, 172, 206
Strauss, David Friedrich,
    178-79, 207-14, 240, 258,
    300-301, 304, 320
Strauss, Leo, 145n. 1, 157n.
    22, 166n. 43, 191n. 38
suicide, 247, 262, 268, 308
    Christian vs. Epicurean,
        93-94, 99
Supreme Court, 165
sympathy/sentiment, 247-48,
    251, 253, 260, 262, 265-
    66, 298
Tertullian, 97
theology
    natural, 26, 36, 45, 77,
        103, 105
    revealed, 26, 36, 77, 103-
        5, 167
Theophilus, 97
Thomas Aquinas, Thomism,
    35-36, 48-49, 81n. 5, 103-
    4, 130, 151, 171, 238-39

Thompson, J. J., 291
Thomson, Arthur, 267
Tiberius, 211, 276
Tindal, Matthew, 204
Toland, John, 204
Tooley, Michael, 303, 318
Toulmin, Stephen, 119
tranquility, 33-34, 47, 53, 65,
    67-68, 73, 98, 145, 153,
    157, 160-62, 174, 176,
    179-81, 186, 192
Traversari, Ambrogio, 107
true holiness shuffle, 185
two realities doctrine (reli-
    gion and science), 193-200
two-platoon strategy, 149,
    168, 214. *See also* Machia-
    vellianism
Unitarianism/anti-Trinitari-
    anism
    of Darwin's family, 236-37
    of Jefferson, 207
    of Newton, 204
Valla, Lorenzo, 109-10
values, 24
    fact/value distinction, ori-
        gin in Hobbes, 160n. 30,
        297
Voltaire (François-Marie
    Arouet), 205
Waal, Frans, de, 313-14
Wallace, Alfred, 216
Ward, Peter, 42
Watson, James, 303
Wedgwood, Josiah, 236
Wells, H. G., 269, 273
Wells, Jonathan, 259n. 7
Wells, William, 216
Wheeler, William, 276-77
Wigner, Eugene, 121n. 15
William of Occam, 104-6
World Trade Center, 150
Zeno, 206

SCRIPTURE INDEX

GENESIS
1—2, *80*
1:2, *182*
1:14-19, *80*
2, *81*
2:7, *183*
3:14-24, *84*
3:16-19, *83*
3:17-19, *169*
12:1-9, *82*
17:1-14, *82*

EXODUS
3:1—14:31, *84*
20:1-17, *82*

DEUTERONOMY
5:6-21, *82*

JUDGES
3:10, *183*
6:34, *183*
11:29, *183*

PSALMS
8:3-5, *319*

ISAIAH
11:2-3, *182*
53, *210*

MATTHEW
5:22-30, *83*
10:28, *83*
10:38, *308*
16:21, *84*
16:24, *308*
18:9, *83*
25:46, *83*

MARK
8:31, *84*
8:34, *308*
9:11, *84*
9:42-46, *83*
10:2-9, *87*
10:17-30, *83*

LUKE
4:1, *183*
9:2, *84*
9:23, *308*
10:15, *83*
12:5, *83*
14:27, *308*
17:25, *84*

18:18-30, *83*
22:3-4, *185*

JOHN
3:15, *83*
6:27-55, *83*

ROMANS
1:18-21, *82*
6:5, *309*
8:17, *309*
8:18-25, *84*

1 CORINTHIANS
15:44, *184*

2 CORINTHIANS
1:3-7, *84*
1:5, *309*

GALATIANS
5:20, *90*

COLOSSIANS
1:24, *84*

TITUS
2:11-14, *83*

1 JOHN
4:2, *183*